LEO STRAUSS ON RELIGION

SUNY SERIES IN THE THOUGHT AND LEGACY OF LEO STRAUSS
KENNETH HART GREEN, EDITOR

LEO STRAUSS ON RELIGION

Writings and Interpretations

EDITED BY SVETOZAR Y. MINKOV
AND RASOUL NAMAZI

Cover Credit: Handwritten manuscripts of Leo Strauss. © Leo Strauss Center at the University of Chicago. Used with permission.

Published by State University of New York Press, Albany
© 2024 STATE UNIVERSITY OF NEW YORK PRESS
All rights reserved
Printed in the United States of America

No part of this book may be used or reproduced in any manner whatsoever without written permission. No part of this book may be stored in a retrieval system or transmitted in any form or by any means including electronic, electrostatic, magnetic tape, mechanical, photocopying, recording, or otherwise without the prior permission in writing of the publisher.

Links to third-party websites are provided as a convenience and for informational purposes only. They do not constitute an endorsement or an approval of any of the products, services, or opinions of the organization, companies, or individuals. SUNY Press bears no responsibility for the accuracy, legality, or content of a URL, the external website, or for that of subsequent websites.

For information, contact State University of New York Press, Albany, NY
www.sunypress.edu

Library of Congress Cataloging-in-Publication Data

Names: Minkov, Svetozar, 1985- editor. | Namazi, Rasoul, 1982- editor.
Title: Leo Strauss on religion : writings and interpretations / edited by
    Svetozar Y. Minkov and Rasoul Namazi.
Description: Albany : State University of New York Press, [2024] | Series: SUNY
    series in the thought and legacy of Leo Strauss | Includes bibliographical
    references and index.
Identifiers: LCCN 2024003475 | ISBN 9781438499413 (hardcover) | ISBN
    9781438499420 (ebook) | ISBN 9781438499406 (paperback)
Subjects: LCSH: Strauss, Leo. | Religion and politics. | Philosophy and religion.
Classification: LCC B945.S84 L457 2024 | DDC 201/.61--dc23/eng/20240702
LC record available at https://lccn.loc.gov/2024003475

CONTENTS

Acknowledgments — ix

Series Editor's Introduction — xi
Kenneth Hart Green

Editors' Introduction — xxi
Svetozar Y. Minkov and Rasoul Namazi

PART ONE

Transcript 1: Leo Strauss, Notes on Lessing's *Nathan the Wise* (1940 and 1942) — 3

Reflections on Leo Strauss, His Notes on Gotthold Ephraim Lessing, and "Nathan der Weise" — 21
Till Kinzel

Leo Strauss on the Philosophical Character of Lessing's *Nathan The Wise* — 37
Martin D. Yaffe

PART TWO

Transcript 2.1: Leo Strauss, On the Plan of the *Kuzari* (c. 1941–1942) — 65

Transcript 2.2: Leo Strauss, On the *Kuzari* (c. 1941–1942) — 73

On Yehuda Halevi's "Spiritual Hell" — 79
Ralph Lerner

91	Proclaiming Dangerous Teachings to the World: Why Would Strauss Reveal the Religious Heterodoxy of the Falāsifa? *Alexander Orwin*

PART THREE

109	Transcript 3: Leo Strauss, "Abraham and Maimonides" (1953)
113	Dichotomies of Understanding Religious Law in Leo Strauss's Lecture "Abraham and Maimonides" *Yehuda Halper*
129	Reason and Law *Joshua Parens*

PART FOUR

147	Transcript 4: Leo Strauss, On Spinoza (c. 1959)
157	Strauss's "Fresh Study" Manuscript *Steven Frankel*
175	The Charity of Spinoza's *Democracy* *Andrea E. Ray*

PART FIVE

191	Transcript 5.1: Leo Strauss, Notes on Plato's *Symposium* (c. 1959)
199	Transcript 5.2: Leo Strauss, *Notes on Agathon's Speech in Plato's Symposium* (c. 1959)
209	Transcript 5.3: Leo Strauss, Two Letters on Plato's *Symposium* (1959)
215	Leo Strauss on Agathon's Theology in Plato's *Symposium* *Svetozar Y. Minkov*

Leo Strauss's Intention with Plato's *Symposium*   233
Alex Priou

PART SIX

Transcript 6: Leo Strauss, Selections from "Seminar in Political Philosophy: Rousseau" (1962)   253

Leo Strauss and Jean-Jacques Rousseau: Ancients and Moderns, Esotericism, and the Challenge of Religion   259
Rasoul Namazi

"Truly a Civil Religion": Leo Strauss Teaches the Profession of Faith   273
John Ray

PART SEVEN

Transcript 7.1: "Religion and the Commonweal in the Tradition of Political Philosophy": The Lecture (1963)   289

Transcript 7.2: Leo Strauss, "Religion and the Commonweal": The Manuscript (1963)   321

Leo Strauss on Religion and the Commonweal   329
Nathan Tarcov

Leo Strauss on Civil Religion   337
Philipp von Wussow

Appendix: Strauss's Confrontation with Pascal   355
Svetozar Y. Minkov

Notes on Contributors   383
Index   387

ACKNOWLEDGMENTS

We would like to thank Jenny Strauss Clay and Nathan Tarcov for their permission to publish the Strauss materials, Ralph Lerner for making the "Abraham and Maimonides" typescript available to us, Kenneth Hart Green for being a strong supporter of this project, Michael Rinella for being an excellent editor, and two anonymous reviewers of State University of New York Press for their helpful comments on the manuscript. We would also like to thank John P. Gibbons, Wiebke Meier, and Stuart D. Warner for their assistance.

KENNETH HART GREEN

Series Editor's Introduction

LEO STRAUSS ON RELIGION:
SOME INTRODUCTORY CONSIDERATIONS

LEO STRAUSS WAS ONE OF the premier political philosophers of the twentieth century. To those who pursue scholarly work in the wake of his philosophic thought, he is often considered one of the greatest political philosophers since Machiavelli. He is also known as one of the most original thinkers and scholars of Judaism in the twentieth century, challenging conventional approaches and uncovering hidden depths, evidenced especially in his insightful explications of the chief texts of Moses Maimonides. In recent years, his broader writings on Judaism and Jewish thought have also begun to be better known. In addition, the unmined treasures of his unpublished writings, together with transcripts of his classroom lectures, are gradually being brought to light. Little doubt remains about what can only be called Strauss's genius. As the prolific fruits of his writing and teaching show, he kept single-mindedly focused on his chief concerns: the history of political philosophy, and Jewish thought especially in its deeper Maimonidean form.

And yet the pieces in this volume disclose that Strauss never quite limited himself in his thought either to political philosophy or to Judaism narrowly construed. The simple fact is that he also reflected deeply about religion in general, from his first scholarly works to his last—from his debut book, *Spinoza's Critique of Religion*, to one of the last pieces he wrote for publication, "Preliminary Observations on the Gods in Thucydides' Work." In other words, while working through his penetrating readings of the great books of political philosophy, he evidently considered religion to be also one of the most requisite, decisive, and weighty issues for anyone who thinks seriously about the goods of human life, the order of society, and the best political regime. In terms of religion, certainly Judaism as an ancient historical tradition was his personal point of origin and deep concern: he never ceased to be morally and passionately bound to it, and yet to meditatively struggle with it. But he also clearly regarded religion in general as well as other specific traditions as distinct phenomena of great profundity and power, which still have much to teach in the study of political philosophy. Passing remarks in his treatment of the great political philosophers show he considered each tradition as it addresses God, man, and the world in its own unique fashion, and as it touches on political life at critical points. As I would further suggest, he viewed it as the duty, if not also the need, of every researcher but also every thinking human being to confront the great religions and to determine how they variously affect human life and deal with human fate. Indeed, the very fact that modern man has tended to dismiss God—as something extraneous, irrelevant, or optional at best—made it of even greater concern to Strauss, putting it among those key facets of human life that modern man has often tended to confuse, if not to get plainly wrong.

He seems to have been compelled to investigate the mysterious sphere of religion as a universal phenomenon, but also as it expresses itself in particular traditions, since each one teaches its own singular approach to Being as seen in the light of God. In focusing on specific traditions as they emerge in the books of the great philosophers (from Plato to Heidegger) and as viewed from each great thinker's unique vantage point, he naturally tended to have the most to say about the polytheism of the Greeks and the Romans, and about the monotheism of the three great scriptural faiths (recently dubbed "Abrahamic"). He recognized that religion in general has occupied an enormous place in human life; indeed, it has normally played an immense role in directing the ordering of human affairs in the political realm. And as he also showed himself keenly aware, beyond (or beneath) its political vocation and on the personal level, this is a potent force and an encompassing domain that has challenged, fascinated, and terrified human beings from time immemorial. Only ideological blinkers, willful blindness, or wishful thinking could prevent an honest mind, even modestly knowledgeable about human beings and history, from admitting that this is so. As Strauss taught, even if one chooses to suspend judgment about the question of God, one cannot do the same with regard to the problem of religion: it is absolutely essential to know about it if one wants to comprehend the human, never mind the political.

At the same time, it must be acknowledged that Strauss himself questioned the modern category of "religion" (starting with Judaism) as assiduously as did the postmodernists, although he held to a position that has little if anything in common with that ideological camp. This is because he recognized the category of "religion" as a thoroughly modern one. Yet as moderns, he also acknowledged that it is almost impossible for us to avoid employing such a category, even if we must also recognize it as a more or less irrelevant classification prior to the sixteenth century, when what we call religion—that is, organized worship of or focused reverence for *God* or *the gods*—was simply a given, as self-evident as the sun that shines on us in every place where we human beings develop a society. If Strauss as a scholar and thinker researched the history of religion in the context of addressing the history of political philosophy, he never limited himself to one dimension of religion, and as such never shied away from asking the seemingly simple and obvious—but actually rather obscure and difficult—questions of *what religion is* and *why it is* (however little he is appreciated for that perceptive querying). He asked what the origins of religion in man are, why it is such an essential element of human life, and why it is so differently deployed in different times and places. As examples of the far-reaching style and manner of his thought, it will be instructive to consider two seemingly casual remarks he makes about the nature of religion itself, revealing how seriously he took this human phenomenon and how far he allowed himself in his thinking to probe it, and to reflect on what he discovered by such probing.

First: "Humanly speaking, the unity of fear and pity combined with the phenomenon of guilt might seem to be the root of religion."[1] This unique insight into what the origin of religion in man may be—as he prefaces his remark with great self-awareness: "humanly speaking," that is, viewed solely as a human phenomenon—seems to relate it to Greek tragedy in all its profundity, especially as explicated by Aristotle. But here simultaneously Strauss may also be playfully echoing the language by which religion is commonly dismissed. By rooting religion in a mixture of psychology and morality, he may also be poking fun at the banal and reductive way by which religion is often discarded in the modern period, as if we can now dispense with such primitive and unneedful passions as guilt once we perceive them as such, since science can "cure" us of them.

Second: In an effort to comprehend the ancient city as a key to grasping how political philosophy arose and became what it is, he deals in *The City and Man*—in reverse historical order—with the thought of Aristotle, Plato, and Thucydides. However, what is most curious for our purposes is how he ends the same book. He concludes by addressing perhaps the most fundamental "religious" problem for philosophy (Plato and Aristotle) as well as for history (Thucydides)—if not for man as man—which happens to be deep-rooted in the very emergence of the ancient city. That question is: *Quid sit deus*?; or, "What is a god?"[2] As this would seem to imply, the concern with religion and especially with God or the gods is never far from the consideration of what philosophy is, and also simultaneously of what makes man's civilized political life possible. Thanks precisely to this key pointer, Strauss also causes us to ask: *Why* should that be so? In other words: *Why* is the presence of God in the city so decisive?

This question, a dramatic last statement to his book, is not only a pointer but also a provocation by which he prods his readers to think more deeply and less conventionally in order to resolve that fundamental perplexity, which has not yet been answered satisfactorily. We are helped to make sense of his highlighting this fundamental perplexity by turning to Strauss's biography. His best friend for most of his life was Jacob Klein, whom he met during his apprentice years (in 1919 in Marburg, Germany), and to whom he remained closest until his demise (in 1973 in Annapolis, Maryland). In a retrospective view, Klein had this to say about Strauss in his youth: "His primary interests were two questions: one, the question of God; and two, the question of politics."[3] Klein is careful to add that "these questions were not mine." I think it is safe to say that for Strauss these two questions did not accidentally intersect but were integrally and even essentially related to one another: they are, as it were, naturally intertwined. I would suggest that this linked pair of questions never ceased to be the key issues that guided and animated his thought. Indeed, one question to which he frequently alluded, as one of his ultimate concerns, was the problem of how precisely the lowest and the highest in human life are related or interconnected. From his youth he seems to have already judged these two poles of human nature to be somehow inextricably bound to one another. However, he was also almost unique in *not* assuming that this being bound together self-evidently and necessarily proceeds in a single direction (as the moderns tend to almost dogmatically conceive), namely: things move from the low to the high in such a way that this renders everything high a mere shadow or at best a projection of the low. It should be no surprise then that he spoke often about there being a permanent and undisputable fact that he called "the theological-political predicament," implying by this key-term that for him politics and religion cannot ever be neatly separated, or treated as virtually self-sufficient, or merely reduced to one another. According to Strauss, any honest searcher for the truth (whether philosopher, scientist, or scholar) who is considering the political will almost by necessity have to also consider the religious—and, significantly, vice versa. But along with this, it is also impossible to presuppose or decree ex cathedra (as some philosophers and academic researchers are wont to do) that the religious is always a mere function or creature of the political, the former being altogether dependent on the latter. This would seem to further imply that Strauss rejected the dogmatic atheism that is built into most modern approaches to religion, based as they are on such a presupposition or decree.

By contrast, Strauss maintained that the modern attempt to neatly separate politics (philosophically elaborated) and religion, and to subordinate the latter to the former, is also not so simple. Moreover, he perceived that one of the key endeavors of modernity is the effort to escape the grave implications of such an unbreakable bond. This led Strauss to also question whether it is adequate to refer to all phenomena related to God (or the gods) as "religion," which is the predominant modern approach: awareness of God (or the gods) would seem to be essential to man as man, that is, to be humanly ubiquitous, and it precedes as well as continues to exist beyond the bounds of the formal establishment of "religion." Just because this is so, the modern approach (which reduces all such awareness, and the phenomena to which it is a response, to "religion") considers these matters solely from the point of view of the subjective human respondent, rather than paying utmost attention to the unresolved problem of the truth of the "objective" divine referent, namely, God. Can we consider God only insofar as He fits the modern category of "religion"? And if we do so, then have we not also already made an advance decision in favor of the view that there is no reality in God? Have we not already rejected the most fundamental problem, namely, the truth of God, and have we not reduced Him to a figment of human production (mostly in the imagination), for whatever reasons we may hypothesize that this figment or at best idealization was produced? And can we do proper justice to the thing we are supposedly studying, "religion," if we already presuppose that this *ultimate* of almost every religion—God (or the gods)—is false, a mere myth or fairy tale? If we are to attain a deeper beginning-point for consideration of this essential matter, it seems that Strauss would suggest to us that we are better to commence the study of religion in its modern form with something like Cicero's *De Natura Deorum* (*On the Nature of the Gods*) or his *Republic*. At least Cicero in this book refuses to evade the question of the truth of divine being in considering the question of religion. (It helps to make better sense of his "The Dream of Scipio.")[4] Strauss would compel us to ask whether the study of religion as a modern "science" is not already built on assumptions about the unreality of God, which cannot be avoided by resorting to the usual "idealized" study of religion (i.e., even if conceived as an impressive human product), since to presuppose God as a figment of the human mind is to construct the so-called science on a circular basis. We cannot seem to *know* by self-analysis whether we may well be aware of God (or the gods) because of His presence in our mind or soul, in our common life, and in the natural world. This is a fundamental question that must be penetratingly searched for, and that elementary fact disallows an answer arbitrarily asserted or defensively decided on.

This brings us to one of the most crucial aspects of Strauss's thought on religion, insofar as we are considering the powers of the human mind and their differing impact on human life. However, in this case it encompasses philosophy as well. I refer to his repeated insistence (as it first emerged in his thought of the 1930s) on the prevailing duality of "Jerusalem and Athens" as the very heart and soul of Western civilization. The phrase "Jerusalem and Athens" was not for Strauss just the names of two ancient cities yoked together by an "and," but rather it represents in its full flowering the two fundamental alternatives in the soul of man. It is an expression of the hitherto—and perhaps permanently—unresolved dividedness of the human soul, which Strauss occasionally speaks about as "the heart" and "the mind."[5] As such, it animates the very search for and debate about the truth that has uniquely defined Western civilization. This phrase, "Jerusalem and Athens," serves of course as a sort of composite or abbreviation for those other dualities that are well known to anyone who is familiar with Strauss's thought: reason vs. revelation, faith vs. science, the Bible vs. philosophy, God of the philosophers vs. God of Abraham, Isaac, and Jacob. However much the names may change in different historical situations, for Strauss these are unavoidable, fundamental, and (I emphasize) *irreducible* human dualities, although some versions of the duality may well stand closer to the truth than others. Just as an aside, in one passage Strauss avers that he thinks Maimonides was the greatest analyst ever of this elemental human duality, especially as it manifests itself in its uniquely "Western" form.

For Strauss, the valiant attempt to fully understand both Jerusalem and Athens is the most significant and noblest occupation a human being can pursue in life. It has focused, if not preoccupied, the "spiritual" life of Western man since "Athens" first encountered "Jerusalem." (He never quite determines a historical date, figure, or event for their first encounter.) However, to perceive each side of the duality correctly, since both assert the singularity and unity of truth, one is forced, according to Strauss, ultimately to choose between one side or the other, seemingly overturning the duality and yielding a monism. But this is not quite the case that Strauss makes: each one chooses with reason, be it only "the reasons of the heart" (Pascal), a "higher" reason being claimed by faith than reason itself. And since neither the one nor the other can produce absolute (as opposed to relative) proof of, or a mutually persuasive reason for, its superiority in the realm of truth, intellectual honesty—unconditionally revered by both sides—obliges that each one's critical examination of and encounter with the other continue. This obligation results from the fact that neither the one nor the other can prevail at least in terms acceptable to both; at best, their encounters end with a stalemate. This, according to Strauss, is the fate of Western man, which has a somber sound to it, although he also suggests that this is not such a bad fate. Indeed, for him it is *the source of life* of Western civilization, even if both sides would and should prefer to vanquish their opposites. Love of truth compels both religion and philosophy to respect the other, insofar as each one shares certain notions with the other, especially but not only in the area of morality.

Likewise, both search for *wisdom*, a term, a realm, and a goal absorbing to both sides, but they reach different results about what it is—albeit results that are not unqualifiedly different.[6] Both sides agree on the view that there is only one truth, and only one right way of life; what they disagree on is what that truth is, and what this right way of life is, *in terms of which one is primary*, so that this makes it impossible to absolutely deny the truth of its opposite, only to subordinate it. Hence, what is curious and striking about this conflict is that each one is not willing to *entirely* reject the other; each one rejects not the whole, but certain—perhaps decisive—parts of the other. To be sure, each one thinks the other can be useful to it if put in a subsidiary position. But both cannot accept compromise on the matter of the truth. This seems to be why, according to Strauss, they also can never achieve a complete and total *synthesis* in the manner of Hegel: each one will try to dominate the other, because each contends that it is ultimately truer than the other and holds to something fundamental that is diametrically opposite to the other. But each one may also recognize significant elements of truth in the other. As Strauss construes "Jerusalem and Athens," it is a complicated and tense marriage, conflicting and yet affectionate. But precisely because they are both fighting for and lovers of the truth, and so "cannot vanquish by the sword" (as Maimonides puts it) if they are to genuinely defeat their opponent, it is never merely a matter of who rules or who is in power; each one may only subdue the other by argument or demonstration, however those are defined. And so both Jerusalem and Athens are locked in a vivifying and tense relation, an astonishingly vital embrace of what he calls two "spiritual powers" contending with one another.[7] For Strauss, it is not only an enchanting conflict and a unique conversation, but it also happens to be the "secret" of the very survival of the West, which must be kept vital and in motion if the West is itself to be kept vital and in motion. Strauss leaves much for his readers to reflect on and to work through, in order to resolve this "spiritual" dialectic (if not often a spiritual combat) that he portrays as almost a lovers' quarrel.

And hence the long tradition of conversation and argument that has characterized the relations between religion and philosophy in the West, occasionally friendly, but often antagonistic. This is something that is unavoidable, considering the nature of each. In Strauss's perspective, religion *can* be analyzed by philosophy in terms of its political function: most political philosophers contend as a universal truth that every healthy society will maintain some type of religion; what the philosophers debate among themselves is about which type of religion is best for a particular form of society. But in Strauss's view, this analysis (however much it seems to legitimate religion) will never be enough to do justice to religion especially insofar as it is biblical religion. That religion is of a type that maintains its superiority *in truth* to philosophy, and not just in political power. And although Strauss was interested in types of religions and types of gods, and how they uniquely characterize, or at least contrarily manifest themselves in, the order of different regimes—even so authentic biblical religion will reject any and every regime that is not ultimately beholden to the divine as biblical religion defines it, that is, as higher than and transcendent of man or any regime. Although Strauss was of the opinion that the political measure can never be a fully adequate way of comprehending the biblical type of religion (even if often attempted), nonetheless he also ventured to comprehend in a study of the book of Genesis what it is in the notion of God constitutive of a certain biblical theology that makes it so resistant to being encompassed by politics, and so also philosophy.

Although Strauss's interest in religion was broadly based, he was likewise especially drawn toward the effort to cognitively fathom how it is that biblical religion in the West rejects the unconstrained philosophic search, that is, the philosophic way of life, as ultimate, even though the same religion is not opposed to the life of thought, if rooted in and animated by proper piety. This brought him to the careful examination of other issues that he tenaciously pursued: the seeming irrefutability of revelation by philosophy or science; the nature of religious experience and whether its interpretation is determined solely by such things as language and tradition; the phenomena of "the presence" and "the call" in religion as key aspects of how the divine being penetrates the heart and guides the soul of human beings; the fraught yet inextricable bond between morality and religion. Although these are only a few of the topics that manifest themselves repeatedly, and are pursued determinedly, in Strauss's writings on religion (appearing in the midst of his writings on political philosophy), none of them quite exhaust Strauss's interest in matters of religion, toward which he tended to maintain a buoyant curiosity and a gracious open-mindedness. In other words, he was almost completely free of the "antitheological ire" that he recognized as most characteristic of the modern philosophers, even though he was not always free of a pointed criticism of certain forms of religion. But he couched these criticisms in the subtlest of terms and conveyed them by the most nuanced modes of communication, not primarily from any fear of persecution, but rather from a prodigious desire to bring the debate (as a lovers' quarrel) to flourishing life again, which compels criticism of religion to be made secondary, and hence subordinate to the fair-minded openness toward and consideration of religion. If Strauss's powerful thought on religion is ever to be comprehended fully and properly, it will require a thorough engagement with his views on the many themes and issues of religion that permeate his writings. This is the stirring and rousing challenge that a book like the present one presents to its readers. If they so choose, it may even set them on an illuminating path of uncovering some of the deepest and most acute dimensions of Strauss's thought.

Notes

1. Leo Strauss, "Progress or Return?," in *Jewish Philosophy and the Crisis of Modernity: Essays and Lectures in Modern Jewish Thought*, ed. Kenneth Hart Green (Albany: State University of New York Press, 1997), 108-9.

2. Leo Strauss, *The City and Man* (Chicago: University of Chicago Press, 1977), 241.

3. Jacob Klein, with Leo Strauss, "A Giving of Accounts," in *Jewish Philosophy and the Crisis of Modernity: Essays and Lectures in Modern Jewish Thought*, ed. Kenneth Hart Green (Albany: State University of New York Press, 1997), 458.

4. See Cicero, "Somnium Scipionis" [The Dream of Scipio], in *De re publica* [*The Republic*], vi.9-29. See especially Leo Strauss, *Seminar in Political Philosophy: Cicero*, ed. James H. Nichols (The Estate of Leo Strauss, 2016), 16, 23-24, 81-83, 92-107, 110. In this context, Nichols notes that in the last session Strauss mentions "an issue on which [Strauss] has changed his judgment," which I would call a truly fundamental issue. Based on statements made by the character Scipio in the *Republic*, he is no longer certain whether or not Cicero "ultimately supported the superiority of the philosophic life" as a knowable truth, in contrast with the life of the legislator or the statesman. Regarding what Cicero thought, "the question remains open for him." See Nichols, iv, and Strauss, 318-19.

5. Perhaps the closest that he gets to an unambiguous statement of this issue is as follows: "Ultimately, I think, one would have to go back to a fundamental dualism in man in order to understand this conflict between the Bible and Greek philosophy, to the dualism of deed and speech, of action and thought—a dualism which necessarily poses the question as to the primacy of either—and one can say that Greek philosophy asserts the primacy of thought, of speech, whereas the Bible asserts the primacy of deed." Leo Strauss, "Progress or Return?," in *Jewish Philosophy and the Crisis of Modernity: Essays and Lectures in Modern Jewish Thought*, ed. Kenneth Hart Green (Albany: State University of New York Press, 1997), 120. For the way of conveying the "fundamental dualism in man" as an opposition of "heart" and "mind," see in the same book 108-09, 159, 319, 475.

6. Leo Strauss, "Jerusalem and Athens: Some Preliminary Reflections," in *Jewish Philosophy and the Crisis of Modernity: Essays and Lectures in Modern Jewish Thought*, ed. Kenneth Hart Green (Albany: State University of New York Press, 1997), 379-80.

7. For the "two spiritual powers," see Leo Strauss, "Appendix 1: Plan of a Book Tentatively Entitled *Philosophy and the Law: Historical Essays*," in *Jewish Philosophy and the Crisis of Modernity: Essays and Lectures in Modern Jewish Thought*, ed. Kenneth Hart Green (Albany: State University of New York Press, 1997), 468.

SVETOZAR Y. MINKOV AND RASOUL NAMAZI

Editors' Introduction

THE SCHOLARSHIP ON A CLASSIC PHILOSOPHER is often concerned with real or apparent contradictions in that philosopher's thought: What is Aristotle's view of the happy life? Is it one of a political man dedicated to virtuous practical activity or is it that of a philosopher contemplating the eternal beings? Is Adam Smith's thought founded on the self-interest of individuals, as it seems from his *Wealth of Nations*, or sympathy, as one can deduce from *The Theory of Moral Sentiments*? Was Thomas Hobbes an authoritarian monarchist or a liberal individualist? The scholarship on the thought of Leo Strauss turns around similarly polarizing questions about his position on some topics at the heart of his thought.[8] Among such controversies, perhaps the most famous one concerns the question of religion. The controversy is born out of one fundamental and indisputable element in Strauss's thought: Strauss subscribed to the idea that there is a radical opposition between philosophy and religion, or reason and revelation, or symbolically between Athens and Jerusalem.[9] Considering the explicit claims made by Strauss in his writings, the attribution of this idea to Strauss is not contested by any of his readers. The controversy concerns where Strauss's sympathies lie in this opposition between philosophy and religion. Considering the radical character of the opposition between philosophy and religion depicted in Strauss's writings, one can immediately conceive two possibilities: either Strauss (1) subscribed to the camp of philosophy, thereby rejecting religion, or vice versa (2) he embraced religion, consequently renouncing philosophy.

The first possibility, which one can perhaps crudely describe as that of Strauss the atheistic philosopher, has some concrete evidence to rely on.

As it appears from biographical evidence, Strauss did not claim to be an Orthodox Jew nor did he show signs of adhering to some other religion. It even seems that during his lifetime, Strauss acquired a reputation in some circles as an atheist.[10] The reputation seems to have inconvenienced some of Strauss's more religiously inclined students who could not follow their teacher in his supposed atheism as in other matters.[11] The second possibility, again crudely speaking, Strauss the religious thinker, has also some biographical evidence to rely on: in 1959, in a note that circulated among his students and in reaction to David Spitz's article, which claimed that "Strauss ... rejects God," Strauss seems to deny that he is an atheist.[12]

The evidence available for these two positions is not limited to biographical anecdotes, obviously. More theoretical evidence has been advanced by different scholars to buttress the claims of these two opposing "camps," though perhaps the military metaphor is not apt. Heinrich Meier is the most thoughtful representative of "Strauss the atheistic philosopher" camp. The major challenge that Meier encounters and takes upon himself to overcome is the fact that Strauss was also explicit in claiming that religion is not a weak but rather an formidable opponent of philosophy whose claims are difficult, nay, impossible, to reject. Meier's solution is to state that such radical claims for religion on the part of Strauss are highly rhetorical and employed for pedagogic or prudential reasons.[13] The camp of "Strauss the religious thinker" is well represented by Susan Orr—although considering Strauss's lifelong philosophic perspective, one can say that she is almost unique in advocating for this view.[14] The same statements of Strauss that are considered by Meier as rhetorical are exploited to the full in bolstering the thesis of Strauss as a religious thinker by Orr. In her view, Strauss's claims about the strengths of the religious view must be taken seriously: they in fact point to Strauss's deepest thought, that is that revelation and religion can provide man with the firm ground that reason and philosophy are incapable of offering.[15]

These two camps are not the only available options either: there are several other options of less radical character that somehow synthesize the two heads of the eagle, philosophy and religion. One claims that Strauss subscribed to a *"modus vivendi* for the two antagonists, rather than a final settlement between them."[16] Others have claimed that Strauss found himself in an impossible situation born out of his claim that neither of the alternatives, philosophy or religion, could refute the other; facing this situation, Strauss, in this view, took a leap of faith and embraced philosophy without having any argument to do so. In other words, on this view, Strauss embraced philosophy knowing "that it is as arbitrary as it accuses religion of being."[17] Strauss was aware of this weak-kneed dodge. Speaking of the predominant tendency of thinkers throughout the ages to harmonize and reconcile philosophy and religion, Strauss explained this tendency by writing that "we do not like the suggestion that we have to make an irrevocable choice between two things which for all we know are both of supreme goodness or beauty." A decisionism described above amounts to saying that "all our actions or thoughts may ultimately be based on a blind choice, on a leap into the dark." For Strauss, we tend to do what we can to avoid clearcut alternatives through different forms of harmonization and synthesis, which "allow us to believe that we are the masters of the situation."[18] In Strauss's view, harmonizations and syntheses are of very different forms, but what perhaps explains all of them is our "human and all-too-human desire to eat the cake and have it."[19] Of course, it is possible that Strauss did not actually believe that this unsatisfactory predicament is capable of being resolved. And perhaps he believed that we can't solve the riddle but can only articulate it most clearly. In this regard, Strauss might have been imitating his Plato:

> Plato composed his writings in such a way as to prevent for all time their use as authoritative texts. His dialogues supply us not so much with an answer to the riddle of being as with a most articulate "imitation" of that riddle. His teaching can never become the subject of indoctrination. In the last analysis, his writings cannot be used for any purpose other than for philosophizing. In particular, no social order and no party which ever existed or whichever will exist can rightfully claim Plato as its patron.[20]

Whether this passage explains the reason for the controversy around Strauss's view of religion or perhaps Strauss has provided in his writings clues for definitively resolving the issue remains to be seen. This short introduction is neither the place nor is it our intention in this book to resolve this complex question and to put an end to the controversy around Strauss's view of religion, one way or another.

This volume, containing texts from and on Strauss touching on the question of religion, has instead the intention of providing supplementary material to study this question if not to fan the flames of the debate in the scholarship on this subject. We are well aware of Vladimir Nabokov's objection to the use of scraps and unvetted materials as a way of plumbing the depths of a great author: "Rough drafts, false scents, half explored trails, dead ends of inspiration, are of little intrinsic importance. An artist should ruthlessly destroy his manuscripts after publication, lest they mislead academic mediocrities into thinking that it is possible to unravel the mysteries of genius by studying canceled readings. In art, purpose and plan are nothing; only the results count."[21] But Strauss, in sharp contradistinction to Nabokov, placed the highest importance on "purpose and plan": see the chapters with "Intention" in their titles in *Thoughts on Machiavelli*, as well as his 1947 "On the Intention of Rousseau." As for sleuthing for the architecture of a work, consider also Strauss's August 19, 1939 letter to Jacob Klein: "Immerhin habe ich inzwischen die Memor. ganz verstanden, wenn ganz verstehen bei solchen Büchern identisch ist mit: den Aufbau verstehen" [In the meantime I have fully understood the *Memorabilia* if a full understanding with such books is identical with: understanding the plan/structure].[22] Drafts, presentations, and other archival materials may provide helpful sidelights to Strauss's intention. Of course, pride of place and the utmost attention should be given to Strauss's fully considered and finished published writings. So in the case of Lessing, one should study Strauss's introduction to Mendelssohn (see Martin Yaffe's edition of *Leo Strauss on Moses Mendelssohn*); in the case of the *Kuzari*, one should study chapter 3 of *Persecution and the Art of the Writing* (as Ralph Lerner has done below); in the case of Maimonides, one should concentrate on the 1963 "How to Begin to Study the *Guide of the Perplexed*" in *Liberalism Ancient and Modern* or "Maimonides' Statement on Political Science" in *What Is Political Philosophy* or on the Maimonides pieces in *Studies in Platonic Political Philosophy* (see Yehuda Halper's and Joshua Parens's reflections below); in the case of Spinoza, one should pore over the Strauss "Autobiographical Preface" to the 1965 edition of *Spinoza's Critique of Religion* (as Steve Frankel has done); in the case of Rousseau, there is the *Natural Right and History* subchapter and "On the Intention of Rousseau." But one should not be churlish and deny oneself access to the riches the unpublished materials provide. And when it comes to Plato's *Symposium* and Pascal's *Pensées*, the informal texts (notes and transcripts) are all we have.

The volume includes ten transcripts by Strauss divided into eight groups (including an appendix on Pascal), each group dealing with a specific thinker or theme. Each group of transcripts is followed by two interpretative essays by two different scholars. In this way, the readers have not only access to a considerable number of writings by Strauss dealing with religion, but they can also see how different scholars engage with them in their interpretative essays.

Notes

1. Leo Strauss, "Progress or Return?," in *Jewish Philosophy and the Crisis of Modernity: Essays and Lectures in Modern Jewish Thought*, ed. Kenneth Hart Green (Albany: State University of New York Press, 1997), 108-9.

2. Leo Strauss, *The City and Man* (Chicago: University of Chicago Press, 1977), 241.

3. Jacob Klein, with Leo Strauss, "A Giving of Accounts," in *Jewish Philosophy and the Crisis of Modernity: Essays and Lectures in Modern Jewish Thought*, ed. Kenneth Hart Green (Albany: State University of New York Press, 1997), 458.

4. See Cicero, "Somnium Scipionis" [The Dream of Scipio], in *De re publica* [*The Republic*], vi.9-29. See especially Leo Strauss, *Seminar in Political Philosophy: Cicero*, ed. James H. Nichols (Chicago: Leo Strauss Center, 2016), 16, 23-24, 81-83, 92-107, 110. In this context, Nichols notes that in the last session Strauss mentions "an issue on which [Strauss] has changed his judgment," which I would call a truly fundamental issue. Based on statements made by the character Scipio in the *Republic*, he is no longer certain whether or not Cicero "ultimately supported the superiority of the philosophic life" as a knowable truth, in contrast with the life of the legislator or the statesman. Regarding what Cicero thought, "the question remains open for him." See Nichols, iv, and Strauss, 318-19.

5. Perhaps the closest that he gets to an unambiguous statement of this issue is as follows: "Ultimately, I think, one would have to go back to a fundamental dualism in man in order to understand this conflict between the Bible and Greek philosophy, to the dualism of deed and speech, of action and thought—a dualism which necessarily poses the question as to the primacy of either—and one can say that Greek philosophy asserts the primacy of thought, of speech, whereas the Bible asserts the primacy of deed." Leo Strauss, "Progress or Return?," in *Jewish Philosophy and the Crisis of Modernity: Essays and Lectures in Modern Jewish Thought*, ed. Kenneth Hart Green (Albany: State University of New York Press, 1997), 120. For the way of conveying the "fundamental dualism in man" as an opposition of "heart" and "mind," see in the same book, 108-9, 159, 319, 475.

6. Leo Strauss, "Jerusalem and Athens: Some Preliminary Reflections," in *Jewish Philosophy and the Crisis of Modernity: Essays and Lectures in Modern Jewish Thought*, ed. Kenneth Hart Green (Albany: State University of New York Press, 1997), 379-80.

7. For the "two spiritual powers," see Leo Strauss, "Appendix 1: Plan of a Book Tentatively Entitled *Philosophy and the Law: Historical Essays*," in *Jewish*

Philosophy and the Crisis of Modernity: Essays and Lectures in Modern Jewish Thought, ed. Kenneth Hart Green (Albany: State University of New York Press, 1997), 468.

8. For an overview of such controversies around Strauss's positions on different issues, see Michael Zuckert and Catherine Zuckert, *The Truth about Leo Strauss. Political Philosophy and American Democracy* (Chicago: University of Chicago Press, 2006), 58–80; Michael Zuckert and Catherine Zuckert, *Leo Strauss and the Problem of Political Philosophy* (Chicago: University of Chicago Press, 2014), 311–38.

9. Leo Strauss, *Natural Right and History* (Chicago: University of Chicago Press, 1953), 74–76; Leo Strauss, "The Mutual Influence of Theology and Philosophy," *Independent Journal of Philosophy* 3 (1979): 111–18; Leo Strauss, "Reason and Revelation (1948)," in *Leo Strauss and the Theologico-Political Problem*, ed. Heinrich Meier, trans. Marcus Brainard (Cambridge: Cambridge University Press, 2006), 149.

10. In 1954, Karl Jaspers describes Leo Strauss as "an orthodox Jew." Jaspers apparently didn't know Strauss and had formed an opinion of him only on the basis of Strauss's book on Spinoza. Arendt, who appeared to know Strauss personally, informs Jaspers that Strauss "is a convinced orthodox atheist." Hannah Arendt and Karl Jaspers, *Correspondence 1926–1969*, ed. Lotte Kohler and Hans Saner, trans. Robert Kimber and Rita Kimber (San Diego: Harvest Book, 1992), 244, 247. See also the discussion of David Spitz below (note 12) and Gershom Scholem's comment on Strauss's *Philosophy and Law* in Heinrich Meier, "How Strauss Became Strauss," in *Reorientation: Leo Strauss in the 1930s*, ed. Martin D. Yaffe and Richard S. Ruderman (New York: Palgrave Macmillan US, 2014), 21. See also Strauss's conflictual relationship with Nahum Norbert Glatzer in Susanne Klingenstein, "Of Greeks and Jews," *Washington Examiner*, October 25, 2010, https://www.washingtonexaminer.com/magazine/565347/of-greeks-and-jews/.

11. Werner J. Dannhauser, "Athens and Jerusalem or Jerusalem and Athens," in *Leo Strauss and Judaism: Jerusalem and Athens Critically Revisited*, ed. David Novak (Lanham, MD: Rowman and Littlefield, 1996), 155–71.

12. David Spitz, "Freedom, Virtue, and the New Scholasticism: The Supreme Court as Philosopher-Kings," *Commentary* 28, no. 10 (1959): 313–21. Strauss's note is quoted in full and discussed in Kenneth Hart Green, *Jew and Philosopher: The Return to Maimonides in the Jewish Thought of Leo Strauss* (Albany: State University of New York Press, 2012), 237n1; Hilail Gildin, "Déjà Jew All Over Again: Dannhauser on Leo Strauss and Atheism," *Interpretation* 25, no. 1 (1997): 125–33.

13. Heinrich Meier, *Leo Strauss and the Theologico-Political Problem*, trans. Marcus Brainard (Cambridge: Cambridge University Press, 2006), 16, 23–24.

14. Orr claims that this view is also shared by Harry Jaffa. Susan Orr, *Jerusalem and Athens: Reason and Revelation in the Work of Leo Strauss* (Lanham, MD: Rowman and Littlefield, 1995), 10–14.

15. Orr, *Jerusalem and Athens*, 149–58.

16. Green, *Jew and Philosopher*, 227n66.

17. Stanley Rosen, "Wittgenstein, Strauss, and the Possibility of Philosophy," in *The Elusiveness of the Ordinary: Studies in the Possibility of Philosophy* (New Haven: Yale University Press, 2002), 151.

18. Leo Strauss, "Jerusalem and Athens (1946)" (New School for Social Research, November 1946), 2. Strauss's lecture was presented on November 13, 1946, when he spoke in the General Seminar at the New School for Social Research in New York. See Meier, *Leo Strauss and the Theologico-Political Problem*, xvi.

19. Leo Strauss, "'Religion and the Commonweal in the Tradition of Political Philosophy.' An Unpublished Lecture by Leo Strauss," ed. Svetozar Y. Minkov and Rasoul Namazi, *American Political Thought* 10, no. 1 (2021): 117. See below 313.

20. Leo Strauss, "On a New Interpretation of Plato's Political Philosophy," *Social Research* 13, no. 3 (1946): 351, or in Leo Strauss's *Published but Uncollected English Writings: 1937–1972*, edited by Steven J. Lenzner and Svetozar Y. Minkov (South Bend, IN: St. Augustine Press), 130.

21. *Eugene Onegin: A Novel in Verse by Alexander Pushkin*, trans. and commented on by Vladimir Nabokov (Princeton: Princeton University Press, 1975), 15.

22. *Gesammelte Schriften*, ed. by Heinrich Meier (Stuttgart/Weimar, 1997), vol. 3, 580.

PART ONE

EDITED BY HANNES KERBER
TRANSCRIBED BY SVETOZAR Y. MINKOV AND HANNES KERBER

Transcript 1

LEO STRAUSS, NOTES ON LESSING'S *NATHAN THE WISE* (1940 AND 1942)

Editorial note: Leo Strauss's notes on Gotthold Ephraim Lessing's 1779 play *Nathan the Wise* were prepared for two different occasions. Strauss wrote the first set of notes (Leo Strauss Papers, Box 18, Folder 7, Hanna Holborn Gray Special Collections Research Center, University of Chicago Library) for a seminar titled "Continental Champions of Freedom of Thought," which he taught at the New School for Social Research in the spring of 1940. The announcement in the 1939/1940 course catalog of the Graduate Faculty of Political and Social Science reads: "410-0. CONTINENTAL CHAMPIONS OF FREEDOM OF THOUGHT—LEO STRAUSS. *Spring term. Fridays, 8:10–10:00 P.M.* The events of the last decades have heightened our interest and increased our understanding of the fight waged by such men as Bayle, Voltaire, and Lessing for freedom of thought. What did they understand by freedom of thought? How did they conceive of its political and institutional implications? To what extent is their view of freedom of thought tinged by the peculiar prejudices of their age? And how did it influence the literary form of their writings?" The second set of notes (Leo Strauss Papers, Box 16, Folder 5) brings together all available drafts for a lecture on "The Political Message of Lessing's *Nathan the Wise*." While the exact date is not known, Strauss's remarks in the notes suggest that he gave, or intended to give, the lecture in the General Seminar, the faculty colloquium of the Graduate Faculty, sometime after March 1942.[1]

All translations are my own. The translations from *Nathan the Wise* are taken from a draft translation of the play that Martin Yaffe and I are preparing for publication. The footnotes as well as the additions in the square […] brackets and translations are by the editor. Angle brackets < … > indicate passages that Strauss crossed out. Strauss's underlinings have been replaced by the volume editors with italics. The editor thanks Jenny Strauss Clay, who gave permission for the publication of these notes and retains her rights to the material.

Notes from a Seminar on "Continental Champions of Freedom of Thought"
(Graduate Faculty, New School for Social Research, 1940)

Nathan der Weise I

A dramatic *poem*—it is not decided whether it is a tragedy or a comedy—only its *dramatic* nature is emphasized.

The occasion: Lessing had been engaged for about 2 years in a violent controversy with the orthodox Lutheranians—his sovereign, the elector of Brunswick, had forbidden him to continue the controversy—he *escaped* into poetry.

(Lessing's ruses: he hid the name of the author of the "fragments," suggesting the name of another dead heretic …)

He escapes into poetry—into a *drama*. What is the peculiar nature of dramatic poetry?

1. The most *vulgar* poetry—it does not even presuppose *reading Hamburgische Dramaturgie*, p.m.[2], p. 91 Ab.[3] 1; 104 col. 1 Ab. 3; 105 col. 1 Ab. 2.[4]
2. In a drama, the poet *never* speaks in his own name. The poet may deceive in particular by the agreement of all *nice* characters …

The subject: The conflict of the 3 great religions is being happily settled in the *holy land* during the *Age of Faith*. The atmosphere of highest religious tensions may be particularly favorable to freedom of the mind—more than the free atmosphere of enlightened 18th century Europe (cf. "Leibniz von den ewigen Strafen": eine Klugheit, für die wir viel zu weise geworden sind [a prudence for which we have become far too wise][5]).

Palestine was then a *Muslim* country > Averroism; Islamic *mono*theism, De tribus impostoribus [Of the Three Impostors].[6]

The leading figure, a *Jew*: the *highest* tension, the highest degree of religious fanaticism may lead to the most radical emancipation > Spinoza—or Maimonides (Leibniz and Mendelssohn).[7]

The Jew is a *merchant*: trade > freedom of the mind.

The action: Nice people belonging to various religions are brought together in an atmosphere hot with religious exclusiveness by a number of strange coincidences, so that they can recognize mutually their *human* dignity, and even their *blood-relationship.*

The action—the happy end—is in accordance with the thesis: Providence, God rewards good actions, done on earth, on earth, "optimism." The religion of providence and optimism is based on *reason* (—nature—charity) ≠ revelation (—miracles—intolerance and pride).

The revelation of that true natural religion is an essential part of the *action*: it establishes the friendship between philosopher and king, without which the happy end would not be brought about.

A number of strange occurrences: *natural* miracles (cf. I 1).

The *real* action is the fate of the hero, Nathan. What happens to him? The first scene exhibits the strength of Nathan's *love* of his foster-daughter (Lessing—Malchen[8]). Cf. 227a, top[9] and 227b.[10] The last scene: Nathan seems to become the father of the Knight as well; but he is, as it were, pushed aside by Saladin and Sittah: he *does* lose his child.

He owes that child, not to nature or chance, but to *virtue* (184b bottom[11])—virtue is *not* rewarded on earth.

What about the statement to the contrary (189a[12])? The context: Nathan's prudent medicines. See also 187a[13] in the middle.

Everything depends on our seeing the *difference* between Nathan and the happy family (Saladin, Sittah, Knight, and Recha), on our seeing the *peculiar* character of Nathan.

The perfectly happy end would have been possible *without* Nathan's discussion with Saladin: the Knight is indifferent to religion independently of Nathan (II 5)—Saladin and Sittah are no fanatic people—Recha is so much in love with the Knight that she would have married him anyway.

"Nathan the Wise"—sounds like the name of a king or of a prince (cf. 194b[14]) (—Friedrich der Weise[15]—Friedrich der Grosse[16])

But why Nathan?

The *prophet* Nathan—the prophet who admonished, and reprimanded, those oriental despots David and Solomon (2 Sam 7,12; 1 Kings 1).

— The *wise* Nathan—he does *not* reprimand Saladin—191a[17] (I 3)—his prudence.

— Patriarch → the fight between Pope and Emperor > cf. Jacobi's "Etwas das Lessing gesagt hat [Something Lessing Said]."[18]

The inferiority of the "family" at the end as compared with Nathan:

the *child* p[19] etc.)
the *young* Knight—he is rash (cf. 232b[20])
    the *confused* Saladin, the bad chess player
    the calculating *woman* Sittah.

Only these 4 people, and *not* Nathan, prove to be blood-relatives—this alone shows that the *natural kinship* of all men is *not* considered by Lessing the last word. It is not without good reason that the solution given in the *Nathan*, is so different from that of the *Tempest*: not upon an island, but in the "holy land." The relation of the "ideal" to "reality" is much more directly a *question* in the *Nathan*.

The deeper problem: it is perfectly understandable that Saladin, Knight and Recha, in order to prove to be relatives, ought not to be married—but why is Sittah necessary? Nathan and the 4 others have *no prospect of progeny* → closed and open society, the open society is impossible. Cf. 206b.[21]

The basic miracles: Recha's life is a *gift* of the Knight—the life of the Knight is a *gift* of the Sultan

everyone's life is a *gift* of his father 203b,[22] 204a top,[23] 223b bottom[24]
    → the radical *dependence* of man on man—the radical *servitude* of man to man

The significance of the *Dervish* (206a[25])
    Nathan's *prudence*: his manner of teaching (with what ease does he tell stories ...). 186b,[26] 187a.[27]

The conflict of Nathan with the Knight: 217b top, 218b top.

Der Tempelherr—der deutsche Bär [the German bear] (195b top[28])—cf. Tellheim[29]—"der menschliche Held [the human hero]" (*Laocoon* IV (10b top))[30] distinguished from, and opposed to, the *Stoic* (the *ideal* philosopher), but also from the *prudent* philosopher Nathan: who is not a "German," but very, very strange: a "Jew."

Nathan der Weise II

The 3 *central* scenes (III 5–7)[31]—in the center of which is the *only monologue* of Nathan.

Saladin has been described in II 1–2 (cf. 205b middle[32]) as a *bad* chess player—Nathan is a *good* chess player (199b[33]).

234a bottom and b top[34]

Saladin believes in vox populi vox Dei [the voice of the people (is) the voice of God]

Saladin's *question*: "What *faith*, what *law* has convinced you?"

The story of the *ring*—what is a ring? a thing which is highly valuable; not easy to destroy or to break; very close to the body, to the naked skin—surrounding it, covering a part of it; an ornament, and not a utensil; an ornament to which a very great usefulness is *ascribed*; *inherited*; an *artificial* thing.

(cf. the comparison of revelation to *chiro*mancy—Hempel XV 267f.[35])

(cf. the explanation of sceptres in *Laocoon* XVI[36])

What Nathan says to begin with, is not much: two rings are forged, only one is genuine—this corresponds to what all Jews, Christians, and Muslims say—he diverges from that view only by saying that it is *almost* impossible to detect the right belief (212a[37]).

(The father = the God of the revealed religions: he loves his sons according to their obedience to him (211b[38])).

He goes one step further: he, Nathan, does not dare to make a distinction between the 3 rings—for *God* made them undistinguishable.

They cannot be distinguished, they are identical, as far as their *reasons* are concerned—they are based on history, on tradition, on faith: everyone must trust most *his* tradition, *his* father (212a[39]).

The Judge does not give his *sentence*, he merely gives his *advice*—he states his sentence surreptitiously: all three rings are not genuine—his *advice* is that each seek to prove the genuine character of his ring by *good actions*, good morality. The sentence will be pronounced by the *Messiah* in 1000 years.

Earlier Draft for the Beginning of a Lecture on "The Political Message of Lessing's *Nathan the Wise*"
(General Seminar, New School for Social Research, 1942 or 1943)

Beginning—Many sermons have been preached by liberal rabbis and by liberal ministers, I say nothing of adherents of ethical culture—sermons extolling the lofty message of Lessing's immortal play. I shall not speak of its lofty message, but only of its pedestrian message, its political message. For apart from the fact that I hate to be a bore, I wish to remain within the boundaries of my competence as far as possible. It is unfortunate for you and even more so for myself, that I have to go beyond these borders on more than one point.

For: The thesis which I am submitting to you in this lecture—to say nothing of the lecture itself—is the product of hours of leisure, not of years of work. It is the thesis, not of [a] scholar, but of an amateur, of a lover. It is uncertain however whether only scholarly work of many years gives a man a right to talk about any subject of more than ephemeral significance; but certain it is that one cannot become a genuine scholar in any field, if one has not been in the first place, and if one does not become again and again, an amateur, a lover. At least potential scholars have the privilege, amounting to a duty, that their leisure alone can justify their work.[40]

Some time ago, I delivered in this seminar a lecture which seemed to some people to reveal an anti-German bias.[41] I am glad to have this opportunity of expressing in a way which, I hope, will not be considered obtrusive, my personal gratitude and my gratitude as a Jew, to a great son of the German nation, to that German whom I happen to love more than any other German, i.e. from whom I learned more than from any other German. That people like myself should avail themselves of opportunities such as these, might well seem to be a duty—in particular in this moment, now extending itself over 10 years, of parting.[42]

When reading, and trying to understand, a work such as the *Nathan*, one ought not to forget—in fact, one cannot forget—for a single moment that the author silently tells us all the time: Tua res agitur: it is *thy* case which is under examination.

This means two things: First, one has to apply to oneself the lesson of the *play*—that lesson is, as everyone knows, tolerance and toleration and charity. But the author cannot possibly tell us how we, how each of us, can best apply it in one's own case. Circumstances are decisive in all practical questions, and the circumstances of each of us are different at different times, in different human relations. The translation of the universal principle into a rule sufficient for guidance for an individual situation, this is the practical problem, and this practical problem is *not* solved by the lesson of the play, because the action of the play is of an *idealized* character: that action is as ideal, as unreal as a fairy-tale. There is, however, another lesson, apart from the lesson of the play itself, implied in the play: the lesson of the *author* of the play; by *writing* the *Nathan*, L. shows us how he, this individual, living in these individual circumstances, applied to himself and to his circumstances the universal rule of tolerance, toleration, and charity. *This* action of the man Lessing, as distinguished from the fairy-tale action of the play, is not ideal nor idealized: it is an actual fact of human experience, hence an *example* which we can try to imitate directly if intelligently. For the thinking reader, at least, the lesson given by the writer is more important than the lesson provided by the characters of the play.

Does this mean that we should have to close the book and study Lessing's life? This would be absurd—for what is Lessing's life except the external conditions for Lessing's thought, and of Lessing's thought we can know practically nothing except for his *books*, and in particular for his *Nathan*. No, we must read and reread the *Nathan*, but we must read it as the work of *Lessing*. This is still very obscure. What I mean is this: We have to consider just one fact of L.'s life, not mentioned at all in the *Nathan*, one fact extraneous to the play itself, which is of decisive importance for the understanding of the play: the fact, I mean, that Lessing was a *Christian*.

Later Draft for the Beginning of a Lecture on "The Political Message of Lessing's *Nathan the Wise*"
(General Seminar, New School for Social Research, 1942 or later)

The political message of Lessing's *Nathan the Wise*.

1. The contrast between Lessing's plea for universal religious toleration and the anti-Christian bias of his play.
2. The pro-Jewish bias of the play and its historical reasons.
3. The practical reasons of the pro-Jewish bias: the relation of money and wisdom, or of commerce and open-mindedness.
4. Nathan and the Dervish: the relation between prudent wisdom and imprudent wisdom.
5. Nathan and the Templar: the relation between prudent wisdom and the voice of the heart.
6. Nathan and Saladin: the gulf between the Wise and the enlightened despot.
7. Why does the play not end with a marriage: the limits of tolerance or the nature of political community.

The universal religion of the *Nathan* and L.'s private belief: Introite nam et hic Dii sunt [Enter, for here too are gods].[43] (the *plural*.) The motto of the play: (cf. the change of the motto from Euripides *Ion*[44]).

* * *

The *Nathan* is a plea for mutual toleration of all historical religions, a plea based, not on any particular historical religion, but on universal, rational religion. As regards the different historical religions—Christianity, Judaism, Islam—the *Nathan* is strictly speaking neutral. In spite of that fundamental neutrality, however, we observe a definitive anti-Christian bias: the most superior people of the play are a Jew (Nathan) and a Muslim (Dervish), and no Christian reaches their stature. The least sympathetic man: the Patriarch, is a *Christian*. How is that anti-Christian bias, which seems contradictory to L.'s freedom from prejudice, to be accounted for?

a) L. had to choose the most significant *setting* as regards both place and time: the Holy Land—the Age of Faith—the time of the Crusades—at that time, the intellectual superiority of Islam and Judaism to Christianity was a fact: Averroes and Maimonides precede in time Thomas Aquinas.

But this is not a sufficient explanation: Lessing had the poetic freedom to emancipate himself from the historical accidents.

b) L. was a Christian, writing in a Christian country for Christians—a pro-Christian bias was to be expected on all sides. To counteract the pro-Christian bias, it is not enough to speak without any bias—cf. the principle of moral education in *E.N.* II[45]—an anti-Christian bias was called for—L. and his contemporaries had to go through the anti-Christian bias to become truly free from their pro-Christian bias. They had to see Christianity from an anti-Christian angle, from a Jewish or Muslim angle, before they could see it without *any* bias, or before they could see it *philosophically*. (Application to *Merchant of Venice*.) This fact lays a heavy obligation on those interpreters of Lessing who are not Christians—e.g., on those interpreters who happen to be Jews. The *Nathan* has not only a general anti-Christian bias, it has even a pro-Jewish bias (L. was calumniated that he had got money from rich Jews[46]): after all, the hero is a Jew, and Nathan is much more important than the Dervish (so much so that Mr. Bruckner felt himself entitled to omit him altogether from his stage-presentation in the New School).[47] Now, a Jew must be expected to have a pro-Jewish bias if he is not perverted human being—and if he wants to learn anything from L., he must be on his guard exactly against that pro-Jewish bias. There is just the possibility to interpret the *Nathan* as a praise of *the* Jews—hence, the *Nathan* appeals to Jewish self-complacency, which is as natural and as illegitimate as any other self-complacency. Any over-emphasis on the pro-Jewish bias of the *Nathan* is not only a grave misinterpretation of Lessing's intention but, if done by a Jew, a sign that he has learned *nothing* from L.: *the* attitude of L. toward Christianity must be the model for the attitude of the Jewish interpreter of L. toward Judaism.

I would like to say one more word about this point which you may be inclined to dismiss as merely methodological or moral—because it is not always considered in any discussion bearing on the Jewish question. Jews, I feel, are under a particular obligation not to be self-complacent—self-complacency is the characteristic feature of the Philistine—Jews are not Philistines, in fact, they are enemies of the Philistines since time immemorial: Samson—but they are *neighbors* of the Philistines. Now, *Vayehi beshallach Par'oh* ... [And it was in Pharaoh's sending-away ...][48]—Jews are always in danger to prefer the short way through the land of the Philistines to the long way through the desert—sometimes, they succumb to that danger, and then something happens which reminds us, to quote Jeremia—*Zakharti lakh chesed ne'urayikh, veg[omer]* [I remember for you[r sake] the kindness/grace of your youth etc.].[49]

Why did L. choose a Jew as the hero of his play?—The particular character of the Jews: why is a Jew the ideal representation of "Wisdom"? The particular *difficulty* for Jews: the Tempelherr's remark on the Jews' responsibility for intolerance (εὐσέβεια [piety] περισσότης[50] [superfluity, excess]): it is particularly *difficult* for Jews—and hence, it is *most convincing* if a Jew can do it. The comedy *The Jews* and J. D. Michaelis' reaction to it.[51] L. knew better: his friendship with Moses Mendelssohn (he was L.'s best friend, in spite of the remarkable difference of intellectual level). More important: Maimonides, the greatest Jew of the Middle Ages, and perhaps of the whole post-Biblical period of Judaism, and Leibniz' judgment on him.[52]

PART IV
NOTE ON *NATHAN*

The *most common* aspect of the Jews: traders, merchants, financiers—money—what have *these* things to do with wisdom? Are they not connected rather with *worldly prudence*, not to say with slyness? Or should there be a profound connection between wisdom and prudence? The relation between philosophy (freedom of mind) and trade: Athens vs. Sparta; modern western philosophy vs. monasteries.

Nathan and the Dervish:

> Nathan wise *and* prudent
> the Dervish merely wise.

L.'s teaching is that wisdom and prudence are not separable, that wisdom without prudence is available, but not really wise. (Socrates did not separate from each other wisdom and σωφροσύνη [prudence]).

N.'s wise prudence "in action": his educating Recha etc.

More general remark: the error to identify the teaching of the *Nathan* with Lessing's own belief—cf. Fittbogen[53] and F. H. Jacobi[54] on the relevance of the *Nathan*. Mendelssohn.[55]

L.'s belief: his conversation with Jacobi
— there is no other philosophy than that of Spinoza—[56]
— philosophy is in *no* book—*not* in the *Ethics*—[57]

non ridere, nec lugere, non indulgere, sed intelligere [neither to laugh nor to cry nor to pander, but to understand].[58]

Then raise from practice to speculation.

Application to the lesson of the *Nathan*: tolerance—to be considered in the light of the action: the happy family—but no prospect of progeny—"Ernst und Falk" on *the* political problem: (you can be a left-wing Tory or a right-wing Whig—but no wise man will be a right-wing Tory or a left-wing Whig.)[59]

Lessing's alleged sentimentality—
MM's [Moses Mendelssohn's] remarks on his coldness
(see laments of MM in Kayserling[60]).

Notes

1. On Strauss's lectures in the General Seminar, see Hannes Kerber, "'Jerusalem and Athens' in America: On the Biographical Background of Leo Strauss's Four Eponymous Lectures from 1946, 1950, and 1967, and an Abandoned Book Project from 1956/1957," in *Journal for the History of Modern Theology / Zeitschrift für Neuere Theologiegeschichte* 29, no. 1 (2022), 90–132, especially 95–100 and 124–26.

2. In his private notes, Strauss uses "p.m." (penes me, Latin for "in my possession") to refer to books from his personal library.

3. "Ab." is short for "Absatz" (German for "paragraph").

4. Strauss refers to sections 2, 11, and 12 in Lessing's *The Hamburg Dramaturgy*. The edition he uses is *Gesammelte Werke in zwei Bänden* (Leipzig: Göschen'sche Verlagshandlung, 1855), vol. 2.

5. The passage from Lessing's *Leibniz on Eternal Punishments* reads in full: "[Leibniz] did no more and no less than what all the ancient philosophers used to do in their *exoteric* presentation. He displayed a prudence which our most recent philosophers have, of course, become far too wise to employ. He willingly set his own system aside and tried to lead each individual along the path to truth on which he found him."

6. The rumor of a treatise entitled *Of the Three Impostors* surfaced in the thirteenth century and circulated through the eighteenth century. The treatise was said to deny the truth of Christianity, Judaism, and Islam, with the "impostors" of the title being Jesus, Moses, and Muhammad. See Leo Strauss to Jacob Klein, February 16, 1938, in *Gesammelte Schriften*, ed. Heinrich Meier (Stuttgart: Metzler, 1997), vol. 3, 549: "You know the rumor (*Rede*) of the book *De tribus impostoribus*, which the bibliographers are looking for in vain: supposedly, it was written by Frederick II of Hohenstaufen, by Averroes etc. etc., but it does not exist. (The book by the same title was written by the end of the 17th century.) Well—one does not find 'De tribus impostoribus' for the simple reason that one is *searching* for it while it is in everyone's hands: it is the *Moreh* (resp. the works of Averroes and Farabi, not to speak of other surprises which are possible in this regard—I do not want to ask too much of my reluctant pen)."

7. See below, note 52.

8. Lessing was strongly attached to his stepdaughter Amalie "Malchen" König, who, aged sixteen when her mother (and Lessing's wife) Eva died in childbed in 1778, took over his household. Lessing repeatedly denied rumors that he intended to marry her after his wife had passed away.

9. "And although sevenfold love soon bound me to this solitary foreign girl; although the thought kills me that in her I am to lose my seven sons once more:—if providence demands her out of my hands again—I shall obey." (IV/7, v. 694-99.)

10. God! if after all I could still keep the girl and purchase such a son-in-law for myself besides!" (IV/7, v. 740.)

11. "Everything else I that own, nature and fortune have allotted to me. This possession alone I owe to virtue." (I/1, v. 33-36.)

12. "For God rewards a good done here, yet here too." (I/2, v. 358-359)

13. "Nathan: Yet if only a human — a human as nature grants them every day provided you this service: he'd have to be an angel for you. He'd have to be and would be. Recha: Not an angel in that way; no! a real one; he was for certain a real one! — Haven't you, you yourself taught me it's a possibility that angels do exist, that God could also do miracles to benefit those who love him? I do love him. Nathan: And he loves you; and does in every hour miracles for you and those like you; yes, did them for you already from all eternity. Recha: I like hearing that. Nathan: What? Since it would sound totally natural,

totally mundane, if an actual Templar had rescued you: should it be therefore any less a miracle? — The greatest of miracles is that true and genuine miracles can become and should become so mundane for us. But for this general miracle, a thinking person would hardly ever have dubbed miracle what only children should so call, who, gawking, follow only the most unusual, only the most novel." (I/2, v. 201-24.)

14. "Daja: His people worship him as a prince. But that they call him the wise Nathan, and not instead the rich one, has often surprised me. Knight Templar: To his nation rich and wise are possibly the same. Daja: But above all they should have called him the good one. For you cannot imagine at all how good he is." (I/6, v. 738-43.)

15. Frederick III (1463-1525), Elector of Saxony, known as "Frederick the Wise."

16. Frederick II (1712-1786), King of Prussia, known as "Frederick the Great."

17. "Enough! stop! ... Al-Hafi, make sure to go back into your desert soon. I'd fear precisely among humans you might forget to be a human." (I/3, v. 490, 496-99.)

18. In *Something Lessing Said: A Commentary on Journeys of the Popes* (1782), Friedrich Heinrich Jacobi reports the following anecdote: "This I heard Lessing say: What Febronius and his followers maintained was shameless flattery of the princes; for all their reasons against the rights of the pope were either no reasons or else twice and thrice as applicable to the princes themselves. Everyone was capable of grasping this; and the fact that no one among the many whose urgent business it would be to point this out has yet said so publicly, with all the conciseness and sharpness such an issue permits and deserves, was odd enough and an extremely bad sign."

19. "Recha: My father, if I'm wrong, you know I don't like being wrong. Nathan: You rather do like being taught." (I/2, v. 275-77.)

20. Reference to V/5, v. 311-49.

21. Reference to III/1, v. 16-64.

22. Reference to II/5, v. 504—II/6, v. 541.

23. "It is not enough that I still exist by his behest, that I still live because of his will: now I must also await him to tell me according to whose will I have to live." (II/7, v. 577-80.)

24. "What right would Nathan have to her, if he is not her father? The one who saved her life becomes the sole heir to the rights of him who gave it to her." (IV/5, v. 462-66.)

25. Reference to II/9, v. 713—III/1, v. 16.

26. Reference to I/1, v. 144—I/2, v. 187.

27. Reference to I/2, v. 188-227.

28. "Then go, you German bear! Go!—And yet I must not lose track of the animal." (I/6, v. 786f.)

29. Major von Tellheim is one of the two key figures in Lessing's 1763/1767 play *Minna von Barnhelm or the Soldiers' Happiness*.

30. "While the lamentations are those of a human being, the actions are those of a hero. Both combined make up the human hero, who is neither womanish nor hardened, but appears at one moment the former, at another time the latter, just as nature demands him to be at one time, and principles and duty demand at another. He is the highest being that wisdom could conceive and art could imitate." The page number refers to the edition mentioned in note 4.

31. In a footnote at the bottom of the page, LS corrects himself: "Not quite correct—the 3rd act has *10* scenes—the *two central* scenes (III 5–6) *precede* the scene where the story of the rings is told (= III 7)."

32. "Al-Hafi: He heeds me not at all, and with contempt throws the whole game into clumps. Nathan: Is that possible? Al-Hafi: And says: he'd simply want it to be checkmate, he'd want! You call that playing? Nathan: Hardly so, you call it gaming the game." (II/9, v. 682–86)

33. "He possesses understanding; he knows how to live; he plays chess well." (II/2, v. 276.)

34. Reference to V/6, v. 400–466.

35. At the end of the first section of his *Counter-Propositions* to the "Fragments by an Unnamed Author," Lessing compares theological and chiromantic proofs: "It is at least certain that the transition from purely rational truths to revealed ones is enormously disagreeable if one has become spoiled by the precise as well as comprehensible proofs of the former. One then expects and demands the *same* clarity and comprehensibility from the proofs of the latter, and one holds anything not proved *in the same way* not to be proved *at all*. I recall here what happened to me in my youth. I wanted to study mathematics, and I was given the elder Sturm's *Tables*, in which chiromancy was still included among the mathematical sciences. When I encountered this, I did not know what hit me. My limited understanding [*Verstand*] suddenly ceased to operate altogether; and although an art which promised to acquaint me with my future destiny held no small attraction for me, I felt as if I had exchanged a pleasant wine for insipid sugar-water when I transferred my attention to it from geometry. I did not know what to think of a man who had combined two such disparate things in *one* book; I took my leave of him and sought another teacher instead. But had I been obliged to regard this man as infallible, the question-begging principles of chiromancy, whose arbitrariness was so apparent to me, would have filled me with fear and distrust toward those mathematical truths which were so comfortable to my understanding [*Verstand*], even though I had grasped some of them only by memory. I could not possibly have regarded them both, geometry, and chiromancy, as equally certain; but I might well have come to regard chiromancy and geometry as equally uncertain. I hardly think it worth the effort to repudiate the suspicion that I am trying to insinuate that the proofs of revelation and the proofs of chiromancy are of equal weight. They are, of course, not of equal weight; their specific weights are unequivocally incommensurable; but both proofs nevertheless belong to one and the same class, both are based on testimonies

and on empirical propositions. And the contrast between the strongest proofs of this kind and proofs which flow from the nature of things is so striking that every art designed to reduce this striking divergence and to smooth it out by introducing all kinds of intermediate gradations is futile."

36. In section XVI of his *Laocoon*, Lessing gives the following explanation of Homer's account of Agamemnon's shield (*Iliad* 2.101–108): "I should not be surprised to discover that one of the ancient commentators of Homer had admired this passage as the most perfect allegory of the origin, the progress, the establishment and the hereditary succession of royal might [*Gewalt*] among men. Admittedly, I should smile if I were to read that the maker of the shield, Vulcan, (as the fire, as that which is most necessary for the preservation of man) points to the elimination of wants as such which moved the first men to subject themselves to one individual;—that the first king was a son of Time (*Zeus Kroniōn*), a venerable old man, who wished to share his power [*Macht*] with, or wholly confer it to, an eloquent, prudent man, a Mercury (*Diaktorōi Argeiphontēi*);—that the prudent orator relinquished his supreme might [*Gewalt*] to the bravest warrior (*Pelopi plēxippōi*), when the young state was threatened by foreign enemies;—that the brave warrior, after subduing the enemies and securing the kingdom, passed it on to his son, who, being a peaceful ruler, as a benevolent shepherd of his peoples (*poimēn laōn*), made them acquainted with luxury and abundance, whereby after his death the wealthiest of his relatives (*poluarni thuestēi*) had the way open to acquire by means of presents and bribes that which hitherto confidence had conferred and which merit had considered more a burden than an honor, and to secure it forever as a kind of purchased estate of his family. I should smile, but I would, nonetheless, be confirmed in my esteem for the poet, from whom so much can be loaned."

37. Reference to III/7, v. 432–76.

38. "So now this ring came, from son to son, ultimately to a father of three sons, all three of whom were equally obedient to him, all three of whom he consequently could not help loving equally." (III/7, v. 413–16.)

39. "Now whose trust and faith does one then least raise doubt about? Isn't it of those who are one's own? isn't it of those whose blood we are? isn't it of those who've given us tokens of their love from childhood on? who never have deceived us except where being deceived was more salutary for us? — How can I believe my fathers less than you do yours? Or the reverse. — Can I demand of you that you give the lie to your forebears in order not to contradict mine?" (III/7, v. 463–73.)

40. Cf. Leo Strauss, "Eine Erinnerung an Lessing," in *Gesammelte Schriften*, 2nd ed., ed. Heinrich Meier (Stuttgart: Metzler, 2013), vol. 2, 607: "The present explanation of Lessing's intentions is the attempt of an amateur, not a scholar; it is the fruit of hours of leisure, not years of labor. It is uncertain whether only years of scholarly labor earn one the right to an amateurish exposition. But certain it is that no one becomes a proper scholar without having been an amateur at first and becoming an amateur over and over again. Scholars in

the making have the obligatory privilege that only their leisure justifies their labor."

41. Strauss here refers to his "German Nihilism" lecture, delivered on February 26, 1941, in the Graduate Faculty's General Seminar. See Leo Strauss, "German Nihilism," ed. David Janssens and Daniel Tanguay, *Interpretation* 26, no. 3 (1999): 353–78, with Wiebke Meier, "Corrections to Leo Strauss, 'German Nihilism,'" *Interpretation* 28, no. 1 (2000), 33–34.

42. Cf. Leo Strauss, "Eine Erinnerung an Lessing," 608: "Besides, the author was not unmindful of the obligation of thanks which is owed by his nation to that great son of the German nation, especially at this moment of parting and of farewell."

43. This is the motto of Lessing's *Nathan*. Lessing consciously misattributes this line to Aulus Gellius ("Apud Gellium"), indicating that he is aware that Aristotle attributes it to Heraclitus (*De partibus animalium*, 645a15–23).

44. For the Greek motto of his unpublished fragment *Bibliolatry*, Lessing makes free use of three verses from Euripides's *Ion*: "Noble, O Christ, is the labor I perform in front of your house to honor the prophetic place."

45. Aristotle, *Nicomachean Ethics,* probably bk. 2, ch. 1.

46. In *Further Correction of the Tale of 1,000 Ducats, or Judas Iscariot the Second*, Lessing denies the rumor that the Jews of Amsterdam had paid him money to publish the anti-Christian "Fragments by an Unnamed Author."

47. In March 1942, Ferdinand Bruckner's free adaptation of *Nathan the Wise* played eleven times at Erwin Piscator's Studio Theatre at the New School for Social Research. According to the New School's Bulletin (February 16, 1942), this performance was "the first professional performance in English of 'Nathan the Wise.'" It was adopted by the Belasco Theatre on Broadway. In February and March 1944, Piscator staged the same version of Lessing's play again at the Studio Theater.

48. Strauss here quotes the beginning of Exodus 13:17: "And it was in Pharaoh's sending-away [the people, that God did not lead them by way of the land of the Philistines though it was near ...]."

49. Strauss here quotes the ninth through twelfth Hebrew words of Jeremiah 2:2

50. Strauss's 1948 notebook on Plato's *Euthyphro* revolves around the question whether piety is "περιττόν [superfluous]." See *Leo Strauss on Plato' "Euthyphro": The 1948 Notebook, with Lectures and Critical Writings*, ed. Hannes Kerber and Svetozar Y. Minkov (University Park: Pennsylvania State University Press, 2023), 49–50, 124, and 127–28.

51. Lessing's one-act *The Jews* attempts, as he himself puts it, "to show virtue to the vulgar in a place where they did not suspect to find it at all." Johann David Michaelis famously faulted the play for a highly improbable presentation of a Jew with an impeccable moral character: "It is indeed not impossible, but all too unlikely that such a noble temperament could have as it were formed itself among a people whose principles, way of life, and education color their dealings with Christians all too noticeably with animosity,

or at least with a decided cold-bloodedness against Christians. This implausibility was a hinderance to our pleasure, the more so that we wish this noble and beautiful image had truth and reality to it. But even mediocre virtue and honesty are so rarely to be found among this people that the few examples cannot diminish as much as one would like the hatred felt against them." *Göttingische Anzeigen von gelehrten Sachen* 70 (June 13, 1754), 621.

52. On the first sheet of his extensive excerpts from Maimonides's *Guide of the Perplexed*, Leibniz notes: *Egregium video esse librum Rabbi Mosis Maimonidis, qui inscribitur Doctor perplexorum, et magis philosophicum quam putaram, dignumque adeo lectione attenta. Fuit in philosophia, mathematicis, medica arte, denique sacrae scripturae intelligentia insignis.* [...] *Profitetur se parabolarum legis veram intelligentiam aperire; timuisse scriber quia, inquit, talia sunt de quibus nullus ex gente nostra in hac captivitate quicquam scripsit hactenus.* ("I find the book by Rabbi Moses Maimonides, entitled *Guide of the Perplexed*, is excellent and more philosophical than I had suspected, worthy of attentive reading. He was distinguished in philosophy, mathematics, the medical art, and finally his understanding of Sacred Scripture. [...] He promises to reveal the true understanding of the parables of the law. 'I fear to write,' he says, 'since these are things of which none of our people in captivity has hitherto written anything.'") Gottfried Wilhelm Leibniz, *Philosophische Schriften* (Berlin: Berlin Akademie, 2006), vol. 4, pt. A, no. 424, 2484.

53. See Gottfried Fittbogen, *Die Religion Lessings* (Leipzig: 1923), 148–82.

54. In *Against Mendelssohn's Imputations Regarding the Letters on the Doctrine of Spinoza* (1786), Jacobi explains his interpretation of *Nathan the Wise*: "The intention [*Absicht*] of this poem is so clear as day that it comes to every reader on its own; the intention to make suspect the spirit [*Geist*] of all revelation and present every system of religion, without any distinction, *as a system* in a hateful light."

55. In his *Morning Hours or Lectures on God's Existence* (Berlin: 1786), 268f., Mendelssohn interprets *Nathan the Wise* as "a kind of *Anti-Candide*" and a "glorious paean in praise of providence (*Lobgedicht auf die Vorsehung*)" (*Morgenstunden oder Vorlesungen über das Daseyn Gottes*, 129f.).

56. In the anonymously published *On Spinoza's Doctrine in Letters to Mister Moses Mendelssohn* (1785), Jacobi reports that Lessing told him in 1780: "There is no other philosophy but the philosophy of Spinoza."

57. Jacobi records the following conversation in *On Spinoza's Doctrine*: "Leßing: Then we shall not fall out over our credo. I: Let's not do that in any case. But my credo is not to be found in Spinoza. Leßing: I hope it's not to be found in any book. I. Not just that. I believe in an intelligent personal cause of the world. Leßing. Oh, so much the better! Then I must get to hear something quite new."

58. Spinoza declares in the *Political Treatise* (I, 4, 10, 2) that he carefully attempted "neither to laugh at nor cry about nor to despise, but to understand human actions (*humanas actiones non ridere, non lugere, neque detestari, sed intelligere*)."

59. At the beginning of the second dialogue of Lessing's *Ernst and Falk: Dialogues for Freemasons*, the freemason Falk calls himself a "heretical (*kätzerischer*) freemason."

60. See, for example, Meyer Kayserling, *Moses Mendelssohn: Sein Leben und Wirken*, 2nd ed. (Leipzig: Hermann Mendelssohn, 1888), 55, 263, 366, 368, and 445.

TILL KINZEL

Interpretative Essay

REFLECTIONS ON LEO STRAUSS,
HIS NOTES ON GOTTHOLD EPHRAIM LESSING,
AND "NATHAN DER WEISE"

Die Gabe sich widersprechen zu lassen, ist wohl überhaupt eine Gabe, die unter den Gelehrten nur die Toten haben.... Ich will nur sagen, daß es sehr gut sein würde, wann auch noch lebende Gelehrte, immer im voraus, ein wenig tot zu sein lernen wollten.[1]

LEO STRAUSS WAS A PHILOSOPHER who presented to the world the image of a scholar, but he was also a scholar who did not hide his interest in philosophy. Although he never spoke of himself as a philosopher—perhaps not too surprising in an age full of those claiming to be philosophers—he suggested that scholarship and philosophizing are not unrelated. In fact, under the peculiar conditions of modernity and the attendant forms of thinking that can be called the historical ("historicism" or *Geschichtlichkeit*) as well as the sociology of knowledge, only through a combination of philosophical thinking and scholarship is there any chance to escape the constraints of one's own living conditions. When Strauss suggested, in *Persecution and the Art of Writing*, that his project was part of what he called the sociology of philosophy, he was, on the one hand, harking back to the intense debate in the late Weimar years particularly in the wake of Karl Mannheim's *Ideologie und Utopie* (1929) to which not only people like Hannah Arendt and Günther Stern (Anders) had contributed but also important representatives of the Frankfurt School like Max Horkheimer and Theodor Adorno or someone like Hans Speier, later Strauss's colleague at the New School for Social Research (as well as a contributor to the Strauss-Festschrift *Ancients and Moderns*).[2] Strauss himself wrote a critique of Mannheim at the time that indicates sufficiently how much he was aware of the necessity to come to terms with this particular view of society.[3]

But Strauss was also speaking somewhat tongue in cheek in this matter because when he spoke of the sociology of philosophy he was also trying to suggest that what he called the class interest of philosophers *as* philosophers transcends the usual way of thinking about more or less Marxist views (to which, in some form or other, many of the contributors to the debate mentioned above subscribed) concerning the determination of one's consciousness by one's position in the social structure of a class society. It is of some significance, though as yet perhaps insufficiently understood, that Strauss, in the very same years that he was developing his peculiar approach to the "sociology of philosophy," should have been engaged in a very careful and extensive study of Lessing and his works. This kind of engagement or confrontation with Lessing that takes him seriously as a philosopher in his own right was not self-evident, and one can point only to very few other thinkers and contemporaries of Strauss who attempted it.[4]

This study of Lessing was on the one hand a scholarly duty in connection with his editorial work on Moses Mendelssohn for the so-called *Jubiläumsausgabe* edited by the Akademie für die Wissenschaft des Judentums. Lessing provided, together with Friedrich Heinrich Jacobi, a focal point for understanding not only what was at stake in late eighteenth-century debates concerning Spinozism, philosophy, revelation, and theology. In a letter to Ernst Simon from March 1937, on which Thomas Meyer reports, Strauss expresses his view that there was no mind freer in intellectual terms in the whole of modernity than Lessing's. And he there even made the astonishing claim that Lessing will be still read in the future when nobody will anymore be interested in Johann Wolfgang von Goethe or Friedrich Schiller.[5]

Lessing was, furthermore, also a thinker who according to Strauss could only be understood in light of his rediscovery of esotericism. In his letter to Alexander Altmann on May 28, 1971, Strauss noted that both he and Altmann seemed to agree on the existence of an esoteric teaching by Lessing ("die Existenz einer esoterischen Lehre Lessings"), even though the question would then still remain what the precise character or content of this teaching might be.[6] If Lessing has some kind of esoteric teaching, the question arises of in what kind of works he might possibly have tried to express or transmit such a teaching. This question is particularly relevant with regard to the different kinds of texts Lessing wrote not only as a scholar but also as a poet and playwright.

In Lessing's work, the interest in scholarship is from early on accompanied by a critique of scholarship or of the particular kind of person that purports to be a scholar. Thus, in one of his early comedies, *Der junge Gelehrte* (*The Young Scholar*), Lessing caricatures the pretensions of scholarship while at the same time engaging himself in scholarly pursuits for the whole of his life.[7]

It thus makes a lot of sense when Strauss, in his 1939 unpublished essay "Exoteric Teaching," speaks of the "divergent qualities of the philosopher and the scholar" that Lessing united in himself.[8] Scholarship is not the same as philosophizing, and under normal circumstances, the scholar is rarely a philosopher, whereas the philosopher is only accidentally also a scholar. That Lessing should have united in himself the qualities of the scholar and the philosopher is a plausible interpretation, but it cannot be the whole truth. (For Lessing also was a poet and playwright, and Strauss begins his commentary on Lessing in his class on "Continental Champions of Freedom of Thought" by pointing first to the [dramatic] poet Lessing before talking about anything else.)

Strauss's thankfulness toward Lessing in the grave matter of the relationship between (philosophical) reason and revelation was a key point in his notes on the topic. Here he explicitly refers to Lessing and specifies what kind of Lessing he is speaking about: "I do not mean the Lessing of a certain tradition, the Lessing celebrated by a certain type of oratory, but the true and unknown Lessing."[9] The Lessing mentioned here is not the author of edifying, if necessary, pleas for tolerance but rather the scholar who chose to opt for philosophy. This option for philosophy is, on the face of it, not edifying, because "Lessing's attitude was characterized by an innate disgust against compromises in serious, i.e. theoretical, matters."[10] Lessing the philosopher, one would assume, needs to express this particular kind of intellectual disgust in a way that makes philosophical readers aware of the crucial theoretical distinctions. However, as Strauss notes right away, when Lessing embarked on writing *Nathan der Weise*, he wrote under very specific circumstances that need to be considered when turning to his play. Strauss notes that Lessing actually escaped to or into poetry because he had been forbidden by his employer, the Duke of Brunswick, to continue the theological controversies in which he was engaged due to his publication of the fragments from Hermann Samuel Reimarus's deistic critique of revelation.

Strauss has claimed that Lessing was particularly important for him in his discovery or rediscovery of esotericism. Strauss seems to have believed that Lessing learned about esotericism directly from the ancients, but this may only be half the truth. For Lessing was so widely read in ancient and modern literature that there are indications that he may well have known about discussions of esotericism in the works of a then-famous contemporary of Leibniz, namely John Toland (whose writings, as one should keep in mind, were known to Hermann Samuel Reimarus as well, as Lessing would most certainly have known. Likewise, Toland was in contact with Leibniz who was of special interest to Lessing in connection with his own elaboration of esotericism.[11]) As for Strauss, he could have come across important references and discussions of esotericism in connection with Toland in at least three books that he studied for his early works, especially the study on *Die Religionskritik Spinozas als Grundlage seiner Bibelwissenschaft*.[12] To my knowledge, Strauss nowhere in his writings, not even in *Persecution and the Art of Writing*, refers to Toland, but he may have come across Toland's notion of an exoteric and esoteric philosophy in either or all of the books he quotes at one point or another.[13] Though there is fairly good reason to believe that he will have come across these pertinent passages, it may still be true that in the 1920s he still did not recognize the significance of these discussions.[14] It is unfortunate that Strauss did not pursue the issue of Lessing's esotericism in greater detail.

Lessing's own education in esotericism proceeded in a way that is still a matter of research and debate.[15] So here a few suggestions have to suffice. Lessing's intense interest in fables is well known. Likewise, his intense interest in English literature and aesthetics, and his Anglophilia, play an important role in his mindset. It is thus somewhat surprising that Lessing scholarship in recent decades has paid only slight attention to Lessing's confrontation with and translation of Samuel Richardson's *Aesop's Fables*, the original version now (2012) being for the first time available in a critical edition. The particular rhetoric of Aesopian writing seems to me of more than passing relevance to a better understanding of Lessing's approach to hermeneutics and theologico-political questions. The rich and diverse scholarship of Aesopian writing particularly in Early Modern English culture might be profitably employed to analyze Lessing's own appropriation of Aesopian writing in his work, examining the thesis that this approach to Richardson and Aesop can be regarded as perhaps the first step in Lessing's self-education in what he would later regard as the esoteric-exoteric double structure of philosophical communication, for example, in his *Leibniz von den ewigen Strafen* and the dialogue *Ernst und Falk*.

Whatever Strauss took from earlier interpretations of Lessing, he was mostly critical of those interpretations insofar as they had contributed to, and strengthened, a *traditional* view of Lessing. This seems also to include the Lessing interpretation of the supervisor of his dissertation, Ernst Cassirer, who had written about Lessing in his book *Freiheit und Form* as well as in another essay from 1929 on "Die Idee der Religion bei Lessing und Mendelssohn" that Strauss must have seen as it was published in the *Festschrift* on the occasion of the tenth anniversary of the Akademie für die Wissenschaft des Judentums. Cassirer only briefly touches on *Nathan der Weise*, but draws together various strands of Lessing's engagement with "religion."[16]

Strauss implicitly suggests that Lessing's play belongs to the more exoteric ways of presenting his thoughts, although a closer look might lead one somewhat into confusion. For on the one hand, according to Strauss, Lessing escaped into poetry by writing *Nathan der Weise* because he was no longer allowed to speak freely about religious matters in scholarly contexts. He thus had to retreat from his scholarly mode of communication to a form of writing that could make use of more indirect presentations of one's thoughts. On the other hand, Strauss emphasizes that what Lessing chose was in fact the most vulgar kind of poetry. Why does he call a play "vulgar"? Because "it does not even presuppose *reading*." A play is something presented to the eyes as performance and to the ears as sound. The words of the play are thus subject to the passing of time, the audience is not at their free will to ponder any statement within the play for long if it does not want to lose sight of the plot and the flow of arguments.

This suggestion by Strauss might be thought to be somewhat in tension with the fact that Lessing seems not to have expected a theatrical performance of this particular play any time soon.[17] In one letter to his brother Karl (April 18, 1779), Lessing explicitly plays with the notion that it may well be that his "Nathan," if put on the stage, would on the whole not effect much. He also adds in this context that it will perhaps never happen that the play was actually going to be staged. At this point, Lessing seems to stress the nature of this particular drama as a closet drama by noting that it would be enough if the play was read with interest, especially if among one thousand readers there would be a single one who came to the conclusion of doubting the evidence and universality (*Allgemeinheit*) of his religion.[18]

Lessing clearly envisions the possibility that the play will not be staged—and if that were the case, some kind of esotericism would be at play, so to speak, insofar as only a minority of readers would then draw the radical conclusion Lessing mentions in his letter to Karl. However, there is also evidence that Lessing's decision to write a play was clearly tied to his career as a dramatist, as his formulation shows in which he suggests returning to his "old pulpit" the theatre ("alte Kanzel"), a terminus that combines the theatrical performance with a sort of preaching in church, that is, a kind of rhetoric that is addressed to the whole community.[19] In his letter to Elise Reimarus, the daughter of the "Unnamed" man whose deistic writings Lessing had published in the course of the so-called *Fragmentenstreit*, he alludes to censorship when he says that has to make the attempt to find out whether the authorities will at least let him use the theatre "to preach unmolested" (*ungestört predigen*). More, he then suggests, will be revealed in oral communication to her.[20]

How does Strauss touch on the issue of esotericism in his class on Lessing? Surprisingly, he seems to do so very early on. For when characterizing the play as the most vulgar kind of poetry, he adds the more general remark that in "a drama, the poet *never* speaks in his own name. The poet may deceive in particular by the agreement of all nice characters." Now, where the poet in fact never speaks in his own name, none of the statements within the play can be unequivocally attributed to him in person (although this is exactly what even scholars have again and again tried to do). Even when the poet lets all so-called nice characters, that is, those that the audience would credit with speaking the truth, agree on a given topic, there is no way of telling what the poet himself truly thinks about it. It is thus the audience that he deceives, or who lets itself be deceived, by suggesting agreement that may be no more than popular or vulgar agreement. But Strauss, as one would expect, is always aware of two kinds of audiences. And he then singles out "the thinking reader" (not, at least not explicitly, the thinking theatergoer): "For the thinking reader, at least, the lesson given by the writer [Lessing] is more important than the lesson provided by the characters of the play." The thinking reader, therefore, is the one who manages to go beyond the words on the page attributed to individual speakers. He thus needs to consider not just the text of the play but the writer. However, for Strauss, it would be absurd if that resulted in a merely biographical study of Lessing.

But Strauss does not leave it at trying to understand the play on its own terms. He also takes into consideration some very topical concerns. Let me just mention one important issue. That Leo Strauss should have put so much emphasis on the issue of Jewish self-complacency is quite remarkable. For the suggestion that *Nathan der Weise* was at the time of particular relevance as a pro-Jewish play would have surprised no one, as it would have accorded with the very strong feeling on the part of the German Jewish community in the 1930s, but also already in earlier decades, that the play *Nathan der Weise* was, in a sense, "their" play.[21] Strauss may well have been aware of the efforts of the Jüdischer Kulturbund Berlin in the 1930s to put their production of the play into the service of some kind of pro-Jewish propaganda directed against the intolerant antisemitism of the National Socialists. In this connection, *Nathan der Weise* clearly fulfilled its function as a means for Jewish self-assertion while also maintaining the German Jews' connection to the German mind properly understood, even though some Jews criticized the staging of the play for this very reason.[22] When Strauss refrains from doing what would have been the natural thing—namely reading the play merely as an uplifting plea for tolerance and humanity—he gives the play by Lessing a nonobvious twist, thereby furthering not only Jewish but especially philosophical self-knowledge.

This approach in no way diminishes the significance of *Nathan der Weise* for the Jews in times of distress and persecution. (In fact, it was the case that National Socialist interpretations of Lessing and especially his play pointed out the unambiguously pro-Jewish dialogue and plot of *Nathan der Weise*, concluding on this basis that staging the play was an "impossibility" in the Third Reich.[23]) But it circumvents or prevents single-minded attention to the play as a contribution to, or commentary on, the Jewish question. This latter seems to be present or at least indicated by a fact parenthetically noted by Strauss: the Austrian playwright Ferdinand Bruckner (whose real name was Theodor Tagger) left out of his version of the play, produced in New York by Erwin Piscator in the theater of the New School for Social Research, the Muslim character of the dervish Al-Hafi.[24] This is not just a minor adaptation to the circumstances of the time of the production. For it is Al-Hafi who, according to Strauss, also represents a particular kind of wisdom that has significant relevance within the economy of thinking within the play. In this view, Al-Hafi represents wisdom without prudence—which cannot be regarded as wisdom in the full sense of the term, according to Strauss. This Piscator performance in New York would thereby also have occluded for its viewers the presentation, highlighted by Strauss in his notes, of the comparative weighing of the religious alternatives represented by Jews, Christians, and Muslims within the play. Al-Hafi the dervish as the representative of wisdom opens up, or makes it easier, to regard *Nathan der Weise* as an obviously pro-Islamic play.[25]

This prompts further questions that would go beyond that with which Strauss was concerned in his notes: What is the precise relationship of the plea for tolerance to the pro-Jewish and pro-Islamic position attributable to the play? Does toleration imply or necessitate some kind of appreciation of other religions? Does one (e.g., as a Christian) have to be in some sense pro-Islamic or pro-Jewish in order to be properly tolerant? And what about the attitude of Jews and Muslims toward Christianity? In the context of the Bruckner performance, leaving out the Muslim dervish underscores the edifying pro-Jewish interpretation of the play that Strauss would regard as a form of self-complacency. Thus, when Christians first had to see Christianity from an anti-Christian viewpoint, such as the Jewish or Muslim viewpoint, before being able to transcend bias as such, he makes clear how difficult a truly philosophical reading of Lessing`s play is. In any given historical situation, bias can only, but not in all respects, be countered by another bias, in order to later view it objectively or philosophically. This movement from bias to philosophy Strauss would later call "attachment to detachment," which is the most elevated form of theoretical engagement with a given problem.[26]

When Strauss notes that Lessing had set the play in the "*holy land during the Age of Faith,*" he also claims that the "atmosphere of highest religious tension may be particularly favorable to freedom of mind"—a view that Strauss explicitly juxtaposes to the situation in the eighteenth century. And rightly so, for even though Lessing had encountered some kind of theologico-political censorship that put a stop to his public engagement not only with Reimarus but also with the Hamburg main pastor Johan Melchior Goeze, he never was in any physical danger himself. Likewise, many theologians of his time no longer pursued religious discussions with fanatical zeal. So in order to find a historical place in which he could seriously contrast the three major religions, the Middle Ages in the Holy Land was the best choice—for here issues of religious diversity could easily and quickly turn into matters of life and death. The patriarch's repeated cries for having the Jew burnt at the stake is a case in point, but also the fact that Nathan had lost his whole family through the violence produced by religious fanaticism.

Taken by themselves, the notes by Strauss sometimes do not give sufficient information about which lines of thought he may have pursued in more detail orally. He refers only very briefly, to give one example, to the interpretations of *Nathan der Weise* by Lessing's contemporary Friedrich Heinrich Jacobi as well as by Strauss's contemporary, the scholar Gottfried Fittbogen. The latter was one of the few writers on Lessing, together with the theologian Friedrich Loofs, who had expressed some insight into the esotericism of Lessing himself. Strauss refers to Lessing's belief by noting "his conversation with Jacobi," but how exactly one should understand this conversation is a matter for debate. This conversation is often quoted by many scholars, including Strauss, for the statement, ascribed by Jacobi to Lessing, that "there is no other philosophy than that of Spinoza," combined with Lessing's other remark that this philosophy, to be precise, cannot be found in any book and therefore also not in the *Ethics*.

These two statements underscore the possibly ironic way of speaking that Lessing employed in the face of someone like Jacobi who had his own philosophical preoccupations but also had a knack for forcing them on others. We have no way of knowing what Lessing may have thought about Jacobi's views and questions independently from Jacobi's own report. The evaluation of what Lessing may have really thought about the issues raised by Jacobi was, perhaps, still to be further explored by Strauss. In his notes, he refers both to "Lessing's alleged sentimentality" and to Moses Mendelssohn's remarks concerning Lessing's "coldness." One wonders how these two different states of mind and soul may be combined if they can be regarded as accurate descriptions. As Strauss speaks of Lessing's "alleged" sentimentality, it is clear that he is of a different opinion, but there is no indication of how he evaluates the so-called coldness of Lessing. Maybe one should draw a connection here to the Spinozan words quoted a few lines above in Strauss's notes: "non ridere, nec lugere, non indulgere, sed intelligere." It is most likely that in this regard Strauss linked Lessing and Baruch Spinoza in this very philosophic attitude so that what can appear to be coldness is in fact the attachment to detachment mentioned earlier, referring to a detachment that does not disregard the world of practice. For Lessing's play turns the religious question concerning the truth of a particular revelation into a kind of long-running game or competition in which practical behavior in terms of humane morality will decide (but when?) which of the three religions implicitly referred to in the parable of the ring can claim to be the true religion.

In the ring parable, Nathan tells the story in such a way as to suggest that the issue still centers around the question of which of the three rings representing the three major religions can be the true one. In the logic of the narration, one ring has to be the original one, but it is at the same time made clear that they cannot be distinguished at all. That there are limits to this indistinguishableness is immediately noted by the Sultan—he knows that as a matter of fact, that is, phenomenologically speaking, the three religions do markedly differ. But the indistinguishable appearance of the rings does not symbolize the exterior aspect of the different religions' rituals, prayers, and other practices but the interior truth.

As Strauss correctly notes, the judge does not arbitrate the quarrel concerning the genuine ring but rather defers the answer to the query by offering his advice. This advice seems to rest on the presupposition that all three rings may well be fakes, so it is a hopeless undertaking to find the genuine ring by examining the rings themselves. In fact, the "genuine" ring can only reveal itself through some obscure causal connection, namely by producing "good morality." This answer, however, although Strauss does not explicitly say so, implies the three sons' freedom of will—for if they want to prove their respective rings to be the genuine one, they obviously need to make an effort. The deferral of the actual judgment to the Messiah in 1,000 years underscores the lack of clear and plain standards for what actually counts as good morality in these particular sons. In view of this future sentence, the morality in question cannot be just individual morality, but it has to be some kind of collective morality. But how can collective (family) morality be regarded as conclusive evidence for anything? In light of the fact that the rings look all the same, one might be tempted to ask: How visible is morality? And how moral would or could a kind of morality be that was merely engaged in to prove one's superior morality? If practical morality becomes the main concern of the "believers," how does this reflect on the "truth value" of the religions? Obviously, Lessing seems to have had in mind the moral doctrine that no homogeneity of opinions is essential for the common good but rather, as he had already maintained in a 1751 review, a consensus in terms of moral or virtuous actions "which render the world quiet and happy."[27]

Strauss esteemed Lessing much more than Moses Mendelssohn whom he did not regard as a first-class thinker. It would have been natural and understandable for Strauss to take Mendelssohn as his model, but he did not do so. What he called, somewhat ironically, the sociology of philosophy motivated him to look for a thinker who was able to critically look at his own religion in a way that does not presuppose anything. By singling out Lessing as exactly such a thinker, Strauss in a way demonstrated that his very special sociology of philosophy in fact opens up a way to philosophy proper. Strauss makes this perfectly clear in his draft for the lecture on "The Political Message of Lessing's *Nathan the Wise*" by saying something that reminds one of the distinction between unrealistic edification and actual reality. The lesson that those—and Strauss addresses them and his audience ("we") explicitly as "readers"—who are clearly meant to include the "thinking readers" should take away from Lessing's play is a lesson of universal relevance "implied in the play": "the lesson of the *author* of the play: by *writing* the *Nathan*, L. shows us how he, this individual, living in these individual circumstances, applied to himself and to his circumstances the universal rule of tolerance, toleration, and charity." But this lesson is ultimately not limited to historically understanding what Lessing did when he wrote this "dramatic poem." This lesson is, on the deepest level, a lesson that can guide our own actions: "This action of the man Lessing, as distinguished from the fairy-tale action of the play, is not ideal or idealized: it is an actual fact of human experience, hence an *example* which we can try to imitate directly if intelligently." Of course, by using the word "intelligently" in connection with imitation, Strauss suggests that "we" cannot imitate Lessing by doing *exactly* what Lessing did. This follows directly from Strauss's earlier remark that circumstances "are decisive in all practical questions, and the circumstances of each of us are different at different times, in different human relations." This can be said to be the crucial insight into the sociology of philosophy that reopens the question of the possibility of philosophy—for if Lessing was able to achieve what he did, "we" may also do so, provided that we correctly analyze the circumstances (the "society") under which we live.

Strauss has moved from his view that Lessing wrote a piece of "vulgar" poetry that "does not even presuppose *reading*" to the admonition that "we must read and reread the *Nathan*"—he does not suggest repeated visits to the theatre here. But he does suggest that merely reading the play as such is not enough. For the play is the work of Lessing and Lessing, according to Strauss, "was a *Christian*." The play does not stand for itself, it is the product of someone with a particular creed. But Strauss merely points to this fact without exploring it in this context. We, therefore, need to consider what Strauss's reference actually means. For further questions immediately come to mind: What kind of Christian was Lessing? That Lessing was a Christian is stated by Strauss as a fact of his life, but the precise nature of this fact remains in dispute. Not only did the Hamburg pastor Johan Melchior Goeze draw into question the nature of Lessing's true beliefs, but other contemporaries of Lessing such as Johann Georg Hamann were quite sure that Lessing was in fact no longer a Christian. Hamann regarded "enmity towards Christianity" as the foundation of Lessing's position, referring to Spinozan pantheism in the context.[28] Strauss's notes thus leave a serious gap that needs to be investigated further with a view to Lessing's confrontation with contemporary apologetical literature on "the truth of the Christian religion," a literature about which Lessing was extremely disillusioned.[29] Whatever the results of such a study might be, Strauss's reading of Lessing strongly suggests that this eighteenth-century playwright and "lover of theology" was one of the most important models of the theoretical life.

Notes

1. Gotthold Ephraim Lessing, "Rettung des Horaz," in *Werke. Dritter Band: Frühe kritische Schriften*, ed. Karl S. Guthke (Munich: Hanser, 1972), 591.

2. See Leo Strauss, *Persecution and the Art of Writing* (Chicago: University of Chicago Press, 1988), 7–8, 21; Volker Meja and Nico Stehr, eds., *Der Streit um die Wissenssoziologie: Rezeption und Kritik der Wissenssoziologie*, 2 vols. (Frankfurt am Main: Suhrkamp, 1982); Wolfgang Martynkewicz, *Das Café der trunkenen Philosophen: Wie Hannah Arendt, Adorno & Co. das Denken revolutionierten* (Berlin: Aufbau-Verlag, 2022).

3. See Leo Strauss, "Der Konspektivismus (1929)," in *Philosophie und Gesetz— Frühe Schriften*, ed. Heinrich Meier with Wiebke Meier, Gesammelte Schriften 2 (Stuttgart: Metzler, 1997), 365–75.

4. See, e.g., Till Kinzel, "Karl Jaspers über Lessing als 'großen Philosophen': 'Das Ewige im Vergänglichen'," *Lessing Yearbook* 49 (2022): 169–87.

5. Regrettably, Meyer does not quote the letter verbatim; it appears to have remained unpublished so far. See Thomas Meyer, "Leo Strauss und die Aufklärung," in *Vertriebene Vernunft? Aufklärung und Exil nach 1933*, ed. Christoph Schmitt-Maaß and Daniel Fulda (Paderborn: Fink, 2017), 49–67, here 52.

6. See Alexander Altmann, "Vorbemerkung," in Moses Mendelssohn, *Schriften zur Philosophie und Ästhetik III,2*, Bearbeitet von Leo Strauss (Stuttgart: Frommann-Holzboog, 1974), 8.

7. Thomas Assinger and Daniel Ehrmann, "Zur Einführung: Gelehrsamkeit zwischen Gelehrtenkultur und Wissenschaftskultur," in *Gelehrsamkeit(en) im 18. Jahrhundert: Autorisierung—Darstellung—Vernetzung*, ed. Thomas Assinger and Daniel Ehrmann (Heidelberg: Winter, 2022), 9-10; Conrad Wiedemann, "Polyhistors Glück und Ende: Von Daniel Georg Morhof zum jungen Lessing," in *Grenzgänge: Studien zur europäischen Literatur und Kultur*, ed. Renate Stauf and Cord-Friedrich Berghahn (Heidelberg: Winter, 2005), 107-30.

8. Leo Strauss, "Exoteric Teaching (1939)," ed. Hannes Kerber, in *Reorientation: Leo Strauss in the 1930s*, ed. Martin D. Yaffe and Richard S. Ruderman (New York: Palgrave Macmillan, 2014), 276.

9. Leo Strauss, "Notes on Philosophy and Revelation," in Heinrich Meier, *Leo Strauss and the Theologico-Political Problem* (Cambridge: Cambridge University Press, 2006), 178.

10. Leo Strauss, "Notes on Philosophy and Revelation," in Heinrich Meier, *Leo Strauss and the Theologico-Political Problem* (Cambridge: Cambridge University Press, 2006), 178.

11. See Till Kinzel, *Lessing und die englische Aufklärung: Bibelkritik und Deismus zwischen Esoterik und Exoterik*, Wolfenbütteler Vortragsmanuskripte 12 (Wolfenbüttel: Lessing-Akademie, 2011), 17-19.

12. See Leo Strauss, *Die Religionskritik Spinozas als Grundlage seiner Bibelwissenschaft: Untersuchungen zu Spinozas Theologisch-politischem Traktat*, in *Gesammelte Schriften I*, ed. Heinrich Meier with Wiebke Meier (Stuttgart: Metzler, 2008), 79 (Mauthner), 99, 125 (Lechler), 145 (Lange).

13. A brief reference can be found in Lechler's presentation of the history of deism; see Gotthard Victor Lechler, *Geschichte des englischen Deismus*, ed. Günter Gawlick (Hildesheim: Olms, [1841] 1965), 473. The second reference can be found in Fritz Mauthner, *Der Atheismus und seine Geschichte im Abendlande*, vol. II (Hildesheim: Olms, [1921] 1985), 437, 441-42. The third reference to Toland's esotericism is in Friedrich Albert Lange, *Geschichte des Materialismus und Kritik seiner Bedeutung in der Gegenwart: Erstes Buch—Geschichte des Materialismus bis auf Kant*, ed. Alfred Schmidt (Frankfurt am Main.: Suhrkamp, [1866] 1974), 285-86.

14. He once admitted, in a letter to Seth Benardete cited by Heinrich Meier, that he actually cited a passage of John Calvin's about the question *quid sit deus* "en pleine ignorance de cause," that is to say without understanding what this question truly implied. See Heinrich Meier, *Leo Strauss and the Theologico-Political Problem* (Cambridge: Cambridge University Press, 2006), 27.

15. The most recent contribution is Eleonora Travanti, *Lessings exoterische Verteidigung der Orthodoxie: Die Wolfenbütteler Beiträge gegen die Aufklärungstheologie (1770-1774)*, Frühe Neuzeit, 251 (Berlin: De Gruyter, 2023); see also Daniel Zimmermann, *Göttliche Zufälligkeiten: G. E. Lessings Vernunftkritik als Theodizee der Religionen*, Collegium Metaphysicum, 29 (Tübingen: Mohr Siebeck, 2023), 3-5.

16. Ernst Cassirer, "Die Idee der Religion bei Lessing und Mendelssohn" (1929), in *Lessings Nathan der Weise*, ed. Klaus Bohnen (Darmstadt: Wissen-

schaftliche Buchgesellschaft, 1984), 94-115. Cassirer does not draw on *Nathan der Weise* but only on his theory of tragedy in his attempt to characterize Lessing's style of thinking. See Ernst Cassirer, "Lessings Denkstil" (1917), in *Gotthold Ephraim Lessing*, ed. Gerhard Bauer and Sibylle Bauer (Darmstadt: Wissenschaftliche Buchgesellschaft, 1968), 54-73.

17. On the instructive contemporary debates concerning the issue of stage play versus closet drama ("Bühnenwerk oder Lesedrama"), see Hans-Friedrich Wessels, *Lessings "Nathan der Weise": Seine Wirkungsgeschichte bis zum Ende der Goethezeit* (Königstein: Athenäum, 1979), 243-47.

18. *Briefe von und an Lessing 1776-1781*, ed. Helmuth Kiesel (Frankfurt am Main: Deutscher Klassiker Verlag, 1994), 247.

19. *Briefe von und an Lessing 1776-1781*, 193.

20. *Briefe von und an Lessing 1776-1781*, 193.

21. This was already true of the generation of Sigmund Freud. See, most recently, Yvonne Wübben, "Inzest in der Literatur: Freud liest Lessings *Nathan der Weise*," in *Gotthold Ephraim Lessing*, ed. Dominic Angerloch and Ortrud Gutjahr (Würzburg: Königshausen & Neumann, 2022), 291-93.

22. See the instructive remarks in Sylvia Rogge-Gau, *Die doppelte Wurzel des Daseins: Julius Bab und der Jüdische Kulturbund Berlin* (Berlin: Metropol, 1999), 78-86.

23. See the remarks in Elisabeth Frenzel, *Judengestalten auf der deutschen Bühne: Ein notwendiger Querschnitt durch 700 Jahre Rollengeschichte* (Munich: Deutscher Volksverlag, 1942), 58. This book, which was listed in the official "N.S.-Bibliographie," also explicitly noted that the play had been understood and exploited in a philosemitic way (58).

24. On the details of Bruckner's *Nathan the Wise* as a literary presentation of exile as well as the actual performance referenced by Strauss, see Kristina-Monika Kocyba, *Nathan auf Reisen: Stationen einer transatlantischen Rezeptionsgeschichte* (Dresden: Thelem, 2017), 99-152, especially 126-45. When Piscator had the chance to stage *Nathan der Weise* in his hometown of Marburg in 1952, he considered using the Bruckner version but finally decided to stage Lessing's text as more appropriate and he focused more on the pogrom scene marginalized by Bruckner (Kocyba, *Nathan auf Reisen*, 151-52). Cf. also the contemporary reviews in *Lessing im Spiegel der Theaterkritik 1945-1979*, ed. Diedrich Diedrichsen and Bärbel Rudin (Berlin: Selbstverlag der Gesellschaft für Theatergeschichte, 1980), 197-99.

25. See Karl-Josef Kuschel, *Vom Streit zum Wettstreit der Religionen: Lessing und die Herausforderung des Islam* (Düsseldorf: Patmos, 1998), 231-63.

26. See Leo Strauss, "Notes on Lucretius," in Leo Strauss, *Liberalism Ancient and Modern* (Chicago: University of Chicago Press, 1989), 76-139, here 85.

27. Gotthold Ephraim Lessing, *Frühe kritische Schriften*, ed. Karl S. Guthke (Munich: Hanser, 1970), 55. See also Peter J. Brenner, *Gotthold Ephraim Lessing* (Stuttgart: Reclam, 2000), 294-95.

28. Till Kinzel, *Johann Georg Hamann: Zu Leben und Werk* (Vienna: Karolinger, 2019), 119; see the letter from Hamann to Friedrich Heinrich Jacobi

(December 5, 1784) printed in Johann Georg Hamann, *Briefwechsel: Fünfter Band 1783-1785*, ed. Arthur Henkel (Frankfurt am Main: Insel, 1965), 274.

29. See Till Kinzel, "Aufklärungstheologie, christliche Apologetik und Freiheit der Untersuchung im transnationalen Kontext: Zur Rezeption von William Warburtons *Divine Legation of Moses* und John Jortins *Abhandlung über die Wahrheit der christlichen Religion* bei Gotthold Ephraim Lessing und Johann Arnold Ebert," in *Religion und Aufklärung: Akten des Ersten Internationalen Kongresses zur Erforschung der Aufklärungstheologie (Münster, 30. März bis 2. April 2014)*, ed. Albrecht Beutel and Martha Nooke (Tübingen: Mohr Siebeck, 2016), 561–73; see also the extremely subtle study by Hannes Kerber, *Die Aufklärung der Aufklärung: Lessing und die Herausforderung des Christentums* (Göttingen: Wallstein, 2021).

MARTIN D. YAFFE

Interpretative Essay

LEO STRAUSS ON THE PHILOSOPHICAL
CHARACTER OF LESSING'S *NATHAN THE WISE*

> The good author—be he of whichever genre he would—if he writes not merely to show his wit and his learning, always has in view the most enlightened and best of his time and his country, and he deigns to write only what can please them and can touch them. Even the dramatic author, if he stoops to the crowd, stoops only to enlighten and to better it—but not to confirm it in its prejudices and its ignoble mode of thinking.
> —GOTTHOLD EPHRAIM LESSING, *HAMBURG DRAMATURGY* #1

> When reading, and trying to understand, a work such as the *Nathan*, one ought not to forget one fact: one cannot forget for a single moment that the author silently tells us all the time *Tua res agitur*: [it] is *thy* case which is under examination.[1]
> —LEO STRAUSS, UNPUBLISHED LECTURE AT THE NEW SCHOOL FOR SOCIAL RESEARCH, CA. 1942–1943

I

Shortly after 1938, when he began his decade-plus at the New School for Social Research, Leo Strauss jotted down extensive notes on Gotthold Ephraim Lessing's dramatic poem *Nathan the Wise* (1779). The several pages containing them are in Strauss's minuscule, all-but-illegible handwriting, consisting of crowded paragraphs and miniparagraphs, isolated sentences, numbered lists, bullet points, small flowcharts, textual citations, and the like—ably deciphered and transcribed for this volume by Svetozar Y. Minkov and Hannes Kerber. Included in the notes are an unevenly elaborated sketch of a syllabus for a 1941 course on *Nathan* and semidetailed plans for a General Seminar lecture given around 1942-1943. These invite further probing, as may be gathered also from Strauss's two closely contemporaneous writings about Lessing—his 1937 "Introduction to [Moses Mendelssohn's] *Morning Hours* and *To the Friends of Lessing*"[2] and his 1939 fragment "Exoteric Teaching"[3]—intricately engaging and informative as each is. In what follows, I look at what the 1937 and 1939 writings call attention to in Lessing for provisional guidance, before exploring the unwritten connections to be found among the notes themselves.

II

Lessing shows up in Strauss's introduction to *Morning Hours* and *To the Friends of Lessing* (1785 and 1786), if largely indirectly, throughout the elaborate give and take of Mendelssohn's notorious confrontation with Friedrich Heinrich Jacobi, which came to be called the Pantheism Quarrel. Jacobi's *On Spinoza's Doctrine, in Letters to Mr. Moses Mendelssohn* and *Against Mendelssohn's Accusations apropos the Letters on Spinoza's Doctrine* (1785 and 1786)[4] proffered the morally shocking disclosure that the recently deceased Lessing, Mendelssohn's oldest and dearest friend and the German Enlightenment's leading literary figure and theological polemicist, secretly and unbeknown to Mendelssohn had late in life become a doctrinaire Spinozist—by which Jacobi, like his theologically minded contemporaries, meant a (morally deplorable) atheist. Mendelssohn, on reflection, countered that he was long familiar with Lessing's distancing himself from theism toward Spinozism but, pace Jacobi, Lessing had "purified" Benedict Spinoza's otherwise objectionable identification of God with nature into a morally harmless pantheism. Strauss finds neither Jacobi's claim nor Mendelssohn's counterclaim sustainable, however. He sees the basic difficulty as follows. Both men understand philosophy exclusively "in the style of the eighteenth century."[5] It is the effort to construct a metaphysical "system" by logical demonstration using clear and distinct concepts. This effort, originating in René Descartes, is carried on above all, with prudent restructuring, by Descartes's epigone Spinoza, and likewise by Spinoza's epigone Gottfried Wilhelm Leibniz—Mendelssohn's chief philosophical authority and, initially at least, Lessing's. Mendelssohn and Jacobi thereby misconstrue the late Lessing in attributing to him a (less than satisfactory) "system."

What is the Lessingian alternative to philosophy as a system? Strauss's Mendelssohn-Jacobi discussion at best intimates it. Both Mendelssohn and Jacobi, he shows, seek to correct Lessing's "system" by way of sound commonsense, though each conceives (or misconceives) his corrective differently.

Jacobi's Lessing-corrective aligns with his radical critique of systems as such, as epitomized by Spinoza's.[6] To aim at demonstrating everything systematically as Spinoza does, says Jacobi, is to construe everything as determined by prior causes, hence as predetermined or fated. It degrades the search for comprehensive wisdom into a search delimited by the concepts in one's use and under one's control. The humble awareness of ignorance that prompts a philosophical inquiry into things thereby gives way in effect to the arrogant search for control over things. Correcting such arrogance, Jacobi submits, requires recovering one's prephilosophical humility—which in turn is possible only by a *salto mortale*, a risky leap or "summersault" back to the systematically abandoned beliefs of sound commonsense and Christian theism. Jacobi's expounding Spinoza's philosophy in this vein, during conversations he reports having with Lessing shortly before the latter's death, occasioned Lessing's striking statement: "There is no philosophy other than the philosophy of Spinoza."[7] Evidently, Jacobi took Lessing's statement to be unqualifiedly doctrinaire—rather than subtly playful, as the course of their conversations might have suggested. Contra Jacobi, Strauss points out that Lessing had qualified his statement by saying earlier, in reply to Jacobi's wondering whether he was more or less in agreement with Spinoza, "*If* I am to name myself after anyone," as well as by replying to Jacobi's subsequently denying that his own credo was in Spinoza: "I would hope that it is not in any book."[8]

In contrast, Mendelssohn immediately recognized Lessing's subtlety and playfulness in the reported profession of Spinozism, without attaching anything further to it—not at first, anyway. Strauss details why Mendelssohn changed his mind and how what he eventually came up with is not as convincing as he makes it out to be. On first being apprised of Jacobi's allegation through a private letter from a close mutual friend,[9] Mendelssohn replied to her "that defending Spinozism could have been a whimsy or a paradox that Lessing posed." His deciding to challenge Jacobi's allegation after all reflects the friend's express worry that it might result in a scandalous exposure of her late father, who had bequeathed in manuscript a radical critique of revealed religion, selections from which Lessing as recently appointed librarian of the ducal library at Wolfenbüttel had published and commented on provocatively as "Fragments of an Unnamed"—and in so doing set off an explosive controversy with a prominent Lutheran pastor anathematizing both Lessing and the (anonymous) "Fragmentist."[10] Mendelssohn's ultimately recasting Lessing's Spinozism as a pantheism compatible for all practical purposes with sound commonsense and Christian theism thus had the pressing aim of both preempting Jacobi's not yet public allegation and putting to rest the Fragmentist backstory. How Strauss sees the recasting as inherently dubious shows up in his assessment of what Mendelssohn says about *Nathan the Wise*.[11]

Where Mendelssohn cites *Nathan* for its compatibility as such with Christian theism, Strauss argues that he should have known—and did know—better. *Morning Hours* characterizes Lessing's "dramatic didactic poem" as a vindication of divine providence, yet does so obliquely, in a fictional dialogue between Mendelssohn and a friendly interlocutor—an articulate devotee of Lessing's oeuvre to whom Mendelssohn (or his persona in the dialogue) has disclosed Lessing's ("purified") Spinozism. The interlocutor overcomes his mild initial shock and, with Mendelssohn's concurrence, reassures himself at some length of his old opinion that *Nathan* vindicates divine providence. Strauss assesses what the concurrence amounts to.

To begin with, he finds Mendelssohn himself clearly aware of the impossibility of inferring from *Nathan* its author's "system." A writing Mendelssohn and Lessing had coauthored at the beginning of their friendship argued that although a "didactic poem" may convey a philosophical teaching, it is not as such the work of a philosopher—by which they had meant, as fellow Leibnizians, "a system brought into a meter"—but "of a 'philosophical poet,' who seeks 'a lively impression rather than a deep conviction' and who for that reason '[has] no other means but to express one truth according to one system and another according to another'."[12] In his own notes on *Nathan*, Strauss will likewise caution that one should not identify the view or views of any of its characters with those of Lessing, nor even with the "optimism" characterizing its dramatic action as a whole, where "[n]ice people belonging to various religions are brought together in an atmosphere hot with religious exclusiveness by a number of strange coincidences, so that they can recognize mutually their *human dignity*, and even their *blood-relationship*."[13]

In the present instance, Strauss points out (in de facto agreement with Jacobi) that while "for Mendelssohn, *Nathan* proved in fact that Lessing agrees by and large with what theism's doctrine of providence 'has of practical relevance'"—namely, "devotion to God"—this same practical consequence (as Mendelssohn implicitly knew) "resulted not only from the theistic doctrine of providence, but also from Spinozism as *amor fati*, to apply Nietzsche's expression."[14] Strauss does endorse Mendelssohn's (or his persona's) calling Lessing's *Nathan* "a sort of Anti-*Candide*," but adds that if this description were sufficient, one would expect to find *Nathan*'s suppressing the moral Voltaire preaches in *Candide* and its underlying Manicheanism[15]—which *Nathan* does not do. Nor, for that matter, does Strauss find any suggestion of *Nathan*'s theism during Mendelssohn's extensive prepublication correspondence with Jacobi (via their mutual friend) concerning Lessing's Spinozism—as there would have been, Strauss implies, had not Mendelssohn resigned himself to the latter once the correspondence got underway.

From the foregoing, Strauss concludes that Mendelssohn's own opinion of *Nathan* is hardly the same as his fictional interlocutor's. Strauss calls the interlocutor's opinion "the popular, exoteric version of the opinion that Mendelssohn had of Lessing's belief originally, i.e., until Jacobi's communication."[16] Calling what Mendelssohn (or his persona) shares with the interlocutor "exoteric" spotlights that it is, as Strauss goes on to say, a "fantasy-image" suited for merely public ("exoteric") use. It brings to the fore *Morning Hours*' overriding popularizing aim. Strauss will elsewhere ascribe a more strictly philosophical aim to exotericism as engaged in by Lessing (and Leibniz). Meanwhile, he intimates what in a private letter of 1971 he says he might have added to his Mendelssohn-Jacobi discussion about "the center of Lessing's thoughts *de Deo et mundo*" if external circumstances had permitted,[17] along with what he says about Lessing's understanding of philosophy—and Leibniz's et al.—in his "Exoteric Teaching" fragment.

III

Exotericism, we learn (as Mendelssohn and Jacobi evidently didn't), is inseparable from Lessingian and Leibnizian philosophy when understood on its own terms. Strauss's "Exoteric Teaching" cites three small writings by Lessing to that effect.[18] Two of these, "Leibniz on Eternal Punishments" (1773) and "Andreas Wissowatius's Objections against the Trinity" (1773), endorse Leibniz's philosophical exotericism in theological matters. The third, "Ernst and Falk" (1777 and 1780), discusses—as clearly and fully as possible, Strauss adds, for someone like Lessing who saw to the need for exotericism in his own case as author—why philosophy is necessarily exoteric. "Exoteric Teaching" expands this point. Following a segue that includes a formidable defense of Plato's exotericism,[19] Strauss recounts how Lessing became aware of exotericism in general, and Leibniz's in particular—by being led to notice, and subsequently to understand, that the views of Leibniz and his philosophical predecessors were characterized by "a sort of prudence" that his Enlightenment contemporaries were overlooking or downplaying.[20] As Strauss's notes on *Nathan* will suggest, the prudence in question characterizes Lessing's dramatic poem as well.

In "Ernst and Falk," a philosophical dialogue whose ostensible topic is "free-masonry,"[21] Lessing entrusts the argument for exotericism to Falk, an untypical free-mason who, in Strauss's words, "expresses himself somewhat evasively and even enigmatically." Strauss tracks the drift of his argument. Free-masonry, says Falk, has always existed and always will. It is the necessary response to the necessary imperfection of all political constitutions, even the best one. A free-mason must therefore know which truths are better kept concealed, inasmuch as free-masonry's good works aim, in Falk's words, "to make good works superfluous." What Falk means comes out in the remainder of his argument. The founder of free-masonry (as an institution), he says, was someone who, having originally planned a scientifically enlightened society for making truths arrived at by speculation useful for practical and political life, conceived of a "society which should raise itself from the practice of civil life to speculation." If and when that stage is reached, the free-mason's "good works" are no longer needed. Meanwhile the concealed reasons for the imperfection of political life as such are that the political life is inferior to the life of contemplation and that the life of contemplation is self-sufficient. It is because conflicts between the two ways of life must arise from time to time that wise men, the men of contemplation—that is, the "free-masons"—need to conceal certain truths (notably, the political life's inferiority to the life of contemplation and the latter's self-sufficiency). Strauss adds that Lessing pointedly ascribes the variety of religions to the variety of political constitutions—so that in his two writings on Leibniz's exotericism, "the problem of historical, positive religion" is "considered by him as part and parcel of the political problem."

The two writings just mentioned apply the views of "Ernst and Falk" to Leibniz's attitude toward religion, as Strauss goes on to spell out. They indicate the motive and reasons prompting his defenses of the orthodox beliefs in eternal damnation and the trinity. In discussing how Leibniz defends the belief in eternal damnation, Lessing identifies Leibniz's peculiar manner of assenting to received opinions with "what all the ancient philosophers used to do in their exoteric speech."[22] The ancient philosophers are said to teach in two different manners, exoteric (or public) and esoteric (or concealed). Leibniz's exotericism is thus to be traced back to that of the ancients. What then, Strauss asks, are its essential features? He indicates two. First, in Lessing's words, Leibniz "observed a sort of prudence for which, it is true, our most recent philosophers have become much too wise."[23] Far from having anything to do with "mysticism," Strauss admonishes, the distinction between exoteric and esoteric speech is a matter of prudence. Subsequently, to illustrate a second essential feature of exotericism, he finds Lessing taking up the difference between exoteric and esoteric speech by showing how an esoteric reason of Leibniz's underlies his asserting the exoteric reason he expresses in defending the orthodox belief in eternal damnation. The "mere possibility" in moral beings of eternally increasing wickedness, Leibniz asserts exoterically, justifies eternally increasing punishment. Although Strauss (unlike Lessing) forgoes mentioning what Leibniz's esoteric reason is, he does emphasize, as does Lessing, that the exoteric reason being asserted is based on eternally increasing wickedness as a "mere possibility" rather than a fact that Leibniz believes to be true. To emphasize this point further, Strauss reproduces a brief dialogue that Lessing anticipates having to engage in if the question were raised, out of a concern for treating believers humanely, "Why frighten with a mere possibility?" Lessing says he would have to reply that the possibility in question can only be frightening to one who has never been serious about self-betterment. To underscore the sense of this reply, Strauss quotes Lessing's instructive appeal to the example of Socrates, who (on the evidence of Plato's *Gorgias* 525b1–c8) "believed in such punishments quite seriously ... at least to the extent that he considered it expedient to teach such punishments in terms which do not in any way arouse suspicion and which are most explicit."[24]

Lessing's rediscovery of the distinction that "all the ancient philosophers" made between their esoteric and exoteric teachings was, in

Strauss's concise but probing account, the result of his own endeavors after having undergone his "conversion" to philosophy, that is, of his "having had the experience of what philosophy is and what sacrifices it requires." This experience, says Strauss pursuant to Lessing, leads directly to the distinction between philosophic and unphilosophic human beings and, with that, to the distinction between the two ways of presenting the truth. The initial evidence Strauss finds for Lessing's rediscovery is the fear expressed in his letter to Mendelssohn of January 9, 1771, that "by throwing away certain prejudices, I have thrown away a little too much that I shall have to get back again."[25] Lessing's statement has been misread, Strauss cautions, as expressing an intent to return from his early "intransigent rationalism" to "a more positive view of the Bible and the Biblical tradition"; but in the immediate context, Lessing is speaking of the truths he noticed "from afar" while looking over the table of contents in Adam Ferguson's *An Essay on the History of Civil Society*[26] (just received from Mendelssohn). Lessing's words are: "truths in the continual contradiction of which we happen to live and we have to go on living continually in the interest of our quietude." The truths he noticed, in other words, concerned "the ambiguous character of civilization"—the theme of Jean-Jacques Rousseau's *First* and *Second Discourses*[27]—which, Strauss surmises, Lessing may have felt he had not considered carefully enough in his youth and which he later formulates "in more precise terms" as the view that "even the absolutely best civil constitution is necessarily imperfect." In short, Strauss infers that what appears to have given Lessing's thought a decisive turn from the philosophy of his enlightened contemporaries toward that of the ancients was the political problem.

Why then did Lessing not stay with the thought of Rousseau, who, says Strauss, "seems to have believed in a political solution to the problem of civilization"? Lessing's distancing himself from Rousseau in favor of Leibniz and the ancients, Strauss suggests, occurred as he recognized, and rejected, the way opened up by Rousseau's Romantic critics toward a putatively "deeper, historical" view of government and religion. To explain, Strauss calls attention to a political remark of Lessing's reported by Jacobi. Lessing reportedly said (in Strauss's paraphrase) that "arguments against papal despotism are either no arguments at all, or else they are two or three times as valid against the despotism of princes."[28] In other words, as Jacobi himself says in a Lessingian spirit elsewhere, "despotism based exclusively on superstition" is not nearly as bad as secular despotism. Strauss interprets Lessing's remark accordingly. Thomas Hobbes, "the classic of enlightened despotism" as Strauss terms him, teaches how secular despotism could be easily allied with the philosophy of (popular) enlightenment, hence with the rejection of exotericism strictly speaking, whereas despotism based "exclusively" on superstition—rather than on force—can be maintained if (and only if) the nonsuperstitious (like Leibniz) are willing to keep from openly exposing and refuting the "superstitious" beliefs. While recognizing Hobbesian despotism's inhospitability to exotericism, Lessing also recognized what Strauss calls the "relative truth" of the Romantics' critique of Rousseau (in their replacing Rousseau's evident attempt at a merely political solution to the ambiguities of civilization with their putatively "deeper, historical" solution, without however freeing themselves from Rousseau's Hobbesianism in theological and political matters)—all this a generation before the (harsh) political experience of Maximilien Robespierre's avowedly secular, antisuperstitious despotism. Differently stated, Lessing's philosophical "experience" concerning the dubiousness of Rousseau's (and his Romantic critics') Hobbesian partnering of popular enlightenment with secular despotism to resolve civilization's ambiguities—during a moment of pivotal insight as disclosed in the exoteric remark reported by Jacobi—enabled him to understand the meaning of Leibniz's aforementioned "prudence," as Strauss puts it forcefully, "in a manner infinitely more adequate than the enlightened Leibnizians among his contemporaries did and could do."

Leibniz, Strauss concludes, was not the only seventeenth-century thinker in the chain of "initiates" into exotericism before Lessing, though he was the nearest link. Preceding Leibniz was Spinoza, whose *Theologico-Political Treatise*, despite its notorious boldness, admitted the necessity of "pious dogmas, that is, such as move the spirit to obedience," as distinguished from "true dogmas";[29] and preceding Spinoza was "the prudent Descartes."[30] Still, Strauss adds, Lessing needn't have relied on the modern and medieval representatives of the exoteric tradition, since he was familiar with its sources thanks to his "intransigent classicism"—"his considered view that close study of the classics is the only way in which a diligent and thinking man can become a philosopher."[31] Strauss's words here seem meant to imply as well that, say, Lessing's *Nathan the Wise* may be designed to repay "close study" similarly. Be this as it may, we turn to the notes on *Nathan* while keeping in mind the provisional guidance Strauss has left us so far. In the wake of his elaborate Mendelssohn-Jacobi discussion, we plan to avoid compressing what counts as *Nathan*'s philosophical teaching into its author's supposed "system." And in the wake of his fragmentary discussion of exoteric teaching, we plan to stay alert for its author's philosophical prudence.

IV

Facing the piecemeal state of Strauss's notes, we can't help focusing initially on what jumps to the eye initially. In and among the notes, we find Strauss asking three broad questions:[32]

A. Why did Lessing choose a Jew as the hero of his play?
B. How is that anti-Christian bias, which seems contradictory to Lessing's freedom from prejudice, to be accounted for?
C. For the thinking reader, at least, the lesson given by the writer is more important than the lesson provided by the characters of the play. Does this mean that we should have to close the book and study Lessing's life?

Each question prompts us to probe further for how we are meant to understand Lessing's teaching in *Nathan the Wise* overall.

A

The 1941 course gets underway by considering why Lessing chose a Jewish hero. Strauss's answer emerges as follows. The subject of Lessing's drama is the conflict among the three great religions "being happily settled in the *holy land* during the *Age of Faith*." Lessing sets the drama in an "atmosphere of the highest religious tensions" (Muslim vs. Christian vs. Jew)—which, more than the free atmosphere of eighteenth-century Europe, may be "particularly favorable to freedom of the mind."[33] Making a Jew the leading figure thus lets him show how "the *highest* tension, the highest degree of fanaticism" may lead to "the most radical emancipation." His Jewish hero is moreover a merchant since trade is also favorable to freedom of the mind. Strauss infers from the foregoing that the "*real* action" of Lessing's drama is not the overcoming of religious differences as such, but the fate of its Jewish merchant Nathan.[34]

What then is Nathan's dramatic fate? Although the drama's first scene shows his strong love for his adopted daughter Recha[35] and its last scene shows his seeming to become as well the father(-in-law) of the Knight (a Christian Templar who had rescued her from a house fire while he was away on a business trip), ultimately Nathan is, in Strauss's words, "as it were, pushed aside" by Saladin (Jerusalem's ruling sultan) and Sittah (the sultan's unmarried sister). The other four prove to belong to a single family, and Nathan thereby loses his child. Since he owes her (as he himself says) neither to nature nor to chance but to virtue, his losing her implies (as Strauss says) that "virtue is *not* rewarded on earth."[36]

Nathan's fate is not exactly tragic, however. "*Everything*," Strauss emphasizes, "depends on our seeing the *difference* between Nathan and the happy family ... on our seeing the *peculiar* character of Nathan." Strauss considers the drama's key features from that point of view. To begin with, he observes that the scattered family could conceivably have been reunited without the drama's pivotal discussion between Nathan and Saladin concerning which religion is most convincing:[37] the Knight is indifferent to religion independently of Nathan;[38] Saladin and Sittah are not religious fanatics; and Recha "is so in love with the Knight that she would have married him anyway." In addition, Lessing's calling his hero "Nathan the Wise" evokes the epithet of a king or a prince;[39] it also recalls the biblical prophet Nathan, "who admonished, and reprimanded, those oriental despots David and Solomon,"[40] although "the *wise* Nathan," guided as he is by "his *prudence*," "does *not* reprimand Saladin"; and it anticipates the drama's implicit comparison between Nathan's risking persecution from Jerusalem's Patriarch (for allegedly having adopted a Christian daughter) and "the fight between Pope and Emperor" such as occasioned Lessing's remark reported by Jacobi (about "superstitious" versus secular despotism).[41] Last but not least, the reunited "family" is markedly inferior to Nathan—Recha being a child,[42] the Knight young and rash,[43] Saladin a bad chess player and confused, and Sittah a "calculating" woman. That these four, unlike Nathan, are related by blood, moreover, suggests that the "*natural kinship*" of all human beings is not Lessing's last word. His including Sittah in the drama's "strangely coincidental" family reunion draws attention to the "deeper problem."[44] Why, Strauss asks, is Sittah needed? Given that it is "perfectly understandable," he reasons, that for the others to turn out to be blood relatives neither Saladin nor the Knight ought to marry Recha, Lessing's having included the unmarried Sittah underscores that the resulting "family" has "*no prospect of progeny*." Put more generally: the inclusion of Sittah indicates that whereas the family qua dedicated to generating and raising offspring is necessarily a "closed" society, the purely "open" society—found here in the "family" of four—"is impossible."[45] Instead the "basic miracles"[46] of the drama--Recha's life as a "*gift*" of the Knight (in rescuing her from the fire), the

Knight's life as a *"gift"* of the sultan (in pardoning him from a beheading), and everyone's life as said to be a *"gift"* of one's father[47]—point to human beings' radical mutual dependence and mutual servitude. Significant likewise, Strauss adds in passing, is the Dervish Al-Hafi (Nathan's comic foil who, having momentarily served as the financially hard-pressed Saladin's overly pressured banker-treasurer, embarks on a pilgrimage to India in order, as he tells Nathan, to avoid living as "another's slave forever").[48] Only Nathan, Strauss implies, confronts wisely and prudently the "deeper problem" of humans' necessary interdependence and rank-ordering, notably during his dialogue with Saladin at the drama's epicenter.[49]

How so? Shortly after connecting Nathan's prudence briefly with his "manner of teaching" and the "ease" with which he tells stories,[50] Strauss turns to the story of the three rings by which Nathan addresses Saladin's sudden question: "What *faith*, what *law* has convinced you?"[51] The story itself, Strauss points out, is not quite at the center of the drama: act 3 has ten scenes, of which the *"two central"* ones, scenes 5 and 6, precede scene 7's *"ring"* story; and scene 6, which is central to these three scenes, contains Nathan's *"only monologue"* (about his being surprised by Saladin's question and, on quick reflection, deciding to answer cautiously by telling a story). Strauss previews Nathan's storyline comparison between the three religions and three rings by asking "What is a ring?" and listing the features of a ring (and, implicitly, of a religion): it is highly valuable, hard to destroy or break, and very close to the body's naked skin that it surrounds and covers; it is an ornament rather than a utensil, though one to which "a very great usefulness is *ascribed*"; it is *"inherited"* and is "an *artificial* thing." In the story, a father in ancient times came into possession of a priceless ring with the hidden force of making its wearer who trusted in it pleasing to both God and men. He wore it always and bequeathed it to his most beloved son, who would in turn become ruler of the household and bequeath the ring likewise to his most beloved son (i.e., not necessarily to the eldest). So the ring passed from generation to generation. Eventually, it came to a father with three equally beloved sons.[52] Unbeknown to them, he had two such rings copied and secretly bequeathed a ring to each son. Each then viewed himself alone as the chosen one. Thus far in the story, Strauss observes, not much more is said than that two of the rings are forgeries and only one is genuine—and this much corresponds to what all Jews, Christians, and Muslims say. Nathan "diverges from that view," however, in saying that it is *"almost* impossible to detect the right belief" (i.e., the genuine ring) and, Strauss adds, "goes one step further" in not daring to distinguish among them, for (as he tells Saladin) "*God* made them undistinguishable."[53] Strauss explains that the three religions are the same "as far as their *reasons* are concerned" inasmuch as each is based "on history, on tradition, on faith" (i.e., not on distinct "reasons" strictly speaking), so that each "must trust most *his* tradition, *his* father."[54]

Nathan's ring story concludes with the three brothers going to court, each seeking to vindicate his individual inheritance claim before a Judge, who however "does not give his *sentence*, he merely gives his *advice*." Even so, as Strauss notes, the Judge "states his sentence surreptitiously." None of the three rings, he tells the sons, is genuine. He advises each son instead to "seek to prove the genuine character of his ring by *good actions*, good morality." "The *Messiah*," he adds, will pronounce his sentence a thousand years hence. With this advice, the Judge surreptitiously changes "the content of the moral teaching." He does so in two ways, Strauss infers—by "depoliticization" and "democratization." The Judge depoliticizes morality by reducing "virtue" to justice and temperance (i.e., to "good actions" understood apart from their particular theological or political setting)—while dispensing with courage.[55] Correspondingly, he democratizes morality by implicitly praising "work" as proof of one's justice and temperance.[56] In short: Strauss finds Nathan's Judge prudently reframing the teaching of the three competing religions by downsizing moral virtue to just and temperate actions for the sake of mutual tolerance.

B

Does the Judge's underwriting his advice by evoking the eventual coming of a judge whom Strauss (unlike Lessing) calls the Messiah, a recognizably Jewish teaching, mean that he takes *Nathan the Wise* to have abandoned religious neutrality after all? Strauss's General Seminar lecture considers what he terms Lessing's "pro-Jewish bias" in connection with the apparent mismatch between the drama's plea for religious tolerance, based "not on any particular historical religion, but on universal, rational religion,"[57] and its seemingly contradictory "anti-Christian bias." Strauss argues as follows. The drama's "least sympathetic" character is the Christian Patriarch,[58] whereas its "most superior people ... are a Jew (Nathan) and a Muslim (Dervish)." A partial explanation for this, he suggests, is Lessing's having chosen "the most significant *setting*" for a drama about freedom from religious prejudice, namely Jerusalem at the time of the Crusades—when "the intellectual superiority of Islam and Judaism to

Christianity was a fact" as evidenced by Averroes and Maimonides preceding in time Thomas Aquinas.[59] But this explanation is not sufficient, Strauss hastens to add, since Lessing as a poet could have freed himself, if he wished, from such historical accidents. For a more clarifying explanation, Strauss turns instead to Lessing's Christian readership.

Writing as a Christian for Christians in a Christian country, Lessing had to confront the thoroughgoing pro-Christian bias of his fellow Christians. He could not counteract it by taking a merely unbiased approach. "Lessing and his contemporaries," says Strauss, "had to go through the anti-Christian bias to become truly free from their pro-Christian bias."[60] Doing so meant having to view Christianity "from an anti-Christian angle, from a Jewish or Muslim angle," before being able to view it "without *any* bias," that is, "*philosophically.*"[61] Strauss has more to say about this last, but waits till addressing the third of the three broad questions I have listed above (about Lessing as author). Meanwhile, he counsels his own audience, particularly his Jewish audience, against construing—or, rather, misconstruing—Lessing's anti-Christian bias from a self-complacently Jewish point of view. Admittedly, says Strauss, any Jew "must be expected to have a pro-Jewish bias" unless there is something "perverted" about him or her as a human being. But this bias must be guarded against, he admonishes, if one "wants to learn anything from L[essing]." What do Jews have to learn from Lessing? As Strauss says strikingly, it is his unself-complacent attitude toward Christianity—which "must be the model for the attitude of the Jewish interpreter toward Judaism."

Lest his audience dismiss this last point as merely methodological or moral, Strauss offers a few personal words about the danger of Jewish self-complacency. "Jews," he remarks as a Jew, "are under a particular obligation not to be self-complacent." This obligation, he points out, dates from time immemorial—showing up biblically in Samson's enmity with the Philistines[62] and in God's not leading the Jews out of Egypt by way of the land of the Philistines even though it was nearer than the long way through the desert.[63] Strauss considers why. Self-complacency, he says, is the "characteristic feature" of the Philistine—both in the biblical account, he implies, and in today's idiom. Jews, however, are "*neighbors* of the Philistines."[64] Hence, he warns, "Jews are always in danger of preferring [the] short way through the Philistines"—and, he adds pointedly, "in danger of succumbing to this danger until someone like Jeremiah reminds them." Strauss rounds out his own (comparatively gentle) Jeremiad by quoting his biblical predecessor in Hebrew: "I remember for your sake the devotion of your youth."[65]

C

"For the thinking reader, at least," says Strauss in the General Seminar lecture, "the lesson given by the writer is more important than the lesson provided by the characters of the play."[66] This does not mean, he is quick to clarify, that we should "close the book and study Lessing's life." After all, he asks rhetorically, what is Lessing's life except the external conditions for his thought—about which "we can know practically nothing except from his *books*," particularly *Nathan the Wise*. Even so, Strauss continues, we must read the *Nathan* while keeping in mind one fact of Lessing's life that, though unmentioned in the drama itself, is of decisive importance for understanding it—namely, "that Lessing was a *Christian*."

In particular, by writing *Nathan the Wise* Lessing "*escaped*" from his "violent" controversy with orthodox Lutheranism over the "Wolfenbüttel fragments," which lasted about two years until his sovereign, the elector of Brunswick-Wolfenbüttel, forbade him to continue. Lessing continued anyway, Strauss adds, thanks to the "peculiar nature" of dramatic poetry. For one thing, it is the most "*vulgar*" (or commonplace) poetry, which "does not even presuppose *reading*" (but can be performed on stage).[67] In addition, the dramatic poet "*never* speaks in his own name" but, as in this case, "may deceive ... by the agreement of all *nice* characters." Here, that is to say, Lessing's deception occurs by way of the drama's happy ending, which "is in accordance with the thesis" that divine providence "rewards good actions, done on earth, on earth," that is, with (Leibnizian) "optimism."[68] Even so, Strauss emphasizes, the "religion of providence and optimism is based on *reason*" rather than on revelation. As we have already seen, the "miracles" integral to the dramatic action are natural ones, allowing in the end for clear explanations, in contrast to revealed miracles, which foster intolerance and pride on the part of believers.[69] "The revelation of that true natural religion," Strauss recapitulates, "is an essential part of the action"—establishing as it does "the friendship between the philosopher [Nathan] and the king [Saladin]," without which there would be no happy ending.

Although (or perhaps because) Lessing thereby smoothed out the surface of his drama to resolve the otherwise unresolved tension between reason and revelation, *Nathan the Wise* did not win immediate approval among his censorious contemporaries. Quite the contrary![70] But what about his more enlightened readers like Mendelssohn and Jacobi, along with others capable of probing more deeply? Here we must recall Lessing's looking to Leibniz et al. to counter his philosophical contemporaries' unphilosophical obliviousness or shortchanging of the need for prudence—for thinking twice about striking details that on closer inspection might be too good to be true, such as those details prompting Strauss's second thoughts about the drama's eventually happy "family." Strauss brings out this point more generally. After quoting Horace to underscore that trying to understand a work such as the *Nathan* means never forgetting for a single moment that its author is silently telling us all the time that our own situation as readers is under examination,[71] Strauss draws two further conclusions. First, the reader is left to apply the lesson conveyed by the drama to oneself. In Strauss's words, the lesson of Lessing's drama is "tolerance and toleration and charity." But this lesson still awaits prudent application to the reader's own particular circumstances at different times and in different human relations—an application that the drama by itself cannot supply, being a merely "*idealized*" action in "unreal" or "fairy-tale" circumstances. Each of Lessing's readers must then translate the intradramatic lesson to address his or her own, often varying, and variable situation. Second, however, another lesson, not explicit but merely implicit in the drama, is the example provided by its "*author.*" "[B]y *writing* the *Nathan*," observes Strauss, "Lessing shows us how he, this individual, living in these individual circumstances, applied to himself and to his circumstances the universal rule of tolerance, toleration, and charity." Lessing's exemplary action as an author is not ideal or idealized but "an actual fact of human experience"—"an *example*," Strauss concludes, "which we can try to imitate directly if intelligently."[72]

Notes

1. Horace, *Epistles* 1.18.84 (emphasis Strauss's): *nam tua res agitur, paries cum proximus ardet, / et neglecta solent incendia sumere vires* [For when a neighboring wall is on fire your own concern is prompted, and flames that are neglected usually gather strength]. See above, page 8.

2. Leo Strauss, "Einleitung zu 'Morgenstunden' und 'An die Freunde Lessings'," in *Moses Mendelssohn Gesammelte Schriften Jubiläumsausgabe*, vol. 3, pt. 2 (Stuttgart-Bad Cannstadt: Friedrich Frommann Verlag Günther Holzboog, 1974) [henceforth JA 3.2], XI–XCV; *Leo Strauss on Moses Mendelssohn*, ed. and

trans. Martin D. Yaffe (Chicago: University of Chicago Press, 2012) [henceforth LSMM], 59-145.

3. Leo Strauss, "Exoteric Teaching," ed. Hannes Kerber, in *Reorientation: Leo Strauss in the 1930s*, ed. Martin D. Yaffe and Richard S. Ruderman (New York: Palgrave Macmillan, 2014) [henceforth ET], 275-86. An earlier version of Strauss's fragment, ed. Kenneth Hart Green, may be found in *Interpretation* 14, no. 1 (1986), 51-59; and a subsequent version, based on Green's, in *The Rebirth of Classical Political Rationalism: An Introduction to the Thought of Leo Strauss*, ed. Thomas L. Pangle (Chicago: University of Chicago Press, 1989), 63-71.

4. Strauss cites as needed Friedrich Heinrich Jacobi, *Über die Lehre des Spinozas in Briefen an den Herrn Moses Mendelssohn*, and *Wider Mendelssohns Beschuldigungen betreffend die Briefe über die Lehre des Spinozas*, in *Werke*, ed. C. J. F. Roth and J. F. Köppen, 6 vols. in 8 (Leipzig: Gerhard Fleischer, 1812-25), vol. 4, pt. 2 [henceforth RK 4.2], 169-232—though wherever possible he prefers to cite *Die Hauptschriften zum Pantheismusstreit zwischen Jacobi und Mendelssohn*, ed. Heinrich Scholz (Berlin: Reucher & Reichard, 1916; reprint, Waltrop: Hartmut Spenner, 2004; see LSMM), 64n29. Cf. Jacobi, *The Main Philosophical Writings and the Novel 'Allwill'*, trans. George di Giovanni (Montreal: McGill-Queens University Press, 1994) [henceforth Gio], 173-251.

5. JA 3.2 CII; LSMM 151. Cf. LSMM 10n23, with 110.

6. For the following, see JA 3.2 XVI-XXX, LXXV-LXXVII; LSMM 65-80, 126-28.

7. Scholz, *Die Hauptschriften zum Pantheismusstreit*, 78; cf. Gio 187.

8. Scholz, *Die Hauptschriften zum Pantheismusstreit*, 77 (Strauss's emphasis), 80n; cf. Gio 187, 189.

9. Mendelssohn had shared with his friend Elise Reimarus his plan (soon to be interrupted) to write *Something about Lessing's Character*, which she amicably and unsuspectingly mentioned to her friend Jacobi (JA 3.2 XV-XVI; LSMM 62-65). The quarrel that Jacobi then began with Mendelssohn over Lessing's putative Spinozism was at bottom, says Strauss, over "just what the meaning of Lessing's legacy was and who—Mendelssohn or Jacobi—had the calling to administer it" (JA 3.2 XXX; LSMM 80).

10. "In the years 1774, 1777 and 1778, under the title 'Fragments of an Unnamed,' Lessing had published a part of the *Apologie oder Schutzschrift für die vernünftigen Verehrer Gottes* [Apology or Defense for the Rational Worshipers of God], whose author was Hermann Samuel Reimarus (1694-1768). Reimarus had been expounding the religion of reason, especially in his *Vornehmsten Wahrheiten der natürlichen Religion* [Noblest Truths of Natural Religion] (1754 and at other times). As concerns revelation, the '2nd Fragment' asserted 'the Impossibility of a Revelation that All Men can Believe in a Justified Mode.' To his edition of the 'Fragments' Lessing had added 'Counterpropositions,' from which it turns out that he did not 'adopt the entire sentiment' of the Fragmentist's.... On the other hand, Lessing had to defend the Fragmentist to Mendelssohn specifically (see his letter to Mendelssohn of January 9, 1771 [JA

12.2 2])" (JA 3.2 125f.; LSMM 63n26). On "the religion of reason" (or "rational religion"), see Strauss, "*Einleitung zu 'Phädon'*," JA 3.1 XVIII–XXV; "Introduction to *Phädon*," LSMM 34-41. For a detailed and penetrating interpretation of the theological issues prompting the emergence of *Nathan the Wise*, see Hannes Kerber, *Die Aufklärung der Aufklärung: Lessing und die Herausforderung des Christentums* (Göttingen: Wallstein, 2021).

11. For the following, see JA 3.2 LXXXV–LXXIX; LSMM 135-39.

12. See also Strauss, "*Einleitung zu 'Pope ein Metaphysiker!'*," JA 2 XV, XVII–XVIII; "Introduction to *Pope a Metaphysician!*," LSMM 7, 9-11.

13. Emphases in this quotation from Strauss's notes are Strauss's. On the difference between the lesson provided by Lessing's drama and the lesson provided by its author, see part IV, section C of the present essay. On Leibniz's "Optimism" (his doctrine that the actual world is "the best of all possible worlds"), see JA 3.2 LXX, CVIII; LSMM 159, 220—with JA 2 XVII; LSMM 9.

14. JA 3.2 LXXXVII–LXXXVIII; cf. LSMM 137-38. On *amor fati* ("love of fate") in Nietzsche, see *Ecce Homo*, "*Warum ich so klug bin*" [Why I Am So Clever], §10 end, in *Werke*, ed. Giorgio Colli and Mazzino Montinari (15 vols.; Berlin: de Gruyter, 1967-1977, 1988), 6:297; trans. Walter Kaufmann in *Basic Writings of Nietzsche* (New York: Modern Library, 2000), 714.

15. JA 3.2 CVIII; LSMM 159: "Voltaire's *Candide* ... is a veiled defense of Bayle's 'Manicheanism' over and against Leibniz's 'Optimism'—Martin, the most rational character in the novel, is a Manichean." On the controversy between Pierre Bayle and Leibniz prompting Leibniz's *Theodicy* (1710), see Strauss, "*Einleitung zu 'Sache Gottes, oder die gerettete Vorsehung'*," JA 3.2 CVI–CIX; "Introduction to *God's Cause, or Providence Vindicated*," LSMM 156-59.

16. JA 3.2 LXXXVIII; LSMM 138. As regards "the emphatically *popular*, 'exoteric' character" of Mendelssohn's widely read, widely praised updating of Plato's *Phaedo*, Strauss says that, in order to defend rational religion's doctrine of the immortality of the soul to his Enlightenment contemporaries by means of "a *proof* as certain as possible, as simple as possible, with as few presuppositions as possible, as *popular* as possible," Mendelssohn "decided in the *Phädon* to philosophize 'exoterically,' to employ 'mere *bon sens*' " (JA 3.1 XXIV, XXV, with JA 3.2 XX; LSMM 39, 41, with 69). As regards Mendelssohn's disagreement with Leibniz's "conviction ... that happiness consists in the observation of the universal order"—and the latter's concomitant "splitting up of the human race into the 'wise' and the 'multitude,' and with this the acceptance of a twofold manner of communicating truths, an esoteric and an exoteric one"—Strauss comments: "Such a distinction Mendelssohn could not accept unreservedly; his presuppositions forced him into popular philosophy" (JA 3.2 CV; LSMM 155).

17. Letter of May 28, 1971, to Alexander Altmann, as editor-in-chief of the republished and resumed volumes of JA (1974 and following, see LSMM 221-23) and literary executor for Strauss's hitherto unpublished introductions, annotations, and the like, to *Morgenstunden / An die Freunde Lessings* and *Sache Gottes* (JA 3.2 VII–IX; LSMM 3-5). See also Strauss's unpublished "Plan

of a Book Tentatively Entitled *Philosophy and the Law: Historical Essays*" (1946), whose concluding chapter was to be on *Nathan the Wise* (Strauss, *Jewish Philosophy and the Crisis of Modernity: Essays and Lectures in Modern Jewish Thought*, ed. Kenneth Hart Green [Albany: State University of New York Press, 1997], 467–70).

18. Strauss cites Lessing's *Werke*, ed. Karl Petersen and Woldemar von Olshausen (25 vols.; Berlin: Bong, 1925) [henceforth PvO], 6:21–60 (for "*Ernst und Falk*") and 21:138–89 (for the two writings on Leibniz).

19. Hannes Kerber, "Strauss and Schleiermacher on How to Read Plato: An Introduction to 'Exoteric Teaching'," in *Reorientation*, 191–216. Strauss's defense of Plato's exotericism occupies the central paragraphs of ET.

20. "Cf. the remarks of the young Lessing on the relevant passage in Gellius (20.5) in the Tenth *Literaturbrief*" (ET 282nXXVII, citing PvO 4:38). Here Lessing notices (without yet fully understanding) Aulus Gellius's *Attic Nights* on what distinguishes Aristotle's "exoteric" teaching from his "acroamatic" (or esoteric) teaching, as that which (quoting Gellius's Latin) "was conducive to meditations on rhetoric, the faculty for nuance, and acquaintance with politics [*civilium*]"—to which Lessing adds: "a philosophy that Aristotle accordingly, under the rubric of *the exoteric* philosophy, separated altogether from the true one; in short, it was the wisdom of the Sophists." See below, page 43, with notes 22–23.

21. Here and for the following see ET 276–77. "The contradiction between the statement made at the beginning that free-masonry is always in existence and the statement made toward the end that free-masonry came into being at the beginning of the eighteenth century enables us to see that 'free-masonry' is an ambiguous term" (ET 277nVII).

22. ET 277 cites PvO 21:147. Cf. above, page 4.

23. ET 278 cites Plato, *Theaetetus* 180c7–d5 and *Protagoras* 316c5–317c5, 343b4–5 (ET 278NXIII).

24. Strauss cites PvO 21:160, with 184, 187 and 189 (on "believing").

25. See JA 12.2 2.

26. 1767. Ed. Fania Oz-Sulzberger (Cambridge: Cambridge University Press, 1995).

27. ET 284. ET 284nXXXIII documents "[t]he influence of Ferguson's mitigated Rousseauism on Lessing."

28. Strauss cites Jacobi's "*Etwas das Lessing gesagt hat*," RK 2:334; "Something that Lessing [has] Said," trans. Dale E. Snow, in *What Is Enlightenment? Eighteenth-Century Questions and Twentieth-Century Answers*, ed. James Schmidt (Berkeley: University of California Press, 1991), 198; with RK 3:469 for the quotation that follows. As Strauss observes, Jacobi quotes Ferguson extensively (ET285nXXXIV).

29. Strauss quotes (in Spinoza's Latin) *Tractatus Theologico-Politicus*, chap. 14, §20 (ed. Bruder); *Theologico-Political Treatise*, trans. Martin D. Yaffe (Indianapolis: Focus Philosophical Library, 2004), 164.

30. "The early Cartesians distinguished the 'exoteric' *Discours de la méthode* from the 'acroamatic' *Meditationes.* Cf. É. Gilson's commentary on the *Discours* (Vrin: Paris 1930), 79. Cf. e.g. *Discours de la méthode*, sixième partie, in princ.: writing, being an action, is subject to religious and political authority, but thought is not" (ET 285n112). For the cited passage, see Descartes, *Discourse on Method*, trans. Richard Kennington (Indianapolis: Focus Philosophical Library, 2007), 48.

31. Strauss cites Lessing's seventy-first *Literaturbrief* ("Certainly criticism considered from this point of view, and the study of the Ancients pursued to this level of familiarity [which Leibniz had with Plato, Aristotle, Archimedes, and Apollodorus], is not pedantry but much rather the means by which Leibniz became who he was") and forty-fifth *Brief antiquarischen Inhalts* ("We see more than the Ancients; and yet our eyes might perhaps be worse than the eyes of the Ancients: the Ancients saw less than we do; but their eyes, especially for reading, might easily have been sharper than ours.—I'm afraid that the whole comparison of Ancients and Moderns might have to come down to this") (ET286nXXXVII).

32. See above, pages 12, 11, and 9, respectively.

33. After citing "Leibniz on Eternal Punishments" on the "prudence" that Lessing's Enlightenment contemporaries considered themselves "too wise" to need to exercise, Strauss notes further that *Nathan*'s Palestine, then a Muslim country, was contemporaneous with Averroism's (prudently communicated) doctrine "of the three impostors"—the view that Muslim "monotheism" was but one of three fraudulent claimants to being the true religion. See above, page 4.

34. Strauss's note points to "Spinoza or Maimonides" and adds in parentheses "Leibniz and Mendelssohn," so as to suggest that the emancipation is either philosophical—that is, the radical intellectual independence from the ruling fanaticism on the part of these philosophers—or, if political, an emancipation at bottom enabled by them. See above, pages 4–5.

35. Strauss cites Lessing, *Werke in zwei Bänden* (2 vols.; Leipzig: G. J. Göschen'sche Verlagshandlung, 1855), vol. 2, 227a top, 227b [henceforth IV/7 Gn2.227a top, 227b; the insertion of act and scene numbers is mine (except where noted otherwise), M.Y.]. (Nathan: "*Und ob mich siebenfache Liebe schon / Bald an dieß einz'ge fremde Mädchen band; / Ob der Gedanke mich schon tödtet, daß / Ich meine sieben Söhn' ihr aufs neue / Verlieren soll:—wenn sie von meinen Händen / Die Vorsicht wieder fordert,—ich gehorche!* [And even though sevenfold love soon bound me to this only one foreign girl; even though the thought kills me that in her I should lose my seven sons once more:—if Providence demands her back from my hands—I shall obey!]" "*Gott! Wenn ich doch das Mädchen noch behalten, / Und einen solchen Eidam mir damit / Erkaufen könnte!*" [God! If after all I could still keep the girl and purchase such a son-in-law (as the knight) for myself besides!])

36. The emphasis is Strauss's. Citing I/1 Gn2.184b bottom (Nathan: "*Alles, was / Ich sonst besitze, hat Natur und Glück / Mir zugetheilt. Dieß Eigenthum allein / Dank' ich der Tugund.*" [Everything else that I own, nature and for-

tune have allotted me. This possession alone I owe to virtue.]), along with a contrary statement at I/1 Gn2.184a (Nathan to Daja on the house fire during his absence: "*Gebe Gott / Daß ich nur alles schon vernommen habe!*" [God grant that I but have already learned everything!]), Strauss says that the prayer he expresses to Daja is "Nathan's prudent medicine . . ." and invites a comparison with I/2 Gn2.187a middle (Recha: "*Habt Ihr / Ihr selbst die Möglichkeit, daß Engel sind, / Daß Gott zum Besten derer, die ihn lieben, / Auch Wunder könne thun, mich nicht gelehrt?*" [Haven't you, you yourself taught me that it's a possibility that angels do exist, that God could also do miracles to benefit those who love him?]). Here and for the following see above, pages 5–6.

37. Cf. note 51, below.

38. Strauss cites parenthetically act II, scene 5, where Nathan eventually persuades the Knight to befriend him since their common humanity transcends sectarian differences. (Knight: "*Doch kennt Ihr auch das Volk, / Das diese Menschenmäkelei zuerst / Getrieben? Wißt Ihr, Nathan, welche Volk / Zuerst das auserwählte Volk sich nannte? / Wie, wenn ich dieses Volk nun, zwar nicht haßte, / Doch wegen seines Stolzes zu verachten, / Mich nicht entbrechen könnte? Seines Stolzes, / Den es auf Christ und Mußelmann vererbte, / Nur sein Gott sey der rechte Gott!—Ihr sturtzt, / Daß ich, ein Christ und ein Tempelherr, so rede? / Wann hat, und wo die fromme Raserei, / Den bessern Gott zu haben, diesen bessern / Der ganzen Welt als besten aufzubringen, / In ihrer schwarzesten Gestalt sich mehr / Gezeigt, als hier, als jetzt?*" [Yet do you know the very nation that first practiced this fault-finding of humans? Do you, Nathan, know which nation was first called the chosen nation? How? what if I did not hate this nation, but could not keep from despising it for its pride? its pride, which it bequeathed to Christian and Muslim that its God alone is the true God! —You're startled that I as a Christian and a Templar talk thus? When and where's the pious rage to have the better God, to impose on the whole world this better one as best, been showing up more in its blackest form than here, than now?]

39. Citing I/6 Gn2.194b (Daja, Recha's Christian nurse, in conversation with the Knight: "*Sein Volk verehret ihn als einen Fürsten. / Doch daß es ihn den weisen Nathan nennt, / Und nicht vielmehr den reichen, hat mich oft / Gewundert.* Knight: *Seinem Volk ist reich und weise / Vielleicht das Nämliche.* Daja: *Vor allem aber / Hätt's ihn den Guten nennen müssen. Denn / Ihr stellt Euch gar nicht vor, wie gut er ist.*" [Daja: His people worship him as a prince. But I have often marveled that they call him the wise Nathan, and not rather 'the Rich'. Knight: To his nation rich and wise are possibly the same. Daja: Above all they should have called him 'the Good'. For you cannot imagine how good he is.]), Strauss adds parenthetically "Frederick the Wise" and "Frederick the Great."

40. Strauss cites 2 Samuel 7 and 12, and 1 Kings 1.

41. See note 28, above.

42. IV/2 Gn2.188a top, etc. (Recha: "*Mein Vater! / Mein Vater, wenn ich irr', Ihr wißt, ich irre / Nicht gern.* Nathan: *Vielmehr, du läßt dich gern belehren.*" [Recha: My Father! My Father, if I'm wrong, you know I don't like being wrong. Nathan: You rather do like being taught.])

Interpretative Essay

43. Cf. V/5 Gn2.232b (Knight, on learning that he must defer to a hitherto unsuspected brother of Recha's, who according to Nathan will always remain worthy of both men's love: "*Sagt / Das nicht! Von meiner Liebe sagt das nicht! / Denn die läßt nichts sich unterschlagen; nichts. / Es sey auch noch so klein!*" [Don't say that! Don't say that about *my* love! For it lets nothing quell it; nothing.])

44. Strauss invites a passing comparison with Shakespeare's *The Tempest*, whose setting is a remote island rather than the "*holy land*," so that "the relation of the 'ideal' to 'reality' is much more directly a question in the *Nathan*.

45. Cf. III/1 Gn2.206b (Recha in reply to Daja's wish that she someday marry a European: "*Wenn mein Vater dich so hörte!—/ Was that er dir, mir immer nur mein Glück / So weit von ihm als möglich vorzuspiegeln? / Was that er dir, den Samen der Vernunft, den er so rein in meine Seele streute, / Mit deines Landes Unkraut oder Blumen / So gern zu mischen?*" [If my Father heard you thus!—What did he do to you, to always picture my own happiness to me as far from him as possible? What did he do to you, to so like mixing the seeds of reason, which he sowed so purely in my soul, with your land's weeds or flowers?]

46. In his General Seminar lecture, Strauss calls them "*natural* miracles." See above page 5.

47. Strauss cites II/7 Gn2.203b (Knight: "*Das Leben, daß / Ich leb', ist sein Geschenk* [The life I'm living is his gift.]), II/7 Gn2.204a top (Knight: "*Nicht genug, daß ich / Auf sein Geheiß noch bin, mit seinem Willen / Noch leb': ich muß nun auch von ihm erwarten, / Nach wessen Willen ich zu leben habe.* [It's not enough that at his behest I still am, in accord with his will I still live: now I must also await him by whose will I'm having to live.]), IV/5 Gn2.223b bottom (Saladin: "*Was hätte Nathan, / Sobald er nicht ihr Vater ist, für Recht / Auf sie? Wer ihr das Leben so erhielt, / Tritt einzig in die Rechte deß, der ihr / Es gab.* [What right would Nathan have to her, now that he is not her father? He who thus brought life back to her becomes sole heir to the rights of him who gave it.])

48. See II/9 Gn2.206a (Derwisch: "*Wer / Sich Knall und Fall, im selbst zu leben, nicht / Entschließen kann, der lebt Anderers Sklav / Auf immer.*" [One who cannot decide come what may to live to oneself lives as another's slave forever.] In his General Seminar lecture, Strauss calls the Dervish wise but not prudent, whereas Nathan is both wise and prudent. See above pages 9 and 12

49. Included in the notes of Strauss's General Seminar lecture are the following subheadings (not spelled out further): "Nathan and the Dervish: the relation between practical wisdom and impractical wisdom"; "Nathan and the Templar: the relation between practical wisdom and the voice of the heart"; "Nathan and Saladin: the gulf between the Wise and the enlightened despot." Cf., respectively, notes 48 and 43, above, and 54, below.

50. By Nathan's prudent "manner of teaching," Strauss may have in mind inter alia his pedagogical appreciation for the story of the three rings in Boccaccio's *Decameron* I:3, on which Nathan models the story he tells Saladin. To document the "ease" with which Nathan tells stories, Strauss cites I/2 Gn2.186b, 187a (Recha: "*Habt Ihr, / Ihr selbst die Möglichkeit, daß Engel sind, / Daß Gott zum Besten derer, die ihn lieben, / Auch Wunder könne thun, mich nicht*

gelehrt? ... Nathan: *Und er liebt dich; und thut / Für dich und deines Gleichen stündlich Wunder; / Ja, hat sie schon von aller Ewigkeit / Für euch gethan."* [Recha: Haven't you, you yourself taught me it's a possibility that angels do exist, that God could even do miracles to benefit those who love him? ... Nathan: And he loves you; and does miracles hourly for you and those like you—indeed, has done them already from all eternity.])

51. Strauss implicitly renders III/5 Gn2.210b (Saladin: *"Was für ein Glaube, was für ein Gesetz, / Hat dir am meisten eingeleuchtet?"* [What faith, what law has convinced you the most?]) (III/5 Gn2.210b) so as to bring out its personal meaning in line with Saladin's intent to test Nathan's character before appointing him his banker-treasurer to replace Al-Hafi. Here and for the following see above, page 7.

52. Citing III/7 Gn2.211b, Strauss mentions that the father—that is, the God of the revealed religions—loves his sons according to their obedience to him (Nathan: *"So kam nun dieser Ring, von Sohn zu Sohn, / Auf einen Vater endlich von drei Söhnen, / Die alle drei ihm gleich gehorsam waren, / Die alle drei er folglich gleich zu lieben / Sich nicht entbrechen konnte."* [Thus came this ring, from son to son, ultimately to a father of three sons, all three of whom were alike obedient to him, all three of whom he hence could not stop himself from loving alike.]).

53. Citing III/7 Gn2.212a (Nathan: *"Kann selbst der Vater seinen Musterring / Nicht unterscheiben."* [Even the father cannot detect his model ring.]).

54. Again citing III/7 Gn2.212a (Nathan: *"Denn gründen alle sich nicht auf Geschichte? / Geschrieben oder überliefert!—Und / Geschichte muss doch wohl allein auf Treu' / Und Glauben angenommen werden?"* [For aren't they all based on history? Written or handed down!—And yet history must presumably be accepted on trust and faith alone?]").

55. Strauss uses the Greek term for "virtue," *arete*—which in the present context would mean the excellence of character rendering each obedient son (Muslim, Christian, Jew) beloved of God for adhering scrupulously to the mores of his inherited religion. Now if, as the Judge implies, what is essential for being beloved of God is justice and temperance rather than adherence to those mores as such, then the virtue required for defending those mores if and as needed, "courage"—for which Strauss here uses the Greek *andreia* ("manliness")—is no longer essential. Likewise "wisdom"—the fourth classical virtue of the soul alongside courage, temperance, and justice (see Plato, *Republic* IV)—which Strauss leaves unmentioned in this context, though see our following note. On the tension between justice and wisdom in theological matters, cf. Strauss's "Introduction to *God's Cause*," which speaks of Leibniz's restoration of natural theology—in response to Bayle's radical critique of revealed theology for inadequately addressing the question of the justice of human suffering in a world created by a putatively beneficent God—"by means of the principle of wisdom, i.e., of regard for the beauty and order of the universe"; even so, Strauss observes, Leibniz's recourse to wisdom to

underwrite God's beneficence required him to reject "the classical concept of justice as a steadfast will to grant each his due" so as to be able to sanction "the elimination of divine justice and punitiveness [i.e., of suffering as God's punishment]" in promulgating the doctrine of "the best of all possible worlds." Nathan's nonpunishing Judge, it seems, concurs in Leibniz's Bayle-induced "distancing from positive religion." See above, notes 13 and 16.

56. Strauss here contrasts, in Greek, *banausia* ("skilled labor," hence "vulgarity") with *kalokagathia* ("gentility"). Cf. his letter of April 22, 1957, to Alexandre Kojève: "in [Plato's] Republic everyone is just and moderate, but only the elite is manly (and wise); manliness and wisdom belong together." (*On Tyranny*, ed. Victor Gourevitch and Michael Roth [rev. ed.; Chicago: University of Chicago Press, 2013], 275, with Strauss's "Restatement," 189–91, 199, 209–11, contra Kojève on "work" vis-à-vis wisdom).

57. See note 10 above. Here and for the following see above, page 10, with page 8.

58. The Patriarch would like to prosecute a non-Christian (in a "hypothetical" case the Knight is asking him about) for having adopted a Christian child, as well as to co-opt the Knight into betraying his gratitude to Saladin (for sparing his life) by secretly conveying to the Crusaders at Acre the Patriarch's assessment of Jerusalem's military vulnerabilities.

59. See notes 33 and 34 above.

60. Strauss mentions in passing the principle of moral education in *Nicomachean Ethics* II (i.e., proper habituation).

61. Strauss notes as an afterthought Shakespeare's *The Merchant of Venice*. On the play's vindication of Judaism vis-à-vis its Christian addressees, see Martin D. Yaffe, *Shylock and the Jewish Question* (Baltimore: Johns Hopkins University Press, 1989).

62. See Judges 13–16. Here and for the following see above, page 11.

63. See Exodus 13:17, whose opening words Strauss quotes in Hebrew: *Vayehi beshallach par'oh* ... "And it came to pass, when Pharaoh had let the people go, that God led them not through the way of the land of the Philistines, although that was near" (Strauss's translation; see Green, 92, 444.)

64. Strauss evidently means both biblical and postbiblical Jews. Cf. also note 1, above: Strauss's lecture quotes from Horace's remark (about a "neighboring" wall on fire prompting active concern) shortly before his present remarks on the nearness of the Philistines.

65. Jeremiah 2:2: *Zakharti lakh chesed ne'urayikh*....

66. Here and for the following see above, pages 4–5, with page 9.

67. Strauss cites parenthetically Lessing's *Hamburg Dramaturgy* #1 (GnI.91 end, the passage I have quoted in the first epigraph, above) and ##11 and 12 (GnI.104 and 105, where Lessing contrasts Shakespeare's dramatically chilling presentation of Hamlet's ghost with Voltaire's sophisticated but dramatically unsatisfactory attempt to present a ghost whose appearance is meant to be consistent with laws of nature).

68. See, however, notes 13 and 36 above.

69. Cf. note 38 above.

70. On the intense personal hostility Lessing faced as author of *Nathan the Wise*, see Mendelssohn's *Morgenstunden*, JA 3.2 130–31 (trans. Altmann, in *Moses Mendelssohn: A Biographical Study* [Tuscaloosa: University of Alabama Press, 1973], 379–80): "after *Nathan* appeared ... intrigue penetrated from studies and bookstores into the private homes of his friends and acquaintances and whispered into every one's ear that Lessing had insulted Christianity—though he had dared to utter some reproaches only against some Christians and Christendom, at most.... Everyone considered as a personal insult whatever reproach he had directed against some of his coreligionists or had expressed through the dramatis personae when castigating self-conceit or narrow-mindedness. He, who used to be made welcome everywhere as a friend and acquaintance, now found everywhere unfriendly faces, reserve, frosty glances, a cold reception, and a ready farewell. He saw himself deserted by friends and exposed to the snares of his persecutors ... and the results this produced in his mind were sad. Lessing, who despite his scholarly work was the most pleasant companion, the most cheerful guest at a dinner party, now lost his jovial mood completely and became a sleepy, insensitive machine."

71. See above, notes 1 and 64. Also, here and for the following see above, pages 8–9.

72. I am indebted to Gisela Berns, Kenneth Hart Green, and Hannes Kerber for pertinent comments.

PART TWO

EDITED AND TRANSCRIBED BY SVETOZAR Y. MINKOV

Transcript 2.1

LEO STRAUSS, ON THE PLAN OF THE *KUZARI* (C. 1941–1942)

Editorial note: The following is the transcript of notes on seven sheets found in Leo Strauss Papers, Box 16, Folder 7, Special Collections Research Center, University of Chicago Library. The first two transcripts are from recto and verso of a single sheet (complemented with the transcript of a separate sheet as identified in the notes) and the other series of notes are transcribed from five other separate sheets. Additions are all indicated by angle brackets. Strauss's underlinings have been replaced with italics.

[Recto]
Plan of the *Cuzari*
I The conversion to Judaism: the Cuzari as a גוי <goy=gentile>

1) Jewish chronology proves beginning of the world, i.e. of the *present* world. I 11–48, and -67.
2) [This might be held on the basis of Epicureanism:]
3) Proof of the truth of revelation by *miracles* I 67–91.
4) Israel's greatness I 92 – end.

{ Plan of I 11 – end.

1. The right method of arguing I 11–25.
2. The election of Israel integrated into the cosmological scheme (the hierarchy of beings) I 26–43.
3. The reliability of the Jewish tradition I 44–59.
4. The tradition of India and of the philosophers I 60–67.

5. How is it possible that God speaks to man? Indirect proof: by rejection of the concept of "nature" I 68-79.
6. The history of the Jewish sharī'a I 80-87.
7. The anthropomorphism of the Jews I 88-91.
8. The disobedience of the Jews I 92.

Question: does the Cuzari raise again the question of how God could talk to men? In II 5: he raised question of the divine *will*.}[1]

II–IV *Institutiones religionis Judaicae: the Cuzari as an Epicurean Jew.* (cf. Haggadah: why do *you* celebrate the Pessach: the question of the רשע {resha, evil})

  a) *Hebraic* questions = *Language* [cf. II 1end and 81]

     1. *Names and attributes* of God. II 2-8.
     2. The *cruelty* of God II 9-25.
     3. The *people* of God II 25.

Hebrew quotations seem to start with II.[2]

  b) The pious man III 1-22.
  c) The Karaites: the tradition III 23-74 }[3] [= *Law*]
  d) Names of God IV 1-24 [= *Roots* of the Law]
  e) The natural sciences IV 25 – end. }[4]

"*Science*" [cf. II 4 end with IV, II 85 & 15] But: II 28, 58, 63 ff., III 32 & context. 39 (190, 191 H.)] cf. IV 15 beg. (IV 5-14: excursus) *the Cuzari as fullfledged Jew* (from IV 26).[5]

V The Kalām

  α) the physical-philosophical structure of theology with occasional criticism of philosophy V 1-14.
  β) The Kalām-theology V 15-19.
  γ) The practical answers to theology ("branch") V 19-20.

Plan in II 81:

  1) Language (= II)
  2) The pious man (=III)
  3) Karaites (=III)

4) Roots of opinions & beliefs = IV 1–24
5) The ancient sciences which remained with the Jews = IV 26–31

Plan in III 74:[6]

1) —{same as in II 81}
2) —{same as in II 81}
3) {same as in II 81}
4) names of God
5) Jewish sciences.

[Verso]
Numbers

Cuzari consists of 5 books and of 331 sections—without the חתימה <khātima = conclusion>, it consists of 323 sections: *19 × 17*

Dialogue between Cuzari and חבר <ḥibr/habr = scholar/sage>—I 11 – V end = 321 sections = *3 × 107*

107 = number of sections of the "Jewish" part of I
Hence:

    A. I 11 – 117.
    B. II 1 – III 26—*see* III 26!
    C. III 27 – V end.

Middle of the whole: sect. 166 = II 49—philosophers vs. sharī'a
Middle of the whole without חתימה <khātima=conclusion> : sect. 162 = II 45—question of Jewish asceticism—cf. IV 18.
Middle of whole Jewish part (= 171)—II 54—the Jews the central fact in the history of human thought.
Middle of Jewish part without חתימה <khātima=conclusion> = *157* = II 40

[Separate sheet]
The *Cuzari* is, not a work of philosophy, but a work of Kalām, and even of an extremely anti-theoretical and fideistic type of Kalām (p. 5f.).[7]

Yet, he corrects the (Karaite) Kalām by basing it on physics (V 2).

Philosophers are so indifferent to religion that they can join any religion, and hence defend any religion (p. 17): a philosopher can *become* a mutakallim. (cf. *Iḥṣa al-Ulūm* {Alfarabi's *Enumeration of the Sciences*} V.)

A philosopher who happens to adhere to a revealed religion, will soft pedal as regards the fundamental difference between philosophy and revelation: he will assert the basic agreement between both (he will say that as regards divine *will*, the crucial question, philosophy and revelation agree—cf. V 18 (IX) with I 1 and II 5 f.

[Separate sheet]
The other way round: the Mutakallim asserts the basic agreement between philosophy and revelation—V 18 (IX). He is a harmonizer. But what is the motive of that harmonization? Intellectual cowardice?

The philosopher in person who ought to know philosophy better, asserts the basic *disagreement* between philosophy and revelation (I 1). The חבר <ḥibr/habr = scholar/sage> calls the philosophers mutakallimūn (V 14; cf. V 1) ....

[Separate sheet]
RMbM[8] & Halevi present two typical attitudes of medieval Jews to philosophy: the two most important attitudes.

> RMbM: harmony between Judaism and philosophy
> Halevi: antagonism between Judaism and philosophy

But things are not as simple as that. Both men are convinced that philosophy as *such* is irreconcilable with Judaism. RMbM admits a higher *degree* of agreement between Judaism and philosophy than does Halevi. RMbM feels that, as matters stand, i.e. owing to the loss of the secret teaching which was caused by the Diaspora, there is no choice for the Jewish élite except to study philosophy. Halevi, on the other hand, thinks that precisely the Jewish élite does not need philosophy at all: pure faith, not based on argument, is absolutely superior to any conviction, arrived at by argument.

When discussing Halevi's attitude toward philosophy, people sometimes identify "philosophy" with "thought" or "reasoning." Since Halevi himself is reasoning all the time, they think that he overstated his critique of philosophy. But this view is wrong. We have to distinguish between two kinds of reasoning: philosophic reasoning and reasoning in the service of the law (in particular: Kalām). Cf. V 16—the conclusion to be drawn concerning philosophy ≠ Kalām: philosophy is *dangerous*.

> It is dangerous in
> its anti-religious character (Socrates—IV 13, V 14).
> its a-social character: IV 18 (ascetic.)
> its a-moral character: IV 13, 16, 19; I 1 end.

The dangerous nature of philosophy determines the *forms* in which philosophy is presented: the disputation between scholar and philosopher is missing. (Cf. the letter of King Joseph to Hasdai ibn Shaprut—no philosopher, but disputatious!).

philosopher cannot be convinced—but the King can. Why? The King is naturally pious.

The argument is convincing, and is meant to be convincing, for naturally pious people only. Naturally pious ≠ naturally faithful—V 2 beg. The scholar *hopes*, hence doubts, as to whether the King is naturally faithful—but is the King not *evidently* a doubter?—No—it depends on whether his conviction was brought about by argument or by the spark (V 16).

The structure of the book: In I, (no Hebrew quotations) the King is a Gentile; in II-IV the King is a *doubting Jew*; in V, the King is a full-fledged Jew. The decisive moment is IV 26.

The law of the book: the more doubt decreases, the more can the essence of philosophy be divulged: presentation of philosophy given only in V. Cf. the two attitudes toward "intellectual laws"—cf. I 81 with II 47 f.

[Separate sheet]
We have emphasized the *anti-philosophic* attitude of Halevi which distinguishes him so characteristically from RMbM. That attitude is due to the recognition of the *danger* of philosophy. We have seen to what extent that realisation determines the peculiar *form* of the work.

But Halevi is famous not only for his theoretical defense of Judaism—he is even more famous as a poet, and in particular as the singer of Zion. What is the connection between the teaching of the *Cuzari* and Halevi's Zionism? Zionism, longing for Zion, *active* longing for Zion, *return* to Zion is the necessary conclusion from the Jewish creed. That is to say: one cannot object to Zionism thus understood on any *Jewish* grounds: any objection to *Zionism* is due to unbelief, i.e. to *philosophy*. Poem n. 6[9]

Or, the other way round: Pure and simple faith is not possible but in Palestine—II 22-23 IV 22-23 V 22-23.

The necessary connection between Judaism and the longing for the return of Jews to Palestine was emphasized equally strong{ly} by RMbM—מלכים ה' <*H' Melakhim*=L' of Kings>[10]— but RMbM laid a great emphasis on the *warlike* character of the Messiah. (Connection with "philosophy"—loss of political freedom due to our sins—i.e. to idolatry, to astrology—i.e. to neglect of arts of war. Restoration due to military efficiency). In accordance with his general view Halevi rejects this military interpretation. Cf. I 3; I 80-84; I 113; II 1 & 14; IV 21-27

There is then a *certain* point of contact between philosophy and Judaism: pacifism and tolerance.

[Separate sheet]
[The problem bothering the King: it is determined by the conflict between his *revelation* and *philosophy*. His revelation (dream, angel): the relevance of (ceremonial) actions—philosopher denies relevance of actions: God does not care for men, God does not speak to men (I 6, 8, 10).

He meets the Jew—the King touched by philosophy is *disgusted* by the extremely obscurantist unphilosophic answer of the Jew; but he is impressed by the fact that philosophy does not lead to *agreement* which is basic for living together. This is the *first* step.

I 12: "you Jew" I 14: "you Jew". I 28: "you Jew". I 82: "you חבר <ḥibr/habr =scholar/sage>"

II 27: "you חבר <ḥibr/habr =scholar/sage>" II 45 ? (not in Arabic).

The *second* step: the Jewish chronology proves that the world has a beginning—limitation of the proof: I 67!

The *third* step: revelation on Sinai shows *miracles* and hence *creation*. Cf. I 84—

The *fourth* step: the wisdom of Israel—legal regime IV 25-26

—

Poem n. 6—cf. Cuzari II 22end-24.

Notes

1. The transcript between the curly brackets is added from a separate sheet by the editors as it complements the plan of the *Kuzari* described here.
2. In the ms. this sentence appears on the right-hand side of the enumeration (here the enumeration is reproduced above it).
3. This curly bracket in the ms. embraces this line and the one above.
4. This curly bracket in the ms. embraces this line and the one above.
5. In the ms. this whole paragraph appears on the right-hand side of the enumeration (here the enumeration is reproduced above it).
6. The plan of III 74 appears in front of the plan of II 81 in the ms. (here reproduced above it).

7. This and the other references below refer to the following: Jehuda ha-Levi, *Das Buch Kusari des Jehuda ha-Levi: Nach dem hebräischen Texte des Jehuda Ibn-Tibbon*, trans. David Cassel (Leipzig: Verlag von Friedrich Voigt's Buchhandlung, 1869).

8. Acronym for Moses Maimonides.

9. Possibly "Excursus: Day of Revelation." See *Ninety-Two Poems and Hymns of Yehuda Halevi: Franz Rosenzweig*, ed. Richard A. Cohen, trans. Thomas Kovach, Eva Jospe, and Gilya Gerda Schmidt (Albany: State University of New York Press, 2000).

10. מלכים ה׳ is the abbreviation of הלכות מלכים and refers to the last section of the last (14th) book of Maimonides's *Mishneh Torah*, the proper title of which is "Laws of Kings and Their Wars." Strauss seems to have passages in mind that deal with the nature of the Messiah, and with how the (messianic) return of the Jews to the Land of Israel, their ancestral homeland, will occur in a historical future and in a "naturalistic" fashion. We owe the explanation to Kenneth Hart Green to whom we are grateful. See also Leo Strauss, "Note on Maimonides' Letter on Astrology," in *Studies in Platonic Political Philosophy* (Chicago: University of Chicago Press, 1983), 207; Leo Strauss, "Introductory Essay for Herman Cohen, *Religion of Reason out of the Sources of Judaism*," in *Studies in Platonic Political Philosophy* (Chicago: University of Chicago Press, 1983), 244; *Gesammelte Schriften*, ed. Heinrich Meier, vol. 2 (Stuttgart: JB Metzler, [1997] 2013), 393-436 ("Cohen und Maimuni"); 179-94 ("Der Ort der Vorsehungslehre nach der Ansicht Maimunis," including Strauss's marginal notes ["The Place of the Doctrine of Providence according to Maimonides," trans. Gabriel Bartlett and Svetozar Y. Minkov, *Review of Metaphysics* 57, no. 3, 537-49]); 229-31 (Strauss's marginalia to his Abravanel essay).

Transcript 2.2

LEO STRAUSS, ON THE *KUZARI* (C. 1941–1942)

Editorial note: This is the transcript of a typescript found in Leo Strauss Papers, box 16, folder 6, Special Collections Research Center, University of Chicago Library. In the 1942 Annual Report of the Executive Committee of the American Academy for Jewish Research the following announcement and short summary of Strauss's paper appears:

> Prof. Leo Strauss, "The 'Philosopher' in the Cuzari."
> In discussing the *Cuzari*, one has to consider in particular also its form, i.e. the conversational setting of all statements. The most important feature of that setting is the absence of a discussion of philosophy between the philosopher and the Jewish scholar, i.e. between intellectual equals. This setting is in accordance with the technical rules underlying the Platonic dialogues.[1]

Transcribing the Hebrew passages, we have benefited from the help of Yehuda Halper, Alexander Orwin, Philip von Wussow, and detailed comments by Joshua Parens to whom we are grateful. The numbers in the square brackets refer to the page numbers of the typescript. All additions appear in curly brackets. Strauss's underlinings have been replaced with italics.

[1] *The "Philosopher" in the Cuzari.* Paper to be read at the Annual Meeting of the American Academy for Jewish Research on December 28, 1941.

The intention of this paper is to submit to you certain general considerations, or rather a *sketch* of such considerations, concerning Juda

Halevi's concept of philosophy. A study of this topic is necessary for two different, if closely related, reasons. First, the philosophers are one of the most important, if not the most important, group of men *attacked*[2] by Halevi in his Cuzari; thus, one cannot understand his own position before one has understood fully the character of the position which he attacks so passionately. The second reason is of a more general character. The philosophers whom he attacks, are the Islamic Aristotelians. Many books of these philosophers are accessible in print, and even in translations; and yet it cannot be said that[3] agreement exists concerning the most general character of their teaching. As regards the *fundamental* question, the question of their attitude toward *religion*, toward *revealed* religion, we are, so to speak, completely in the dark. The situation is briefly this. Up to about 90[4] years ago, it was generally, and, I think, universally held that Averroes—that Islamic Aristotelian who was most famous in the Western, Christian, Latin world—was an arch-heretic, a radical unbeliever: he was looked upon as the Voltaire of the MA <Middle Ages>. Since Renan, a radical change of orientation has taken place. Asin Palacios went so far as to describe Averroes as the Islamic Thomas Aquinas. To exaggerate a little in order to clarify: present day scholars consider Averroes et hoc genus omne as believing Muslims. To reconcile this view with the traditional one, which is backed by such authorities as Thomas Aquinas and Dante, the suggestion has been made that the Christian scholastics *mis*interpreted the *Islamic* philosophers by interpreting the latter from a *Christian* point of view. It is perfectly true, it is said by some scholars, that a Christian who would approach revelation in the manner of Farabi and Averroes, would have been a heretic, for Christianity has not only a clearly circumscribed dogma, but also a clearly defined magisterial authority interpreting the dogma, but Islam is in these respects fundamentally different from Christianity, and consequently the latitude permitted to philosophers is much greater in Islam than it is in [2] Christianity. This suggestion is, of course, refuted by the fact that not only Christians such as Thomas Aquinas, but also Jews such as Halevi and Maimonides and Muslims such as Ghazzali considered the Islamic Aristotelians, the falāsifa, to be unbelievers. We are then driven back to the contradiction between the characteristically modern view that the falāsifa were believing Muslims, and the traditional view that they were *not*. The modern view is borne out by a very large number of explicit statements of the falāsifa. The traditional view is supported, to begin with, merely by the authority of such men as Ghazzali, Maimonides, Thomas Aquinas. The question is this: why did these medieval authorities not attach any great weight to the orthodox statements of the falāsifa? The answer is simple: evidently they *did not take seriously* these orthodox statements; evidently they read the statements of the falāsifa in a manner different from the manner of the modern scholars (aliter pueri legunt Terentium, aliter Hugo Grotius); they read *between the lines* of the works of the falāsifa. The falāsifa themselves emphasized time and again the necessity to keep the philosophic teaching a secret, this necessity probably had more than one reason; but there is one possible reason, quite naturally not mentioned by the falāsifa, which is particularly evident. If Ghazzali, Halevi, Maimonides, and Thomas Aquinas were right, if the falāsifa were in radical opposition to revealed religion, to the *sharī'a,* the open presentation of the philosophic teaching was impossible; for it would have been subject to persecution. If this should be the situation, the works of the orthodox proponents of the philosophic teaching would be of paramount important for the historian. For the orthodox writers were under no compulsion to keep the philosophic teaching secret; on the contrary, they had to *divulge* it in order to show how dangerous it is; they had to draw the philosophers out of their corners in order to fight them; they had to state quite openly the implications, carefully concealed by the philosophers, of the philosophic teaching. It is with some open-mindedness as to this possibility that I propose to make some remarks on the philosophers as presented by Halevi, or rather on what I believe to be the right method of understanding these remarks.

[4] p. 3—has been rewritten[5]

and what he claims to be an *actual* conversation between the king and a Jewish scholar. He points out that the story of the conversation is taken from the histories, and as regards the arguments of the חבר {ḥibr/habr = scholar/sage},[6] he asserts that he had heard them. The introductory remarks end with the sentence: וראיתי לכתוב את הדברים האלה כאשר נפנו {I thought that I should record this argumentation just as it took place}. And he adds: המשכילים יבינו {the intelligent will understand]. Since not much שכל {sechel/sekhel = intellect or intelligence}[7] is required in order to see that the arguments of the חבר have been invented by Halevi (But Halevi *lies* – cf. More's *Utopia*'s proof as to the historicity of the account of Utopia—)[8], the שכל which he expects us to use, has to be used for understanding the *reason* of that fiction, or, generally speaking, of the *form* of the work. {The preceding paragraph has been crossed out. – ed.}

If the Cuzari presents indeed the defence of Judaism in its ideal setting, the following three questions take on the greatest significance: 1) By what argument does the חבר first *overcome the prejudice* of the king? (I 14). 2) By what argument or arguments does he convince the king of the *truth* of Judaism? (I 48, note 3, 68, 76, 82, 84) 3) When and why does the king finally cease to consider himself a non-Jew? One word on the third question. The conversation of the king is recorded at the beginning of the 2nd book, but throughout the 2nd and 3rd book and the larger part of the 4th book, he continues speaking of "you Jews," "you, the community of the Jews," "your prayers"[9] and so forth. As late as IV 22, he addresses the חבר יא חבר: אל יחוד {O sage/scholar of the Jews} (Hirschfeld 264, 13).[10] Four sections later,[11] in IV 26, however, he quotes from the shaharit-prayer by saying "*we* are saying" How was this change effected? Possibly by the extensive explanation of the *Sepher Yezira* in IV 25. (Cf. II 63. But it is also possible that it was brought about by the explanation of the unwarlike character of the Jewish nation in IV 23; cf. the last word of the philosopher in I 3).

I cannot dwell on this point—important as it is—if we want to enter into the thought of Halevi. I have to hurry to a somewhat more exact discussion of the central thesis that the setting of the Cuzari is the ideal setting for a defence of Judaism. For this thesis is open to a very grave objection. The ideal defence of Judaism would be one which would convince the most exacting, if fair, adversary. Is the king of Cusar really an exacting adversary? However prejudiced against Judaism the king may be: he meets two conditions which make him, so to speak, an ... [12]

1 II 23 beg.. 29, 45, 47, 57, 63, 65, 73, 79, 81, III 2, 10, 20, 22, 38, 44, 50 IV 10, 12, (14) 22. Apparently no Hebrew quotations in I (apart from proper names)—but: 50, 22 Hirschfeld. No distinction between Cusari and Jews in V.
2 The אצליכם {near you/in your possession} in IV 24 has probably to be corrected with אצלם {near them / in their possession} ---- ענדהם {'inda hum = near them / in their possession}

The Jewish calendar: the מנין {mīnyān = number} convinces him → Sefer Yezirah. But more important: I 62 ff: chronology and creation of the world ≠ eternity of the world. Cf. Wolfson, Proceedings Academy 1941, 110f. {"Hallevi and Maimonides on Design, Chance and Necessity, "*Proceedings of the American Academy for Jewish Research* 11 (1941): 105-63.}

Notes

1. "Annual Report of the Executive Committee," *Proceedings of the American Academy for Jewish Research* 12 (1942): vii.
2. Apart from the title, all other passages in the transcript are underlined in pencil by hand.
3. "that" inserted by hand.
4. "80" is corrected to "90" by hand.
5. Page 3 of the typescript is missing.
6. This is the Judeo-Arabic for a non-Muslim religious authority.
7. This is based on what follows right after the passage immediately quoted before: "and the intelligent will understand" (*Daniel* 12:10). As related to a biblical passage, perhaps the less philosophic translation (intelligence) is preferable to the more philosophic one (intellect).
8. The sentence in the parentheses is inserted by hand.
9. Here "1)" is inserted by hand referring to the handwritten footnote at the end of the ms., reproduced at the end of the transcript here.
10. Here "2)" is inserted by hand referring to the handwritten footnote at the end of the ms., reproduced at the end of the transcript here.
11. "Four sections later" is inserted by hand.
12. The rest of the typescript is missing from the archive.

RALPH LERNER

Interpretative Essay

ON YEHUDA HALEVI'S "SPIRITUAL HELL"

From the point of view of the literary historian at least, there is no more noteworthy difference between the typical premodern philosopher (who is hard to distinguish from the premodern poet) and the typical modern philosopher than that of their attitudes toward "noble (or just) lies," "pious frauds," the "ductus obliquus" or "economy of the truth."[1]

RENOWNED AND BELOVED for the vigor of his defense of his people's religion and the beauty of his words, Yehuda Halevi remains, as he has been from the outset, an object of scrutiny. His life story presents challenges to anyone eager to characterize him in simple, unambiguous terms, and the same is true of his writings.

Shuttling between Spain's Christian north and its Muslim south, this twelfth-century Jew ultimately was at home in neither. His poems bespeak both a passionate yearning for the god of his fathers and an untroubled enjoyment of the earthly pleasures of the flesh. (The instance of John Donne comes to mind.) And his great prose work, the sprawling dialogue generally known as the *Kuzari*, has elicited the most diverse interpretations. Halevi, in his multifaceted complexity, continues to raise questions for those who would discern his innermost intentions and thoughts.

The *Kuzari* is a reenactment of a series of conversations alleged to have taken place some four centuries earlier in a distant land between a pagan king and four learned interlocutors—a philosopher, a Christian, a Muslim, and finally (and reluctantly) a Jew. There are only two brief narrative passages in this text of over two hundred pages. In the first of these,

Halevi appears and speaks in his own voice to set the stage for what follows. He introduces the work by first explaining how it came into being. This book is his response to an appeal from his fellow Jews for arguments with which they might counter an array of separatists, opponents, and critics. Jews are generally regarded as despicable, even loathsome, and deserving of the wrongs and contempt that others visit upon them. This book consists of Halevi's recollection of the arguments that persuaded a disdainful ruler to convert to the despised faith and that put his recurring misgivings to rest. That conversion is attested to by ancient chronicles, and the arguments recorded here purport to be an exact transcript of that earlier exchange.

Such a claim might test the limits of most people's credulity and lead them to deny that any such event as the conversion of a pagan king and his people to Judaism ever occurred. They might incline to treat this dialogue as a philosophical fable and liken it to another twelfth-century Andalusian masterpiece, Ibn Tufayl's *Hayy ibn Yaqzân*. But such a dismissal would be mistaken.

There is an abundance of documentary and archeological evidence that there once was a Turkic people called Khazars living in the much-contested territory between the Black Sea and the Caspian. And further, that there was indeed a mass conversion of a king and his people to Judaism in the eighth century.[2] Yet even if this work has a verifiable backstory, we cannot wholeheartedly credit Halevi's assertion that he has recorded that long-ago argumentation "just as it took place."[3] There is simply too much artfulness on display here, the effect of which is to remind us repeatedly of the author's shaping hand. Questions about the force, adequacy, and even sincerity of the positions staked out by the participants in this dialogue are opened rather than closed. Halevi as much as tips his hand when he follows that bold assertion with a quotation from Daniel 12:10: "And those who understand will comprehend."

A comparable aura of uncertainty surrounds one of the most thought-provoking modern interpretations of Halevi's prose masterpiece. Fortunately, in the case of Leo Strauss, the author had already articulated a rule of reading that not only applied to his reading of the thinkers he studied but may safely be applied by us in our reading of him. Rather than hold fast to your preconceived notions of an author's character, attend if you can to your author's manner of writing. But how? By attending especially to the habits he exhibits when reading the texts he studies. Thus, for example, we gain access to Maimonides's manner of writing by studying how he read the Bible.[4] Or we learn how to read Spinoza by identifying the rules he followed in reading and interpreting scripture.[5] One need hardly add that this counsel is not presented as a universal. But when engaged with the writings of individuals of high intellect, we are well advised to pay very close attention to their manner of writing, for which their manner of reading may provide a clue.

Not the least of Leo Strauss's writings on medieval thinkers that he composed and published while he was living in America is "The Law of Reason in the *Kuzari*."[6] It displays several features that set it apart. It is the only sustained treatment of Halevi's thought in Strauss's entire oeuvre. Rather than evoking a chorus of denials and disbelief such as greeted Strauss's later interpretations of Niccolò Machiavelli and John Locke, this essay was recognized immediately by a knowing judge as magisterial.[7] Notwithstanding its title, the range of issues stirred in the essay extends far beyond the "law of reason" to encompass what it means to be a believer and what it means to be a philosopher. Further, when compared to a later essay, "Notes on Maimonides' *Book of Knowledge*,"[8] this study of the *Kuzari* is strikingly assertive. Both essays exhibit Strauss's customary and complicated way of examining a text in its different facets. But the later essay is studded with hesitations, "seems," "hints," and other locutions that draw attention to things that demand reflection, all the while refraining from pronouncing the author's own conclusions. The *Kuzari* essay surely offers a plenitude of matter for pondering, but its challenges arise more from its declarative statements—and it is to one of the most arresting of these that we now turn.

> To return to safer ground, we start from the well-known fact that Halevi, in spite of his determined opposition to philosophy as such, underwent the influence of philosophy to no inconsiderable degree. What does influence mean? In the case of a superficial man, it means that he accepts this or that bit of the influencing teaching, that he cedes to the influencing force on the points where it appears to him, on the basis of his previous notions, to be strong, and that he resists it on the points where it appears to him, on the basis of his previous notions, to be weak. A confused or dogmatic mind, in other words, will not be induced by the influencing force to take a critical distance from his previous notions, to look at things, not from his habitual point of view, but from the point of view of the center, clearly grasped, of the influencing teaching, and hence he will be incapable of a serious, a radical

and relentless, discussion of that teaching. In the case of a man such as Halevi, however, the influence of philosophy on him consists in a conversion to philosophy: for some time, we prefer to think for a very short time, he was a philosopher. After that moment, a spiritual hell, he returned to the Jewish fold. But after what he had gone through, he could not help interpreting Judaism in a manner in which only a man who had once been a philosopher, could interpret it. For in that moment he had experienced the enormous temptation, the enormous danger of philosophy. The manner in which he defends Judaism against philosophy, testifies to this experience. For if he had presented a disputation between the Jewish scholar and the philosopher, i.e., a discussion of the crucial issue between truly competent people, he would have been compelled to state the case for philosophy with utmost clarity and vigor, and thus to present an extremely able and ruthless attack on revealed religion by the philosopher. There can be no doubt, to repeat, that the arguments of the philosopher could have been answered by the scholar; but it is hard to tell whether one or the other of the readers would not have been more impressed by the argument of the philosopher than by the rejoinder of the scholar. The Kuzari would thus have become an instrument of seduction, or at least of confusion.[9]

This paragraph (the thirteenth in an essay of well over twenty thousand words divided into forty-five paragraphs) is a call to attention. Its immediate effect is to stop the reader in his tracks. Even a mildly curious reader, secure in his point of view, would be prompted by Strauss's language to pause to consider more closely what is going on (and not going on) in Halevi's dialogue. No less is a reader being prompted to attend to Strauss's own plainspoken and radical challenge.

The clear presumption behind Strauss's paragraph is that saying "Jew" is to say nonphilosopher and saying "philosopher" is to say non-Jew. This assertion, expressed more than once in Strauss's writings, appears typically as the opinion of others, leaving the reader uncertain whether Strauss himself holds that disjunction to be true. Speaking of Maimonides's *Guide of the Perplexed*, he states that as a book written by a Jew for Jews, "its first premise is the old Jewish premise that being a Jew and being a philosopher are two incompatible things." Yet can one leave it at this, that "Jews of the philosophic competence of Halevi and Maimonides" could simultaneously straddle both worlds, giving assent as Jews while suspending assent as philosophers?[10] The issue is further complicated by Strauss's assertion in the paragraph quoted above that Halevi underwent a double conversion from believing Jew to philosopher and back again to the Jewish fold. However comforting that thought might be to other believing Jews, the return from heresy or atheism is not a simple retrieval of the erring individual's original position. In a sense the wayward one can never simply go home and be at home again. His exposure to the charms and seditious thoughts attending philosophy is not lightly to be forgotten, let alone overcome. Strauss cites Salo Baron[11] who in turn cites the *Kuzari*: "Who among us is endowed with a soul so steadfast that it is not misled by the opinions that pass through it, such as those of natural scientists, astrologers, believers in talismans, magicians, materialists, devotees of philosophy, and still others besides these?"[12] Let there be no mistaking: for all but a few rare individuals, a person's journey from ignorance to faith is a journey through the hell that is heresy or unbelief. It is no simple matter for the spiritual pilgrim to shake the earthly world's dust from his coattails.

It is safe to assume that it was not beyond the art of a poet of Halevi's caliber to have contrived a full-throated face-to-face confrontation between the two most challenging characters he has fashioned in the dialogue, but that was not to be. Strauss suggests that a sense of responsibility may have led Halevi to hold back from staging such an exchange lest that inadvertently seduce vulnerable minds into disbelief. Fair enough, but that does not preclude another possible explanation for the absence of what would have been the most arresting scene in the drama. It is not altogether far-fetched to imagine that a devotee of philosophy who is also quite visibly an adherent of a revealed religion might choose to prompt some unknown but apt young minds to dig deeper. In effect, by inviting such rare individuals to think through on their own the argument that the character of the philosopher in the *Kuzari* might have made, Halevi would have been offering potential philosophers their first opportunity to catch a glimpse of the forbidden fruit.[13]

But we don't have to dwell on hypotheticals. Strauss states categorically that "Halevi knew too well that a genuine philosopher can never become a genuine convert to Judaism or to any other revealed religion." "The religious indifference of the philosopher knows no limits."

Despite the philosopher's brief and early sole appearance, the memory of his distinctive attitude lingers on long after he left the stage for good. "In a sense, the philosopher is always present in the Kuzari."[14] This philosopher depicted in the dialogue is more than indifferent; he is the very embodiment of denial. His first word is a negation,[15] and his parting shot of advice to the Khazar king is to adopt the stance of a philosopher with respect to religion in general. Never mind the dreams that stirred the king in the first place to seek a way more pleasing to heavenly authority. Continue, if you so choose, practicing the religion of your forefathers—or not. Choose one of the religions currently on offer—or not. Invent a religion of your own—or not. Or follow the way of a true philosopher for whom the one thing needful is philosophizing itself, coming to know the true nature of things. In the latter case, it would not matter whether the king-philosopher were a true believer or an unbeliever. He could be either. His public face, however, would be that of a man who is able and ready to defend a faith he knows to be false but "cannot but call the true faith, not only with the sword, but with arguments, viz., dialectical arguments as well." Strauss puts the matter baldly: "The philosopher as such is a 'zindîq,' an 'apikores'"—in short, an atheist.[16] Yet one should not be shocked on hearing about "adherents of philosophy who belong to the adherents of the religions" (al-mutafalsifûn min ahl al-adyân).[17]

* * *

In trying to come to grips with the argument and the action of a work whose title promises a defense of the "despised religion," one is tempted to take its leading character, the Jewish rabbi, to be Halevi's mouthpiece. In view of the vigor, persistence, and adroitness with which this character mounts his defense, there would seem to be no daylight between him and his author. And yet Halevi almost immediately subverts that easy assumption with a disclaimer. Speaking in his own voice and at the very opening of the *Kuzari*, he declares that he was persuaded by some of the rabbi's arguments as being in accord with his own views.[18] In effect, Halevi gives readers notice that his innermost thoughts are not lying out in the open. Some readers may take that remark as a hint and a challenge to dig deeper and discover more.

There are as well other considerations that might make us hesitant to assert categorically that Halevi and the character he created are as one. It would be as rash, then, to identify Halevi and his character as it would be to take the thoughts expressed by Falstaff or Iago or Macbeth in their soliloquies to mirror those held by the poet who created them.

Nor, finally, is the rabbi's own position free of ambiguity. His large dominant theme is an attack on philosophy and philosophers for what in effect is their subversion of the common morality that helps shape a community and preserves that community over time. But he also sounds a discordant note in an obbligato of sorts when—almost gratuitously—he brings the philosopher's position to the fore again. This move had been prompted by the king's request at the opening of the fifth and final treatise that the rabbi give him a clear, accessible account of the roots and articles of their shared faith following the method of the dialectical theologians (al-mutakallimûn). Although the king had converted to Judaism at the opening of the second treatise and had been intensively tutored by his Jewish interlocutor through all the intervening pages, he evidently still feels his faith needs shoring up. Ultimately the rabbi obliges the king, but not before delivering a lengthy restatement of the philosophic position.[19] His presentation elicits an interjection by the new convert revealing the shakiness of his faith (V 13), and that in turn compels the rabbi to undertake yet another refutation.[20] Only after reiterating earlier arguments about the limits of human understanding and the solid basis provided by a reliance on tradition does the rabbi turn to addressing what the masters of kalâm have to say. But even that lengthy account is preceded by a brief introduction in which the rabbi moves from arguing that the study of kalâm is useless to asserting that it may be downright harmful.[21] You either have what it takes to draw close to God, in which case a mere hint from another naturally gifted person will ignite the divine spark in you—or you don't, and then you will fall back on kalâm reasoning with doubtful results.

The rabbi's protean arguments leave us (readers who dare not presume we are blessed with that divine spark) in something of a quandary. When the rabbi or Halevi argues that the method of the dialectical theologians is good for silencing your opponents but for little else, what are we then to think of this work as a whole? The *Kuzari* is manifestly a work of kalâm, refuting and silencing those who disparage and despise Judaism. Yet Halevi has strewn through this dialogue enough irregularities, contradictions, reversals, and hints for us to suspect—more than suspect—that he wants at least some choice readers to attempt to unearth and reconstruct his innermost thoughts.

* * *

With a few brief strokes at the beginning of the second treatise, Halevi portrays how the Khazar king converted to the despised religion and then went on to create a new Israel with its own replica of the Tabernacle and with a vastly expanded army that enlarged the nation's borders and wealth. Since the king had earlier indicated that he adheres to the principle—cuius regio, eius religio—it follows as a matter of course that he and his inner circle "prevailed over the rest of the Khazars and converted them to the religion of the Jews as well."[22] Halevi's book is clearly an account of conversions—of the king, of his vizier, of his inner circle, and ultimately of the entire Khazar people. It is worthy of note that this quasi-historical account has been composed by an author who has himself experienced more than one conversion. Does that fact cast a different light on how the *Kuzari* should be viewed?

One cannot quite say of the *Kuzari* what Shlomo Pines memorably said of Maimonides's *Guide*—that it "belongs to a very peculiar literary genre, of which it is the unique specimen."[23] Yet there are not many works whose accounts of others' real or legendary conversions might be suspected of having been refracted through their author's own conversion experience. A comparison with an analogous modern example may be suggestive. Edward Gibbon's spiritual journey was checkered and varied. He fled from an inherited Anglicanism to an outlawed Catholicism, only to be forcibly "reprogrammed" back to Protestantism and coming to rest at last in what can charitably be called a tepid Anglicanism. When he turned to writing a memoir of his own life, the great historian faltered, despite numerous attempts, and failed to settle on a clear and coherent account of his religious journey. But when it came to recounting the conversions of early Christians and of the emperor Constantine the Great, the self-styled "philosophical historian" wrote with a bold, cool, and confident irony. For a bookman such as Gibbon, words are deeds. In this respect, at least, his inner life remains obscure and ambiguous, possibly by design, but endlessly controversial.[24]

Halevi presents challenges of a different kind. If he exhibits distance from his subjects, it is covert rather than overt, philosophical rather than ironic. Although he devoted much of his last decade to composing this dialogue, he never ceased being the Hebrew poet of his generation. He sang with great beauty and with a passion that came from the heart and spoke to the hearts of others. For those who recited his poetry, Halevi's yearnings for the God of his fathers, his longings for the Land of Zion (themes that infused his poems both secular and devotional), made him not only a celebrity, but beloved. It is undeniable that Halevi was more than the greatest poet of his generation. He was the greatest Hebrew poet of the millennia stretching from the biblical psalmist David to the emergence in the early twentieth century of Chaim Nachman Bialik and Saul Tchernichovski. Unlike Gibbon, Halevi did not limit his deeds to words. Rather, like the rabbi portrayed at the conclusion of his dialogue, he acted on what he had been singing, leaving family, friends, and homeland, and embarking on the hazardous journey to the Jews' Promised Land.

If we harken back to our earlier uncertainty about the character of Halevi's return to the Jewish fold after dwelling in a "spiritual hell," we have this further complication to ponder. When Strauss wrote "for some time, we prefer to think for a very short time, he was a philosopher,"[25] we readers of Strauss's words have to ask, who is or are that "we"? It is not a *pluralis majestatis*, nor is it readers in general, for why should they care how long Halevi dwelt in what believing Jews regarded as a spiritual hell? When Strauss asserts that it is beyond doubt that the rabbi could have answered the philosopher's arguments, he is not asserting more than that those arguments that might have silenced the philosopher and satisfied the king would not, perhaps, have been equally persuasive to every reader. The speech we never get to hear from the philosopher's lips mirrors the dramatist's silencing of himself. Halevi surely knew that a rejoinder that reduces your opponent to silence hardly constitutes a refutation.

We are left, then, with Yehuda Halevi, an individual of extraordinary complexity: a sometime philosopher who carries within him a persistent awareness of the power of philosophy's ruthless critique of revealed religion; a thinker who may indeed be one of those students of philosophy who chose to embed himself among the adherents of the religion; and a poet who cried out from his heart in his Ode to Zion: " ... when I dream / Of the return of thy captivity, I am a harp for thy songs."[26]

Notes

1. Leo Strauss, "Persecution and the Art of Writing," *Social Research* 8, no. 4 (1941): 488–504. Reprinted in Leo Strauss, *Persecution and the Art of Writing* (Glencoe, IL: Free Press, 1952), 35. Citations to this essay are to the pagination of the reprint edition.

2. Haim Beinart, *Atlas of Medieval Jewish History* (New York: Simon & Schuster, 1992), 24–25; Eric Maroney, *The Other Zion: The Lost Histories of Jewish Nations* (Latham, MD: Rowman & Littlefield, 2010), 53–77, 175–78.

3. Yehuda Halevi, *Kitâb al-radd wa-'l-dalîl fî 'l-dîn al-dhalîl. (The Book of Refutation and Proof on the Despised Faith [The Book of the Khazars] Known as the Kuzari)*, ed. David H. Baneth and prepared for publication by Haggai Ben-

Shammai (Jerusalem: Magnes Press, Hebrew University, and Israel Academy of Sciences and Humanities, 1977), I 1/3: 12–15. Citation is first to the book and traditional section numbers used in this Judaeo-Arabic text and in all other editions and translations. That is followed by the page and line numbers of this critical edition.

4. Leo Strauss, "The Literary Character of *The Guide of the Perplexed*," in *Essays on Maimonides: An Octocentennial Volume*, ed. Salo W. Baron (New York: Columbia University Press, 1941), 37–91. Reprinted in Strauss, *Persecution*, 60–61. Citations to this essay are to the pagination of the reprint edition.

5. Leo Strauss, "How to Study Spinoza's *Theologico-Political Treatise*," *Proceedings of the American Academy for Jewish Research* 17 (1948): 69–131. Reprinted in Strauss, *Persecution*, 144. Citations to this essay are to the pagination of the reprint edition.

6. Leo Strauss, "The Law of Reason in the *Kuzari*," *Proceedings of the American Academy for Jewish Research* 13 (1943): 47–96. Reprinted in Strauss, *Persecution*, 95–141. Citations to this essay are to the pagination of the reprint edition.

7. Shalom Spiegel to Strauss, 11 September 1942, Leo Strauss Papers, Box 3, folder 12, Special Collections, Regenstein Library, University of Chicago.

8. Leo Strauss, "Notes on Maimonides' *Book of Knowledge*," in *Studies in Mysticism and Religion Presented to Gershom G. Scholem* (Jerusalem: Magnes Press, Hebrew University, 1967), 269–83. Reprinted in Leo Strauss, *Studies in Platonic Political Philosophy* (Chicago: University of Chicago Press, 1983), 192–204.

9. Strauss, "Law of Reason," 108–9.

10. Leo Strauss, "Introduction," in Strauss, *Persecution*, 19. Leo Strauss, "How to Begin to Study *The Guide of the Perplexed*," in Moses Maimonides, *The Guide of the Perplexed*, trans. Shlomo Pines (Chicago: University of Chicago Press, 1963), xi–lvi. Reprinted in Leo Strauss, *Liberalism Ancient and Modern* (New York: Basic Books, 1968), 142. Citations to this essay are to the pagination of the reprint edition. Leo Strauss, "Farabi's 'Plato,'" in *Louis Ginzberg Jubilee Volume* (New York: American Academy for Jewish Research, 1945), 374–75.

11. Salo W. Baron, "Yehudah Halevi: An Answer to an Historic Challenge," *Jewish Social Studies* 3 (1941): 243–72, at 259n3.

12. Halevi, *Kuzari*, V 2/191:11–14.

13. Strauss, "Persecution," 24–25.

14. Strauss, "Law of Reason," 104–5, 115, 108n36.

15. Halevi, *Kuzari*, I 2/3:18

16. Strauss, "Law of Reason," 115, 107n34.

17. Strauss, "Law of Reason," 105n29, 115n60; Halevi, *Kuzari*, IV 3/158:26.

18. Strauss, "Law of Reason," 101n17.

19. Halevi, *Kuzari*, V 2–12/191:11–208:19.

20. Halevi, *Kuzari*, V 14/208.22–213:10.

21. Halevi, *Kuzari*, V 18–20/214:7–225:7; V 16/213:13–3.

22. Halevi, *Kuzari*, I 80/21:18; II 1/42:10.

23. Shlomo Pines, "Translator's Introduction: The Philosophic Sources of *The Guide of the Perplexed*," in Maimonides, *Guide*, lxxix.

24. Hugh Liebert, *Gibbon's Christianity* (University Park: Penn State University Press, 2022).

25. Strauss, "Law of Reason," 109.

26. *Selected Poems of Jehudah Halevi*, ed. Heinrich Brody, trans. Nina Salaman (Philadelphia: Jewish Publication Society of America, 1924), 3.

ALEXANDER ORWIN

Interpretative Essay

PROCLAIMING DANGEROUS TEACHINGS TO
THE WORLD: WHY WOULD STRAUSS REVEAL
THE RELIGIOUS HETERODOXY OF THE FALĀSIFA?

THE INTRODUCTION TO A FRAGMENT OF a lecture given by Strauss on Yehuda Halevi has the merit of focusing our attention on a key question that drives Strauss's interpretation of the Muslim *falāsifa*, namely, what is their attitude toward religion? This question derives its force from a revolution in scholarship that occurred in the two generations before Strauss. From medieval times until the nineteenth century, Averroes was thought to be hostile to religion, a view echoed in Muslim, Christian, and Jewish sources alike, but since the time of Ernest Renan, he had come to be accepted as a more or less sincere believer.[1]

In seeking to account for this difference, Strauss develops a theory that would receive due elaboration in subsequent writings: it arises from a change in our manner of reading, owing to which contemporary scholars take the more orthodox statements of the *falāsifa* seriously, while older interpreters did not. The latter "read between the lines of the works of the *falāsifa*," a procedure that seems vindicated by the *falāsifa*'s own preoccupation with keeping "the philosophic teaching a secret."[2] For no prudent philosopher who held the heretical point of view that older critics ascribed to his class would declare it in broad daylight in the overwhelmingly pious societies of medieval times. Strauss fears that this secrecy might make the actual teaching of the *falāsifa* uniquely difficult to fathom. He wonders whether "the orthodox opponents of the philosophic teaching" might have divulged that teaching and its implications more openly than its advocates did, in order to "show how dangerous it is." He resolves to test this proposition, by reflecting on "the philosophers as presented by Halevi," one of their most intelligent critics.[3]

While the introduction to this lecture on Halevi seems tolerably well preserved, the rest consists only of fragments. This makes it impossible to discern from them how Strauss understood Halevi's presentation of philosophy at the time of the lecture. Thankfully, we still possess a writing that grew out of it, namely the chapter of *PAW* titled "The Law of Reason in the *Kuzari*." In this work, Strauss does not present Halevi as somebody who revealed the teaching of the *falāsifa* to all and sundry. While Halevi is more than able to "state the case for philosophy with clarity and vigor," he offers, at least on the surface, only "a summary and very conventional sketch of the philosophic teaching." Indeed, if the philosophical teaching is as dangerous as the orthodox believe it to be, then the most thoughtful and responsible among them would hesitate to declare it from the rooftops, even with the purpose of ultimately consigning it to the trash heap. As Strauss puts it, "In Halevi's age, the right, if not the duty, to suppress teachings, and books, which are detrimental to faith, was generally recognized."[4] In seeking to refute the philosophers, Halevi is thus forced to adopt some of their methods. The most that can be said, in reference to the promise of Strauss's earlier lecture, is that Halevi does succeed in bringing out the "deepest reason why philosophy is so enormously dangerous." Philosophy destroys "genuine morality," since morality needs to be bolstered by the divine revelation at which the philosophers scoff. Yet even this matter must be spoken of with "remarkable restraint," for two distinct reasons: one should tempt neither the ignorant or immoral with the implications of philosophy, nor philosophy's zealous religious enemies with any intellectual weapons that they are likely to abuse. The moral fanatic, no less than the immoral opportunist, poses a menace to society, against which a wise author, be he philosophic or antiphilosophic, must guard.[5]

We conclude that in Strauss's view neither the *falāsifa* nor their enemies revealed the philosophic teaching about religion with any candor in medieval times. This inevitably raises the question of Strauss's own candor. Did he disseminate the *falāsifa*'s teaching about religion to a large and indiscriminate number of readers? In examining this question, we will rely primarily on his writings on Alfarabi. This choice is not entirely arbitrary. Whatever Strauss's final judgment on Maimonides might have been, he portrays him in the present passage less as a philosopher and more as a critic of philosophy.[6] As for Averroes, Strauss mentions him alone among the *falāsifa* by name, as a philosopher on whom scholarly views have recently shifted. This reference is appropriate, since there had been scholarly views on Averroes over the past several centuries; during that same period, Alfarabi remained almost unknown in Europe. It therefore fell to Strauss himself to make extraordinary efforts, philological and philosophical, to resuscitate Alfarabi. The result was a couple of early articles devoted to him, followed by three more mature works, on which a modest amount of scholarship has already been written.[7] References to Averroes published by Strauss during his own lifetime are comparatively scattered and brief. Some rough notes on Averroes's *Commentary on Plato's 'Republic'*, whose debt to earlier work on Alfarabi is acknowledged by Strauss himself, have only been edited this year: they will be occasionally cited to support our argument.[8]

The Cognitive and Practical Value of Religion in "Farabi's Plato"

The question of Alfarabi's attitude toward religion preoccupied Strauss from the very beginning of his attempts to study him. His efforts to determine the contents of many yet-to-be-discovered works by Alfarabi passed through extant medieval Hebrew summaries and translations by Shem-Tov ibn Falaquera. In comparing already extant works by Alfarabi with summaries by Falaquera, Strauss was already able to determine that their respective approach to religion diverged greatly. For example, Falaquera's use of biblical citations has no parallel in Alfarabi, who is known for never citing the Quran. Falaquera omits passages in Alfarabi that subordinate religious sciences to political science, or lend unorthodox meaning to the term *imam*.[9] The later discovery of the text of Alfarabi's *Philosophy of Plato* revealed more of the same: Falaquera had added a reference to this life and the other life, where none existed in the original, and removed the passages that deny the value of religion in philosophic investigation.[10] Rather than rebuke Falaquera for his flagrant distortions of the original, Strauss hints that he is motivated by the considerations discussed in the previous section: the author of a "decidedly Jewish book" who "wrote for a somewhat different public" would have wanted to expose his readers to certain elements of Alfarabi's teaching but not to others.[11]

Strauss justifies those medieval authors who conceal the unorthodox teaching of the *falāsifa* from the public, but he does not always follow them. The treatment of religion in his article "Farābī's Plato" is notoriously outspoken.[12] Strauss does not hesitate to reveal what Falaquera had tried to conceal: Alfarabi ranks religious investigations as "the lowest step of the ladder of cognitive pursuits ... inferior even to grammar and to poetry." They do not come close to providing the knowledge of the beings that Plato seeks.[13] Alfarabi nonetheless left some suspense by considering the value of religion before revealing the superiority of philosophy.[14] Strauss does no such thing. His interpretation of Alfarabi considers religion only after Alfarabi has formulated his philosophic teaching on the supremacy of contemplation: "Theoretical philosophy by itself, and nothing else, produces true happiness in this life, i.e. the only happiness that is possible." It follows that the vast majority of humans, being unphilosophic, are "eternally barred, by the nature of things, from happiness."[15]

Alfarabi nevertheless made some concessions to the dominant religion within his community. Unlike Aristotle, he was compelled "to reconcile [this doctrine] with the belief in the immortality of the soul or with the requirements of faith."[16] Alfarabi performs this task admirably in works such as the *Virtuous City*, *Political Regime*, and *Virtuous Religious Community*, all of which are written in his own name, but he abandons it in his lost *Commentary on the Nicomachean Ethics*: according to Ibn Tufayl, Alfarabi dismisses in that commentary stories of life after death as "old wives tales," while according to Averroes, he denies immortality through any abstract intelligences.[17] The "specific immunity of the commentator," as Strauss aptly describes it, allows Alfarabi to take the same blunt approach in the *Philosophy of Plato*.[18] This practice often entails a peculiar distortion of the original. For while Plato describes life after death in several dialogues cited by Alfarabi, such as the *Gorgias*, *Phaedo*, and *Republic*, Alfarabi removes all mention of it, ascribing a moral but this-worldly meaning to Plato's stories about human transformations into animals after death. By giving "an extremely unliteral interpretation of a most tolerable teaching," Alfarabi insinuates that Plato's teachings about life after death are entirely exoteric. Strauss concludes that the same must apply to Alfarabi's teachings: when there is a contradiction between the dismissal of life after death characteristic of the *Philosophy of Plato* and more or less orthodox teachings about it found in other works, preference must be given to the former: "Compared with the *Plato*, all these other writings are exoteric."[19]

One might object that Strauss never offers a sufficiently detailed interpretation of these other writings to corroborate so sweeping a claim. Strauss anticipates this objection with a philological excuse: "we lack a satisfactory edition" of the *Political Regime*, the work so highly praised by Maimonides.[20] Yet Strauss cites the unsatisfactory edition on numerous occasions throughout his career, not to mention in this very article.[21] Still more problematic is the fact that such considerations did not deter Strauss from interpreting the account of political science in Maimonides's *Logic* in extraordinary detail on the basis of Hebrew translations.[22] Besides, a critical edition was produced, with Strauss's encouragement, by his student Fauzi Najjar in 1964.[23] Strauss lived for several more productive years, without ever returning to Alfarabi. Those who knew Strauss have suggested through oral communication that by this time Strauss's attention had shifted to other things, such as Plato and Xenophon. He also might have trusted Muhsin Mahdi and Najjar, who had superior knowledge of Arabic, to carry the study of the *falāsifa* forward. Even if we grant the significance of these considerations, it still seems that uncovering the secrets of the more "exoteric" works of Alfarabi was never as pressing a priority for Strauss as declaring Alfarabi's most intransigent Platonic teachings.[24]

Having revealed Alfarabi at his most subversive, Strauss nonetheless denies that he disrespected religion. Strauss cites twice a passage in the work directly preceding the *Philosophy of Plato* in which Alfarabi "considers conformity to the laws and beliefs of the religious community in which one is brought up, a necessary qualification for the future philosopher," and attributes this view to Plato.[25] The use of the adjective "future" implies that the philosopher may indeed abandon these beliefs once he is fully mature: Strauss would later speak publicly about his own upbringing in a strictly Orthodox home, and gradual but decisive drift away from it.[26] The context is the philosopher's need to present his thoughts in a manner acceptable to the people, challenging prevailing opinions without immediately shocking or overturning them. In his restatement of this chapter, Strauss would call this "the political aspect of philosophy" and "political philosophy," pursued by combining the way of the philosopher Socrates with that of the rhetorician Thrasymachus and defining "the general character of the activity of the *falāsifa*" as such.[27] A philosopher cannot succeed in this crucial part of philosophy unless he is thoroughly cognizant of conventional religious opinions, and able to appear respectful of them. One might expect Alfarabi to show such respect, whose necessity is merely stated in the *Philosophy of Plato*, in his second Platonic work, namely the *Summary of Plato's "Laws."*[28] We therefore turn to Strauss's interpretation of this work, written shortly after it came out in 1952.

Alfarabi's Platonic *Kalām*

Strauss's later work on Alfarabi is quick to define itself in relation to the former. Strauss shows how thoroughly the terminology of Alfarabi's *Summary of Plato's "Laws"* distinguishes it from his other Platonic work. While the *Philosophy of Plato* is unapologetically a work of philosophy, the *Summary* avoids the very term along with words associated with it, including "essence," "beings" and "multitude." In contrast, it employs roots related to *kalām* twenty-six times, along with terms for God and divine law, none of which occur in the *Philosophy of Plato*. Strauss concludes: "the *Philosophy of Plato* presents Plato's philosophy, whereas the *Summary* presents his art of *kalām*."[29]

So heavy a focus on *kalām* would seem to be propitious for religion. In a passage from the *Enumeration of the Sciences* that Strauss alludes to in the paragraph quoted above and often cites elsewhere, Alfarabi treats *kalām* as a branch of political science devoted to the defense of various religions.[30] In presenting the *Summary* as a work of *kalām*, Strauss leads us to expect something similar. But does *kalām* have this character and purpose in the *Summary*? Plato's version of the art may not be identical to Alfarabi's. The word for religion (*milla*) does not occur in the *Summary*, despite numerous references to related topics, such as God, gods, and law, human and divine.[31] What, then, is Alfarabi's intention with regard to religion? Strauss suggests that Alfarabi "may have rewritten the *Laws*, as it were, with a view to the situation created by the rise of Islam or of revealed religion generally." The following paragraph, however, lists three possible approaches that a medieval Muslim reader of Plato could choose with regard to its relationship to his own religion, without stating which of them was chosen by Alfarabi.[32] Strauss will later justify his failure to determine Alfarabi's choice by invoking our relative ignorance of "the religious situation in Fārābī's age," as something that precludes any further "clarification of Farābī's own position."[33] Due to the paucity of historical sources, this ignorance is unlikely to be lifted any time soon. Given how strongly Strauss emphasizes the reticence of both Alfarabi and Plato, we should hardly be surprised to find him occasionally reticent as well.[34]

Along with philosophy and religion, the term "political science" does not occur in the *Summary*, an omission seconded in Strauss's interpretation, and amplified by its placement directly before a chapter on Maimonides's treatment of that very subject.[35] Since Alfarabi's other extensive treatment of *kalām* presents it as part of political science, this omission should be duly noted. In the absence of any explicit supervision from philosophy, political science, or even religion, what direction would *kalām* assume? Strauss's basic answer to this question is a simple one: the *Summary* and the *kalām* that is its central subject focuses its reflection on the laws as such. Its opening paragraph lays the groundwork for examining the laws, their causes, and their goodness.[36] Neither philosophy nor science, but laws as legislated in actual societies and experienced by the humans who live under them, form the basis of this inquiry.

One cannot defend the law intelligently without understanding it thoroughly. It follows, as Strauss indicates in reference to the opening of the *Summary* proper, that the very superiority of the law cannot be vindicated without a proper examination of it. This thought, being already somewhat subversive, is only "intimated" by Plato.[37] It forces us to consider whether the purpose of this peculiar *kalām* is truly the defense of the laws. There are numerous passages in the *Summary* that seem to serve this purpose. It suffices here to point out chapter 7, which offers a brilliant intellectual defense of Islamic doctrines rather than any apparent summary of Plato.[38] These aspects of the work have been ably interpreted by Joshua Parens, and surely deserve further study.[39] They are not, however, the focal point of Strauss's study, which is geared instead toward Alfarabi's critique of the law. Let us take a closer look.

Questioning the Law

For most medieval readers, the law would be closely connected to religion. The opening story of the *Summary*, to which Strauss draws our attention, presents a conflict between a pious ascetic and the law, represented by the command of the unjust ruler. The ascetic is obliged to lie in deed, pretending to violate the Muslim law against consuming alcohol in the process, in order to outwit the ruler's henchmen and escape. Even a pious person might, on certain occasions, need to engage in deception in order to evade the law and protect himself.[40] No simple equation of piety, honesty, and obedience to the law is possible. This story, as far as we know invented by Alfarabi himself, seems designed to loosen any unquestioning attachment to law, thus preparing the reader for the still more subversive arguments that follow.

Strauss devotes considerable attention to the first chapter: indeed, this is the only one of "the threads of the argument" that he claims to have "succeeded in following."[41] In following this argument, he steers his interpretation in a very pronounced direction. However lofty the origin of the laws may be, they cannot be defended without reference to two extraneous standards, namely the "right reason" with which their stipulations must agree and "the virtuous city" that they are intended to form. Since all laws claim divine origin along with guidance toward the "countenance of God" and "reward in the other life," but not all meet these exalted human standards, Alfarabi and Plato indicate the necessity of distinguishing between "the true legislator" and "impostors."[42] But is the true legislator concerned with "the countenance of God" at all? He is, to be sure, concerned with "divine virtue" as well as "human virtue," but as Strauss has already shown, with due reference to both the *Summary* and *Philosophy of Plato*, the adjective "divine" as employed by Alfarabi often means nothing more than "excellent" in human terms.[43] The legislator must instill human virtue, including science, but define it as divine virtue when it happens to be in obedience to the law. Strauss is quick to conclude: "It would appear that one can acquire human virtue without obeying the law." This argument foreshadows his final statement about the first chapter: "It would seem that reasonable individuals do not need guidance by the legislator." Strauss continues: "we are thus already somewhat prepared for the following remark which occurs unexpectedly in the center of the last chapter and still strikes us as unbelievable," namely, that as Plato explained, the best people can become happy without the assistance of the laws. Alfarabi also indicates, near the end of the same chapter, that neither full obedience to the laws alone nor the punishments that they inflict in this world and the next are sufficient to make defective people happy.[44]

We recall here that according to Strauss, Alfarabi's and Plato's habitual caution allows them to "say explicitly and unambiguously what [they] thought about the highest themes" because few readers will notice or believe these statements.[45] Faithful to the audacity of his predecessors, Strauss concludes his analysis of the *Summary* by calling our attention to just such a statement. It applies to both Alfarabi's time and Plato's, and even Strauss's own: Alfarabi "knew equally well that in other respects which are no less important there was no difference between Greek laws and Islamic laws."[46] The *nomoi* of the polis, *sharīʿa* of the Muslims, and criminal code of the modern Leviathan all share this much in common: they are unnecessary for the happiness of the best people, and necessary for inferior people, but effective with them only to varying degrees.

Where, we might ask, does this leave religion and the *kalām* that is supposed to be the subject of the *Summary*? As much as we might be inclined to distinguish between law and religion, Strauss comes close to equating them: "to be religious means to be virtuous according to the prescriptions of the law." With regard to how this "divine virtue" brings its adherents closer to God than mere human virtue, "Fārābī does not answer this question." And it certainly appears that the legislation of both Zeus and Apollo is defective, the result of victory in war rather than supreme legislative virtue.[47] Strauss reaches a similar conclusion in his reading of Averroes: "There is no significant excess of Islam over merely human laws."[48] If the purpose of Alfarabi's *Summary* is in fact *kalām*, for Islam or even for religion in general, then Strauss appears to have undermined it. It is worth noting that his interpretation of the first chapter is silent about *kalām*. A passage in which Alfarabi uses the term and its cognates four times is summarized by Strauss as follows, with direct citations to the original: "Yet in spite of those doubts of the laws which may have suggested themselves to us, or may still suggest themselves to us (9.13–20), the law in itself is noble and virtuous, and superior to everything which is said for or against it (9.21–22)."[49] The summary captures the spirit of Alfarabi's original, which presents *kalām* as argumentative and untrustworthy, from the point of view of both intellect and the law. It invites another, more truly rational layer of analysis of law, rooted in "training in logic ... and the handling of political affairs." This analysis, however, leads quickly to the conclusion about "the problematic character of law" that we have stated.[50] As carefully as Strauss, following Alfarabi, has avoided the terms "philosophy" and "political science," their presence here is clearly felt.[51] It is no accident that the rest of Strauss's argument is devoted to showing the essential agreement between the *Summary* and the *Philosophy of Plato* on law and questions related to it, his earlier emphasis on their divergence notwithstanding.[52] This conclusion carries over into the next chapter, devoted to Maimonides's political science, in which the only reference to Alfarabi in the body of the text reads as follows: "According to Fārābī, whom Maimonides regarded as the philosophic authority second only to Aristotle, the unchangeable divine law (*sharīʿa*) is only a substitute for the government of a perfect ruler who governs without written laws and who changes his ordinances in accordance with the change of times as he sees fit."[53] But since "the philosophers, as distinguished from the legislators, cannot expect to be deified by the citizens," the superiority of living wisdom to law can never become the official doctrine of any human society.⁵⁴ Philosophy, the exemplar of living wisdom, would therefore seem obligated to offer some defense, however tentative, of prevailing religious law.

Does Strauss Ignore His Own Warnings?

Our analysis, though hardly exhaustive, should suffice to illustrate the extent to which Strauss was willing to reveal the *falāsifa*'s critique of religion, contrary to their own practice or that of their medieval critics as sketched in his fragment on Halevi. Doesn't Strauss thereby risk transgressing the practice of both the *falāsifa* and their opponents, of not disclosing the most subversive teachings of philosophy?

The starting point of any defense of Strauss on this point has to be his historical milieu. The legal and ritual piety that both ennobled and constrained medieval Islamic and Jewish society had mostly vanished, so protecting the faith that informed these "other ages" and "other climates" was no longer a meaningful endeavor.⁵⁵ Amid the carnage and intellectual decay of mid-twentieth-century Europe, other imperatives had replaced it. Strauss notes in the Halevi fragment how quickly scholarly approaches to the *falāsifa* had shifted, or, as we can now see, declined. Strauss responds directly to this predicament in the introduction to *Persecution* that repurposes 'Fārābī's Plato.' Its first and last paragraphs conclude with the word "philosophy."⁵⁶ The elaboration of a "sociology of philosophy" aimed at recovering the true relationship between philosophy and society emerges as the main purpose of Strauss's work on Alfarabi's Plato. This could not be accomplished without refuting the contemporary prejudice in favor of the *falāsifa*'s religiosity, a manifestation of the general sociological prejudice that reduces "the intellectuals of the Sages" to mere exponents of the views of their class and society. In blowing up the myth of the piety of the *falāsifa*, Strauss follows the *falāsifa* in defining and defending the interests of the class of philosophers as such.⁵⁷

Strauss approaches Alfarabi in a manner somewhat comparable to how Alfarabi approaches Plato. In the "interests of philosophy and nothing else," he seeks to restore genuine philosophy, whose meaning "had been blurred and destroyed."⁵⁸ To accomplish this goal, Alfarabi needed to free Plato not only from any whiff of neo-Platonism, but even from any whiff of religious belief. Not wishing to take full responsibility for such radical positions himself, he stated them through the mouth of Plato.⁵⁹

Strauss also seeks to restore the true meaning of philosophy, and in particular to rescue the *falāsifa* from contemporary misunderstandings of them. He pursues these aims through unveiling the more radical aspects of Alfarabi's two presentations of Plato, to which he gives precedence over Alfarabi's more numerous "exoteric" writings. This does not, however, answer the question of Strauss's own attitude toward religion, since one could conceivably ascribe these views to Alfarabi, just as Alfarabi often ascribed his to Plato.

As important and inevitable as this question is, we cannot treat it adequately here. We therefore conclude by noting the obvious: the same thinker who developed such an antireligious interpretation of the greatest medieval philosophic authority for Maimonides was able to establish himself as a respected figure in the world of Jewish thought. While at the University of Chicago, Strauss developed a "close, collegial friendship with Rabbi Maurice B. Pekarsky, Chicago Hillel's founding director," under whose auspices he gave a series of lectures at Hillel House. In the lecture following Pekarsky's death, meant to "pay homage" to his "simple, old-fashioned, chaste, Jewish piety," Strauss discusses the role of religion in public life, from antiquity down to the present, raising the possibility of an atheistic society but treating it with some skepticism.[60] More theoretical lectures about reason and revelation, presented for the first time by Laurenz Denker and his coauthors in the article cited above, grew into familiar texts such as "Jerusalem and Athens" and "Progress and Return." These works do not teach a philosophic atheism or antinomianism anywhere near as explicit as that ascribed by Strauss to Alfarabi; they tend to argue that in the reason-revelation debate, neither side has refuted the other. Yet in the Hillel lecture Strauss adduces, almost in passing, one powerful argument for reason: "Man can live as a philosopher—as far as we know, in this life—man can live as a philosopher *happily*."[61] This unmistakable allusion to views expressed most forcefully in his work on Alfarabi demonstrates that Strauss never forgot their significance.

Notes

1. Strauss, "The 'Philosopher' in the Kuzari," 1–2 (paper to be read at the Annual Meeting of the American Academy for Jewish Research), December 28, 1941. [henceforth *PK*]. See also Leo Strauss, *Persecution and the Art of Writing* (Chicago: University of Chicago Press, 1952), 27 [henceforth *PAW*].

2. Strauss, *PK*, 2–3. Strauss is fond of quoting a passage from Ibn Tufayl that ascribes veils and contradictions to the writings of Alfarabi, Avicen-

na, al-Ghazali, and Ibn Bajja alike: see *PAW*, 14, 111. Strauss also cites Aquinas and Dante as examples of the older view. Despite the help of experts, I have been unable to locate any passages in either author that openly call Averroes a nonbeliever: this is entirely consistent with Strauss's observation that no author in medieval times exposed the teaching of the *falāsifa* in full.

3. Strauss, *PK*, 3

4. Strauss, *PAW*, 109-11. See also 17: "Some opponents of the *falāsifa* seem to have thought it necessary to help the *falāsifa* in concealing their teaching, because they feared the harm which its publication would cause to those of their fellow-believers whose faith was weak."

5. Strauss, *PAW*, 140-41. In the present volume, Ralph Lerner provides a more in depth discussion of these points (79-89 above).

6. Strauss, *PK*, 2, 3.

7. Leo Strauss, "Ein vermißte Schrift Fārābī's (1936)," in *Gesammelten Schriften: Band 2: Philosophie und Gesetz*, ed. Weibke and Heinrich Meier (J.B. Metzler'sche Verlagsbuchhandlung & Carl Ernst Poeschel GmbH, 2013), 96-106 [henceforth EVSF]. In English: Leo Strauss, "A Lost Writing of Fārābī's," trans. Gabriel Bartlett and Martin Yaffe, in *Reorientation: Leo Strauss in the 1930s*, ed. Martin Yaffe and Richard Ruderman (New York: Palgrave Macmillan, 2013), 255-65; "Quelques remarques sur la science politique de Maimonide et de Farābī (1936)," in *Gesammelten Schriften: Band 2: Philosophie und Gesetz*, 126-58 [henceforth QSPM]. "Fārābī's Plato," in *Louis Ginzburg Jubilee Volume* (New York: American Academy for Jewish Research, 1945), 357-93 [henceforth FP]. Strauss makes "free use" of this article in the preface and introduction to *PAW*, 5-21. "How Fārābī Read Plato's Laws," in *What Is Political Philosophy and Other Studies* (Chicago: University of Chicago Press, 1959), 134-54 [henceforth WPP]. Useful accounts of Strauss's work on Alfarabi may be found in Steven Lenzner, "Strauss's Fārābī: Scholarly Prejudice, and Philosophic Politics," in *Twentieth Century Literary Criticism*, vol. 141, 334-45; Daniel Tanguay, *Leo Strauss: Une Biographie Intellectuelle* (Paris: Éditions Grasset & Farquelle, 2003), and Steven Harvey, "Leo Strauss's Developing Interest in Alfarabi," in *The Pilgrimage of Philosophy: A Festschrift for Charles E. Butterworth*, ed. Rene M. Paddags, Waseem El-Rayes, and Gregory A. McBrayer (South Bend, IN: St. Augustine's Press, 2019), 60-83. Of these scholars, Lenzer engages in the most careful and suspicious reading of Strauss, Tanguay provides a spirited account of the development of Strauss's ideas, while Harvey looks more deeply into the scholarly research behind them. We are dedicated, by the way, to allaying Harvey's fear that Strauss's approach to Alfarabi is "dying a slow and agonizing death" among scholars (Harvey, 60, 82-83). Immediate evidence against such worries is provided by a newly released book by Rasoul Namazi, *Leo Strauss and Islamic Political Thought* (Cambridge: Cambridge University Press, 2022), by far the most comprehensive work to date on Strauss and the *falāsifa*.

8. "Leo Strauss's Notes on Averroes's Commentary on Plato's 'Republic,'" in Namazi, *Strauss and Islamic Political Thought*, 205-15, esp. 206 [henceforth *NACP*]. Namazi offers a thorough and thought-provoking interpretation of these notes on 49-83.

9. Strauss, *EVSF*, 169-70, 175 [Eng. 258, 263-64]. See Harvey, "Strauss's Developing Interest," 69-71.

10. Strauss, *FP*, 371n36, 373n41, 385-86.

11. Strauss, *EVSF*, 169 [Eng. 258], *FP*, 373n41.

12. See, for example, Lenzner, "Strauss's Fārābī," 336-37.

13. Strauss, *FP*, 372-75. See also *NACP*, 209: "The passage which contains an *allusion* to Plato, suggests that belief has no cognitive dignity whatever." A longer, more detailed, and subtler discussion by Namazi nevertheless reaches a similar conclusion: "Strauss left no doubt that Alfarabi rejected Islam and considered its claims to truth entirely worthless" (Namazi, *Strauss and Islamic Political Thought*, 144).

14. Alfarabi, *Philosophy of Plato and Aristotle*, trans. Muhsin Mahdi (Ithaca: Cornell University Press, 2001), 55-56, 60.

15. Strauss, *FP*, 370, 381. The quotation from Lessing, "von den ewigen Strafen," that headlines the article (357), draws our attention to the question of what eternal punishment might mean. For an excellent account of its larger context, see Namazi, *Strauss and Islamic Political Thought*, 136-39.

16. Strauss, *FP*, 370-71.

17. Strauss, *FP*, 372n39, 381n58.

18. Strauss, *FP*, 375. Strauss describes Alfarabi's use of Plato's *Laws* as follows: "He may have desired to ascribe a revised version of Plato's teaching to the dead Plato in order to protect that version, or the sciences generally speaking, especially by leaving open the question of whether he agreed with everything his Plato taught" (*WPP*, 144).

19. Strauss, *FP*, 358, 374-75. In note 43, Strauss observes that Averroes "directly attacks" Plato's teaching on life after death (see also *NACP*, 212).

20. Strauss, *FP*, 357-59. Namazi and Lenzner share our skepticism of this argument: see Namazi, "Strauss and Islamic Political Thought," 123-24; Lenzner, "Strauss's Fārābī," 335, 342-43n9. Strauss's dismissal of the *Harmonization of the Two Opinions of the Divine Sages, Plato and Aristotle*, which was already available at the time, as a purely "exoteric treatise" is also noteworthy: see Harvey, "Strauss's Developing Interest," 73-74, 80-81.

21. Strauss, *FP*, 372, *QPSM*, 133-36, *PAW*, 64n79, *WPP*, 156, 159, 163. This list is not exhaustive.

22. Strauss, *WPP*, 156.

23. Najjar publicly credits Strauss with providing intellectual and financial support: see *Kitāb al-Siyāsa al-Madaniyya*, ed. Fawzi M. Najjar (Beirut: Dār al-Mashriq, 1986), 10.

24. I propose here a provisional answer to a question that has long puzzled me: see my earlier bewilderment in Alexander Orwin, *Redefining the Muslim*

Community: Ethnicity, Religion and Politics in the Thought of Alfarabi (Philadelphia: University of Pennsylvania Press, 2017), 7-8.

25. Strauss, *FP*, 373n41, 383-84, cf. Alfarabi, *Philosophy of Plato and Aristotle*, 48.

26. Leo Strauss and Jacob Klein, "A Giving of Accounts," in *Jewish Philosophy and the Crisis of Modernity*, ed. Kenneth Green (Albany: State University of New York Press, 1997), 457-66, esp. 459-60.

27. Strauss, *FP*, 383-84, *PAW*, 16-18. Since this remark suggests that political philosophy does have an important role in "Farābī's Plato," I am not entirely persuaded by Parens's critique of this work for neglecting it. See Joshua Parens, *Leo Strauss and the Recovery of Medieval Political Philosophy* (Rochester: University of Rochester Press, 2016), 5, 108, 123-24. Another intriguing critique, by Christopher Colmo, posits that reconciling the theoretical and political aspects of Alfarabi's philosophy is impossible on the basis of Strauss's analysis. See Christopher Colmo, *Breaking with Athens: Alfarabi as Founder* (Lanham, MD: Lexington Books, 2005), 70-75. Neither Parens nor Colmo deals adequately with Strauss's second major treatment of Alfarabi. Strauss's silence about political science or political philosophy in this later chapter, despite the title of the volume in which it appears, along with the lack of detailed studies by Strauss on works of Alfarabi that by his own admission treat theoretical and practical philosophy in a different manner, makes this question difficult to resolve (see Strauss, *FP*, 366, *WPP*, 134-54).

28. Alfarabi, "Summary of Plato's Laws," In *The Political Writings, Part II*, trans. Charles Butterworth (Ithaca: Cornell University Press, 2015), 97-173.

29. Strauss, *WPP*, 138-40, see also *PAW*, 99.

30. Strauss, *QSPM*, 136n43, *FP*, 372, *PAW*, 13.

31. Strauss alludes to this absence by omitting religion from his list of important terms (*WPP*, 139).

32. Strauss, *WPP*, 144. Namazi plausibly argues that Strauss prefers the central reason: even if true, this manner of stating his preference is highly oblique (Namazi, *Strauss on Islamic Political Thought*, 190).

33. Strauss, *WPP*, 150.

34. Strauss, *WPP*, 135-37. In many passages, Strauss appears to tell us how to read Alfarabi without directly telling us what to think about what we read. See, for example, 140-41, 147-50, along with Harvey, "Strauss's Developing Interest," 76-77. A full understanding of Strauss's position would require a more thorough examination of his meticulous textual references than we can undertake here.

35. Strauss, *WPP*, 155-69.

36. Strauss, *WPP*, 140, 141, 150. See also Alfarabi. "Summary of Plato's Laws," 1.1. Arabic readers should consult the otherwise obsolete Gabrieli edition, cited in Strauss's first note, to trace Strauss's abundant references.

37. Strauss, *WPP*, 141, 150. Butterworth translates "intimated" (*awmā*) as "pointed out" (Alfarabi, "Summary of Plato's Laws," 1.1, 1.3).

38. Strauss, *WPP*, 143-44. Section 7.8 of the *Summary*, for example, seems to refer to the Quranic stories of the destruction of the Hud, Ud, and Thamud, while 7.11-12 allude to the core Muslim doctrines of Islam as the restoration of previous monotheistic faiths and Muhammad as the seal of the prophets.

39. Joshua Parens. *Metaphysics as Rhetoric: Alfarabi's Summary of Plato's 'Laws'* (Albany: State University of New York Press, 1995), 3-11, 40-54. Parens says surprisingly little about Strauss's interpretation of the *Summary*.

40. Strauss, *WPP*, 135-36. Alfarabi, "Summary of Plato's Laws," intro, 1.

41. Strauss, *WPP*, 150-52.

42. Strauss, *WPP*, 150-51.

43. Strauss, *WPP*, 148-49.

44. Strauss, *WPP*, 151-52, see 145, top, Alfarabi, *Summary*, 9.9. Namazi concludes his discussion with a fine interpretation of this passage. He argues that it is designed to cast doubt on the notion of the "divinity of laws" while indicating its social necessity, especially for "the ignorant and children" (Namazi, *Strauss and Islamic Political Thought*, 201-3). This points to Strauss's (or Alfarabi's) even more shocking statement about the limitations of law as such (Namazi, *Strauss and Islamic Political Thought*, 201-3).

45. Strauss, *WPP*, 137.

46. Strauss, *WPP*, 145. Compare Strauss's "still strikes us as unbelievable" on 152 with Alfarabi's "continues to be" in *Summary* 9.9.

47. Strauss, *WPP*, 151.

48. Strauss, *NACP*, 215.

49. Strauss, *WPP*, 151-52, Farabi, "Summary," 1.17.

50. Strauss, *WPP*, 152. See also the gentler phrase "masterful epitome of the problem of revelation," with which Strauss describes Maimonides's political science (*WPP*, 169). The fact that Strauss was raised a Jew and had a large Jewish audience surely complicates his presentation of Maimonides.

51. Other, more narrowly political constraints on law to which Strauss points include that it cannot adjust to great variations in customs across large geographical areas (Strauss, *WPP*, 146-47) or endure over a long periods of time (145). And since law, in its origin, requires forcing people of disparate natures and habits to submit to a single rule, it is usually preceded by tyranny (142-43, 146).

52. Strauss, *WPP*, 152-54, cf. 138-39.

53. Strauss, *WPP*, 163. Strauss's footnote cites passages from the *Virtuous City* and *Political Regime*, allegedly among Alfarabi's more "exoteric" works.

54. Strauss, *WPP*, 154.

55. Strauss, *PAW*, 8. Namazi goes so far as to suggest that the strident unbelief of "Farabi's Plato" appeals to the prejudices of Strauss's likely readers (Namazi, *Strauss and Islamic Political Thought*, 145). Elsewhere, Strauss evinces nothing but contempt for the argument that "the survival of Western civilization depends on belief in revelation." See Laurenz Denker, Hannes Kerber, and David Kretz, "Leo Strauss's 'Jerusalem and Athens' (1950): Three Lectures

Delivered at Hillel House, Chicago," *Journal for the History of Modern Theology* 29, no. 1: 133-73, esp. 164.

56. Strauss, *PAW*, 7, 21. See also Tanguay's gloss on the importance of what he christens Strauss's "Farabian turn," which "reveals what seems to be the key to Straussian thought. Strauss's defense of the intellectual life ultimately rests on a radical and elitist form of intellectual eudaimonism" (Tanguay, *Leo Strauss*, 168).

57. Strauss, *PAW*, 7-8, 21. I owe part of this argument to Lenzner's fine article, which persuasively explains many of the peculiarities and excesses of Strauss's argument as directed against contemporary scholarship (Lenzner, "Strauss's Fārābī," 334-35, 339-40.

58. Strauss, *PAW*, 18, Alfarabi, *Philosophy of Plato and Aristotle*, 49-50.

59. Strauss, *FP*, 362, 373-75, *PAW*, 14-15.

60. Hannes Kerber, "'Jerusalem and Athens' in America: On the Biographical Background of Leo Strauss's Four Eponymous Lectures from 1946, 1950, and 1967, and an Abandoned Book Project from 1956-57," *Journal for the History of Modern Theology* 29, no. 1, 90-132, esp. 108-9, and Svetozar Minkov and Rasoul Namazi, "Religion and the Commonweal in the Tradition of Political Philosophy: An Unpublished Lecture by Leo Strauss," in *American Political Thought* 10 (Winter 2021): 86-120, esp. 92-93, 110, 112.

61. Strauss, "Progress and Return," in *JPCM*, 130-31, cf. Denker et al., "Jerusalem and Athens," 172-73.

PART THREE

Transcript 3

LEO STRAUSS, "ABRAHAM AND MAIMONIDES" (1953)

Editorial Note: The following document was originally typed by Ralph Lerner, transcribing handwritten notes that he had taken in the course of the evening seminar held on April 30, 1953 at the University of Chicago's Hillel Foundation (Strauss's seminar was the second in a series called "Abraham in the Jewish and Christian Tradition"). The various references that are listed are accurate reproductions of what Mr. Lerner heard Strauss say. But none of the statements should be mistaken for direct quotations; they are all paraphrases. The transcript has been improved with the help of Joshua Parens. Numbers in square brackets refer to the page numbers of the original typescript, and numbers in curly brackets refer to the paragraph numbers of the original typescript. The underlinings in the typescript have been replaced with italics."

[1] 30 April 1953
Abraham and Maimonides
(Hillel Seminar)

{1} Abraham ibn Daud, *Emunah Ramah*, is a reply to Halevi's *Kuzari*. Classes of laws or *miṣvot*: known reasons; unknown reasons (e.g., ritual slaughter, sacrifices), which aim at absolute faith. Full obedience requires acceptance of commandment without knowing the reason (ʿaqedah, binding of Isaac). Full obedience is imitation of Abraham's acts.

{2} In letter to the Rabbis of Southern France, RMBM says he has given reasons for *all* the *miṣvot*. This is his last statement. What is the significance of the Abraham story? In the *Mishneh Torah* (M.T.), M distinguishes *miṣvot sikhliot* (rational commandments) and *miṣvot shimiʿot* (proclaimed commandments). In *More Nebukhim* (M.N.) all laws have knowable reasons.

{3} Traditional religion: it is good that reasons are not given since knowing reasons leads men to argue. (Cf. Solomon on *mishpaṭ ha-melekh*, regulation of the king's way of life.) The real difficulty is sacrifices. M cannot explain every particular difference, but can do so for the principle. Sacrificial law was adaptation to the customs of the times. M depreciates the significance of sacrifices, yet regards it as an integral part of the future in the M.T. If paganism is an eternal danger, protection will still be needed. The "days of the Messiah" is an imperfect period. (Only one statement saying it will last thousands of years.)

{4} M.T., *Hilkhot Yesode Ha-Torah* 7: prophecy of Moses is superior to all those before and after him. This view is borrowed from *Mishnat Rabbi Eliezer* VI; but there, it is preceded by a separate section dealing with prophecy of the patriarchs claiming it is superior in respects. Why did M drop the statement praising patriarchs while preserving praise of Moses? Two ways of understanding Judaism: Mosaic and Abrahamic. M—deliberate Mosaisation of Judaism. According to Ibn Daud, it was not a progress of [2] revelation from Abraham to Moses in the telling of "I shall be what I shall be." In the time of Moses, publicity was needed. But cf. M.N., II 35—Moses was superior. II 39—Why? Moses is the only *legislating* prophet. This bringing of divine law is essential. (Cf. Islamic view of Mohammed as peak.) Law is decisive. M denied the legal character of what is given to Abraham. M.T., *Hilkhot Deʿot* I (7): Private instruction needed to bring felicity for himself. Not the function of law. Abraham does not obey in order to improve a social order. M.N., II 39:[1] Abraham uses only argument; he convinces men. No compulsion. Moses brings the law to perfect society. In Abrahamic order, no society is involved. Insofar as law is full perfection of man, role of Moses is raised and that of Abraham is lowered. Abraham's work is preparatory, but not so Moses'. M.T., Hilkhot ʿAbodah Zarah I (2f.): three stages of mankind—wives and children, priests, few who understand. Work culminates in Moses. Predecessors of Abraham lived in idolatrous community without protesting. Abraham's iconoclasm started the work. (The isolated predecessors account for Aristotle.) Abraham was the first teacher of monotheism. M.T., *Haqdamah*, 1b, motto—"In the name of the Lord, God of the world" (*El ʿolam*); same motto in M.N. from Gen. 21:33. M uses an expression from the Abrahamic story. "God of the Cosmos"?

{5} In one way, emphasis is on legislative prophet as consummation. Therefore Abraham is subordinate. But mottoes indicate that this is not last word. Problem of law: law is superior to instruction of clan. What is the function of law? M.T., *Hilkhot Yesode Ha-Torah* 4 (13): (form of the chapters: 1&2 deal with *ma'aseh merkabah*; 3&4 with *ma'aseh bereshit*; Ezek. 1&10 was regarded as more exalted than Gen. 1-3; M's 1&2 summarize Aristotle's *Metap.*; 3&4 summarize Aristotle's *Phys.*) Four men entered *pardes* (garden; Paradise), but not all could grasp it completely. *I* say it is not proper to walk in paradise without first feeding oneself. Quotes sages: great thing is *ma'aseh merkabah* and small thing is legal discussion. But M says legal discussion [3] is prior; commandments serve immediate purpose of making social life possible. M admits crucial importance of law, but it is not the end; commandments only create a condition so that end can be reached by new and independent effort—'*iyyun* (speculation). Most important thing—speculation—was in Abraham. Fulfillment was already in Abraham

{6} (*El 'olam*=177=*gan 'eden*. True knowledge is knowledge of *El 'olam*)

{7} M.N, III 24—'*aqedah*. Trials seem to imply finding out how far Abraham will go. Incompatible with omniscience. God knew, but others didn't know. Two lessons: 1) lesson for all men; 2) demonstration of certainty of prophetic vision. How did Abraham receive commandment? Through angel, not directly from God. Every prophetic vision and audition led to action—an act of the imagination, not of reason.

{8} Is Abraham story a symbol or a historical fact? Traditionally, it is a fact. But what about modern theology? M is aware of the theoretical problem involved.

{9} In case of Sodom, Abraham argues. He has no attachment to them. In case of '*aqedah*, he has love and does not argue. Unconditional obedience to God does not lead to unconcern with others, but rather self-abnegation. Story of '*aqedah* expresses notion of absolute obedience to God's revealed will. But then how can he argue with God? A divination of the unrevealed will of God. This allows him to appeal to God's love. Bible is not simply orthodox. '*Aqedah* is great symbol of orthodoxy. But the feeling that there is something else too is expressed by mysticism. There is the other element of arguing with God. Abraham is certain that God is merciful and just. It is possible for man to know what God would never ask prior to meeting God.

{10} Cf. Deut.: "This is your wisdom in the eyes of the nations." This is M's justification for a rational explanation of the *miṣvot*. This wisdom is certainly visible to the wisest pagans. Hence Aristotle's system can be used. Main question: do we know anything as to how we should live without [4] direct religious experience? Buber says no; then there is nothing which can be said before that experience. The Sodom story bears on this and balances the ʿaqedah. Miraculous grace of God accounts for Isaac: natural course of events would have led to Abimelech's taking of Sarah; saving of Isaac from the ʿaqedah leads to a second birth.

{11} In *gan ʿeden*, Adam has understanding to understand God's command. This is Biblical answer to Aristotle's *Metap.*, I 1; man has natural desire to see (with eyes and mind). Not everything, however, is revealed which is God's will; it could be part of man's nature. Cf. Cain's knowing that he had done wrong. There is a reasonable transition from M's way of looking at things to[2] the Bible's. Adam in Paradise was trans-moral; morality is a means to recover that paradise. M denies the rational basis of moral principles. Platonic view—man is a compound of form and matter. Highest perfection of intellectual rational soul is understanding. To understand, man must behave tolerably. Rational proof is possible. But man's body requires society which in turn requires habits. Man's bodily perfection requires virtues too. Yet M does not say that morality is rational. The two moralities overlap but do not coincide. Common-sense morality has two separate roots.

Notes

1. In the typescript "I 39" but this seems to be a typo and "II 39" is meant.
2. "and" in the original typescript.

YEHUDA HALPER

Interpretative Essay

DICHOTOMIES OF UNDERSTANDING
RELIGIOUS LAW IN LEO STRAUSS'S LECTURE,
"ABRAHAM AND MAIMONIDES"

I

The surviving remnants of Ralph Lerner's notes documenting Leo Strauss's lecture, "Abraham and Maimonides," given at the University of Chicago Hillel House on April 30, 1953, are difficult reading, largely because they are somewhat fragmentary. In particular, they lack any kind of unifying thesis statement. Still, these notes present with relative frankness Strauss's understanding of the purpose of religious law according to Maimonides and raise the question of the connection between metaphysical speculation about the divine and religious law. Strauss's frankness here is reflected in the fact that these notes do not mention the esoteric vs. exoteric or hidden meanings of any kind.

Strauss's lecture focuses on a series of dichotomies: Abraham vs. Moses, blind obedience vs. knowing the reasons for the laws, argument vs. legal compulsion, and Abraham ibn Daud vs. Moses Maimonides. The first of these is particularly important. Indeed, in the central paragraphs of the talk, paragraphs 4–6, Strauss goes so far as to talk about "two ways of understanding Judaism: Mosaic and Abrahamic."[1] These two ways of understanding Judaism are primarily based on Maimonides's *Mishneh Torah*, Book of Knowledge, Laws of Idolatry I, and *Guide of the Perplexed* III 29. In both places, Maimonides presents a purportedly historical account of Abraham's attacks on paganism and then Moses's attacks and implementation of the Law.[2] Strauss highlights that for Maimonides the difference between Abraham's Judaism and Moses's Judaism is that the latter is a *legislating* Judaism, that is, it involves the Law. According to Strauss, Maimonides "denied the legal character of what is given to Abraham." While Moses brought Israel the law, Abraham gave "private instruction needed to bring felicity for himself." In this connection, Strauss mentions Maimonides's *Mishneh Torah*, Book of Knowledge, Laws of Deʿot I, 7. There Maimonides discusses accustoming oneself to various habits and says that this is the path that Abraham taught his sons, quoting Genesis 18:19.[3] Indeed, habituation is a major theme of the Laws of Deʿot and legal compulsion is absent from the first four chapters. Thus, Strauss sets us up to contrast two different "understandings of Judaism." One is the legal understanding, associated with Moses and apparent in the various laws of the Torah and in the majority of the *Mishneh Torah*. The other is Judaism as a system of habituation, as described in Law of Deʿot I-IV, in the *Eight Chapters*, and perhaps also in Aristotle's *Nicomachean Ethics*.

These two "understandings of Judaism" are also aimed at different groups. Abraham's Judaism is aimed at his sons and household (cf. Genesis 18:19), which Strauss considers Maimonides to extend to the "clan." Moses's Judaism is aimed at what is here termed "society." "Society" and its similar "social order" are modern terms without clear parallels in biblical or Maimonidean Hebrew or in Maimonides's Arabic, but here they seem to refer to a large group governed by law. Moses brings the Law, viz. the Torah, to the Israelites to perfect their society and to give them the tools to keep up that perfection by maintaining the Law. In contrast, Abraham "uses only argument; he convinces men." Indeed, he convinces "wives and children, priests, [and the] few who understand."

This method of persuasion is, in fact, antithetical to the society around Abraham. Indeed, it seems likely that what is here called Abraham's "iconoclasm" led Abraham to direct confrontation with society. In *Mishneh Torah*, Laws of Idolatry I, Maimonides says that Abraham, even before reaching adulthood, began "to wander about in his views and to consider day and night how it would be possible for this planetary sphere to run its course eternally without something that made it run its course."[4] This leads Abraham to discover the Creator, Who makes the world run its course, and to discover that there is no other besides Him.[5] Following these considerations, Abraham "came to know that the entire people were in error"[6] as a result of their worship of the stars. This led Abraham to "give responses to the people of Ur Kasdim and to conduct a discussion with them."[7] Further, Abraham recommended destroying the idols of Ur and directing worship solely at the One God. Maimonides continues, "Since [Abraham] prevailed over them with his proofs, the king sought to kill him. A miracle happened for him and he went out to Ḥarran."[8] Subsequently, people continued to ask Abraham questions and to join his cause, or perhaps to join what Strauss's lecture calls his "clan." Maimonides here describes Abraham using the language of questioning and responding and prevailing over people with proofs—all language typical of dialectical argument.[9] Abraham of the *Mishneh Torah* could thus appear to be a dialectical arguer whose arguments were threatening to the king of Ur Kasdim and to idolatrous society. Despite Abraham's initial success, according to the *Mishneh Torah*, the Israelite descendants of Abraham turned to idolatrous practice after spending considerable time in Egypt.[10] It was only when God sent Moses to Israel that proper worship of God was restored; that is, when God [through Moses] "crowned them with commandments, let them know the way of worshipping Him, and what judgment would apply to foreign worship and to all those who err after it."[11] That is, this section of the *Mishneh Torah* gives us the clear contrast Maimonides sees between the legal approach of Moses and the argumentative or dialectical approach to the Judaism of Abraham. Abraham's approach can be destructive (perhaps, Moses's can too, but this does not figure in Maimonides's account here), and while both approaches can be constructive, only Moses's is truly lasting.

Maimonides also discusses Abraham's approach to Judaism in *Guide of the Perplexed* III 29, beginning with an account attributed to the Sabian book, *Nabatean Agriculture*.[12] According to this account, Abraham was born in Kūthā, not Ur Kasdim, where he "disagreed with the community and asserted that there was an agent other than the sun."[13] That is, according to the Sabian view, which is inaccurate with respect to Abraham's birthplace, there is nothing specifically monotheistic about Abraham's view. Still, as a result of this view and Abraham's arguments in its favor, "the king became afraid that [Abraham] would ruin his [i.e., the king's] polity and turn the people away from their religions and [so the king] banished [Abraham] toward Syria."[14] According to Maimonides's presentation of the Sabian account, then, Abraham's religious approach is politically destructive because it attacks political religion, but at the same time the Sabians do not clearly see it as fundamentally different from polytheism.

In contrast, according to Maimonides's own account of the Abraham story in *Guide* III 29, the discovery of monotheism is Abraham's primary contribution. "It became clear to him that there is a separate deity that is neither a body nor a force in a body and that all the stars and the spheres were made by Him."[15] Moreover, according to Maimonides, this monotheism is expressed in what Strauss's lecture calls Abraham's "motto," viz. Genesis 21:33: "In the name of the Lord, God of the world," or as it appears in these lecture notes, "God of the cosmos." In fact the Hebrew term ʿolam used in Genesis 21:33, translated as "world" by Shlomo Pines and "cosmos" in these notes, probably meant "of long duration" or "eternal" originally.[16] Still, it is clear from the context that Maimonides must understand the term according to its later meaning of "world" since Abraham inferred the principles of monotheism from examining the world or the cosmos. Maimonides's account of Abraham's arguments with the Sabians occurs somewhat later in the chapter, suggesting that this is a separate activity from the theoretical activity of discovering the principles of monotheism. This second activity is also described in dialectical, or even rhetorical terms: "*Abraham our father* began to refute these opinions by means of arguments and feeble preaching, conciliating people and drawing them to obedience by means of benefits." Maimonides contrasts this with the approach of Moses who "perfected [Abraham's] purpose in that he commanded killing this people [viz., idolaters], wiping out their traces, and tearing out their roots."[17] That is, Abraham's dialectical/rhetorical approach that makes use of habituation is in contrast with Moses's use of what Strauss's lecture calls "compulsion," that is, employing the full arm of the law.

The primary difference between Maimonides's own perception of Abraham's approach to Judaism in both the *Mishneh Torah* and the *Guide* and Maimonides's perception of the Sabian perception of Abraham's approach to Judaism in the *Guide* lies in their theoretical understandings of God's role in the world. Both perceptions see Abraham as a dialectical arguer whose arguments are potentially destructive of the monarchy. Yet, in Maimonides's account of the biblical stories, Abraham arrives at his understanding of monotheism by examining the world, the stars, the planetary spheres, and making inferences about their causes. According to Maimonides's account of the Sabian view of Abraham, Abraham's conclusion that there is "an agent other than the sun"[18] is of far less theoretical moment. This may be because, as Maimonides says, "the utmost attained by the speculation of those who philosophized at those times (ואגיא מא אנתהי אליה נט'ר מן תפלסף פי תלך אלאזמנה) consisted in imagining (תכיל) that God was the spirit of the sphere and that the sphere and the stars are a body of which the deity, may He be exalted, is its spirit."[19] Accordingly, the people of Abraham's time were in no position to understand his monotheistic arguments and could only understand that he was denying the sun, or perhaps the spirit of the sun, as a cause of the world.

In what we have of his lecture, Strauss points to the different practical approaches of Abraham and Moses through habituation and dialectic (Abraham) and Law and compulsion (Moses), yet he notes that the two approaches are unified in the "most important thing," viz., ʿiyyun, speculation. ʿIyyun is not a concept associated with the biblical Abraham or even with Maimonides's Hebrew, but was used by Samuel Ibn Tibbon to translate the Arabic نظر, a term often associated with the Greek, θεωρία. The English translation of ʿiyyun here as "speculation" accords with Shlomo Pines's translation of نظر, and refers to scientific speculation, particularly of physical or metaphysical things. Here it is associated with the Account of the Beginning and the Account of the Chariot, which Maimonides associates with physics and metaphysics, respectively, in the introduction to the first part of the *Guide*. Moreover, as Strauss notes, the Account of the Beginning and the Account of the Chariot figure prominently at the opening of the Laws of the Foundations of the Torah in *Mishneh Torah*. These accounts are not, in fact, associated with Abraham directly, though it is possible they are covered somehow in Abraham's statement in Genesis 21:33, "In the name of the Lord, God of the world." Strauss probably alludes to this in his parenthetical note in paragraph 6 that the Hebrew of "God of the World" and the "Garden of Eden" have the same numerical valuation of 177. Strauss notes Maimonides's association of Paradise (*ha-pardes*) with the Account of the Beginning and the Account of the Chariot in *Mishneh Torah*, Laws of the Foundations of the Torah IV.13, and the context suggests that Strauss identifies the Garden of Eden with Paradise.

The result of this is that Strauss suggests a kind of theoretical unity shared by Abraham and Moses that is in both cases derived from the study of the world and making inferences about God, through physics and metaphysics. The differences between Abraham and Moses are practical. Abrahamic Judaism is a religion that utilizes habituation and dialectic, while Mosaic Judaism is a "society" that utilizes compulsion and law. True fulfillment comes from the theoretical, says Strauss, and so either approach to Judaism can reach it. Yet, in order to achieve the theoretical, certain social conditions must exist. The achievement of these social conditions would seem to have worked for Abraham's clan, but not to have been long lasting. Moses's Law is clearly longer lasting and applicable to what Strauss calls "society," viz., all who are bound by that Law.

II

The different practical approaches Strauss sees in Maimonides's Abrahamic and Mosaic religion entail different ways of understanding the practices, that is, different political sciences. According to Strauss's understanding of Maimonides, the Laws of Moses are all rationally comprehensible, while Abraham's revelation is beyond human comprehension, even if his arguments appeal to rationality.

Strauss points out that Maimonides sees the Law of Moses as rationally comprehensible. Indeed, the majority of the third part of the *Guide* is dedicated to explaining the commandments. This is based on Deuteronomy 4:6: "For this is your wisdom and understanding in the eyes of the all the peoples who will hear all of these statutes and say, only a wise and understanding people which is this great nation." In *Guide* III 31, Maimonides cites this verse in order to show that "even all the *statutes* [ḥuqqim] will show to all the nations that they have been given with *wisdom and understanding*."[20] That is, that even those laws which are sometimes considered impossible to understand, viz. *statutes* (ḥuqqim), do according to the Mosaic system have a rational reason. If so, then certainly the *mishpatim*, which all consider to be understandable, should have rational reasons behind them. Thus, Strauss points to Maimonides's "Letter to the Rabbis of Southern France," that is, to the *Letter on Astrology*. There Maimonides says, "It became clear to me what the reason is for all those commandments that everyone comes to think of as having no reason at all other than the decree of Scripture."[21] There Maimonides refers the rabbis of Southern France to the *Guide of the Perplexed*, though noting that it was in Arabic and so inaccessible to them.

More significantly, Maimonides states in both the *Letter on Astrology* and in part III of the *Guide* that the reasons for the commandments become clear when compared with the practices of idolatry. In other words, in order to understand the reasons for the commandments, one must undertake an investigation of the kind that Abraham undertook while still in Ur of the Chaldees. One should interrogate the laws and their relationship to scientifically or theoretically understood notions about the world and God. Doing so is a dialectical process that, according to Strauss's lecture notes, "leads men to argue" (para. 3). Such arguments can potentially undermine the Law, just as Abraham's arguments against the Chaldeans undermined their polity. Yet, at the same time, understanding the reasons for the commandments is to move toward rationality and wisdom. This wisdom, according to Strauss's lecture notes (para. 10), is "visible to the wisest pagans. Hence Aristotle's system can be used." Accordingly, it seems that for Strauss, studying the reasons for the commandments leads to rationality and wisdom, particularly about scientifically understood notions, such as physics and metaphysics, and so to understanding them according to Aristotle. In other words, it leads to philosophy proper.

In contrast, Abraham's nonlegal, ethical approach does not in itself lead to philosophy. Indeed, while Abraham did not shy from interrogating the laws of the Chaldeans, he does not do so for his own commandments. Thus, he accepts without question the ʿaqedah. This, says Strauss, is the "great symbol of orthodoxy" and derived from Abraham's certainty "that God is merciful and just." Where Abraham argues with God, that is, in the case of Sodom in Genesis 18, it is for people for whom "he has no attachment." That is, he is ready to argue about someone else's decree, but not his own. When it comes to his own life, Abraham adopts an attitude of absolute, unquestioning subservience to God, even when asked to bind his own son for sacrifice. Even still, Strauss suggests that Abraham's argument with God about Sodom is for the purpose of obtaining "a divination of the unrevealed will of God." In this case, it is not a destructive argument of the kind Abraham undertook with the Chaldeans, but part of a quest for "divine love" and "mysticism."[22]

For Abraham, according to Strauss's reading of Maimonides, God's command is inherently nonrational. Indeed, drawing on *Guide* III 24, Strauss notes that the ʿaqedah is in fact "incompatible with omniscience." This is presumably based on the difficulty seen in Genesis 22:12, where God says, "Now I know that you are God fearing...." If God did not know this beforehand, as would seem to follow from the biblical verse, then He is not omniscient. Such a difficulty is inherent in the very notion of a divine test, as Maimonides explores in *Guide* III 24. Strauss alludes to the interpretation Maimonides gives there, which also follows Saadia's *Tafsir* on Genesis 22, according to which God does not say "now I know," but rather, "Now I make others know." That is, God does not gain knowledge through the divine test, but rather others, viz., those who hear of the test, gain knowledge. What knowledge do these others gain? According to Strauss's lecture, they gain a "demonstration of the certainty of prophetic vision." This demonstration is apparently Abraham's willingness to sacrifice Isaac on the basis of a prophetic vision. This prophetic vision, which grants Abraham this orthodox certainty, comes through an angel, not directly from God, and is "an act of imagination, not of reason."[23]

Abraham and Moses thus present opposite views of Judaism. For Abraham, God's revelation is based on imagination and is not subject to argument, while the religious laws of others are subject to argument and should be rejected on the basis of reason. In contrast, Moses's laws are subject to reason and so can be a source of argument.[24] On the other hand, Moses's laws forbid studying idolatry and encourage attacking rather than arguing with idolaters.[25] Still, Strauss notes that it is the wisdom of the reasons of the commandments that form common ground between wise Jewish and non-Jewish people. While both approaches are compatible with philosophical speculation, ʿiyyun, such speculation occupies a different place in each system. In Abrahamic Judaism, insofar as revelation is imaginative and not rational, philosophical speculation is outside of the religion itself, and only shows up in the context of debates with other religions. In Mosaic Judaism, however, philosophical speculation is internal, discovered through exploring the reasons for the commandments.

III

In light of the fact that most of the lecture apparently concerns Strauss's interpretation of Maimonides's views of the biblical Abraham and Moses, we might be inclined to explain the title of the lecture, "Abraham and Maimonides," as a reference to Maimonides's account of the biblical Abraham and the latter's "understanding of Judaism." Yet, Strauss begins his lecture not with the biblical Abraham, but with Abraham ibn Daud, a twelfth-century, older contemporary of Maimonides. Indeed, this opening suggests that Strauss's title could refer to a contrast between Abraham ibn Daud and Moses Maimonides. This suggestion is particularly mystifying since Strauss writes considerably less about Abraham ibn Daud than he does about Maimonides. Still, if we glean Strauss's understanding of Ibn Daud from his other writings, we find a fairly straightforward view of Ibn Daud. This view is quite different from that which has emerged in recent years in Ibn Daud scholarship.[26] Strauss's view, indeed, is undoubtedly based on a much more limited range of sources. Whether or not Strauss's Ibn Daud is an accurate reflection of the historical figure, it is clear that he sees Ibn Daud as holding a view of Judaism that is not too far from that which Strauss sees in Maimonides's portrayal of the biblical Abraham.

Thus, for example, "Spinoza's Critique of Maimonides," which Strauss originally published in German in 1930, gives the following description of Ibn Daud: "Abraham Ibn Daud, Maimonides' forerunner, justifies the superiority of the revealed commandments, which are beyond human understanding, to the rational commandments. The high example is the obedience of Abraham who made ready to sacrifice his son at the command of God, even though God had promised him that his son should be his heir, even though Abraham, had he wished to pretend to wisdom, could not but find that command absurd."[27] Thus does Strauss see Ibn Daud as placing the highest value on those commandments that cannot be explained, with special emphasis on the ʿaqedah. Indeed, this is quite close to Strauss's depiction of Maimonides's Abraham in this lecture with the exception that according to Strauss, Maimonides's Abraham is actively involved in intellectual speculation, while Ibn Daud's Abraham does not seem to be involved at all in wisdom.

This view of Ibn Daud may help explain Strauss's enigmatic statement that Ibn Daud's *Emunah Ramah* is "a reply to Halevi's *Kuzari*." This is because, according to Strauss, Ibn Daud sees two kinds of commandments, rational and nonrational, and maintains the superiority of the nonrational. This view suggests that Ibn Daud is a man of faith, a believer in the superiority of faith to reason. Strauss also points out Halevi's use of a similar distinction between rational and nonrational commandments in his 1943 essay, "The Law of Reason in the *Kuzari*."[28] Strauss's Halevi associates the rational commandments, "the laws of reason," with the Philosopher of part I of the *Kuzari* and since such commandments can be understood by reason alone, they are also a kind of "natural law," that is, a "natural morality." The nonrational commandments cannot be understood in themselves. These nonrational commandments, we learn from the end of Strauss's essay, though discovered only through divine revelation, are what make up an objective morality, what he calls "categoric imperatives." Throughout the essay, in fact, Strauss depicts Halevi as grappling with these two views of morality—objective and rational, that is, somewhat relative (or at any rate adaptable to various situations). Strauss may believe that Halevi himself ultimately believes in the rational view of morality, but he still presents Halevi as taking the religious view of absolute morality as a serious, perhaps irrefutable opponent. Ibn Daud, it would seem, is an answer to Halevi insofar as he takes the absolute, religious morality as unquestionably superior to a relative, rational morality.

According to Strauss then, Halevi emerges as a representative of a middle position between the positions of Ibn Daud and Maimonides. Strauss's Ibn Daud is an adherent of an absolute, religious morality whose divine origin places it beyond human understanding, that is, beyond reason. Strauss's Maimonides, as we have seen, sees Mosaic religious law as given to reasoning and indeed considers that such reasoning about the law will give rise to theoretical speculation about physics and metaphysics. Halevi apparently sees both views as possibilities: there is both a religious law that is beyond reason and a rational law, albeit not one that is identical with Mosaic religion.

Accordingly, it would seem that Strauss sees Maimonides's *Guide* (and perhaps *Letter on Astrology*) as a reply to Abraham ibn Daud's *Emunah Ramah*, suggesting rational law as the counterpart to transcendent moral imperatives. This is so, even though Maimonides acknowledges the undercurrent of Abrahamic morality in the Mosaic law. This shows up in paragraph 2 of the lecture notes, where Strauss answers the question, "What is the significance of the Abraham story [for Maimonides]?," with the distinction between rational commandments and proclaimed commandments in the *Mishneh Torah*. In fact, the categories of *miṣvot sikhliot* and *miṣvot shimiʿot* are not found in the *Mishneh Torah*—Maimonides does not even use the Hebrew *sikhli* in this way.[29] Still, not all commandments are explained in the *Mishneh Torah* and, as we have seen, Maimonides alerts his readers to an earlier, pre-Mosaic, Abrahamic Judaism that, it would seem, followed a divine morality that went beyond rationality. That this Abrahamic Judaism was replaced by Mosaic Judaism is mirrored, to my mind, in the way Strauss sees Moses Maimonides's understanding of rational law as an answer and replacement to Abraham ibn Daud's understanding of divine law as beyond rationality.

IV

I noted earlier that this view of Abraham ibn Daud is not the view of modern scholars. It is, perhaps more significantly, not a view that can be found in Strauss's predecessors. Indeed, most of Strauss's predecessors apparently see Abraham ibn Daud as a champion of the rationalist approach to law. Thus, for example, Julius Guttmann's chapter on Ibn

Daud in his *Philosophies of Judaism* presents a far more intellectualist and philosophical Ibn Daud than we find here.[30]

In his 1942 *The Reasons for the Commandments*, which is based on lectures given in Breslau in the 1930s, Isaac Heinemann describes an Ibn Daud that is somewhat similar to that we find in this lecture. According to Heinemann, "Ibn Daud attributes special value to those mitzvot whose reasons we do not understand ... in performing them a person shows that he is heeding the word of his God, without questioning His ways." That is, for Heinemann's Ibn Daud, there is value in commandments that are beyond rationality. Abraham is an example of this approach: "When the patriarch Abraham was commanded by God to sacrifice his son, he did not second-guess and argue, asking what had happened to all the promises and hopes that God had implanted in him."[31] Still, according to Heinemann's Ibn Daud, this does not mean that the unquestioning approach to commandments is necessarily *superior* to the rational approach that seeks the reasons behind the commandments. While it is true that "[t]he essential pillar of the Torah is faith,"[32] Heinemann understands this "faith" (*emunah*) to be essentially rational in character. As he notes, Ibn Daud says this faith is attained by studying the sciences in hierarchical order. Moreover, "Our overall purpose on this earth is to perfect our intellect generally and to acquire true knowledge of divine matters in particular. Therefore the most important part of the Torah is that which enables us to acquire correct knowledge of the blessed God."[33] Thus, for Heinemann, Abraham ibn Daud does not himself agree with his portrayal of the biblical Abraham that the most important kind of belief is the unquestioning acceptance of prophetic truths. Moreover, Heinemann criticizes those "critical scholars" of the "modern period" who distinguish between prophetic and legalistic Judaism and claim to follow Ibn Daud in accepting only adherence to the prophetic, while neglecting or even rejecting the legalistic.[34] That is, Heinemann apparently criticizes those who read Abraham ibn Daud in the way Strauss does, as advocating unthinking acceptance of the moral law alone.

In his note to this section, Heinemann mentions Hermann Cohen.[35] In fact, in *Religion of Reason out of the Sources of Judaism*, we find another depiction of Ibn Daud. There Cohen points to Ibn Daud's division of the laws of the Torah into parts of unequal value and cites the same sentence we saw would later be central for Heinemann: "The main point of the Torah and of the worship is the faith (in God)."[36] Cohen takes this view of faith to be connected to what he calls "fundamental laws," which he opposes to "the commandments, the causes of which are not rational" and as an example of which he gives the sacrifices. Indeed, according to Cohen, Ibn Daud, following the distinction present in Deuteronomy between ordinances (*ḥuqqim*) and judgments (*mishpaṭim*), "distinguishes those regulations according to the distinction introduced by Saadiah between principles of reason (*sikhliot*) and prescriptions of obedience (*shimiʿot*)."[37] That is, according to Cohen what is most important for Ibn Daud is the rational, fundamental commandments, those which can be described by reason. Seen in this light, the biblical Abraham is not important for his willingness to sacrifice Isaac, but only for "binding" him. Through this binding, says Cohen, Abraham comes to be commanded to reject human sacrifices and idolatry in general and to adhere further to the rationalism behind the law.[38]

Conclusion

I believe it is clear that Strauss's Ibn Daud is not only different from Cohen's, but a symbol of the contrary position. For Cohen, Ibn Daud is important for dividing the commandments into rational and for obedience only, while clearly preferring the rational. For Strauss, Ibn Daud prefers the nonrational, even absurd commandments, accepted without wisdom. Moreover, it is Maimonides, according to Strauss, who divides the commandments into rational and for obedience only, even while ultimately rejecting this distinction in favor of the claim that *all* of the commandments are rational. Neither of these claims, viz. that Ibn Daud prefers the nonrational commandments, nor that Maimonides divides the commandments in this way, are correct. As I see it, this suggests that Strauss is making a point here that is simply not simply in scholarly exegesis of Ibn Daud and Maimonides.

This point may be alluded to in the final paragraph of the lecture notes, where Strauss mentions, but does not develop, a dichotomy between morality and social laws. Strauss suggests that according to Maimonides there is no "rational basis of moral principles." It is only societal laws that can be understood rationally, according to Strauss's Maimonides. This would seem to be a reply to Hermann Cohen, arguing that morality simply is not rationally understood. So, would Cohen's Ibn Daud actually be the same as Strauss's, acting on the basis of a divinely prophesized morality that is in fact highly irrational? It is this view of morality as predicated in the first place on experience of the divine that Strauss attributes to Martin Buber in paragraph 10 of the lecture notes. This kind of experience, Strauss notes there, is directly opposed to "the natural course of events" and so not accessible to Aristotelian reason. The way to rationality is, in fact, to follow Strauss's Maimonides in studying the reasons for *all* of the commandments in their societal and legal contexts. These reasons, according to Strauss and Strauss's Maimonides, ultimately lead to theoretical speculation, including physics and metaphysics, in a way that morality simply will not.[39] Accordingly, we may add a final dichotomy to Strauss's lecture, albeit not one explicitly mentioned in the lecture notes: Hermann Cohen vs. Leo Strauss.

Notes

1. Quotations from "Abraham vs. Moses," refer to the text reproduced in this volume, with the understanding that they reflect Ralph Lerner's typed account, and perhaps not Strauss's actual formulation word for word.

2. On the historical Sabians, who are apparently mentioned only thousands of years after the biblical Abraham, and their connection to Maimonides's understanding of paganism, see Sara Stroumsa, *Maimonides and His World: Portrait of a Mediterranean Thinker* (Princeton: Princeton University Press, 2009), 84–124.

3. Genesis 18:19 actually refers to Abraham *commanding* (יצוה) his sons and his household, which might seem to refer to compulsion, rather than habituation.

4. Moses Maimonides, *Mishneh Torah*, ed. Yohai Makbili, 3rd ed. (Haifa: Mishne Torah Project, 2009), Laws of Idolatry I.3: התחיל [אברהם] לשוטט בדעתו והוא קטן, ולחשב ביום ובלילה ולהיאך אפשר שיהיה הגלגל הזה נוהג תמיד ולא יהיה לו מנהיג. This passage is particularly difficult to translate. The Hebrew word לשוטט is particularly difficult because of its similarity to the Hebrew word for "fool" or "idiot," שוטה. I have translated it "to wander" because of the association of this term with the Hebrew שיטה, whose primary meaning is apparently "line" and which is used for "line of thought" as well as "trajectory of the planets." My translation of this term as "to wander about" was influenced, albeit with no real linguistic basis, by Plato's use of the Greek term πλανᾶσθαι in *Alcibiades I* 117a–118a to refer to wandering or wavering of the kind one does when one thinks one knows something, but does not in fact know. The solution to this predicament is to learn and to discover the truth.

5. Maimonides, *Mishneh Torah*, Laws of Idolatry I.3: אין . . . אלוה חוץ ממנו.

6. Maimonides, *Mishneh Torah*, Laws of Idolatry I.3: וידע שכל העם טועים.

7. Maimonides, *Mishneh Torah*, Laws of Idolatry I.3: להשיב תשובות על בני אור כשדים ולערוך דין עמהם.

8. Maimonides, *Mishneh Torah*, Laws of Idolatry I.3: כיון שגבר עליהם בראיותיו, בקש המלך להרגו; נעשה לו נס ויצא לחרן.

9. Cf. al-Farabi, *Art of Dialectic*, an edition and translation of which is in Dominique Mallet, "La Dialectique dans La Philosophie D'Abū Naṣr Al-Fārābī," (PhD diss., Université Michel-de-Montaigne, 1992).

10. Maimonides does not mention the part slavery may have played in this.

11. Ibid. הכתירן במצוות, והודיען דרך עבודתו, ומה יהיה משפט עבודה זרה וכל הטועין אחריה.

12. Pines notes that by the term "Sabians" Maimonides "designates the pagans." See Moses Maimonides, *Guide of the Perplexed*, trans. Shlomo Pines (Chicago: University of Chicago Press, 1963), 514n1.

13. Pines trans., 514.

14. *Guide of the Perplexed*, Pines trans., 515.

15. Pines trans., 516.

16. See Francis Brown, S. R. Driver, and Charles A. Briggs, *A Hebrew and English Lexicon of the Old Testament* (Oxford: Clarendon Press, 1951), 761–63.

17. Pines trans., 517.

18. See note 13 above.

19. Pines trans., 515.

20. Pines trans., 524.

21. Translated in Ralph Lerner, *Maimonides' Empire of Light: Popular Enlightenment in an Age of Belief* (Chicago: University of Chicago Press, 2000), 180. Hebrew text in *Letters and Essays of Moses Maimonides*, ed. I. Shailat (Ma'aleh Adumim: Ma'aliyot, 1995), 481. While much of the Letter on Astrology draws on Avicenna's *Refutation of Astrology*, this statement is not found in Avicenna. See Elon Harvey, "Avicenna's Influence on Maimonides' Epistle on Astrology," *Arabic Sciences and Philosophy* 29 (2019): 171–83.

22. Para. 9.

23. Para. 7. Cf. *Guide* II 36.

24. Cf. Para. 3: "knowing reasons leads men to argue."

25. Cf. Yehuda Halper, "Does Maimonides' Mishneh Torah Forbid Reading the Guide of the Perplexed?," *AJS Review* 42, no. 2 (November 2018): 351–79.

26. For a concise overview, see Resianne Fontaine and Amira Eran, "Abraham Ibn Daud," Stanford Encyclopedia of Philosophy (Spring 2020), ed. Edward N. Zalta, https://plato.stanford.edu/archives/spr2020/entries/abraham-daud/.

27. *Leo Strauss on Maimonides: The Complete Writings*, ed. Kenneth Hart Green (Chicago: University of Chicago Press, 2013), 156. For the original German, see Leo Strauss, *Die Religionskritik Spinozas als Grundlage seiner Bibelwissenschaft: Untersuchungen zu Spinozas "Theologisch-Politischem Traktat* (Berlin: Akademie-Verlag, 1930), 166.

28. *Proceedings of the American Academy of Jewish Research* 13 (1943): 47–96. This essay was reprinted without significant changes as chapter 4 of Leo Strauss, *Persecution and the Art of Writing* (Glencoe, IL: Free Press, 1952).

29. He prefers forms of the word *deʿah*. It was the Hebrew translators of the *Guide*, Samuel Ibn Tibbon and Judah Al-Ḥarizi, who associated the Arabic *ʿaql* with the Hebrew *sekhel*. On Maimonides's discussion of the Hebrew term *deʿah*, see Yehuda Halper, "'For the Earth Shall Be Filled with *Deʿah*': Terminological Ambiguities and the Connection between Knowledge and Actions in Maimonides' *Commentary on the Mishnah* and *Mishneh Torah*?," in *Officina Philosophica Hebraica I: Studies in the Formation of Medieval Hebrew Philosophical Terminology*, ed. Reimund Leicht and Giuseppe Veltri (Leiden: Brill, 2019), 76–103.

30. Julius Guttmann, *Philosophies of Judaism*, trans. David Silverman (Garden City, NY: Anchor Books, 1964), 162–72. Cf. Julius Guttmann, "Abraham Ibn Daud Halevi," in *Jewish Ecyclopedia* (1906), vol. I, 101–3.

31. Isaac Heinemann, *The Reasons for the Commandments in Jewish Thought from the Bible to the Renaissance*, trans. Leonard Levin (Boston: Academic Studies Press, 2008), 88.

32. Apparently citing Abraham ibn Daud, *Emunah Ramah,* ed. Weil, 103: עיקר התורה ועמודה הוא האמונה. Weil adds a note here that this belief is belief in God.

33. Heinemann, *Reasons for the Commandments*, 91.

34. Heinemann, *Reasons for the Commandments*, 89.

35. Heinemann, *Reasons for the Commandments*, 192, referring to *Maimonides* (1908), vol. I, 80.

36. Hermann Cohen, *Religion of Reason out of the Sources of Judaism*, trans. Simon Kaplan (Atlanta: Scholars Press, 1995), 352. See note 31 above.

37. Cohen, *Religion of Reason*, 352.

38. Cohen, *Religion of Reason*, 397.

39. Strauss gives a more detailed critique of Cohen and his notion of morality, with a focus on the unintended inescapability of the Law for Cohen's system in his introductory essay to Cohen's *Religion of Reason* printed in the English translation of the volume cited here. In that essay, Strauss notes the different view Cohen had of Ibn Daud (xxvii–xxviii) and the consequence that "the religion of reason leaves no place for absolute obedience" such as the binding of Isaac (xxviii).

JOSHUA PARENS

Interpretative Essay

REASON AND LAW

IN HIS 1953 UNIVERSITY OF CHICAGO HILLEL SEMINAR, titled "Abraham and Maimonides," Strauss explores the extraordinary range of meaning ascribed to the biblical patriarch Abraham by Maimonides. The patriarch appears variously, in relation to the binding of Isaac (*akedah*) as the representative of unquestioning obedience, on the one hand, and as the representative of "speculation," on the other. Over the course of these notes on the seminar, taken by Ralph Lerner, Strauss touches on the biblical bases for this opposition. Judaism has long been fascinated by the gap between, on the one hand, the obedient Abraham who is willing to sacrifice his one and only son if the one and only God demands it of him (para. 1), and, on the other hand, the righteous Abraham who demands of God that He temper His righteous anger toward, at least some of, the inhabitants of Sodom (and Gomorrah) (para. 9).[1] How well this gap lines up with the gap between obedience and philosophic speculation we hope to determine in this essay.

At first somewhat oddly, Strauss places Abraham within a frame established not by Maimonides but by his older and far less well-known contemporary Abraham ibn Daud (ca. 1110–1180; Maimonides 1137/38–1204), noting that Ibn Daud's *Emunah Ramah* (The Exalted Faith) was written as a "reply to Halevi's *Kuzari*." Anyone familiar with Strauss's "The Law of Reason in the *Kuzari*"[2] expects here to find something like the discussion there of the relation between Maimonides and Halevi. But that published discussion is far too complicated and subtle for this setting.

Its subtlety is due to the fact that Halevi's position, though deeply influenced by the Mu'tazilite *kalām*'s rational law teaching, especially as it was taken up into the Jewish tradition by Saadia Gaon, is not simply equivalent to that teaching. At least Halevi's Jewish scholar holds a position described by Strauss as that of an "atypical" *mutakallim*.[3] And then there are the contrasts between Maimonides, especially his critical response as expressed in his *Eight Chapters*[4] to the rational law teaching of Saadia in the opening pages of "Law of Reason." It is worth observing that Lerner's notes never suggest that Strauss references explicitly *Eight Chapters* in this seminar. Instead, he cites only the introduction (*hakdamah*) and the first volume of the *Mishneh Torah* and explicitly cites only three chapters from the *Guide of the Perplexed*.[5]

Because this seminar is a conversation with a somewhat general audience at the University of Chicago's Hillel House, many of the subtleties found in "Law of Reason" about the rational law background and Halevi's unique stance are set aside or merely alluded to. Having said that, Ibn Daud seems to be identified with the rational law tradition from which Halevi departs quite subtly. More broadly than as regards rational law, the *Exalted Faith* contains strands of the Mu'tazilite *kalām* tradition together with Aristotelian ones.[6] Strauss appears to be alluding to the former when he distinguishes between *mitzvot* or laws with "known reasons" as opposed to laws with "unknown reasons." The latter, exemplified by animal sacrifice as practiced in the Temple in Jerusalem, by virtue of the unknown character of their reasons, seek to instill "full obedience." It is this that Abraham's binding of Isaac is meant to exemplify.

When Strauss[7] turns from Ibn Daud to Maimonides in the second paragraph, he appeals to a responsum that Maimonides sent to the "Rabbis of Southern France" in which he claimed to have "given reasons for *all*[8] the *mitzvot*," evidently in the *Guide*.[9] Although it might be difficult to confirm that Maimonides gives reasons for every last *mitzvah*, we can at least confirm that he takes the opposite approach to those who have a sickness in their souls that leads them to embrace things that are irrational or meaningless.[10] Maimonides's claim regarding the *Guide* appears at first glance to be partially opposed to Ibn Daud's *kalām* reference to laws with "unknown reasons"—though "unknown reasons" remain reasons nonetheless. According to Strauss, in his *Mishneh Torah* Maimonides echoes the rational law tradition's contrast between "rational commandments" (*mitzvot sichliot*) and "proclaimed commandments" (*mitzvot shim'iot*).[11] Proclaimed commandments are sometimes referred to as "non-rational" or "irrational" commandments. Despite echoing this pairing of commandments in the *Mishneh Torah*, according to Strauss in "Law of Reason,"

Maimonides undercuts it in *Eight Chapters*, chap. 6, and in *Guide* 2.33, when he identifies "the first two propositions [in the Decalogue as] . . . rational," while the rest are "generally accepted," on the one hand, and "traditional opinions," on the other.[12] Of course, those first two "propositions" refer to what theologians would dub God's existence and nature, and their status as "commandments" has long been debated in Judaism and beyond. In the *Guide* and *Eight Chapters*, then, the primary opposition regarding commandments proper is between generally accepted and traditional opinions or laws; in Ibn Daud, Saadia, and evidently even the *Mishneh Torah*, the contrast, following the Mu'tazilite *kalām*, is between rational and proclaimed. The moniker "rational" in both the *Guide* and *Eight Chapters* is reserved for rationally demonstrable claims such as that God exists. Maimonides's more considered rejection of the traditional opposition between rational and proclaimed laws should neither be ignored, nor should it be interpreted to suggest that he intends to denigrate "generally accepted" opinions or laws. That laws traditionally identified as "rational" are labeled "generally accepted" by Maimonides must be squared with his insistence to the Rabbis of Southern France that *all* the laws have reasons. That a law cannot be demonstrated does not mean that it cannot serve a useful (and in that limited sense "rational") purpose.

The heading of paragraph 3 is "Traditional religion"—in other words, the following explains the underlying traditional rationale for denying that laws have reasons. As Strauss puts it, "Knowing reasons leads men to argue." To eliminate disagreement, it appears to at least some of the rabbis that one shouldn't seek the reasons for any of the commandments. Unquestioning obedience is what "proclaimed" or "irrational" or "traditional laws" or *ḥuqqim* most obviously demand. The exemplar of this pole in law are Abraham's binding of Isaac and the laws concerning Temple sacrifice. Here, Strauss references the difficulty in explaining "every particular difference" as opposed to the "principle" (1). This contrast seems to allude to *Guide* 3.26's contrast between knowledge of the generalities or universals of the law and of the particulars—especially in the case of the *ḥuqqim* (statutes, as opposed to the *mishpatim*, judgments).[13] On the one hand, in *Guide* 3.32, the famous divine ruse chapter, Maimonides seems to anticipate a time when sacrifices will be transcended—to which Strauss alludes without citation of the *Guide*—literally, Maimonides "depreciates the significance of the sacrifices"; on the other hand, he devotes an entire volume of the *Mishneh Torah* (*Korbanot*) to envisioning the reconstitution of the Temple service. The biblical teaching on the sacrificial service stands as "protection" against the "eternal danger" posed by "paganism" (1). Evidently, Maimonides is not sanguine about how widespread or long-lasting wisdom will be in the "'days of the Messiah.'"

Strauss turns somewhat abruptly to what he characterizes over the course of paragraph 4 as Maimonides's "Mosaisation of Judaism." One could perhaps view the first three paragraphs of these seminar notes as introductory. Here then would begin the seminar proper. Strauss begins with the clear privileging of Mosaic prophecy in "Laws concerning the Foundations of the Torah," that is, in the first part of the first volume of the *Mishneh Torah*. According to Strauss, Maimonides had precedent for this "Mosaisation" in the Midrashic or Aggadic work called *Mishnat Rabbi Eliezer*, with the noteworthy difference that Rabbi Eliezer acknowledged the superiority of the biblical patriarchs over Moses in certain respects. And Rabbi Eliezer was not alone, so too did Ibn Daud, according to Strauss, note that the move from patriarchs to Moses was not a "progress of revelation." Nevertheless, Maimonides begins his code of law by stating somewhat hyperbolically the superiority of Mosaic prophecy over all others. In *Guide* 2.35, which is cited here in Lerner's notes, Maimonides seems to say something similar in pronouncing the uniqueness of Mosaic prophecy, uniqueness that is so great that Maimonides insists none of what follows about prophecy will refer to Moses, though in 2.39, he explains "why" Moses is unique: because he is the legislating prophet. The emphasis on Moses's uniqueness and superiority seems intended to reinforce the authoritativeness of the Law. Despite claims to the contrary, Maimonides cannot stop talking about Moses—often in ways that seem to undercut the claim of superiority —sometimes indirectly but often not. The opening three paragraphs of Lerner's notes on Strauss's seminar seemed to center at least as much on law as they did on Abraham. In the binding of Isaac, Abraham exemplifies unquestioning obedience to God's decree or law. Yet whether God or law must only be obeyed or may be questioned is what Abraham also exemplifies. From the start, we cannot but suspect that there is more to Abrahamic prophecy than Maimonides's insistence on the uniqueness of legislating prophecy would seem to allow. Indeed, it is hard to escape the sense that Abraham is the secret hero of the *Guide*, despite the greater authoritativeness of law.

Still in paragraph 4, Strauss underscores the nonlegal character of Abraham's mission.[14] He uses only "eloquent speeches"[15] rather than "compulsion."[16] As Strauss puts it compactly: "Moses brings the law to perfect society. In [the] Abrahamic order, no society is involved." Here the

Abrahamic order is presented as presocial and in that respect imperfect in comparison with the Mosaic order. Citing again the *Mishneh Torah* (MT) volume one, now "Laws concerning Idolatry," Strauss articulates Maimonides's three stages: family, priests, and the "few who understand." Already here, though, the merely presocial role of Abraham is in doubt. The seeds of said doubt are sown more deeply by reference to "predecessors of Abraham" who are obviously what is meant by "the few who understand." Those predecessors lived "in idolatrous communit[ies] without protesting." Abraham's predecessors include Aristotle! Consequently, the motto that greets the reader of both the MT and the *Guide*, quoting Abraham, "In the name of the Lord, God of the World" (Gen. 21:33) references the "God of the Cosmos" rather than the God of Creation. We find the basis of our suspicions that the superiority of the Law over Abrahamic questioning is not what it seemed at first. Abraham is not merely presocial. He fits well Aristotle's description of the human being beyond law as either a beast or a god.[17]

What we have begun to suspect about Abraham is confirmed in paragraph 5. Abraham, at least Maimonides's Abraham, will come to exemplify not only speech rather than compulsion but also "speculation" (*iy[y]un*). Consequently, Strauss begins this paragraph with the acknowledgment that "in one way," that is, in comparison with the legislating prophet, Abraham appears less than the "consummation" of Judaism and as "subordinate" to Moses. Yet the mottoes tell another story. Here, Lerner's notes are especially succinct: "Problem of law: law is superior to instruction of clan. What is the function of law?" Why the former is a problem of law is not immediately evident. After all, the superiority of law over instruction of [the] clan stems from the fact that the law is political, while the clan is subpolitical.[18] Could it be that though law must possess superior authority than clan rules that which rules the clan still possesses a certain superiority due to the greater flexibility of a human ruler of a clan? The much larger question (rather than "problem") is "what is the function of law?": the question that the rest of this paragraph (para. 5) as well as the following single-sentence parenthetical paragraph are concerned with. The answer is somewhat startling. Maimonides elaborates his answer in "Laws concerning the Foundations of the Torah" with the most philosophic opening to any code of Jewish law. Strauss starts by anticipating the conclusion with reference to chapter 4 (of "Laws c. the Found. of the Law"), where Maimonides invokes rabbinic authority that law is a small thing and the Account of the Beginning and the Account of

Interpretative Essay

the Chariot are a big thing.[19] Ultimately, how one interprets this rabbinic claim hangs on the meaning of each term of the contrast. We will eventually have to ask ourselves whether the rabbis consider these two accounts as something distinct from the Law rather than its culmination. That Maimonides considers them distinct is readily apparent. Strauss does not flinch from the trajectory set already by his identification of Abraham with Aristotle. Chapters 1 and 2 of "Laws concerning the Foundations of the Torah" contain the Account of the Chariot (*Ma'aseh Merkabah*), which is traditionally identified with Ezekiel chapters 1 and 10; chapters 3 and 4 contain the Account of the Beginning (*Ma'aseh Bereshit*), which is traditionally identified with Genesis 1 through 3. Not surprisingly, because in keeping with the opening identification of the former with divine science (or metaphysics) and the latter with natural science in *Guide* part 1, introduction (Pines, 6), Strauss states parenthetically that Maimonides's Account of the Chariot "summarize[s]" Aristotle's *Metaphysics* and his Account of the Beginning "summarize[s]" Aristotle's *Physics*. Some may quibble about this identification of natural science and divine science with those of Aristotle. However, evidence abounds that this is what Maimonides has in mind, so long as one acknowledges that, for example, the very opening of "Laws concerning the Foundations of the Torah" begins with a variation on an Aristotelian argument, the so-called necessary existence argument.[20]

Following Maimonides, Strauss identifies the two accounts with the Talmudic vision of *Pardes*.[21] As Strauss explains parenthetically, *Pardes*, which has come into our language as paradise and which clearly references a or the garden, will come by the end of this paragraph to bespeak the identification of the Garden of Eden, that to which the pious Jew aspires to return,[22] with speculation about the God of the Cosmos. This means that when the rabbis claimed that "knowledge of what is permitted and what forbidden" is "a small thing," but the Account of the Beginning and the Account of the Chariot are "a great thing," they were divining the superiority of speculation over the law as end. In effect, the "function of law" is to make "social life possible." It is a means and not the end.

Paragraph 6 consists of a one-sentence parenthesis, which confirms the aim of paragraph 5, namely, the identification of the true human end as speculative knowledge, that is, knowledge of the God of the Cosmos. Whether it was intentional on Lerner's part or not, this single-sentence paragraph is the middle of these eleven paragraphs of notes on Strauss's seminar:

"(*El olam* = 177 = *Gan Eden*. True knowledge is knowledge of El olam.)"[23]

Paragraph 7 is the first moment in this seminar that Strauss focuses with care on a chapter of the *Guide*—the chapter on Abraham, 3.24. Previous *Guide* citations (of 2.35 and 39) were to place Abraham in relation to Moses or to law. Lerner offers as Strauss's "chapter heading" "M.N., III 24—*akedah*." And the topic of this chapter is "trials," the first word of Lerner's second sentence. Trials seem according to a literal reading of the Bible intended to reveal something about a human being to God. That is, of course, incompatible with the divine omniscience ascribed to God by traditional Jewish theology.[24] Rather "God knew, but others didn't know." Trials teach lessons to human beings; God does not learn anything new. There are two lessons.[25] First is a "lesson for all men," the lesson of the *akedah*, that is, of obedient love of God. It may be significant that, at least initially, Strauss does not mention the content of that lesson. Perhaps, though, that is merely because it has been the clearer of the two lessons taught by the example of Abraham throughout this seminar.

The second lesson (or notion) is "demonstration of certainty" about a "prophetic vision." Maimonides writes with unusual ambiguity in this moment of the *Guide*. First, he refers to what comes to "prophets" (*anbiyā'*) being viewed by them as true,[26] then to the generic Hebrew phrase "*in a dream and in a vision*" (*biḥalom vebimar'eh*) and finally as "*a vision of prophecy*" (*mar'eh hanabu'ah*). We would not mention these details, passed over by Strauss, if he had not confirmed so flat-footedly the striking conclusion to this paragraph that Abraham's vision in the *akedah* was "an act of imagination, not of reason." This is the shocking significance of this moment of the *Guide*, which runs deeply counter to previous accounts of Abraham's prophecy, making this one of those startling reversals that are all too common in the *Guide* and especially in conjunction with prophecy. At the risk of repeating too much I quote Lerner's seminar notes in full: "How did Abraham receive commandment? Through [an] angel, not directly from God. *Every* prophetic vision and audition led to action—an act of imagination, not of reason."[27] In *Guide* 2.36, Maimonides set forth the paradigmatic account of prophecy as overflow from the Active Intellect to the human intellect and then to the imagination. Subsequently, this peak seems to elude nearly all if not all prophets. In *Guide* 2.41, a *vision* of prophecy appears to be opposed to a *dream* as overflow to reason is opposed to overflow to the imagination.[28] And in *Guide* 2.45, dreams are clearly treated as lower than visions. Out of the eleven degrees of prophecy, the lowest and first two are discounted (note that Moses appears in his early career in these ranks), the third degree through the seventh are prophetic *dreams* (very surprisingly the seventh rank—the middle of the third through eleventh ranks—includes Isaiah's Account of the Chariot, treated at length in *Guide* 3.1–7) and the eighth through eleventh degrees are prophetic *visions*. Every example of a prophetic vision (but one) is had by Abraham. This makes the affirmation of the merely imaginative and practical nature exemplified by Abraham's prophetic vision in the *akedah* all the more surprising. There is a simple explanation for all this: the *akedah* does quite literally involve an angel (Gen. 22:11, "Then an angel of the Lord called to him from heaven: 'Abraham! Abraham!'"). Whether a vision or a dream from a cherub or an angel—from reason or imagination—the prophet views all such experiences as a "certain truth" (ḥaqq yaqīn).

Despite the imaginative character of Abraham's vision of the angel, Strauss turns from Maimonides to musings about our own ways of thinking about this event. In paragraph 8, he raises the question, "Is [the] Abraham story a symbol or an historical fact?" From this moment forward Strauss seems to oscillate between Maimonides and contemporary views on the matter of "religious experience." After all, that is the baggage that his audience is likely to bring to this seminar. They are the kinds of issues that he contended with in *Philosophy and Law* and that would recur at least in the background of his autobiographical preface to the Spinoza book.[29]

To repeat, the original question was, is the *akedah* "a symbol or an historical fact?" The traditional answer is that "it is a fact. But what about modern theology?" (para. 8). Over the course of paragraphs 9 and 10, Strauss will muse about modern theology and its concern for "religious experience" (para. 10). In doing so, of course, he repudiates the contemporary (post-Enlightenment) prejudice in favor of the superiority of "modern theology." The theoretical question implied by the opposition between symbol and fact is a problem that Maimonides "is aware of." We should not presuppose that as a premodern thinker he is naïve about the inherited or traditional character of the revealed sources.[30]

In paragraph 9, Strauss engages the contrast between Abraham's questioning of God in the case of Sodom and Gomorrah and Abraham's obedience in the case of the *akedah*. We have already seen that obedient love fits with the authority of the Law, and that introducing reasons especially in connection with the Law may well give rise to disagreements. At this point, it is worth recalling Strauss's observation that Abraham's mission is presocial—and to that extent it is prelegal. It would be a mistake to assume that the biblical Abraham's questioning of God—no matter how readily it might remind us of "speculation" (*iyyun*)—is a foreshadowing of theoretical speculation from within the Bible itself.[31]

The initial contrast between Abraham's actions in relation to Sodom and the *akedah* in paragraph 9 is between a context in which he argues and one in which he does not. In the case of Sodom, Abraham has "no attachment" to those to be punished by God. In the case of the *akedah*, he loves his only son more than himself. This willingness to obey God's command proves Abraham's "absolute obedience to God's revealed will." Yet that willingness to obey absolutely does not result in a Stoic attitude toward all humankind. Abraham is willing to give up his son as the greatest act of sacrifice of which he is capable for the one thing he loves even more than his son, namely, God. That does not mean that he will stand by while injustices are committed. His pleading on behalf of the potentially just among the Sodomites does not stem from love for them so much as it stems from "a divination of the unrevealed will of God." Why God's will is revealed in the case of the binding but unrevealed in the case of Sodom may stem from the difference between a command and a punishment. A command tells Abraham to bind and sacrifice his only son. The punishment of Sodom is, till God performs the act of punishment, not yet a revelation of a will but merely a feared punishment.

In staying God's "hand" from the most severe punishment, Abraham "appeal[s] to God's love" (para. 9). God's leniency regarding Sodom is "not simply orthodox," it reveals some slippage in absolute obedience. This gap or wedge in obedience Strauss here relates not to philosophic speculation but to "mysticism." Aside from God's love, there is Abraham's "certain[ty]" that God is "merciful and just." It is this conviction that spurs Abraham on to argue with God. This is not the height of speculation. The opposition between obedience and arguing—though it was used so artfully by Strauss to link the case of Sodom to Abraham's role in both the *Mishneh Torah* and the *Guide* as someone engaged in philosophic speculation like Aristotle—is not as clear an opposition as that between law and philosophy. Abraham thirsts for justice, not for the truth. As Maimonides shows in *Guide* 3.22 in connection with Job, it is not until Job sees the matter of his own suffering through a theoretical lens that he can grasp it properly. Seen through the lens of justice, the suffering of the innocent can hardly be accepted. Abraham's argument with God in the name of justice ultimately falls within what will become the Law.

In paragraph 10, the previous allusions to "modern theology" (in para. 8) and "mysticism" (in para. 9) reappear in the guise of Martin Buber's assertion that Judaism is at its heart "religious experience." In the view of "modern theology" Sodom and the *akedah* are viewed as symbols. Within this interpretive matrix, what we learn from Judaism depends on our "direct religious experience" of the meaning of such symbols. Merely inherited reports will not suffice, even if they testify to the reasonableness of the laws. In contrast, Maimonides interprets Deuteronomy 4:6[32] as upholding his view that there are reasons for all the commandments. For Maimonides, obeying these laws has a rational purpose understood as the well-being of society. For Buber, only religious experience can inspire or motivate us to obey. Subsequently, Lerner's Strauss says compactly: "The Sodom story bears on this and balances the *akedah*." He then proceeds to recount how matters might have occurred differently in relation to the *akedah* without divine intervention (or grace). The antecedent of "this" in the sentence quoted just above is not clear. It seems to refer to the disagreement between Maimonides and Buber over reason and religious experience, but I cannot be certain. How that relates to the balancing of the Sodom story and the *akedah* is far from obvious.

The concluding paragraph, paragraph 11, returns to the framing question about the rationality of law. We recapitulate the numerous overlapping but not synonymous options with which we initially addressed the rationality of law: known reasons vs. unknown reasons; rational laws vs. proclaimed laws; generally accepted opinions vs. traditional laws. In retrospect, one begins to wonder whether Buber's late modern confidence in the superiority of "religious experience" is not an odd and very remote effect of the ancient divisions at least between rational and nonrational laws. A striking result of the irrationalism of late modern thought is that such thought appears on surer footing when dealing with the miraculous and mystifying aspects of Judaism, such as the sacrificial service. After all, what is it that late moderns seem to long for but some sort of reenchantment of the world after centuries of modernity's disenchantment?

In paragraph 11, Strauss turns back to the opposition between Aristotle and the Law. In the Garden of Eden, "Adam has understanding to understand God's command." This biblical response to philosophy hints once again at the gap between "speculation" (*iyyun*) and the biblical view of human understanding. According to the latter, we understand in order to obey. Even if we argue, our argument should not be with the order of the whole—but in the name of the righteousness that the Law came eventually to serve. Whether the order of the whole is providential down to the last particular is assumed; however, it is also "God's will" that "not everything ... is revealed." In contrast, in Aristotle's *Metaphysics* to be divine the divine does not concern itself with every particular.

Paragraph 11 is punctuated by Strauss's assertion: "There is a reasonable transition from M[aimonides]'s way of looking at things to the Bible's. Adam in Paradise [viz., in the Garden] was trans-moral. Morality is a means to recover the paradise." Maimonides's way of looking at Adam in paradise is presented in *Guide* 1.2. The view of Adam presented there couldn't be further from the suggestion that he has understanding to obey. On the contrary, his understanding is presented as originally theoretical. His failure is in following his desires for imaginary goods. His punishment is that he should become obsessed with practical and moral matters. Morality is a means to recover paradise because human beings require society in order to engage in "speculation" (*iyyun*).

Although morality is a means to the best life, "M[aimonides] denies the rational basis of moral principles."[34] Maimonides's teaching about the rationality of law is not that law is itself inherently rational or demonstrable nor is it that law is somehow possessed in advance or intuitively by all human beings in their reason. Rather, suddenly following Plato, our highest perfection is the perfection of our rational soul. According to Strauss, "to understand, man must behave tolerably." This could mean that a minimum of morality as established by the law is required to be able to engage in speculation, or it could perhaps mean that a philosopher must behave tolerably, lest he face the fate of Socrates. What "behaving tolerably" might mean is exemplified by the problem of Socrates. From a certain point of view, he behaved far more justly than any other man, but was his behavior "tolerable"?—evidently not in the eyes of Athens. Again the compactness of these seminar notes precludes certainty about Strauss's intention: "Rational proof is possible." Presumably, he means that it can be proven rationally that behaving tolerably is a requirement if one wants to speculate. Although *rational* proof of the necessity of "behaving tolerably" can be produced, in addition, "man's body requires society," which requires habits. And the perfection of the body also requires virtues.[35] As Strauss brings out more at the end of these notes than the beginning, "M[aimonides] does not say that morality is rational."[36] Indeed, in comparison even with Aristotle, he seems to demote morality as it might relate to the soul. Maimonides's demotion is the necessary complement to his historically unprecedented elevation of theoretical inquiry in

Judaism. Despite this departure from the Law, Maimonides preserves the "overlap" between the morality he outlines and that of the Bible. When Strauss concludes by asserting "common-sense morality has two separate roots," he appears to be revisiting his own claim that the West exists in the tension between Athens and Jerusalem.[37]

Notes

1. It is worth acknowledging that Lerner's notes reference only "Sodom" and not Gomorrah. Perhaps that's because these are Lerner's seminar notes, so that "Sodom" could be an abbreviation of "Sodom and Gomorrah." Another possible consideration is that all the action directly connected with Lot in the biblical story appears to take place in Sodom.

2. Leo Strauss, *Persecution and the Art of Writing* (Glencoe, IL: Free Press, 1952; Chicago: University of Chicago Press, 1980), 95–141. Note that "The Law of Reason" was originally published in the *Proceedings of the American Academy for Jewish Research* 13 (1943): 47–96.

3. Strauss, "Law of Reason in the *Kuzari*," in *Persecution and the Art of Writing* (Glencoe, IL: Free Press, 1952; Chicago: University of Chicago Press, 1980), 138n136.

4. As the introduction to Maimonides's commentary on the portion of the Talmud called *Pirqei Avot* (Ethics of the Fathers), the *Eight Chapters*, like the *Guide*, is written in Judeo-Arabic. There are reasons to believe that, despite having been written before the *Mishneh Torah*, the *Commentary on the Mishnah* may have had a more elite audience than the *Mishneh Torah*. Among the most obvious reasons is that the *Mishneh Torah* is written in more accessible Mishnaic Hebrew; the *Commentary on the Mishnah* is written in Judeo-Arabic. See *Eight Chapters*, chap. 6 in *The Ethical Writings of Maimonides*, ed. and trans. Raymond L. Weiss and Charles Butterworth (New York: New York University Press, 1975; New York, Dover Publications, 1983).

5. Those three chapters are on Moses (2.35 and 39) and on Abraham (also 2.39 and 3.24). The reference to 1.39 in paragraph 4 is a typo. See note 12 below. Since this piece is based on Ralph Lerner's notes on this seminar, we should not infer too much from the presence of these citations. The author of this interpretative essay cannot know whether these citations were given by Strauss or supplied by Lerner.

6. See Terrence Kleven's review of T. A. M. (Resianne) Fontaine, *In Defence of Judaism: Abraham Ibn Daud. Sources and Structure of "ha-Emunah ha-Ramah"* (Assen: Van Gorcum, 1990), in *Interpretation* 25 (1998) 3: 331–65.

7. From this point forward, I will stop inserting references to Ralph Lerner as notetaker, except where it seems necessary.

8. Lerner's report of Strauss's emphasis.

9. In keeping with contemporary typographic conventions, I italicize things that Lerner underlines. The responsum Strauss appears to be referenc-

ing is the "Letter on Astrology" in Ralph Lerner, *The Empire of Light* (Chicago: University of Chicago Press, 2000), 178-87, esp. 180.

10. In *Guide* 3.31, Maimonides inveighs against those Jews who resist any and all attempts to understand the reasons for the commandments. Cf. what appears to be Alfarabi's characterization of the Ash'arite *kalām* in *Enumeration of the Sciences*, chap. 5 on dialectical theology with Maimonides's characterization of it in *Guide* 3.17.

11. Or *shim'iyot*. To my knowledge, the closest Maimonides comes to affirming this rational law opposition would be his discussion of the Noahide law in the final volume of the code, *The Book of Judges*, Laws concerning Kings and their Wars, chaps. 8 through 9. For authors who present Maimonides as a natural law (essentially the same as a "rational law") theorist, contra Strauss, see David Novak, *Natural Law in Judaism* (Cambridge: Cambridge University Press, 1998), esp. chaps. 4 and 6, and "Maimonides' Theory of Noahide Law," in *The Image of the Non-Jew in Judaism* (Cambridge: Cambridge University Press, 2019), 153-175; and Jonathan Jacobs, *Law, Reason, and Morality in Medieval Jewish Philosophy* (Oxford: Oxford University Press, 2010).

12. "Law of Reason," in *Persecution*, 96-97n4.

13. Strauss does not reference 3.26 here. This contrast echoes loudly the contrast between natural political right and conventional political right in Aristotle, *Nicomachean Ethics* 5.7.

14. Either Strauss stated or Lerner inserted the mistaken "M.N. [Moreh Nebukhim], I 39" when the correct reference would be "M.N., II 39."

15. Citing *The Guide of the Perplexed*, ed. Shlomo Pines (Chicago: University of Chicago Press, 1963), 379.

16. By the time we reach 3.29, which is obviously correlated numerically to 2.39, Abraham's speeches are characterized by reference to the MT as "feeble preaching" (Pines, 517)!

17. Aristotle, *Politics* 1.2, end.

18. See Plato, *Laws* 3, esp. 680d-681c.

19. In Laws concerning the Foundations of the Law, chap. 4, sect. 13. See footnote 21 for the Talmudic basis for this.

20. Although strictly speaking this argument is usually traced only back to Avicenna, it is a simple enough argument to be compatible at the same time with the sense of *Metaphysics* 12.6 (as opposed to chaps. 7 and 8, the arguments from motion).

21. Again, this is from Laws concerning the Foundations of the Torah, chap. 4, sect. 13, here referencing BT, Ḥagigah 14.

22. See Strauss, "Progress or Return?" in *Jewish Philosophy and the Crisis of Modernity*, ed. Kenneth Hart Green (Albany: State University of New York Press, 1997), 87-136.

23. The numerological value of God of the World (*El olam*) and Garden of Eden (*Gan Eden*) is 177.

24. In his outline of the *Guide* in the Pines edition, Strauss summarizes the relevant chapters from the fifth section of the *Guide*, the one on particular

providence, in this way: "3. The philosophic arguments against omniscience (III 16).... 5. Jewish views on omniscience and Maimonides' discourse on this subject (III 19–21)."

25. Pines has literally "two great notions that are fundamental principles of the Law" (500).

26. Here Pines takes an unhelpful liberty by adding the word "revelation."

27. The italics here are mine.

28. This seems to confirm a distinction Maimonides drew early on between an angel as the imagination as opposed to a cherub as the intellect (2.6, 264–65, and 2.12, 280).

29. Strauss, *Philosophy and Law*, trans. Eve Adler (Albany: State University of New York Press, 1995); Strauss, "Preface to *Spinoza's Critique of Religion*," in *Liberalism Ancient and Modern* (New York: Basic Books, 1968; Ithaca: Cornell University Press, 1989), 224–59.

30. A strong piece of evidence in support of this view are the anachronisms in the lineage Maimonides presents in the introduction to the *Mishneh Torah* for the chain of custody of the Oral Law. That is, part of the confirmation of the authoritativeness of the Talmud is the claim that this chain is traceable back to Moses for the revelation of the Oral Law together with the Written Law, which is the Torah. That chain has noticeable anachronisms in it.

31. Although this view is common in Jewish circles, I don't believe that it is what Strauss intends in his account of Abraham as engaging in speculation in paragraph 5. I would accept such an interpretation of Abraham if I really believed that what the rabbis of the Talmud meant by the Account of the Beginning and of the Chariot was Aristotle's *Physics* and *Metaphysics*, respectively.

32. Strauss quotes from earlier in the biblical verse: "This is your wisdom in the eyes of the nations." Maimonides in *Guide* 3.31, which we cited earlier as inveighing against fideism, references the end of this verse in favor of the notion that God has reasons for every commandment: "'*Which shall hear all these statutes [ḥuqqim] and say: Surely this great community is a wise and understanding community.*' Thus it states explicitly that even all the *statutes [ḥuqqim]* will show to all the nations that they have been given with *wisdom and understanding*."

34. This in a sentence is the upshot of Strauss's "Law of Reason in the Kuzari." See especially Strauss, *Persecution and the Art of Writing*, 114.

35. See *Guide* 3.27–8.

36. See note 12 above.

37. See "Jerusalem and Athens: Some Preliminary Reflections," in *Studies in Platonic Political Philosophy*, ed. Thomas L. Pangle (Chicago: University of Chicago Press, 1983), 147–73, esp. 147, and "Progress or Return," 105–11. I thank Svetozar Minkov for reminding me that Strauss reproduces nearly this exact language of "common-sense morality has two separate roots" in an even more revealing comparison than that of Jerusalem and Athens in *What Is Po-*

litical Philosophy? (Chicago: University of Chicago Press, 1988), 166–67. See also Joshua Parens, "Strauss on Maimonides's Secretive Political Science," in *Leo Strauss's Defense of the Philosophic Life: Reading "What Is Political Philosophy?"*, ed. Rafael Major (Chicago: University of Chicago Press, 2013), esp. 127–28.

PART FOUR

Transcript 4

LEO STRAUSS, ON SPINOZA (C. 1959)

Editorial note: The following is the transcription of a typescript found in Leo Strauss Papers, Box 18, Folder 17, Special Collections Research Center, University of Chicago Library. On the basis of the content, one can surmise that this transcript is from the period of Strauss's seminar on Spinoza offered in the autumn quarter of 1959 at the Political Science Department, the University of Chicago. Significantly, this is also the period in which Strauss was working on the autobiographical preface to his 1930 *Spinoza's Critique of Religion*.[1] In this regard, the allusion to the question of *bontà* in Machiavelli and Cicero (p. 4 of the transcript below) is crucial. Strauss refers to the same point in his 1959 course on Cicero.[2] Numbers in the angle brackets refer to the page numbers of the typescript. Additions are all in curly brackets. The underlinings in typescript have been replaced with italics.

<1> Choice of subject: not to repeat what I said in the print: fresh study: I just happen to have studied Spinoza again.

Status of political theory: alleged failure of original theory of democracy (democracy as *the* state of virtue and reason) but: electoral apathy as support of democracy; elites (oligarchies) an indispensable element of democracy. More fundamental: facts ≠ values → political theory = ideology.

What was the meaning of the *original* theory of democracy? Spinoza the first *philosopher* of political democracy.

I) General description of his political philosophy: rejection of all earlier political philosophy—in particular Aristotle Plato—*the*[3] predecessor praised by him: Machiavelli (politician ≠ philosopher). *Tractatus Politicus* I = *Prince* XV: realistic doctrine, not utopian, men as they are. But also: Hobbes (state of nature, right of nature ≠ law of nature)[4] → by nature right = might. Yet: liberal democracy—how? his Ethics (Stoa)[5] --- but this is too general. His political books. Difficulty: the one which is completed is *Tractatus Theologico-Politicus*, and his *Tractatus Politicus* incomplete.

II) *Tractatus Theologico-Politicus*—biblical context, Christian context. Typical: modern thought secularized biblical thought. But what does secularization mean? Secularization of monasteries—but secularization of thought? Surely a modification: a) corruption b) perfection (cf. Hegel: reconciliation of the gospel with the world ≠ original antithesis) → what is the character of the secularization effected by Spinoza? Is it corruption or perfection?

Extreme biblicism (Socinianism): but the bible contains *the* saving truth which is super rational: its revealed and hence supra-rational character guaranteed by miracles. No speculative truth. Only the moral teaching authoritative → God demands only charity → the sin is <2> persecution—the right conduct is tolerance, in particular also for philosophers[6] → *Liberalism* (the right to think what one pleases and to say what one thinks) → everyone equally the judge in speculative matters— no hierarchy (no ecclesiastical authority)—if everyone is autonomous in matters spiritual, all the more in matters temporal → *democracy*.[7] This teaching is theological, based on authority of the bible. That charity is necessary and sufficient condition of salvation, for the bliss is not known to reason. Hence: charity as demanded by bible possible only in the spirit of *obedience*. It is on this ground that Spinoza demands the separation of philosophy from theology: philosophy → speculative truth or simply the truth—theology → charity is a spirit of obedience. Rationality ≠ obedience (*Tractatus Politicus* II 20). Close inspection shows that this simple juxtaposition of philosophy and theology is not possible: philosophy lays claim to the whole realm of truth. On the other hand demand for charity rests on speculative premises and those premises as much a part of bible as command of charity itself → the 7 dogmas in chapter 14 (existence of God, providence etc.): limitation of freedom of thought and speech. But. freedom of *interpretation*[8] of these dogmas --- matter must be *called* "God." And democracy requires a sovereign in the most radical Hobbian sense— charity demands unqualified obedience to sovereign (XIX 22ff.) in matters spiritual as well as temporal—but: the sovereign himself cannot possibly *obey* (→ he cannot possibly be charitable).

III) Biblical teaching confirmed by miracles—but miracles are impossible and/or not knowable → revelation is impossible for it is a miracle—God does not have organs of speech → no verbal inspiration—<3> one cannot even in strict language speak of God having a *mind*;[9] and Bible does not contain authentic records of revelation (Moses not author of Pentateuch = no authentic record of the alleged miracle of revelation)—and textual difficulties: bible poorly compiled and poorly preserved → bible does not possess any authority. Intervening stage: the moral teaching of bible (= charity) authenticated by moral character of prophets—but this presupposes that moral teaching bible is *true* moral teaching. Yet true moral and political teaching *follows* from true *speculative*[10] principles—and bible sets forth an untrue speculative teaching (providence: God rewards the just and punishes the unjust but in fact one fate meets the just and the unjust; no traces of divine justice are found except where just *men* rule) → the biblical moral teaching ≠ the rational moral teaching. While not being true it is eminently useful—but in what way? E.g. do not resist evil (VII 31-34) only for corrupt societies—"turn the other cheek": incompatible with civil society → need for national religion—hate thine enemy → biblical teaching of some usefulness for private people, for people not engaged in political activity (on the death-bed and in churches): or rather: what Spinoza calls the biblical teaching is useful as long as the authority of the bible is recognized, as a protection against theological persecution.

Clearest formulation of Spinoza's position is supplied by an equation which he first suggests and then retracts:

No charity proper: charity proper (to love the other like oneself) is impossible. But even if it were possible it would be possible only <4> for

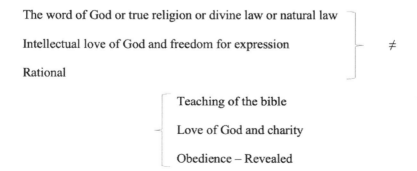

Figure 1. A diagram of Spinoza's equation. Source: Created by the author.

a few, it would be of no political significance—it has validity only on the deathbed and in churches (*Tractatus Politicus* I 5)—it is an untrue and misleading teaching (= Machiavelli)

Summary: Spinoza's *Tractatus Theologico-Politicus* teaching a secularized version of the bible which consciously falsifies the bible—it presents a break with the bible in the disguise of a perfection of the bible—a conscious transformation of biblical teaching or use of biblical teaching for non-biblical ends. Cooperates with sincere simpletons.

The doctrine that man can achieve his bliss by charity is in Spinoza a *kalon pseudos* {noble lie} in the Platonic sense. Fundamental kinship with Plato: the divine or natural law → intellectual love of God—but this a preserve[11] of the few (V 35-36, 40, 44). Natural inequality → *contempt for the vulgar*[12] [frequently plebs in derogatory meaning (IV 35; XVII 44, 103; XVIII 11, 23, 25; XIX 40; XX 8, 21, 31, 33, 42; but: *Tractatus Politicus* VII 27)][13] → *destruction of the base of democracy*[14] → contempt for politics: the rational life possible in every society (XVI 34n.) (government of the solitary: divine law has nothing to do with human laws. [*Tractatus Theologico-Politicus* IV]).[15]

Difference between Plato's and Spinoza's kalon pseudos {noble lie in Greek – ed.}: social hierarchy =[16] natural hierarchy—but more simply *Phaedo* 82b justice and moderation =[17] the virtues common to all classes in the *Republic* which do not presuppose specific physis {nature} (cf. *bontà* in Machiavelli - Cicero) → moderation replaced by charity (→ "the severe and restrictive virtues"[18] replaced by *humanité*[19]—Burke)

But agreement with Hobbes (justice and charity *De Homine* XIII 9) yet in Hobbes this is serious—for he rejects the theoretical ideal and virtues = means of self-preservation (violent death) → Spinoza more in agreement with Plato than with Hobbes. Agreement with Kant, but in Kant impossibility of *theoria* → supremacy of moral virtue[20] <5> i.e. especially justice (different from happiness).—no esotericism. Difference from Plato in exoteric teaching → difference in esoteric teaching: intellectual love of God the theme of natural law = divine law—but for Spinoza this natural law is only a *human* law, a free human project—there is no natural law which men can transgress—for: no teleology.

IV) Since argument in favor of liberal democracy as hitherto discussed was based on theological teaching, what happens to liberal democracy? Spinoza rejects extreme Platonic suggestion (rule of philosophers and practically no freedom of speech for the non-philosophers) for the reason that the rule of philosophers is impossible (VII 79): the multitude of non-philosophers will never bow to the philosophers. But that multitude is in need of government, of compulsion, of law; yet it resents compulsion especially if it comes from equals [margin of the typescript: *Politikos* {Plato's *Statesman* – ed.}] (the unreasonable unreasonably regard the reasonable as their equals)—hence either fraudulent presentation of one or a few unreasonable men as superior, as gods or sent by gods, or else democracy—either untrue inequality (rule of priests) or acceptance of the untrue premise of equality—in the former case cooperation of the fraud from above (priestcraft) with the fanaticism of the many (V 20 - 25). Spinoza the *philosopher* rebels against the rule of priests → democracy, itself based on a crude doxa the only alternative to rule of priests open or disguised.

V) This is very sweeping: what about a strictly secular monarchy of oligarchy? Spinoza himself presents (*Tractatus Politicus*) what he regards as the best form of monarchy which is characterized by absence of established religion. He implies: a *republic* requires established religion and he indicates that if that religion is not indigenous (like the pagan state religions) but imported (like Christianity) <6> the teachers of that religion possess an independent authority dangerous to that of sovereign. (XVIII 25, XIX 29) → an indigenous established religion in oligarchic republic (limitation of freedom of speech) is a valid alternative to the rule of priests.

Spinoza disregards these possibilities for the following reasons: monarchies inferior to good republics; indigenous religion in republic out of the question now: one has to accept imported religion as a fact—by giving everyone the right to interpret the bible as he sees fit one prevents the rule of priests → the sufficient reason for democracy is *not* that it is the only alternative to the rule of priests. Spinoza's indication that democracy is the only alternative to the rule of priests foreshadows the demand for universal enlightenment as the basis of sound political order. But while he tends in this direction, he does not go so far: he is held back by the contemplative ideal (→ gulf between wise and vulgar). Cf. in this context Spinoza's Baconianism (Descartes) re science.

VI) The philosophic or the purely rational doctrine in the *Tractatus Politicus* (also in parts of the *Tractatus Theologico-Politicus*). Gulf between wise and vulgar—but: liberal democracy → Spinoza must have found a common ground for the wise and the vulgar (*Tractatus Politicus* I 7). Politics quest for *universal* laws ≠ traditional *lex naturalis* which is inapplicable, not realistic—universal laws which man cannot transgress—laws of *behavior*

(≠ duties derived from telos). Yet radical difference between behavior of the wise and behavior of the vulgar, between the law of reason and the law of irrational appetite → Spinoza prefers the latter (for:[21] "realism") but then doctrine not universal → can there be universal laws of behavior? Madmen.

VII) Basis: right = might—there is no natural law but only natural right—man has by nature the right to everything he pleases—every man equally. But this is true not only of men but of brutes <7> and inanimate beings as well → natural right has no human meaning. Yet not entirely: generally speaking men are stronger, especially if united than all other earthly beings → men can conquer nature (jus in naturam)—the only right on earth which counts is that of men. And: no right which is not backed by force → no rights of men which are not backed by the force of men, by the armed interests of men (≠[22] God) → all right is social right. Spinoza ≠ Hobbes: natural right remains intact → Spinoza's doctrine not legal; civitas is a *res naturalis* (≠[23] artificial body). → democracy: the greatest right of the greatest might =[24] the greatest number (*Tractatus Politicus* VII 18) /if they are enlightened/

VIII) Self-interest induces almost all men to prefer society to the state of nature—the interest in peace and security—those who reject peace and security are both foolish and few → the majority have the right and the might to compel them to submit to society. Everyone has equally the right to peace and security. But man wants more: happiness → right of each to pursue happiness as he sees happiness—this is not compatible with the same right of everyone else, especially if one considers also happiness of afterlife → such right only to the extent to which it is compatible with the same right of everyone else. All men are capable effectively to desire peace and security, at least through compulsion—and peace and security are objectively to the advantage of each—in this respect all men, the wise as well as the unwise, are equal. Peace and security is only the lower part of the highest good but it is a genuine part of it. Let us call that part the universal sub-rational good. It supplies Spinoza with the necessary standard.

IX) To achieve that good, need for government. For the rational insight into the need for society is too weak: need for supporting <8> passions. What reason prescribes can be brought about only by non-reason—general importance: need for coincidence of public interest and private interest in office holders (not counting on virtue and public spirit—cf. Federalists). Availability of religion or superstition, but this a dangerous means—the remedy: freedom of thought, freedom of speech. Natural right of freedom of speech—for: speech expression of thought, and thought not subject to sovereign—but indirect means (propaganda supra-liminal and sub-liminal). Must be granted because of men's incontinence (XX 8-9). But also: for the sciences and arts; otherwise hypocrisy (26-30). Spinoza tends toward complete freedom of speech: only actions are to be forbidden—but he must admit that certain opinions cannot be tolerated, e.g. anarchism (not atheism)—empirical proof of possibility of freedom of speech: Amsterdam (20-22, 39-42, 46)—yet he submits his book to the judgment of the sovereign. Only reasons of expedience of course—therefore not universally valid—ultimate right of the sovereign to permit or forbid any opinions he sees fit. Spinoza's strongest motive: to counteract the power of religious orthodoxy.

X) As for the form of government, democracy. Strange: contempt for the many—democracy → rule of the *wrath*[25] of the plebs (XVII 23-24, XIX 40 end, XX 33-34)—the mind of the vulgar: XVII 9-10, 14-16—he sides with the aristocratic Sadducees against the plebian Pharisees XVIII 11—plebs almost always a term of contempt → the ruling men must be the more prudent sort. But if the demos is weaned away from the clergy and the kings, if it is brought to see its true interests, it supplies the basis of the best and most rational society → the demos is to be weaned away from the promised goods [note below the page: IV 35, XVII 44, 103; XVIII 11, 23, 28; XIX 40; XX 8, 21, 32, 33, 44—*but: Tractatus Politicus* VII 27] <9> of the thereafter to the solid goods of this life—heaven on *earth*.[26]

The foundation of this: democracy most *natural*—by nature all men are free and equal, for by nature no one is subject to anyone else, for by nature no one is *ordered* towards something → democracy the regime in which natural freedom and equality are preserved to the highest degree (XVI 36, XVII 26, *Tractatus Politicus* VIII 12) → Rousseau who was more convincing than Spinoza because he questioned the value of "the marvels of the intellect."

And: democracy most *rational* (XVI 28-30, 34, XIX 10, *Tractatus Politicus* II 21): a large multitude cannot be united but in what is rational, the passions being divisive—especially: democracy → peace (XVII 74, XVIII 15, 18-19, *Tractatus Politicus* VII 5). Dubious character of the proof of the rationality of demos → Spinoza's notion of a democracy: the actual government not in the hands of the demos: preponderance of the rich, the only ones who have time for public office (to say nothing of the exclusion of servants =[27] workers from citizen rights). Spinoza thinks of a regime in which the commercial patriciate in fact predominates—not Rome which was a tyranny of a few (XVIII 35)—cf. XVIII 2, *Tractatus Politicus* VII 7, 8.

XI *Tractatus Politicus* X 5-8 a) Mere[28] laws are not good enough: the right spirit—[education to virtue—one form: sumptuary laws] b) No, for laws which can be violated without injury to others are despised; the only effective limitation of human desires is horizontal, not vertical. c) The vices of peace (loss of public spirit, effeminacy) cannot be forbidden directly but only indirectly → the majority must be induced to live, not wisely (this is impossible) but prompted by those passions from which the commonwealth derives great benefit → the rich must be induced to be avaricious: if access to public office is made dependent on wealth—on the other hand no special <10> public honor by statues etc. to anyone. Avarice is of course a vice, and despised and rejected in the *Ethics*—but the motive power of society ≠[29] the motive power of the wise.

"Freedom" at the price of the weakening of true morality. Cf. Kant: moral philosophy teaches that lying is absolutely evil; political philosophy teaches that the basic freedom which one's highest moral duty to uphold, includes freedom of speech =[30] freedom to lie. Both in Spinoza and Kant freedom for the highest is demanded in such a way as to include freedom for the lowest—is the primary motive, as they claim, concern with the highest?

Notes

1. Leo Strauss, *Spinoza's Critique of Religion*, trans. Elsa M. Sinclair (New York: Schocken Books, 1965). The preface is also reprinted as Leo Strauss, "Preface to Spinoza's Critique of Religion," in *Liberalism Ancient and Modern* (Chicago: University of Chicago Press, 1995), 224-60.
2. Leo Strauss, *1959 Course on Cicero Offered at the University of Chicago*, ed. James H. Nichols (Chicago: University of Chicago Press, 2016), 239.
3. Underline inserted by hand.
4. "e)" inserted by hand.
5. The typescript is corrupt: it reads "how question his Ethics (Stoa)" and "question" is crossed out by hand.
6. "philosophy" is replaced with "philosophers" by hand.
7. Underline inserted by hand.
8. Underline inserted by hand.
9. Underline inserted by hand.
10. Underline inserted by hand.
11. "in presence" crossed out by hand.
12. Underline by hand.

13. Square brackets by hand.
14. Underline by hand.
15. Reference, square brackets, and parenthesis inserted by hand.
16. Equal sign inserted by hand.
17. Equal sign inserted by hand.
18. Scare quotes inserted by hand.
19. Acute accent inserted by hand.
20. "moral virtue" inserted by hand.
21. Colon inserted by hand.
22. Not equal sign inserted by hand.
23. Not equal sign inserted by hand.
24. Equal sign inserted by hand.
25. "wroth" corrected by hand.
26. Underline inserted by hand.
27. Equal sign inserted by hand.
28. "More" corrected to "Mere" by hand.
29. Not equal sign inserted by hand.
30. Equal sign inserted by hand.

STEVEN FRANKEL

Interpretative Essay

STRAUSS'S "FRESH STUDY" MANUSCRIPT

THE DISCOVERY OF THE "FRESH STUDY" document at the University of Chicago archives provides further evidence that Strauss maintained a lifelong interest in the political philosophy of Spinoza. Moreover, the document supports the view that Strauss's studies of Spinoza were a catalyst for his philosophical thought, including his view of the conflict between ancients and moderns, the conflict between Jerusalem and Athens, and his discoveries in the art of philosophical writing. His first book focused on the sources and meaning of *Spinoza's Critique of Religion* (1930; henceforth SCR), and he continued to revise and revisit his position.[1] His discovery of a philosophical art of writing led him to revise his account of Spinoza in *Persecution and the Art of Writing* (1948; henceforth PAW). At the same time, he then turned to a new project on Spinoza, which presented the *Theological Political Treatise* (henceforth TTP) as an introduction to philosophy. Though he abandoned the project, parts of this book were incorporated into *Natural Right and History* (1951; henceforth NRH), including the first ten paragraphs of chapter 3. These themes are revisited in this new project, even though Strauss promises "not to repeat what I said in the print."

Instead, he offers the book as a "fresh study" motivated by the fact that he "just happen[ed] to have studied Spinoza again." Strauss then offers a detailed outline for an article or book. Although the outline is not dated, it seems likely that the proposal was written some time around 1960–1961. The evidence for this is the way Strauss's analysis in the outline reiterates many of the points made in his fall 1959 seminar on Spinoza's political philosophy.[2] Since this seminar is the only occasion that Strauss taught

Spinoza at the University of Chicago, it seems likely that this was the occasion for studying Spinoza that he refers to in his introduction.

The fact that Strauss studied the work afresh, made a detailed outline of the findings of the study, and proposed a new project makes it all the more curious that he abandoned the work. Although we do not know Strauss's precise explanation for this decision, we do have an excellent clue: soon after proposing and abandoning the "fresh study," Strauss wrote an extensive study of Spinoza as an autobiographical preface to his first Spinoza book (August 1962). This publication would prove to be one of Strauss's last essays focused on Spinoza. Strauss turned his attention to the study of classical political philosophy and did not publish again on Spinoza.[3] By comparing the "fresh study" outline with the autobiographical preface, we can discern the reasons for Strauss's decision to abandon the project and instead pursue the preface. As we shall see, the fundamental difference between the two works is not the content; to the contrary, his interpretation of Spinoza remains consistent. Instead, Strauss chooses to emphasize the theological, rather than the political, dimension of Spinoza's project.

Strauss's "Fresh Study" Proposal

Strauss begins his outline with a justification of the study of Spinoza. The call for a "fresh study" reminds one of his justification for his earlier study of Spinoza in the 1940s: "What are the reasons that cause us to study an historical figure like Spinoza? The reason why a *fresh investigation* of Spinoza's TTP is in order is obvious. The chief aim of the *Treatise* is to refute the claims which had been raised on behalf of revelation throughout the ages; and Spinoza succeeded ... his book has become the classic document of the 'rationalist' or 'secularist' attack on the belief in revelation" (emphasis added, PAW 142). This reason for studying Spinoza is to evaluate his critique of scripture, which has become a dogmatic certainty and therefore no longer problematic.

In contrast, Strauss justifies this new "fresh study" by emphasizing politics rather than theology. The focus here is on the justification and the arguments on behalf of democracy.[4] This emphasis on the political question is confirmed in the first section, where Strauss raises the basic questions on ancients versus moderns and Spinoza's relation to Thomas Hobbes and Niccolò Machiavelli. Strauss claims that he must consider the TTP because Spinoza died before he was able to finish writing his

Political Treatise. Since we have only the complete edition of the TTP, we must begin with that text and, as a result, consider the relation of theology to politics.

Strauss does not wholly neglect theology. But rather than approach it initially as does Spinoza in terms of prophecy and law, he takes up the question of secularization posed by several of Strauss's contemporaries such as Carl Schmitt in *Political Theology* and Karl Löwith in *Meaning in History:* "What is the character of secularization affected by Spinoza?" Strauss's answer is original and interesting. Rather than accept the contention that the main concepts of modern politics are secularized versions of medieval theology, Strauss reopens the question of whether "secularization" refers to the corruption or perfection of the Bible. In section three, Strauss presents his novel thesis that Spinoza presents his corruption of the Bible as its perfection: Spinoza "presents a break with the bible in the disguise of a perfection of the bible—a conscious transformation of biblical teaching or use of biblical teaching for non-biblical ends." In short, even when examining the theological issues in the TTP, Strauss remains firmly focused on politics.

The Main Themes

Strauss begins in section two by using the break between the ancients and moderns as a point of departure for considering democracy. His initial suggestion is that Spinoza, along with Machiavelli and Hobbes, offers a "rejection of all earlier political philosophy. He cites the beginning of Spinoza's *Political Treatise*, which explicitly rejects ancient philosophers as builders of unrealistic cities in speech and cites Machiavelli as the statesman who best understands the constraints of political life. He also borrows from Hobbes concepts such as the state of nature, natural right, and the general view of nature. But Strauss admits that this overview is "too general," and in the course of the study, he will revise it considerably.

The Analysis of Theology

Spinoza begins the TTP by devoting nearly half the book to a discussion of theology. "Fresh Study" follows Spinoza's own outline by beginning with an extended discussion of Spinoza's analysis of the Bible. But, rather than focus on theological questions regarding providence, law, and miracles as he does in his earlier work on Spinoza, Strauss examines instead the ways in which Spinoza's broader political project shapes his theology. Strauss distinguishes liberalism from democracy and asserts that the development of liberalism precedes the defense of democracy.[5] He defines liberalism using Spinoza's terms, that is, "the right to think what one pleases and to say what one thinks," the title of chapter 20 of the TTP.[6] That Strauss fixes the meaning of liberalism in this way emphasizes his willingness to follow Spinoza's argument wherever it leads. In NRH, where Strauss follows Hobbes, he defines liberalism differently, as "the political doctrine which recognizes as the fundamental political fact the right, as distinguished from the duties, of man and which identifies the function of the state with the protection or safeguarding of those rights."[7] Freedom of speech and thought, Strauss suggests, is the primary motive for Spinoza's theological-political project. This freedom includes the freedom to philosophize.[8]

Such freedom presumes that everyone is equally competent to judge the teachings of the Bible or, more generally, speculative matters. This is, to say the least, problematic for Spinoza. As Strauss emphasizes throughout, Spinoza is aware that people are superstitious and prone to fanaticism, that is, that freedom of speech will likely lead to instability and violence. The theological teaching of the TTP aims at setting limits on free speech so that some equality of judgment will be possible. To do so, Spinoza reduces the Bible's essential teaching to a single moral teaching: the practice of charity and toleration is sufficient for salvation.[9] As for other speculative claims, including those advanced by priests and theologians, scripture allows a wide variety of views and thereby leaves men free to interpret and consider. Of course, the view that one is saved through the practice of charity rests on other beliefs, including the existence of a providential god who rewards just men. These form the basis of his seven dogmas of universal faith. Too, there must be a sovereign power to avoid chaos and allow for the practice of charity. In this way, Spinoza's theology supports liberalism and equality on apparently biblical grounds.

Strauss devotes the remainder of his treatment of Spinoza's theological project to showing why it is provisional and ultimately, as a civil religion, unable to support an increasingly secular polis. He argues that the separation of philosophy and revelation, which Spinoza proposes in chapter 15, is not tenable: "Close inspection shows that this simple juxtaposition of philosophy and theology is not possible." For one thing, the domain of philosophy "lays claim to the whole domain of truth." This means, in practical terms, that philosophy determines the speculative beliefs that undergird the practice of charity, including the belief in a providential god.[10] Similarly, philosophy alone determines the limits of charity including those moments when the practice of charity might undermine its theoretical basis. In order to preserve the belief in salvation, philosophy must determine both the limits of free speech as well as the power of the sovereign (to avoid charity for the sake of the polis).

The harsh foundation of Spinoza's account is, according to Strauss, that the Bible is entirely false. Its claim to truth is confirmed by miracles; in fact, the idea that God has a mind or can speak is itself a miracle. Such claims cannot be proven and the Bible does not attempt to prove them. What is worse, the Bible cannot prove anything; it is not even a coherent or unified text. Rather, it is a hastily compiled set of fragments that reflect the incomplete work of the compilers or the superstitions of its authors. Because the Bible continues to exert influence on political life, Spinoza tries to extract useful political teachings from it. Unfortunately, many of the clearest teachings to "turn the other cheek" and "love thy neighbor" are incompatible with a healthy civil society. The goal of Spinoza's theology is to present an interpretation of the Bible that provides support for his novel political founding.

The theology seems to be "useful" as a temporary measure, while men are still prone to believe in God, but Spinoza does not address the viability of liberalism in an entirely secularized society. This is in sharp contrast to medieval philosophy, whose divine law pointed toward intellectual perfection. Spinoza is well aware of the medieval tradition, but he abandons it. He presents the medieval version of divine law in chapter 5 by describing "love of God" in terms of knowledge of God. Later, in chapter 12 of the TTP, intellectual virtue drops out entirely in favor of moral virtue or the practice of charity. The reason that Spinoza abandons the medieval tradition is that he intends to replace it with a novel political teaching that aims at freedom rather than virtue. Strauss uses this moment to suggest a monumental change in political philosophy and turn to a comparison of Plato and Spinoza.

The Political Teaching of the TTP

Surprisingly, Strauss begins by emphasizing how much Spinoza shares with Plato, including the view that intellectual perfection is the highest virtue, superior to moral virtue, and that men are naturally unequal in terms of their intellect. They also agree on their approach to political life, namely that the reliance of the multitude of men on their passions is a perpetual stumbling block to peace and stability. Strauss even describes Spinoza's interpretation of scripture is "a *kalon pseudos* in the Platonic sense." Indeed, Spinoza is "more in agreement with Plato than Hobbes" who "rejected the theoretical ideal" (3). What then is the fundamental difference between Plato and Spinoza?

For Plato, there is a natural law that points toward the highest, best way of life, namely philosophy. "[F]or Spinoza, this natural law is only a human law, a free human project—there is no natural law that man can transgress—for: no teleology."[11] Strauss turns in sections four and five to Spinoza's rejection of the Platonic philosopher-king. Oddly, Strauss appears to abandon the theme of natural law as a human project in favor of the practical consideration that "the multitude of non-philosophers will never bow to the philosophers" (5). This is in keeping with Spinoza's argument in chapter 5 of the TTP. But, in light of Strauss's earlier emphasis on philosophy as the pursuit of theoretical wisdom, Strauss's readers are invited to wonder whether Spinoza's break from Plato is merely practical. To put this same question differently, What is the status of philosophy as the best way of life? Strauss raises the question here without resolving it. This will prove to be deliberate, and the question at the heart of Spinoza's defense of democracy..

The rejection of the philosopher-king takes the form of a rejection of rule of the priests. Their claim to authority rests on a superior relation to God or superior knowledge of scripture. As with his 1959 seminar, Strauss pays special attention to Spinoza's unusual typology of political regimes in chapter 5 of the TTP.[12] Spinoza suggests that, in practical terms, there are only two possible regimes, democracy and theocracy. Most people, Spinoza explains, are irrational and need to be compelled to obey the law. The most effective form of compulsion is fear of divine punishment or the "crude doxa" that all people are equal. In Strauss's playful phrase, "the unreasonable unreasonably regard the reasonable as their equals" (5). Strauss explains in section five of his outline that other regimes, such as monarchy or oligarchy, require "an indigenous established religion" (6). With the advent of Christianity, this is "out of the question now." Only a republic can resist the rule (or tyranny) of priests who possess an authority that is both independent of and higher than the regime.

For many modern thinkers, the preference for democracy goes hand in hand with universal enlightenment in order to justify freedom of thought and speech. Spinoza "is held back" from advocating such a view because, like Plato, he is deeply convinced of the permanent "gulf between the wise and the vulgar" (6). Strauss then presents Spinoza's case for democracy in light of his questionable support for equality. But that support is not based on natural law, hierarchy, or teleology. Rather, his account of equality rests on a doctrine of natural right that refers to the fact of self-preservation, namely that everything in nature is striving to preserve itself by using whatever power is available to it. While it is true that the few individuals who follow reason, rather than "irrational appetite," adopt more effective strategies for survival, power—not reason—is ultimately more critical for survival: "generally speaking, men are stronger, especially if united than all other earthly beings" (6, 7). Since democracy unites the greatest number, it has the greatest might or (which is the same thing) right.

Why are democracies more united than other forms of government? Strauss discovers Spinoza's novel formula for directing self-interest toward an "enlightened" end (7): "All men are capable effectively to desire peace and security, at least through compulsion—and peace and security are objectively to the advantage of each." All men do not agree that theoretical virtue is the greatest good, but all men see the value of peace and security. Strauss calls this point of agreement "the universal sub-rational good." [13] It is a standard that all can recognize, even if it is not the highest good. The goal of political life must be lowered so that men can unite to embrace this subrational good.[14]

Achieving this modest good still requires government; yet men resent this power and, without the support of the passions, will resist it. Religion is able to harness these passions to support government but this solution, dependent upon irrational superstition, is "a dangerous means" (8).[15] Instead, Spinoza offers "freedom of speech" as a passion that proves difficult to control or suppress. While propaganda and control of information can limit people's freedom of speech, such means are usually not more powerful than people's inability to control their tongue.

> What does [Spinoza] say? "For even the most experienced, to say nothing of the plebs, do not know how to be silent." This is a common vice of men, that they trust their thoughts, their plans, even when secrecy is needed, to others. In other words, a failing, a vice of man which is so powerful—that is very strange. You know that if right is based not on a virtue but on a vice, that is very remarkable. Spinoza doesn't say this in vain.[16]

In addition, freedom of speech also promotes the flourishing of the arts and sciences and thus protects philosophy. Strauss emphasizes that "Spinoza's strongest motive [is] to counteract the power of religious orthodoxy" (8).

In the penultimate section, Strauss summarizes Spinoza's argument on behalf of democracy as the best regime. He does not mitigate Spinoza's "contempt for the many" or suggest that they can be enlightened to pursue theoretical virtue. At most, they can be "weaned away from the clergy and the kings" and made to see their self-interest in terms of "the solid goods of this life" (9). Nature does not provide any structure, telos, or ordering toward the good. Spinoza preserves this same freedom from ends, and subsequent equality of all beings, in his democratic political teaching. (As an aside, Strauss mentions that Spinoza's preference for the theoretical life is not altogether consistent with his praise of the intellect. Rousseau is more consistent and convincing on this point.) Democracy is also more rational than other regimes because it is the most peaceful regime, focused on the acquisition of wealth and comfort.

The proposed study concludes with an assessment of Spinoza's case for democracy. It is true that the laws do not educate the citizens toward virtue, but such laws are not ultimately effective. As for the "vices of peace," namely, that they induce apathy toward the common good and an unwillingness to sacrifice oneself for the benefit of others, this is partly true. But democratic regimes can encourage a kind of public spiritedness through the passions, especially by combining the desire for wealth and comfort with honor. This falls short, of course, of intellectual and moral virtue. Still, liberal democracy allows people the freedom to pursue virtue. The outline ends with a question: "freedom for the highest is demanded in such a way as to include freedom for the lowest—is the primary motive, as [Spinoza] claims, concern with the highest?" (10).

Strauss's Defense of Democracy

From this brief account, we can observe that the intention of Strauss's analysis is to explain and defend Spinoza's justification of liberalism. Although philosophers do not rule directly, the multitude is weaned away from superstitions toward the practice of charity. Loosened from the control of manipulative priests whose authority depends on ridiculous fear and vain hope, the multitude is free to pursue the subrational goods of comfort and security. While such goals fall short of the highest good, the pursuit of security and comfort is not entirely irrational. Philosophy also benefits from greater toleration. Spinoza's achievement is further enhanced by Strauss's comparison with Plato. The two share a similar analysis of the political problem and the dangers that the city poses to philosophy, but Spinoza discovers a practical solution. Directing the passions, especially the desire for acquisition, toward peace, the multitude can be taught to pursue interests that benefit everyone. Spinoza, it seems, has succeeded in grafting a modern view of politics, that is, the promotion of rights at the expense of natural law, in order to protect philosophy more securely from persecution.

Strauss also mutes the problems with Spinoza's justification. It is true that Spinoza "falsifies" the Bible, but he does so in order to create a theology that supports liberal democracy. Moreover, by claiming that only philosophy can make claims that are true, theology is forced to sacrifice any truth claims. The leaves civil religion to defend itself only as a useful fiction, which promotes political stability. Charity and kindness may help pacify the citizens, but they are not the path to either political or intellectual salvation. Strauss does not conceal these points, but neither does he accentuate them. One consequence of "falsifying" the Bible and directing the multitude's passions toward comfort is the confusion of the high and low. Strauss's last word of the "fresh study" is "freedom for the highest is demanded in such a way as to include freedom for the lowest—is the primary motive, as they claim, concern with the highest?"[17]

The Themes of the Autobiographical Preface

That the "fresh study" ends with a question rather than a conclusion indicates the direction of Strauss's dissatisfaction with his account. To be sure, Strauss does not reject the details of his mature reading of Spinoza's theological-political project. The autobiographical preface presents the same account of Spinoza's theological political analysis as the "fresh study." Nonetheless, whereas the "fresh study" leads one to celebrate Spinoza's achievement as the founder of liberal democracy, the autobiographical preface is far more ambivalent, not to say pessimistic, about this achievement. Indeed, Strauss chooses Weimar as the setting for the autobiographical preface, a moment when liberal democracy was on the verge of a spectacular collapse: "[T]he election of Field-Marshall von Hindenburg to the presidency of the German Reich in 1925 showed everyone *who had eyes to see* that the Weimar Republic had only a short time to live."

Strauss subsequently elaborates on the blindness of his contemporaries in Weimar, paying special attention to the Jewish community in Germany, which tragically did not see its imminent destruction.[18] One reason for this extraordinary blindness is that the community was "the grips of a theological-political predicament." "[M]ost German Jews believed that their problem had been solved in principle by liberalism," that is, they believed that Spinoza's TTP had provided a theologico-political blueprint for creating a society that was indifferent to the distinction between Jews and Christians (4). Following the ambiguity in Spinoza's analysis of the Bible, the German Jews divided into two camps: one believed that liberalism was the perfection of the Bible; the other that liberalism surpassed the Bible with its political teaching. Despite this division, both camps believed that "the millennial antagonism between Judaism and Christianity was about to disappear": "Spinoza had become the symbol of that emancipation which was to be more than emancipation but secular redemption. In Spinoza, a thinker and a saint who was both a Jew and a Christian and hence neither, all cultured families of the earth, it was hoped, will be blessed. In a word, the non-Jewish world having been molded to a considerable extent by Spinoza, had become receptive to Jews who were willing to assimilate themselves to it" (17).

This view of Spinoza sets the stage for Strauss's account, which takes the form of an odyssey to escape from the "theological-political predicament." Strauss first comes to see that liberalism cannot solve the Jewish problem when he discovers the Zionist critique (see ¶¶ 1–13). But, despite this cogent critique, Zionism ultimately embraces liberalism and thus fails to escape its horizons, particularly the view that the divine claims of scripture have been refuted. This causes Strauss to wonder whether it is possible to return to Jewish belief (see ¶¶ 14–23). Modern theology however proves to be steeped in liberalism, even when it is critical of Spinoza, so Strauss finally considers the return to orthodoxy or "unqualified Jewish belief." The confrontation with Spinoza's critique of the Bible (see ¶¶ 24–39) unexpectedly opens up a new horizon, a return to "Jewish medieval rationalism and its classical (Aristotelian and Platonic) foundation" (see ¶¶ 40–42).

"Fresh study" begins with the "alleged failure" of liberal democracy and of Spinoza's account. Ostensibly, the goal of the study is to defend both. The autobiographical preface, on the other hand, begins with the concrete failure of liberalism in Weimar, and with the celebration of Spinoza, which blinds its celebrants to the coming storm. Both accounts consider Spinoza's theology, but in a markedly different fashion. In the "fresh study," Strauss shows how Spinoza's theological arguments are designed to make possible freedom of speech and liberal democracy. The preface examines theology as part of Strauss's broader personal quest that includes philosophy. Finally, in the "fresh study," liberal democracy and Spinoza's analysis are vindicated as a novel solution to the theological-political problem. The liberal regime allows freedom for the promotion of philosophy and science, while promoting the equality of all citizens. In sharp contrast, the autobiographical preface exposes the political and intellectual problems with liberal democracy. It also emphasizes how the dogmatic attachment to liberal democracy blinded the Jewish community to the regime's weaknesses and prevented them from taking steps to avert the gathering storm. In this way, the preface urges us to look for a solution that, at least theoretically, moves beyond liberal democracy toward a return to classical political philosophy.

This last difference can be clearly seen in their distinctive accounts of Spinoza's relation to Plato. In the 1959 seminar, Strauss remarks on his renewed interest in Spinoza: "The notion which characterized the classical position was [that] speculation, or theory, *theoria*, contemplation, was the highest [good]. Spinoza grafts this notion of the supremacy of contemplation on a Machiavellian-Hobbesian basis.... Spinoza restores an important part of the classical heritage but on the modern basis, and this is the reason why I myself am now interested in Spinoza."[19] In other words, Strauss's renewed interest in Spinoza is motivated by his return to classical political philosophy in order to assess its current prospects. The "fresh study" suggests that Spinoza's liberalism is a qualified success. It protects the freedom to philosophize and aligns the regime with a set of subrational goals. Strauss allows, in his conclusion, that liberal citizens likely do not recognize contemplation as humanity's highest activity, but as we have seen, he reassures his readers by stressing the kinship between Plato and Spinoza. The ambiguity about the origins and nature of the highest good appeared to be the source of liberalism's blessings by recognizing the limitations of politics and its superstitious citizens. Rather than invite controversy about the highest good or justice, liberalism discovers a common good that all people can agree to, security and comfort.

Strauss abandons this confidence in liberalism to protect contemplation in the autobiographical preface. Instead, he shows that liberalism's attempt to avoid questions about the highest good does not silence the debate. To the contrary, by suggesting that the highest good is merely a human imagining, they impel the regime toward ever more extreme solutions. At the same time, liberalism obscures these dangers from its potential defenders (e.g., the Jewish community) who are busy enjoying its fruits. Finally, the theoretical life succumbs to a vicious confusion of the high and low in the name of "intellectual probity." Such freedom offered by liberalism is a risky bargain: "It is safer to try to understand the low in the light of the high than the high in the light of the low. In doing the latter, one necessarily distorts the high, whereas in doing the former one does not deprive the low of the freedom to reveal itself fully for what it is." The alleged safety of liberalism turns out to be an illusion for the Jewish community in Germany. Moreover, it was a mirage for philosophy as well. As Emil Fackenheim points out, Strauss's assertion here "is clearly Platonic."[20] Plato suggested a natural hierarchy based on an account of the highest or best way of life. The perpetual tension between the needs of the city, political life, and the goals of the philosopher, the theoretical life, has a moderating effect on the political aspirations of philosophers. In contrast, Spinoza claimed that contemplation is the highest activity of humans but such a claim reflects his "free human project" rather than a reflection on human nature. The autobiographical preface suggests that this is the central question for grasping (and escaping) the predicament that is Spinoza's legacy, a legacy that blocks the paths to Jerusalem and to Athens.

The TTP as "the True *Protreptikos*"

The "Fresh Study" was not the only proposal on Spinoza that Strauss abandoned. Strauss proposed a similar project in the mid to late 1940s. The remains of that manuscript in the Chicago archives show that Strauss had been thinking about Spinoza's relation to Plato for decades.[21] Strauss planned to compare their distinctive approaches to divine law as an introduction to philosophy: "[T]he introduction to philosophy which must repeat the original discovery of philosophy, must take on the form of a theologico-political consideration. The classical introduction to philosophy did have that character. The classical introduction was the *protreptikos*, the speech that urges men on, or impels them, to philosophize."[22] For Strauss, the path of return to the original discovery of philosophy is ever the same. It requires compelling an individual to recognize that their opinions about the most important things are largely unexamined because they have been established by a divine text or constitution. Such opinions "are necessarily concerned with sacred or divine things, and they ultimately derive their authority from the sacred or divine things which are their objects"—that is, they are necessarily concerned with what Strauss calls "the high." Once the potential philosopher examines these opinions independently, he recognizes their "self-contradictory character." The speech that generates philosophy must therefore begin with the theological and political premises of the regime. From this vantage point, we can see that the differences between Plato and Spinoza can be understood as the result, at least in part, of the premises that each inherited.[23]

One result of the success of liberalism is that Western citizens find themselves in an unusual position. The dominant dogma is the belief in science as a substitute for the divine: "[W]e are irreligious because fate forces us to be irreligious and for no other reason."[24] This atheism dominates our institutions, "even the highest lawcourt in the land is more likely to defer to the contentions of social science than to the Ten Commandments as the words of the living God."[25] Our atheism, supported by the belief that natural and social science are viable substitutes for wisdom, prevents us from returning to classical philosophy and, according to Strauss, "a *fresh understanding* of classical political philosophy ... may be an indispensable starting point" for understanding our present situation.[26]

Strauss's decision to abandon his "fresh study" manuscript and to pursue a critique of atheism in the autobiographical preface does not indicate any dramatic change in Strauss's thought. Instead, it indicates a change in strategy for writing a *protreptikos* in a regime where liberalism, including atheism, has become a dogmatic opinion. In such a situation, Strauss attempts to "prove the legitimacy of philosophy partly by appealing to the authority of the Bible and partly by questioning the authority of the Bible."[27]

Notes

1. "My study of Hobbes began in the context of an investigation of the origins of biblical criticism in the seventeenth century, namely, of Spinoza's *Theologico-Political Treatise*. ... Since then the theological-political problem has remained the theme of my investigations." Strauss, "Preface to *Hobbes Politische Wissenschaft*," in Kenneth Hart Green, ed., *Jewish Philosophy and the Crisis of Modernity* (Albany: State University of New York Press, 1997), 453.

2. This seminar can be found at https://leostrausscenter.uchicago.edu/spinoza-autumn-1959/. An additional piece of evidence that suggests that it was written around the same time is that Strauss makes the point about bontà in Machiavelli in connection with Cicero, but on page 240 of the Cicero transcript from 1959 Strauss expresses a regret that he did not quote Cicero in this connection (https://leostrausscenter.uchicago.edu/cicero-spring-1959/). Thanks to Prof. Svetozar Minkov for bringing this to my attention.

3. Strauss turned his attention increasingly to the study of Platonic political philosophy. As Peter J. Ahrensdorf notes: In 1957, "Strauss had not yet published a commentary on the *Republic* or indeed on any Platonic dialogue. Strauss went on to publish commentaries on 7 dialogues: first, relatively short, separate commentaries on The *Republic*, the *Statesman*, and the *Laws* in his chapter on Plato in *The History of Political Philosophy* (1963); then, a longer commentary on the *Republic* in the *City and Man* (1964); and later, commentaries on the *Minos* (1968), on the *Euthydemus* (1970), and on the *Apology* and the *Crito* (1976), and a book on the *Laws* (1975)." Ahrensdorf's introduction to Strauss's seminar on Plato's *Republic* can be found on page 1 at https://wslamp70.s3.amazonaws.com/leostrauss/s3fs-public/pdf/transcript/Platos_Republic_1957.pdf.

4. This emphasis on democracy is novel. Strauss's previous studies of Spinoza focused on his atheism and relation to ancient thought (SCR), the deliberate contradictions in his work and the tradition of hiding philosophy because of its tensions with the city (PAW). For more on Strauss's "fresh investigation" and the differences between his various interpretations of Spinoza, see Laurence Lampert, *The Enduring Importance of Leo Strauss* (Chicago: University of Chicago Press, 2013), chapter 7, especially 224.

5. For a fuller account of Strauss on the meaning of liberalism, see *Liberalism: Ancient and Modern* (New York: Basic Books, 1968).

6. "Look at the heading of chapter 20: 'It is shown that in a free commonwealth everyone is entitled to think what he wishes and to say what he thinks.' These words are literally taken from Tacitus, the Roman historian. There are many more quotations from Tacitus and other ancient writers. You must not forget that Spinoza meant this seriously: to restore a freedom which existed in classical antiquity. I have spoken of this prejudice of the seventeenth-eighteenth centuries on a former occasion—you know, the belief that there was perfect tolerance or something approaching perfect tolerance in classical antiquity; and only under the influence of the Bible, this tolerance was destroyed." (*1959 Spinoza Seminar*, 155).

7. NRH, 181–82. Nathan Tarcov has identified at least six different ways that Strauss employs the term "liberalism" in a single text, *Liberalism: Ancient and Modern*. See Nathan Tarcov, "Leo Strauss: Critique and Defense of Liberalism," page 8 of a paper delivered at the conference on Leo Strauss: Religione e Liberalismo, Fondazione Magna Carta, Rome, May 13, 2011.

8. However, the freedom to philosophize cannot be the ultimate justification for the political teaching, since Spinoza observes in a footnote that philosophy can be practiced in any regime. (Strauss too notes this footnote in this outline.) Moreover, Spinoza rejects the notion that philosophy can rule over superstition and thereby secure its independence. In other words, freedom—including freedom to philosophize—is not the ultimate justification for the political teaching. See the *1959 Seminar on Spinoza*, 211-12, for a discussion of political freedom and philosophy.

9. In his lecture, "Why We Remain Jews," Strauss accepts part of Spinoza's view on the apparent indifference of nature to charity. But he brilliantly reverses or inverts the logic of Spinoza's claim so that revelation represents a great and noble attempt to establish some basis for decency: "The one thing needful is righteousness or charity; in Judaism these are the same. This notion of the one thing needful is not defensible if the world is not the creation of the just and loving God, the holy God. The root of injustice and uncharitableness, which abounds, is not in God, but in the free acts of His creatures—in sin. The Jewish people and their fate are the living witness for the absence of redemption. This, one could say, is the meaning of the chosen people; the Jews are chosen to prove the absence of redemption."

10. "In other words, what he suggests (and this had a terrific success): here is reason, and here is revelation; they have nothing to do with each other. Nothing. No conflict. But unfortunately truth belongs only here, with reason. Of course what he says in so many words [is that] they have everything in common, namely, the claim to the truth, and they contradict each other in this respect. But he expresses it peacefully by saying they live on different planets." (*1959 Spinoza Seminar*, 159.)

11. Emphasis in the original, 5. See also *1959 Spinoza Seminar*, 257-58.

12. Strauss covers much the same material in session four of his 1959 Spinoza seminar. See also 56, 216.

13. The "subrational good, as I call it (which is not an irrational good—it is rational, but not fully rational), comfortable self-preservation, that we should try to get by all means, and Spinoza tries to answer the question: How can we get that? ... How must the government be constructed to give us the maximum guarantee that this sensible, low but solid good, comfortable self-preservation, will be made possible?" (*1959 Spinoza Seminar*, 198.)

14. Interestingly, Strauss also calls this "the lower part of the highest good," which also suggests a kinship with Plato. On lowering the goals, see "The Three Waves of Modernity," in *Introduction to Political Philosophy*, ed. Hilail Gildin (Detroit: Wayne State University Press, 1979), 86-88; *What Is Political Philosophy? And Other Studies* (New York: Free Press, 1959), 41; and *Natural Right and History*, 178.

15. Individuals driven by their passions are not naturally united toward a particular end; in fact, they are more easily divided toward a host of supersti-

tious ends. This is one reason why it is critical for Spinoza to neutralize the power of priests and theologians.

16. *1959 Spinoza Seminar*, 234.

17. "What Spinoza tries to do is to find a unitary formula which [does] not pin the argument purely on the highest good, nor pin it entirely on this subrational good, but on something which is equally applicable to both, you see, to get a truly universal doctrine. Why does he do that? First of all, there is this interest in a universal doctrine stemming from the theoretical conception altogether.... The highest good does not necessarily require political freedom. This good, the subrational good, does not have an essential relation to the freedom of the mind. It could perhaps include it among many other things, but it has no essential relation to it. That is unsatisfactory; therefore he is trying to find a principle which applies equally to the highest human possibility and to the lowest which is defensible, the subrational good, comfortable self-preservation." (*1959 Spinoza Seminar*, 248–49.)

18. "The German-Jewish problem was never solved. It was annihilated by the annihilation of the German Jews" (preface to SCR, 4).

19. *1959 Spinoza Seminar*, session 1. See also David Wollenberg's introduction to the seminar: "This interest in the possibility of restoring elements of classical thought on the basis of modern science is understandable. After all, in *Natural Right and History*, Strauss writes: 'Natural right in its classic form is connected with a teleological view of the universe ... [which] would seem to have been destroyed by modern natural science.... The fundamental dilemma, in whose grip we are, is caused by the victory of modern natural science.'" It would appear that the solution to this dilemma is either a refounding of classical thought on a modern view of the universe, or else, which would appear more challenging, a restoration of the classical view of the universe in the face of modern science. Spinoza is one of the few great thinkers who attempts the former, to restore core elements of classical thought—most notably the primacy of contemplation—on the "foundation of the new Galilean-Cartesian science."

20. Fackenheim continues: "You understand the perverse state of the tripartite 'soul' in terms of its healthy state. Perversity and chaos come in many forms, and you recognize them for what they are. It seems to me that there are limitations here. The limitation is that there is one low that cannot be understood, or does not fully reveal itself, if looked at from the standpoint of the high." See *Jewish Philosophers and Jewish Philosophy*, ed. Michael Morgan (Bloomington: Indiana University Press, 1996), 97–105. For an alternative view that suggests any such hierarchy is part of a mythical account, see Lampert, *Enduring Influence of Leo Strauss*, chapter 5.

21. I thank Professors Svotzar Minkov and Rasoul Namazi for bringing this manuscript to my attention. According to Prof. Minkov, the first section of the proposed book was incorporated into the first ten paragraphs of chapter 3 of *Natural Right and History*.

22. Leo Strauss Papers, box 18, folder 17, Special Collections Research Center, University of Chicago Library.

23. Strauss writes in the same manuscript: "Since the philosopher addresses it, not to philosophers, but to citizens, he has to follow the example of Odysseus and start from premises that are generally agreed upon; he has to argue, at least to begin with, not apodictically or scientifically, but 'dialectically.' We contend, and we shall later show, that Spinoza's *Treatise* meets the requirements of the true *protreptikos*."

24. *The City and Man* (1964), 1.

25. *The City and Man* (1964), 1.

26. *The City and Man*, 11; emphasis added. As Strauss remarked thirty years earlier: "The Enlightenment won the freedom from traditions ... we are *completely free*. But free *for what*? Have the principles of the tradition been replaced by other binding principles? In no way. We therefore do not *know* at all *what* we are free *for*, what we live for, what the right and good is according to which we can be in harmony with ourselves." In "The Intellectual Situation of the Present" (1932) in *Reorientation: Leo Strauss in the 1930s*, ed. Martin Yaffe and Richard Ruderman (London: Palgrave Macmillan, 2014), 246–47.

27. "Divine law" manuscript from the mid-1940s, 3.

ANDREA E. RAY

Interpretative Essay

THE CHARITY OF SPINOZA'S *DEMOCRACY*

FROM THE BEGINNING OF THIS MANUSCRIPT, Strauss emphasizes that in returning to Spinoza, he seeks to accomplish something new, to undertake a "fresh study" rather than to merely "repeat" what he had previously put forth in print.[1] The extent to which what follows in the manuscript can be said to be genuinely new or novel to readers of Strauss on Spinoza is perhaps questionable. As Steven Frankel notes in his essay in this volume, one can read Strauss's interpretation of Spinoza as basically remaining consistent between this unpublished manuscript and the 1962 preface to the second edition of *Spinoza's Critique of Religion*.[2] This is further supported by the fact that it is likely that the manuscript represents a draft of an outline for an article or book project born of Strauss's autumn 1959 course, "The Political Philosophy of Spinoza."[3] Hence, it seems plausible that within the context of Strauss's work on Spinoza, this manuscript was drafted at some point between 1959 and 1962 and represents an earlier attempt at revisiting Spinoza, a project that Strauss ultimately undertook through the 1962 preface instead.

However, in what follows we will take a naïve reading of Strauss's claim and explore what can be gleaned from the manuscript should we take Strauss at his word. Doing so will allow us here to limit our focus to a much narrower question prompted by the manuscript itself—namely the role and importance of charity in Strauss's reading of Spinoza as presented within the manuscript. In the manuscript, Strauss repeatedly returns to the question of charity, both in the biblical sense and with regard to the way in which Spinoza takes up charity in his own work. We will therefore consider charity in light of a broader question that Strauss uses to frame the subsequent discussions in the manuscript: "What is the character of secularization effected by Spinoza? Is it a corruption or perfection?"[4]

Charity and Tolerance

Strauss first introduces the issue of charity by outlining what he sees as the basic argument from charity to tolerance, an argument that can then be extended into an argument for democracy. In doing so, Strauss sketches the first of two competing but interwoven understandings of charity that he suggests are at play in Spinoza's political philosophy. Identifying this first position as beginning from "extreme biblicism," Strauss suggests that, from the claim that "God demands only charity," one may infer that "the sin is persecution" and thus that tolerance is "the right conduct" for all, including for philosophers.[5] Notably this implies an extraordinarily close relation between charity and tolerance. God's demand for charity implies a universal duty of tolerance. It may be too strong to say that such an argument suggests that charity *is* tolerance, but it is at least the case that tolerance is an expression of charity according to this view and that intolerance is incompatible with God's fundamental demand on man. Furthermore, depending on how much weight we give the phrase "the sin," here, there may even be reason to suspect that Strauss is sketching out an argument for a much stronger claim that identifies charity as tolerance.[6] Unfortunately, this section of the manuscript is too breezily outlined to come to a definitive interpretation.

Nonetheless, Strauss suggests that Spinoza builds on this argument to argue that the fundamental demand for charity in turn implies an argument for democracy. Because charity requires universal tolerance, the demand for charity yields an argument for liberalism, under which each may think and speak as he pleases, that is, under which each tolerates and is tolerated. Consequently, there is therefore implicit in the demand for charity a deeply antihierarchical impulse, as everyone is "equally the judge."[7] Strauss suggests that this impulse is fundamentally first a theological one, according to which the demand for charity is primarily a demand for religious toleration, and thus of the individual's freedom to judge for himself with regard to spiritual concerns rather than deferring to a specified ecclesiastical authority. Yet, as temporal matters are necessarily of lesser importance than spiritual ones within the context of an argument that begins from God's demands on man, this antihierarchical impulse extends to apply not only to spiritual matters but also to temporal ones. It thus implies an argument for democracy as the form of government that both explicitly allows for the freedom of thought and speech of its citizenry and best expresses this deeply antihierarchical impulse.

Charity and Obedience

However, Strauss immediately extends from this argument to one that appears to conflict with it. Rather than arguing for charity as requiring universal *tolerance*, Strauss suggests that Spinoza ultimately builds to argue for charity as requiring universal *obedience*. Because the argument for charity as requiring tolerance derives from a demand by God, it is at its basis a theological teaching, rather than a rational one. This is to say that it relies on the authority of the Bible rather than on that of reason, and thus implicit in it is an assumption of a "spirit of obedience"[8] on the part of the one from whom tolerance is required. Strauss suggests that the argument for a requirement of universal tolerance must therefore contradict itself, as the call to recognize the freedom of each to think as he pleases depends on a shared assumption that in being so called, each must acknowledge the authority of God's demands on him, and presumably consequently also acknowledge an authority over him superior to that of his own thought and judgment. Strauss thus argues that, contrary to the claim that the demand for charity implies a form of government under which universal tolerance prevails, the democracy logically required by the divine demand for charity cannot be a democracy within which the open philosopher would be tolerated. This is because "philosophy lays claim to the whole realm of truth,"[9] and thus a philosopher who openly denies any authority outside of reason limiting reason's scope or authority likewise openly denies the fundamental underlying assumption of the government under which he lives and the toleration he both enjoys and is held to owe to others. Instead, therefore, Strauss suggests that the democracy yielded by the demand for charity itself demands certain limitations on freedom of thought and speech rather than universal toleration as Spinoza's argument at first appears to indicate.

Strauss does not fully elaborate his argument for this interpretation within the manuscript, and it is one that might at first strike some readers of Spinoza as odd or discordant given Spinoza's own arguments regarding censorship within the *Theological-Political Treatise*. While the *Theological-Political Treatise* certainly grants that "by right [sovereigns] can consider as enemies anyone who doesn't think absolutely as they do in every matter,"[10] it suggests that to do so is foolhardy and contrary to the sovereign's own self-preservation as sovereign. There are two reasons for this. First, according to Spinoza, "no one can transfer to another person his natural right, *or* faculty, of reasoning freely, and of judging concerning anything whatever. Nor can anyone be compelled to do this."[11] While Spinoza admits that it is of course possible to influence another human being's judgment, this influence "has never reached the point" of wholly overriding that individual's freedom of reasoning. Hence, while Moses "had gotten the greatest prior control of the judgment of his people ... still he was not able to escape murmuring and perverse interpretations."[12] It therefore appears inevitable that even a sovereign capable of the most potent influence over men's minds will still fail to utterly control their thoughts.

Second, not only is it the case that "no one can surrender his freedom of judging and thinking what he wishes," but it is also true that "not even the wisest know how to keep quiet, not to mention ordinary people."[13] Hence, even if a sovereign were to impose limitations on speech, doing so would ultimately be at best a highly ineffective form of censorship, as among those living under such limitations, no one would be able to give up his freedom of thought, and, thinking freely, no one would be able to keep his thoughts consistently to himself. Strikingly, Spinoza here emphasizes that this applies not only to "ordinary people" but also to "the wisest"—thereby specifically highlighting that even the philosophical few cannot be expected to control their speech. Therefore, Spinoza insists that "anyone can think, and judge, and consequently also speak, without infringing on [the sovereign's] right, provided just that he only speaks or teaches, and defends his view by reason alone, not with deception, anger, hatred, or an intention to introduce something into the republic on the authority of his own decision."[14] This statement seems to contradict the assertion that Spinoza's democracy requires that the philosopher's freedom of speech be curtailed, as it is specifically the philosopher who defends his view by reason alone and thus any limitations on speech under such a democracy would appear to be imposed on the irrational multitude rather than on the philosophical few.

Spinoza's Noble Lie

How are we to understand this apparent contradiction? Strauss's solution to this potential problem is to argue that the appeal to charity functions as a noble lie by Spinoza. While charity as tolerance properly understood is undergirded by an assumption of charity as obedience—insofar as it demands that one heed God's demand for charity and thus recognize the ultimate authority of the Bible—and thus must be fundamentally in conflict with philosophy's unbounded reasoning, Spinoza's argument from the demand for charity to democracy elides this conclusion. According to Strauss, in the *Theological-Political Treatise*, Spinoza "teach[es] a secularized version of the bible which consciously falsifies the bible—it presents a break with the bible in the disguise of a perfection of the bible."[15] Hence, Spinoza's use of God's demand for charity to undergird his political project thus constitutes "a conscious transformation of biblical teaching or use of biblical teaching for non-biblical ends."[16] This is to say, rather than drawing forth the true conclusion of his own argument regarding charity and its relation to freedom of thought and speech, Spinoza falsely denies the conflict between the demand for charity and philosophy and suggests instead that they are not only compatible, but that the demand for charity requires that each may think freely and thus that a democracy tolerate philosophy.

However, just why Spinoza would argue for a democracy specifically still requires explanation. The importance of this question is further stressed by the fact that Strauss is clear that by his reading "the doctrine that man can achieve his bliss by charity is in Spinoza a *kalon pseudos* in the Platonic sense."[17] According to Strauss, for Spinoza, "charity proper (to love the other like oneself) is impossible,"[18] and even if it were possible, it would be possible only for a select few and thus of no political relevance. In reading Spinoza in this way, Strauss highlights the extent to which, like Plato, Spinoza is deeply concerned with natural inequality. For both thinkers, the intellectual love of God is both highest and open only to a few.[19] This leads Spinoza's philosophy to be marked throughout by a "contempt for the vulgar."[20] Yet Spinoza's similarities with Plato stand alongside significant differences in the two thinkers' political conclusions. Whereas in Plato natural inequality is accompanied by a parallel political inequality, in the *Theological-Political Treatise* it is noticeably not.

Strauss considers a number of possibilities in attempting to explain this divergence between Spinoza and Plato, and is markedly both more hesitant and more skeptical in his interpretation of Spinoza throughout this portion of the manuscript. While he explicitly considers aspects of Spinoza's argument "dubious,"[21] ultimately, Strauss seems to conclude that Spinoza's support for political equality must be grounded on three claims. First, the vulgar will never accept the rule of philosopher-kings.

They require government and laws, but will resent subjugation to the rational because "the unreasonable unreasonably regard the reasonable as their equals"[22] and thus cannot be expected pragmatically to tolerate the rule of their perceived equals over them. Second, if a society holds universal tolerance as a norm, then the threat of a rule of priests is eliminated for similar reasons, as each, including irrational individuals, will consider himself equally the judge with regard to spiritual matters and not accept the arbitrary rule of priests. This is important because while, as Strauss notes,[23] Spinoza regards rational life as in principle possible in every society, rule through religion or superstition relies on "a dangerous means."[24] Third, there is a good common to the rational and irrational that political equality furthers without hindering the highest good for the rational. This good is that of "peace and security," which are "objectively to the advantage of each—in this respect all men, the wise and the unwise, are equal."[25] While this is not the highest good, it is nonetheless a good and an important one for the pursuit of the highest good by the rational.[26]

This means that through his noble lie, Spinoza is able to construct an argument for a form of government that both acknowledges the infeasibility of rule by Plato's philosopher-kings and opens the possibility for the philosopher to live securely and peaceably in a state free of the threat of rule by religious authorities precisely by using an argument that is in fact grounded on religious authority against that very authority. For Strauss, therefore, the noble lie that the divine demand for charity entails a requirement of universal toleration thus represents an instance of Spinoza cooperating with "sincere simpletons"[27] for his own end of arguing for a form of government that is both feasible and amenable to the rational pursuit of the highest good even at the same time that in doing so he advocates for a form of government that runs contrary to the sincere simpleton's fundamental commitment to the authority of the Bible.

An Alternative Concept of Charity

Yet how ought we to understand this cooperation within Spinoza's thought? Here it is useful to consider the extent to which the characterization of charity as outlined so far corresponds to Spinoza's own thought. Notably, in the manuscript, Strauss explicitly glosses "charity proper" as "to love the other like oneself"[28]—and this is the form of charity that Strauss declares to be impossible from Spinoza's own position. However, turning to the *Ethics* suggests that Spinoza's thought has room for, and perhaps even requires, a distinct form of charity—to love the other not like oneself, but *as* oneself.[29]

Understanding what loving another as oneself means within Spinoza's thought and how such a thing might be possible requires that we first consider Spinoza's concept of love. In the *Ethics*, Spinoza initially defines love in terms of joy. Along with sadness, joy is one of two fundamental affects that form the basis for the *Ethics*' systematic account of human emotions. Joy is "that passion by which the Mind passes to a greater perfection,"[30] whereas sadness is that passion by which the mind passes to a lesser perfection. In other words, when we take ourselves to have been affected such that our power of acting or our power of thinking has increased, we experience joy, and when we take ourselves to have been affected such that such powers are diminished, we experience sadness.[31] For Spinoza, love is "nothing but Joy with the accompanying idea of an external cause."[32] This is to say that according to Spinoza, to put it plainly, I love another insofar as I think of that other as an external object associated with an increase in my power. As Clare Carlisle notes, this means that unlike joy, love is "inherently cognitive, always involving an idea—that is, an act of thinking" for Spinoza.[33] More specifically it involves a judgment concerning the effect of a given external object on one's power.

Notably, this may not seem like a very promising starting point from which to go looking for forms of charity, as it is an account of love that is strikingly oriented toward the self-interest of the individual who loves and contains no reference to the interest of the individual who is loved. Further, by power, Spinoza means the "striving, by which [a thing] strives to persevere in its being"[34]—and hence my power is explicitly defined as that by way of which I further my self-preservation. Hence, in Spinoza's terms, one loves another insofar as one either thinks that this other serves to further one's own self-preservation or simply thinks that other is associated with an increase in one's power.[35]

However, Spinoza builds from this highly individualistic, and perhaps even cynical, definition of love to an account of love that is surprisingly socially robust. The beginnings of Spinoza's development of the social dimensions of love can be seen in part III of the *Ethics*. In Proposition 33, Spinoza could appear to be discussing what Strauss characterizes as charity, writing "when we love a thing like ourselves, we strive, as far as we can, to bring it about that it loves us in return."[36] But, as the demonstration makes clear, this "like" refers not to a similarity between our love for the thing and our own self-regard, but to a similarity between the thing and ourselves. Spinoza argues that "if a thing is like us, we shall strive to affect it with Joy above all others, *or* we shall strive, as far as we can, to bring it about that the thing we love is affected with Joy, accompanied by the idea of ourselves [as cause], i.e. that it loves us in return."[37] This implies that not only do we love those things and persons we associate with an increase in our own power, but, when those things or persons are similar to us, we will strive to increase their power as well—to help them to better further their own self-preservation and to think of us lovingly.

Yet, what does it mean for a thing to be "like us" for Spinoza? In part IV of the *Ethics*, Spinoza makes clear that "any singular thing whose nature is entirely different from ours can neither aid nor restrain our power of acting, and absolutely, no thing can be either good or evil for us, unless it has something in common with us,"[38] and goes on to argue both that "no thing can be evil through what it has in common with our nature; but insofar as it is evil for us, it is contrary to us"[39] and that "insofar as a thing agrees with our nature, it is necessarily good."[40] To understand what these statements mean, we must recall that, for Spinoza, evil denotes simply what we perceive to affect us with sadness and good what we perceive to affect us with joy.[41] Something is known to be truly good or evil only when we have correctly perceived it to affect us with joy or sadness.[42] Hence, something is evil insofar as it diminishes my power, and I call it evil insofar as I recognize it as having done so. Likewise, something is good insofar as it increases my power, and I call it good insofar as I recognize it as having done so. To return to Spinoza's evaluation of the good or evil of singular things, this means that, insofar as something shares something in common with our nature, that thing is good, that is, it increases our power, and that we love it and seek to be good to it in turn, that is, to increase its power as well.

The importance of this becomes clear when we consider the fact that Spinoza holds that "insofar as men are subject to passions, they cannot be said to agree in nature"[43] and "only insofar as men live according to the guidance of reason, must they always agree in nature."[44] This is a crucial step in Spinoza's argument for the sociability of his concept of love, as it explains why the philosopher loves others. To see why, we will consider two kinds of love in Spinoza: the love of the philosopher for fellow reasoners and the love of the philosopher for the irrational multitude.

First, regarding love among the rational, it is helpful to recall that Spinoza asserts that "what we strive for from reason is nothing but understanding; nor does the Mind, insofar as it uses reason, judge anything else useful to itself except what leads to understanding."[45] In other words, when we seek to increase our power rationally, we seek to increase our power of reasoning.[46] This implies that "we know nothing to be certainly good or evil, except what really leads to understanding or what can prevent us from understanding."[47] Because men disagree in nature insofar as they are subject to passion and agree in nature insofar as they "live according to the guidance of reason,"[48] this means that philosophical friendship is both necessary and necessarily good, increasing the power and furthering the self-preservation of each friend. Insofar as they are rational, reasoners "are joined to one another by the greatest necessity of friendship"[49] because what each seeks most of all is to increase his understanding—especially of the one substance God—or, in other words, to better his reasoning and further himself as a philosopher. A rational interlocutor is thus of supreme utility in the pursuit of his own self-interest and serves as an external object rightly associated with joy for the philosopher, and hence must be loved by the philosopher. Furthermore, as it is in the philosopher's interest for his interlocutor to be as rational as possible, it is likewise in the philosopher's self-interest to aid his interlocutor's reasoning as well, just as it is in the interest of the interlocutor to be aided by him and to aid him in turn. Thus, just as each philosopher loves his fellow reasoner, he is likewise loved by a fellow reasoner.

Second, and perhaps more strikingly, the philosopher must in some sense love the irrational multitude as well according to Spinoza. This may seem surprising when considered in light of Spinoza's often expressed contempt for the irrational multitude. As he writes, "[I]t rarely happens that men live according to the guidance of reason. Instead, their lives are so constituted that they are usually envious and burdensome to one another."[50] Yet, Spinoza also holds that "we do derive, from the society of our fellow men, many more advantages than disadvantages." Given that men rarely live according to the guidance of reason, a society of reasoners is almost certainly an impossibility in Spinoza's eyes, and so it must be the case that even the rational derive many more advantages than disadvantages from living among the irrational than they would from solitary life. Spinoza clarifies this point later in the *Ethics*, noting that "[a] man who is guided by reason is more free in a state, where he lives according to a common decision, than in solitude, where he obeys only himself."[51] Given that Spinoza "call[s] him free who is led by reason alone,"[52] this means that the philosopher is more capable of living guided by reason alone when "keep[ing] the common laws of the state,"[53] even though doing so necessarily entails living among the ignorant. As Strauss notes in his manuscript, this is because when considering the need to sustain the body physically in order to persist in one's being, Spinoza holds that "the powers of each man would hardly be sufficient if men did not help one another."[54]

Yet, while this does mean that the irrational multitude increase the power of the philosopher, it would be overly simplistic to read this as merely indicating that the philosopher's love for them amounts to simply recognizing that living among them is better for his physical well-being that living in solitude would be. Spinoza writes that "a free man strives to join other men to him in friendship, not to repay men with benefits that are equivalent in their eyes, but to lead himself and the others by the free judgment of reason, and to do only those things that he himself knows to be most excellent."[55] In other words, the philosopher's love for others leads him to seek to increase their power as well, to lead them to live by the guidance of reason to the extent he can. Importantly, the fact that Spinoza stresses that the free man does not seek to repay men with benefits "equivalent in their eyes" implies that Spinoza here has not only other rational men in mind, but also irrational ones, as those are the men who would hold other benefits to be "equivalent in their eyes" than those that the free man "knows to be most excellent." This implies two things. First, that the philosopher's love for the irrational expresses itself at least in part in a striving to join them to him in friendship, not merely to benefit from the physical security of living among a society. Second, there must be some sense in which the free man considers the irrational to be like him, since in loving them he seeks to increase their power and thus to affect them with joy. The true good of the irrational multitude and of the reasoner is known by the reasoner to be other than what the irrational take it to be, and the reasoner responds to this knowledge when and as he can by repaying the irrational with this true good.

This is not to say that Strauss's emphasis on Spinoza's low opinion of the vulgar is misplaced, but only to suggest that Strauss's account of charity in Spinoza perhaps does not take Spinoza's rosier claims seriously enough. While Strauss rightly identifies a clear disdain for the multitude running through Spinoza's thought, his account of Spinoza's view of charity also downplays the extent to which Spinoza likewise maintains a persistent commitment to the claim that philosophy leads one to love the world, and with it one's neighbors—even including the simpletons.

Rational regard for one's own self-interest leads one to seek the good of others not only as well as one's good, but truly as one's good. Hence, for Spinoza, love of oneself rightly understood entails love of one's neighbors, and therefore while it may be the case that the doctrine that man can achieve his bliss by charity is a noble lie in Spinoza, it is also the case that in Spinoza the only path by which man can achieve bliss entails its own form of charity.

Notes

1. Leo Strauss, "On Spinoza (c. 1959)," in *Leo Strauss on Religion*, ed. Rasoul Namazi and Svetozar Minkov (Albany: State University of New York Press, 2024), 147.

2. Steven Frankel, "Strauss's 'Fresh Study' Manuscript" in *Leo Strauss on Religion*, ed. Rasoul Namazi and Svetozar Minkov (Albany: State University of New York Press, 2024), 157. That the manuscript ends with a lingering question suggests that Strauss was perhaps dissatisfied with aspects of the manuscript, and may help to explain why Strauss abandoned the approach found therein in favor of the approach taken in the autobiographical preface.

3. Leo Strauss, *Autumn 1959 Course on Spinoza Offered at the University of Chicago*, ed. David Wollenberg (Chicago: Leo Strauss Center, 2018).

4. Strauss, "On Spinoza (c. 1959)," 148.

5. Strauss, "On Spinoza (c. 1959)," 148.

6. Notably, Strauss stops short of this claim in the transcripts of his 1959 course, stating only that "charity is incompatible with any intolerance." See Leo Strauss, "Session 6," 84.

7. Strauss, "On Spinoza (c. 1959)," 148.

8. Strauss, "On Spinoza (c. 1959)," 148.

9. Strauss, "On Spinoza (c. 1959)," 148.

10. Benedictus de Spinoza, "Theological-Political Treatise," in *The Collected Works of Spinoza*, ed. and trans. Edwin Curley, vol. 2 (Princeton: Princeton University Press, 2016), 345. I substitute "sovereigns" here for Curley's "supreme 'powers" for the sake of clarity for readers not familiar with Curley's distinction between power (*potentia*) and 'power (*potestas*).

11. Spinoza, "Theological-Political Treatise," 433.

12. Spinoza, "Theological-Political Treatise," 345. In Strauss's autumn 1959 lectures, he emphasizes that, by his interpretation, Spinoza must be understood as indicating that the "self-enforcing natural right for everyone to think as he pleases ... can be rendered nil by subliminal influences" ("Session 13," 234). I take the Moses example to show that while Spinoza fully admits the importance of influence on man's thinking, he also stops short of the view that this right can be "rendered nil" by such influence.

13. Spinoza, "Theological-Political Treatise," 345.

14. Spinoza, "Theological-Political Treatise," 346–47.
15. Strauss, "On Spinoza (c. 1959)," 150.
16. Strauss, "On Spinoza (c. 1959)," 150.
17. Strauss, "On Spinoza (c. 1959)," 150.
18. Strauss, "On Spinoza (c. 1959)," 149.
19. Strauss, "On Spinoza (c. 1959)," 150. Similarly, in the autumn 1959 course, see Strauss, "Session 9," 140: "[Spinoza's] serious teaching is the old one: the perfection of man consists in speculative perfection, in theoretical perfection, and not in moral perfection as such."
20. Strauss, "On Spinoza (c. 1959)," 150.
21. Strauss, "On Spinoza (c. 1959)," 153.
22. Strauss, "On Spinoza (c. 1959)," 151.
23. Strauss, "On Spinoza (c. 1959)," 150.
24. Strauss, "On Spinoza (c. 1959)," 152–153.
25. Strauss, "On Spinoza (c. 1959)," 152.
26. In the 1959 lectures, Strauss frequently refers to this good as a "subrational good." See for example "Session 10," 169: "subrational good—by which I do not mean that it is irrational" and "Session 11," 198: "the subrational good, as I call it (which is not an irrational good—it is rational, but not fully rational."
27. Strauss, "On Spinoza (c. 1959)," 150.
28. Strauss, "On Spinoza (c. 1959)," 149.
29. For a recent alternate interpretation of charity within Spinoza's thought, see Clare Carlisle, *Spinoza's Religion: A New Reading of the Ethics* (Princeton: Princeton University Press, 2021), 97–99. Carlisle suggests instead that charity ought to be understood as human "participation in the love that constitutes God's being" (98).
30. Benedictus de Spinoza, "Ethics," in *The Collected Works of Spinoza*, ed. and trans. Edwin Curley, vol. 1 (Princeton: Princeton University Press, 1985), IIIP11S, 501.
31. Due to Spinoza's parallel doctrine, an increase of one's power of acting must entail an increase of one's power of thinking and vice versa. The same applies with regard to diminution of one's powers. See Spinoza, IIIP11, 500.
32. Spinoza, IIIP13S, 502.
33. Carlisle, *Spinoza's Religion*, 99.
34. Spinoza, IIIP7, 499.
35. Spinoza is clear that we may come to love external objects that do not increase our power in two ways. First, we may be mistaken that a given external object increases our power and thus love something or someone that does not further our self-preservation without realizing it. Second, we may come to love or hate things purely by accidental association. Spinoza argues that if we suppose that one is affected by two things at once, the first of which neither increases nor decreases one's power, and the second of which increases one's power, then the first thing will be associated by one with an increase in one's power. Hence when encountered on its own, this thing will be taken to

affect one with joy such that the "former thing will be the cause of Joy or Sadness—not through itself, but accidentally" (IIIP15Dem1, 503). This accidental association extends to alter our relation to external objects as well, and thus from this "we understand how it can happen that we love or hate some things without any cause known to us" (IIIP15S, 503).

36. Spinoza, IIIP33, 513.
37. Spinoza, IIIP33D, 513.
38. Spinoza, IVP29, 560.
39. Spinoza, IVP30, 560.
40. Spinoza, IVP31, 560.
41. Spinoza, IVP8D, 550.
42. Importantly, Spinoza's account of good and evil allows for the possibility for us to have been affected with joy or sadness without being fully conscious of it, and thus to be mistaken as to whether something is in fact good or evil. See Spinoza, IVP8, 550.
43. Spinoza, IVP32, 561. Spinoza holds this view because to be subject to the passions entails a negation of power, and "things that agree only in a negation ... really agree in nothing." IVP32S, 561.
44. Spinoza, IVP35, 563.
45. Spinoza, IVP26, 559.
46. Another way to express this would be to say that we seek adequate ideas of things, because it is only through adequate ideas of them that we may have certain knowledge of whether they are good or evil. Spinoza regularly characterizes knowledge as both an object to be grasped and the activity by which it is grasped. In IVP27D, 559, he writes, "But the mind has certainty of things only insofar as it has adequate ideas, or (*what is the same thing*) insofar as it reasons" (emphasis added), making clear that he views the two as interchangeable.
47. Spinoza, IVP27, 559.
48. Spinoza, IVP35, 563.
49. Spinoza, IVP71D, 586.
50. Spinoza, IVP35S, 564.
51. Spinoza, IVP73, 587.
52. Spinoza, IVP68D, 584.
53. Spinoza, IVP73D, 587.
54. Spinoza, XXVIII, 593.
55. Spinoza, IVP70, 585.

PART FIVE

Transcript 5.1

LEO STRAUSS, NOTES ON PLATO'S
SYMPOSIUM (C. 1959)

Editorial note: This is the transcript of an untitled typescript found in Leo Strauss Papers, box 18, folder 17, Special Collections Research Center, University of Chicago Library. Based on the content one can surmise that these notes were written sometime in 1959, the period when Strauss was teaching his famous course on Plato's *Symposium*, edited by Seth Benardete and published as Leo Strauss, *On Plato's Symposium* (Chicago: University of Chicago Press, 2001). These notes can be therefore considered a companion piece of that course transcript. Numbers in the curly brackets refer to the page numbers of the typescript. Additions are all indicated by square brackets. The underlinings in the transcript have been replaced with italics.

{1} The proper state of mind in which to approach a Platonic work: not that of a babe in the woods, yet a certain innocence, some sort of virginity. *Monos pros monon* [one alone to one alone]:[1] a judicious disregard of "the results of Platonic research": what we can *know* is ultimately the Corpus Platonicum as it has come down to us from antiquity. That this or that is an *early* dialogue or above all that this or that is a *spurious* dialogue is less certain than that the dialogue in question was regarded as a work of Plato by men who knew Greek better than any classical scholar, to say nothing at present of Plato's school.

3 points to remember when studying any Platonic work: 1) Plato didn't write treatises—"step by step as well as correctly"[2]—but beautiful dialogues, beautiful fictions, beautiful lies. What is the general character of

these beautiful lies? What is *the* beautiful lie? → 2 and 3 2) Logographic necessity—nothing superfluous—everything is meaningful—in the dialogues (≠ the world) there is no *tyche* [chance]—e.g. that Socrates is snub-nosed: so that Aristotle can illustrate by Socrates's snub-nosedness that the ideas are "in matter."[3] 3) No dialogue about the whole—each dialogue deals with a part—the utmost a dialogue can teach is the truth about a part—a partial truth—a half-truth. Every dialogue abstracts from something. If the result of a given dialogue is paradoxical or shocking we ought not to be shocked by it: the paradox will be corrected in other dialogues. For: that is ὀρθή δόξα [orthe doxa = correct opinion]

I) *Symposium*: eros—the *god* eros—the only Platonic dialogue to be devoted to a *god* → *Symposium* the Platonic theology (*Laws* X and *Republic* II belong to a non-theological context). The god chosen for discussion in *the* Platonic dialogue on a god is a little god, {2} a god not worshipped by the city—yet the most plausible god (everyone has *experienced* him). Now, of the only god ever made the theme of a dialogue, *Socrates* says that he is not a god at all but only a demon; and it appears that he is not even a demon, a superhuman willing and thinking being, but = *epithumia* [desire, concupiscence] something which is only *in* mortal animals—which is not self-subsisting.

II) The *theme* of the Symposium is most singular—so is the *title*—the only title of a dialogue which indicates the *occasion*. The only occasion of a dialogue indicated by a title is a *symposion*—*parresia* [speaking candidly]—*hybris* → Socrates's hybris.

Titles: 25 - 7 - 3—*Erastai* the participants → Symposium and Epinomis. Symposium: the Olympian gods are not but there are cosmic gods—Symposium *abstracts* from the cosmic gods [Strauss's note: *Ap. Soc.* 26c-d: S. does not refute the charge that he does not believe in the Olympian gods but refutes the charge that he does not believe in the cosmic gods]: it is atheistic. "Socrates" occurs only in "Apology of Socrates," the *accusation*—not the gods which the city worships = not the Olympian gods. Symposium teaches that Socrates is guilty of that charge—this is Socrates's hybris.

III) Symposium a *narrated* dialogue: 9 of them—3 narrated by people other than Socrates: Parmenides, Phaedo, Symposium. Parmenides and Phaedo present the *young* Socrates: the *physiologos* who turns to teleology—the whole is altogether good, or beautiful → there are no *ideas* of ugly or base things.

Socrates's speech in the Symposium = report of Diotima's speech—addressed to the *young* Socrates → culminates in the vision of the beautiful itself. More than that: central of the 7 speeches in the Symposium is that by Aristophanes—who had attacked the *young* Socrates in the Clouds for saying among other things "Zeus is not."

IV) Symposium *doubly* narrated *and* narrated for the *second time*—this is unique—someone had heard that there were erotic speeches {3} at a dinner at which Agathon, Socrates and Alcibiades had participated and that dinner had taken place a short while ago. The reply: Agathon has left Athens years ago—Agathon's absence from Athens *proves* that the exchange of speeches *cannot* have taken place a short while ago; the other fellow did not know that Agathon had left Athens. The reply does not refer to Socrates: Socrates is always in Athens. But what about Alcibiades? Was not Alcibiades *absent* since 415? The argument doesn't make sense if Alcibiades is not in Athens at the time when the conversations are narrated—and: whether or not *Alcibiades* (≠ Agathon) is in Athens, is of course a matter of public and universal knowledge → 407. The dinner itself: 416. Alcibiades had left or deserted Athens in 415: the mutilation of the Hermae and the profanation of the Eleusinian mysteries. Phaedrus and Eryximachus involved in that scandal → 3 out of the 7 speakers of the Symposium known to be involved in that scandal. And: in the Symposium a divulgation of the mysteries takes place (Aristophanes and especially Socrates) → Symposium tells the true story of what happened in 416. That story can be told now, in 407, after the reconciliation of Athens and Alcibiades and after the Eleusinean procession could take place again thanks to Alcibiades. Story told originally by Aristodemus who was present: he is the leak from those present to the younger comrades of Socrates, and the emotional Apollodorus is the leak from the Socratics to the outside world. Bottleneck: shows that even now the matter is not entirely public. But the story itself: nothing scandalous—everything was decent, no Black Mass—above all Alcibiades came in when everything was over—and no *Athenian* mysteries but *Mantinean* mysteries. Yet: *Socrates* was the culprit → Socrates's hybris → *Plato's* hybris.

{4} V) The original accusation of Socrates's hybris had been made by a poet, Aristophanes' Clouds—generally, the poets accuse the philosophers of hybris (cf. *Laws* X, *Republic* X) → The Symposium meets this accusation. A tragic poet had won in a tragic contest; Symposium the contest of the victorious tragic poet and Socrates with Dionysus as judge → *Frogs*: contest between 2 tragic poets decided with a view as to how they stand to Alcibiades. Plato's contest with Aristophanes' *Frogs*: *after* the contest between 2 tragic poets, a contest between *all* forms of Athenian wisdom, rhetoric, medicine, comedy, tragedy, philosophy, in which Alcibiades as Dionysus is the judge. He crowns *Socrates*.

VI) 6 speeches in praise of eros and one speech in praise of Socrates. Uninspired eros subject to something extraneous to it—gain, virtue (= *nomos* [law, convention]), *techne* [art]; inspired: eros sovereign—ugliness, beauty, the good (inspired by Diotima). Alcibiades's speech inspired by wine.

The central speech: Aristophanes—the only one to deal with the most comprehensive theme, the Olympian gods and the cosmic gods. Man originally descended from the cosmic gods (sun, moon and earth)—their shape (round) and somehow their motion (turning around their axis)—had nothing in common with the Olympian gods except their sexuality. This man shares also with brutes but no mating seasons → specific of man and Olympian gods: sexiness. But man was not meant to live in Olympian bliss: no physis [nature] limitation of his sex life but nomos [law, convention] limitations, i.e. prohibition against incest. This nomos imposed on him by the Olympian gods who are not subject to that nomos and who impose it on man not out of love for man but for *their* own profit: domestication of man. {5} Still, through nomos man becomes human → the cause which makes man human must itself be of human shape: the Olympian gods. Original man is split into 2 and thus acquires erect stature—but not for looking up to the cosmic gods: from the Olympian gods' point of view in order to honor and feed them; from men's point of view for the sake of amorous embrace: men received an erect stature so that they could *lie* together. Eros is distinctly human: eros is a desire for remedying the scission effected by Zeus—the countermove to Zeus's move—rebellion against the nomos. (Biblical: the only action in the performance of which one cannot think of God is the sexual act.)[4]

Eros is seeking the other half—but owing to Apollo's blunder the other half remains skinless and perished → *eros can never reach its goal*: it is essentially tragic. Eros is seeking the other half—one's own flesh and blood → eros is essentially *incestuous*; but also: eros is essentially love for one's own—one's own is necessarily distinguished from the alien → eros for the *fatherland*. [Footnote. Since *the* goal of eros is unattainable, *political* life is the best → Alcibiades: both Alcibiades and Aristophanes are bodily handicapped (concerned with the body). Alcibiades agrees with Aristophanes that Socrates is completely unerotic.]

Agathon: eros of the *beautiful* (≠ one's own)

These 2 conceptions of eros are the most important premises of Socrates's speech on eros. That speech: 7 parts (just as Symposium as a whole - 7 speeches) I) how to praise eros = the true rhetoric (corresponds to Phaedrus' speech → Phaedrus)—silence on the base in eros → Socrates abstracts from that. II) Dialogue between Socrates and Agathon. III–VII) = Socrates's speech: eros is neither love of one's own (Aristophanes) nor of the beautiful (Agathon) but of the good. The exposition of this truth is accompanied by silence {6} about gods, no immortality proper, no pederasty. But in the 3 last parts of Socrates's Diotima speech—a) love in procreation = love of *one's own* b) love of eternal glory (especially the poets) = love of *one's own* c) love of the *beautiful* culminating in the vision of the beautiful itself: restoration of these forms of eros (even of pederasty)—but *no* restoration of gods and immortality proper. [Strauss's note: ἔρως [eros] = maternal instinct—no natural inclination toward moral virtue—cf. ἔρως [eros] of φρόνησις [phronesis=prudence] (Phaedrus) ≠ ἔρως of virtue: Xenophon *On Hunting*—cf. Thomas Aquinas.] Massive contradiction: denial that eros is of the beautiful—and the speech culminates in praise of eros of the beautiful. Why that? Eros is of one's own on the one hand and of the beautiful on the other—in both respects it creates the gods, the Olympian gods: 1) beautiful → beautiful beings—of eternal beauty and youth; 2) one's own → ancestors, fatherland, polis [city], dike [justice]—*avenging* gods mediated by thymos [spiritedness] (not mentioned in Symposium). By recognizing the *grounds* of the Olympian gods in eros, by understanding them as *postulates* of eros one becomes free of them—eros thus becomes fully: *natural* eros—The Symposium presents the catharsis of eros. There is another kind of eros → the good = the true → the cosmic gods—this eros is not in the ordinary sense of the word most beautiful, therefore abstracted from in the *praise* of eros.

VII) The context—contest with poets—the poets do *not* purify eros—they abandon themselves to the demands of eros—either of one's own (comic poet) or of the beautiful (tragic poet) but: they believe in the Olympian gods as little as Socrates. What then is the ground of *Socrates's* superiority to the poets both present and absent? Socrates: philosophic presentation of poetry and poetic presentation of philosophy: the poets *might* give a poetic presentation of philosophy but no philosophic presentation of poetry. Socrates can give a disenchanting presentation of poetry and an enchanting {7} presentation of philosophy. The poets are only enchanters: Socrates is also a disenchanter. The poets are *only* inspired by their madness: Socrates is also sober. We could leave it at that if there were only 1 kind of poetry, but there are 2 kinds, tragedy and comedy; tragedy is enchanting but comedy is disenchanting. *Hen monon sophon* [the one wise thing] wishes and does not wish to be called Zeus[5]—wishes → tragedy, enchanting; does not wish → comedy, disenchanting. The former is higher: Agathon is awake when Aristophanes has already dozed off—but not simply: the technē tragedian [tragedian by art] is also a comedian— the statements cannot be inverted. The poet who is both a tragic poet and a comic poet is *Socrates*—but is this true?

The explicit discussion of the poets: they generate the beautiful— works of immortal beauty—but not out of love of the beautiful but for the sake of their eternal fame: love of one's own ≠ Socrates inspired by love of the beautiful and free from love of his own does not produce works of immortal beauty: he does not *write* → Socrates wins the contest with the poets because his love is *pure*.

But *Plato* wrote. Is it possible that Plato who had realized the true standard should have had the baseness so harmlessly to fall short of it? → Socrates *could* not write—he could not *invent*, he was a midwife, barren— but: the 3 kymata [waves] in the *Republic*. Socrates was rhetor—he could make speeches—and therefore he could have written them down. Socrates's rhetoric and its *limitations*: *Gorgias*—exhibitio ad Gorgiam: his success with Polus, his failure with Callicles—he could not write punitive speeches—*therefore* he did not write. He could have written comedies but the highest is {8} not comedy but tragedy concealing comedy. *The* punitive man, the angry man, Thrasymachus → Farabi.[6] Young Socrates ≠ old Socrates = he discovered the *necessity* of the αἰσχρὸν [aischrón = shameful, base] and ἄλογον [álogon = irrational]—the recalcitrance of the political—. The limitation of Socrates: Plato in Syracuse, Xenophon with Cyrus and almost founder of a city—Socrates was not political enough to write— the contest with the poets simply (≠ the poets present at the Banquet) is won only through Plato.

VIII) Alcibiades's speech 1) Socrates a Marsyas—superior to Marsyas— flutes—the religious and tragic effect of "statues of *gods.*" Socrates's speeches [Strauss's note: but no reference *to* gods] 2) Socrates as Silenus—his *deeds*: outwardly he is erotic and ignorant—inwardly he is full of contempt for all men, even for Alcibiades, and he is full of knowledge— but Alcibiades did not discover that inward or secret knowledge although he slept with Socrates—he is not even aware of his having missed it—he only discovered Socrates's sophrosyne [moderation] = hybris. Socrates guilty of hybris but not guilty of corrupting the young—guilty of hybris: the gods worshipped by the city—but this hybris is identical with his sophrosyne: the fact that his eros has been purified or he does not assert what he does not know: cautious-bold. [Strauss's note: ὕβρις—σωφροσύνη [hybris - moderation] → μανία [mania = madness] of σωφρ.—this primary opposition (thought ≠ speech)—this ultimate identity (the μανία of the pre-Socratics)] 3) the Silenus-like character of Socrates's *speeches*: externally ridiculous, internally "statues of *virtue*" - = *comedies*.

Socrates had presented his eros in his speech as love of the beautiful (≠ one's own)—yet silence on eros in the highest stages there → eros *proper* is for living human beings, the young and beautiful ones with whom one can be present in body Antigone v. 1— the eros for the young which is effective through *writings* is alien to him.

Socrates as presented by Alcibiades: Socrates does not love at all—he despises all men—yet he *cares* for men—? because he loves to *be* loved—his eros is only self-love, love of his own—but: love of what is most his own (his soul) and therefore for his soul being best.

{9} Phaedrus ≠ Pausanias the omitted speeches—how to figure them out? → love of gain.

Eryximachus

Aristophanes ≠ Agathon → love of one's own, of something which is outside the lover

Socrates—Alcibiades → Socrates lover of gain → one should distrust the lover: beginning of *Phaedrus*: the Symposium the beginning of the love affair with Phaedrus (also Isocrates only 20 at date of Symposium).[7]

IX) Alcibiades's speech the satyr play → a *tragedy* preceded it a) the tragedy = Alcibiades's betrayal of philosophy, desertion of philosophy which Socrates was helpless to prevent. b) the *Symposium* a tragedy—Socrates's speech a tragedy—?how this possible? punishment presupposes: dike [justice] or law—tragedy a nomos [law, convention] (*Laws* 817b)—a unity which is as ennobling as it is spurious. This tragedy = nomos is the poetic presentation of philosophy which culminates in the nomos regarding eros (end of Socrates's speech) (cf. Pausanias's deliberative speech): the purport of the nomos: eros proper → human beings, especially males. The reasoning *leading up* to that nomos is Diotima's = young Socrates—the *conclusion* (= nomos) is all Socrates's—but: the cautious formulation ("not easily a better helper")—the cautious formulation does not justify the nomos: Socrates is not a legislator. Alcibiades says in effect: Socrates does not honor eros—he transgresses the law which he himself laid down. The alternative to eros as a helper toward philosophy: dike [*justice*] (*Republic*).

Notes

1. An allusion to Plotinus's statement: the "flight of the alone to the alone." See Plotinus, *Enneads* 6.9.11, 1.6.7, 6.7.34. For Strauss's meaning here, see Leo Strauss, *Xenophon's Socratic Discourse: An Interpretation of the Oeconomicus* (Ithaca: Cornell University Press, 1970), xiii.
2. See Plato, *Symposium* 210e2.
3. Aristotle, *Metaphysics* 1037a20-b7.
4. See Aristotle, *Nicomachean Ethics* 1152b15-20.
5. Attributed to Heraclitus (Diels–Kranz 22 B 32).
6. See Leo Strauss, "Fârâbî's Plato," in *Louis Ginzberg: Jubilee Volume on the Occasion of His Seventieth Birthday* (New York: American Academy for Jewish Research, 1945), 383, or in *Leo Strauss's Published but Uncollected English Writings:1937–1972*, edited by Steven J. Lenzner and Svetozar Y. Minkov (South Bend, IN: St. Augustine Press), 97–98.
7. See Plato, *Phaedrus* 278e.

EDITED AND TRANSCRIBED BY SVETOZAR Y. MINKOV

Transcript 5.2

LEO STRAUSS, NOTES ON AGATHON'S
SPEECH IN PLATO'S *SYMPOSIUM* (C. 1959)

Editorial Note: The following is a transcription of Strauss's notes on Agathon's speech in the *Symposium* that he used in his course on the dialogue in the fall quarter of 1959 at the University of Chicago. The notes are found in Leo Strauss Papers, box 17, folder 6, Special Collections Research Center, University of Chicago Library. Like the transcripts 5.1 and 5.3 in this volume, these notes are published here as a supplement to Strauss's class sessions on Agathon as found in Leo Strauss, *On Plato's Symposium*, edited by Seth Benardete (Chicago: University of Chicago Press, 2001), 155–73. The notes here have the benefit of containing detailed references to the text (with the marginal Stephanus numbers), cross-references, underlinings, and other ways of indicating emphasis, the punctuation, and the general flow of how Strauss connected lines of thoughts and consequences, words in the original Greek, additional observations, and so forth. Numbers in the angle brackets refer to the page numbers of the manuscript. Additions are all indicated by curly brackets. The underlinings in the notes have been replaced with italics.

<28> **Agathon's Speech** (194e4-197e8)
194e4 Agathon is the only one who begins with Εγώ {I}: he *is* beautiful & successful and he *knows* that he is beautiful and successful.
<29> 194e4-5 To speak of how one ought to speak is not truly to speak [unless ῥητορική {art of rhetoric} is based on ψυχολογία {psychology}]

194e5-6 Aristophanes had blamed all earlier *human beings*—Agathon only blames all *earlier speakers tonight* → Agathon is not a revolutionary, an iconoclast, for iconoclasm is αἰσχρόν τι {something/somewhat shameful}.

194e6-195a5 For the first time, the *god himself* becomes the theme—not as something merely existing *in* the souls of men etc. but as *self-subsisting*—of *what quality* he is. *Aristophanes* had almost touched upon this (189d3-5): δύναμις {power} of ἔρως {eros} ≠ the human *nature*, not the *nature* of ἔρως → will Agathon discuss the *nature* of ἔρως?

195a1-3: the *philosophic* character of his speech: the universal statement on *every* praise regarding *every* possible thing → the gifts of ἔρως = that of which ἔρως is the *cause*.

195a5-7 the *plan* of his speech

I ἔρως οἷος {qualities of} 1) κάλλιστος {most beautiful} 195a7-196b5 2) ἄριστος {best} (196b5-197b)

II ἔρως as αἰτία {cause} (197a-e)

the *whole* speech of Agathon is characterized by unusually clear *order*—for τάξις {order} is an element of κάλλος {beauty}.

But: he does not raise the *primary* question—of the τί ἐστι {what is} of ἔρως—i.e. quid sit deus {what is a god?}.

His praise of ἔρως is necessarily a *critique of the other gods*: they all are less than perfect regarding beauty and goodness.

195a7-b5 The first subdivision of ἔρως' beauty is his *youthfulness*—proven by the fact that he is always with the young and runs away from the old—but why is he the *youngest* of the gods? He is *wholly* young, young in every respect—*therefore* the *youngest* (god). Cf. "idea" of beauty = αὐτὸ τὸ καλόν {the beautiful itself}— is of course τὸ κάλλιστον {*most* beautiful}.

All other gods are *older* than ἔρως → all other gods are more or less *old*, and hence more or less *ugly*.

195b5 only love of similar for similar: the theme of the pederasts—but not used by *Agathon* for this purpose: he is *not* concerned with defense of pederasty.

195b6-c6 *What* does he grant to Phaedrus? Cf. 180b6-8. But does he grant that ἔρως is *not* in the beloved?—He disagrees with Hesiod & Parmenides—*not with Homer* although Homer too speaks of θεομαχίαι {battles of gods} (*Rep.* 378d3-5): he does {not—ed.}wish to blame Homer (→ d1) [the *oldest poet*: is there not a contrast between the blame of the old γῆρας {oldness} and the praise of Homer?]

Originally, Ἀνάγκη {Necessity} ruled over the gods, now Ἔρως rules (i.e. *not* Zeus is the king of the gods). If the stories told by Hesiod & Parmenides *are* true, ἔρως vanquished ἀνάγκη - yet ἔρως is the youngest god: he cannot always have ruled →ἀνάγκη must have ruled [→ the stories told by Hesiod & Parmenides *are* true [→the gods other than ἔρως lack ἀρετή {virtue}. Agathon tacitly opposes Aristophanes who implied that ἀνάγκη is stronger than ἔρως-.

Savage beginnings → progress—i.e. good ≠ old—as Phaedrus implied and no one, not even Aristophanes, contested (ἡ ἀρχαία φύσις {the *oldest* nature} is the model)—Agathon contests it (cf. *Legg*. III): the divination of ἀρχή = τέλος {end}. But Aristophanes contested already the assertion that ἔρως is the oldest god—implicitly → there is a progress of enlightenment, a progress of progress in the speeches: Ἔρως the oldest god; ἔρως younger than the Olympian gods; ἔρως explicitly the youngest god; ἔρως not a god at all.

If ἔρως is the oldest god, ἔρως affects *all* things → all things love: ἔρως is *not* specifically human (→ Eryximachus) ≠ ἔρως is not the oldest god: not all things love (Aristophanes: neither the cosmic gods nor the Olympian gods nor even the brutes) → Agathon in {195}e4-7 and 197a1-3.

195c6-e8 Ἔρως is tender, gentle, delicate.

195c7-d7 the praise of Homer (cf. the silence on Homer in c2)—yet: Homer praised not ἔρως, but Ἄτη {Atë}, the god*dess* of mischief [a) not a male god, but a female god, b) not love, but mischief → Homer conceived of ἔρως as something much *sterner* than Agathon does]. With due euphemism, the elegant (εὐσχήμων) poet Agathon suggests that the *oldest* of all poets could not have done justice to the *youngest* of all gods: only the *youngest* poet who is in his way eternally young, can do this. In the thought of the *ancients*, Ἄτη {Ate}, the daughter of Zeus, occupies the place which in the thought of the *moderns* is occupied by ἔρως: the softening of manners. {Note on the back:> no longer "guilt-ridden" and "fear-ridden" → Agathon transforms Ἄτη into ἔρως—something not-beautiful into something beautiful. ≠ Aristophanes: the limping god Hephaestus who was *deceived* by his wife *alone* of the gods understands ἔρως—ἔτι {besides}, Homer places the softness of Ἄτη only in her *feet*, not in her whole being, as Agathon does (e7). Homer Il. 19.92-94 continues: βλάπτουσ' ἀνθρώπους {she who damages/hurts human beings}.

195d7-e8 Another correction of Homer: Ἔρως does not walk on such hard things as heads or skulls.

195e3: souls are the *softest* of beings → e5-6: souls *as souls* are soft, but ἤθη {characters} may be σκληρά {hard}—cf. 196a3—

<30> 195e4-7 Ἔρως does not dwell in the souls of *all gods* and *men*—he does not dwell in the souls of the hard or harsh gods—yet which god is harder and harsher than Ares, and ἔρως dwells in the soul of Ares (cf. 196d2) → ἔρως *makes* all souls soft [Und dennoch hat die harte Brust {Even the hard heart ... —a line from a German folk-song, ed.}]

196a1-7 Ἔρως is ὑγρός (wet, fluid, loose, pliant, serpentine, languishing [melting]) of *shape* (εἶδος)—[*the* εἶδος does not become a theme of Agathon]—therefore, he can pass through every soul, for every soul *as soul* is soft. *This* constitutes his συμμετρία: he makes himself symmetric to everybody—*his symmetry is his all-pliancy*—[by being pliant to all, he is also pliant to the ἄμετροι [measureless]—no distinction between noble and base ἔρως: ἔρως is *as such* noble.]

196a7-b3 ἔρως' beauty of *color* or *complexion*: since he *dwells* among those of beautiful color, he must possess beautiful colors—!

Agathon on ἔρως' *beauty*—i.e. the beauty of his *body*—he is young, delicate, of a pliant shape and of beautiful color—cf. *Rhet.* I 5.11, 13: Agathon omits *strength* and *size*—but: these 4 qualities are not sufficient for making a human being beautiful → *nothing is said of human shape*—ἔρως has the beauty of a *serpent* or a *butterfly* as much as the beauty of a human shape → b4-5: the enumeration of ἔρως' beautiful qualities is not complete.

196b4-5 (cf. 195a7)—Ἔρως' *goodness* is *not* his κάλλος → ἀρετή {virtue} is *not* καλόν {beautiful}—for: beauty = beauty of the *body*.

the 4 parts of beauty —in the sequel, *the 4 parts of goodness*
    youth   justice
    delicacy   σωφροσ. [moderation] for a similar parallel (cf. virtues of the body and the virtues of the soul), s. *Legg.* 631b6ff.

<u>pliancy</u>   ἀνδρεία {courage} (cf. ad c3-d5)
<u>beautiful color</u>   σοφία {wisdom}

196b6-c3 the greatest: not justice, but the combination of justice (not hurting others) and immunity to injustice (not being hurt)

ἔρως rules as a king over the *gods* (195c6) and the laws are the kings of the *city* [there is no connection between these two ruler-ruled relationships—for ἔρως' rule is gentle, and the rule of the νόμοι {laws} is not—Agathon is even more unpolitical than Aristophanes?]

196c3-d5 the argument: a very great coward of the greatest pliancy could control the bravest without *being* the bravest—cf. also the fact that ἔρως cannot be touched by βία {violence} (b9-c1)—Agathon κωμῳδεῖ τὸν θεόν {treats the god comically}

196d1-2 *the transition from the self-subsisting god* ἔρως *to the* ἔρως-*for* in Ares (cf. already c5-6: is ἔρως *a kind* of pleasure?)

196d1-2 the *heterosexual* love—

196d5-6 the account of ἔρως' σοφία {eros' *wisdom*} (≠ of his beauty) claims to be *complete*—silence on the account of his justice, *moderation*, and courage

196d6-e1 Agathon praises his τέχνη as Eryximachus did his → cf. ad e1-6 (≠ his Muse, as Aristophanes)—for Aristophanes did not lay claim to wisdom because his concern was with return to the ἀρχαία φύσις {ancient nature} which antedates the very possibility of wisdom. And:

196e1-6 Ἔρως is wise *first* because he is a poet and the one who makes others poetic [but does not say that ἔρως is indispensable for poetry {LS' note on the back:} → his τέχνη {art} is as love-less as Er[yximachus]→ the φύσει ἄριστοι {best by nature} who are genuinely ἄριστοι {best, pl.} precisely because they are *not* inspired by ἔρως, as Phaedrus said (179a9)—perhaps Homer was such a poet?]

196e6-197a3 Ἔρως is wise *secondly* and *centrally* because the ποίησις {making}, i.e. the γένεσις {generation} and the φύσις {nature}of *all* ζῷα {animals} is his work. Tacit exclusion of pederasty. And: there was no γένεσις and φύσις of *any* ζῷα *prior* to ἔρως—the *gods* did not come into being by generation, through parents—were they *always*? or *how* did they come into being? Agathon does not answer these questions, for he deals only with *one* god, ἔρως: Ἔρως was *not* always, for he is the *youngest* god—he was *not* generated by parents (he agrees with Phaedrus in many things—195b6—and *especially* in this: 178b2-3)—for every generation by parents *presupposes* Ἔρως.

Ἔρως' rule was preceded by that of Ἀνάγκη {Necessity} (cf. ad 195b6-c6): did Ἀνάγκη produce Ἔρως? but if this were the case, how could Ἔρως be simply the *opposite* of Ἀνάγκη?

197a3-b9 Ἔρως is wise *thirdly* by being the inspirer of all *handling* of τέχναι {arts}—

197a3-6 *fame* in any art is due to being touched by ἔρως—e.g. fame in poetry (≠ poetry *itself*)

<31> 197a6-b3 He mentions only *gods* who became famous in the arts—because they were led by ἐπιθυμία {desire} and ἔρως (ἔρως = ἐπιθυμία—not a god). 5 gods and 7 arts.

The central *art* is μουσική [musical] → to make us see the contrast with 196d6-e6: poetry (≠ fame for poetry) does not need ἔρως.

The central *god* is Hephaestus—love for *whom* made him famous in his art? love for his wife Aphrodite? Hephaestus is also famous for the love of his wife Aphrodite for Ares—did *Aphrodite & Ares* become famous as inventors by virtue of their love? what is that ἔρως which inspires the invention of the arts? (cf. also the role of Hephaestus in *Aristophanes'* speech) → Contrary to Aristophanes, Agathon conceives of ἔρως as *civilizing* force. (cf. the silence on ἔρως in b1-3—beginning from "Muses").

197b3 through ἔρως Zeus learned to rule gods and men—Zeus rules men too—but the *cities* are ruled by *laws* (196c2-3) → no clear connection between the rule of Zeus *or* ἔρως and the rule of *laws*.

Zeus rules gods (and men), but Ἔρως rules Zeus (195c6): did Ἔρως teach Zeus how to rule Ἔρως? or is Ἔρως not a god at all? cf. ἐπιθυμία καὶ ἔρως {desire and eros} in a7.

197b3-5 Since ἔρως taught Zeus to rule *gods and men*, there arose friendship and peace among the *gods*: must the gods rule men so that there can be peace among the gods? are men absorbed into the gods or vice versa? Ἔρως is no longer an absolute: but: Ἔρως *of*—i.e. of *beauty*.

197b5-7 He now explicitly grants the truth of the stories told by Hesiod & Parmenides. (cf. 195c3).

197b7-9 Peace & friendship arose among the gods—not since Ἔρως *rules* (195c6) but since this god *came into being* or *sprang forth*—from what or through what? out of nothing and through nothing? then he *is* nothing—as a self-subsisting being. We noted some changes from Ἔρως as a self-subsisting being, i.e. a god, to a ἔρως as an activity *of* the soul or something-*for* → as a *god*, ἔρως is *nothing*, but he *is* most powerfully *in* the souls [*hence he has no human shape*]. As a self-subsisting being, ἔρως is nothing—yet we *speak* of him as a self-subsisting being—πως {somehow} he is a self-subsisting being: he *becomes* a self-subsisting {being} through *poetry*, through *tragic* poetry, for poetry as poetry *precedes* ἔρως (196e1-6) and ἔρως rules Zeus; more simply: the other gods *presuppose* ἔρως—for they have *parents*: *their* self-subsistence breaks down with Ἔρως' self-subsistence.

Ἔρως is ἔρως τοῦ κάλλους {of beauty} or more precisely ἐρᾶν τοῦ κάλλους {loving of beauty}.

Now, we have seen that Agathon uses καλόν only in the sense of bodily beauty—he never applies καλόν to the virtues → *the love of bodily beauty is the ground for everything good for gods & men*. But: ἐρᾶν τοῦ κάλλους {loving the beauty} may also mean: love of *honors* (cf. {Xenophon's} *Memor*. III beg.) → φιλοτιμία {love of honor} is not merely a byproduct of ἔρως (Phaedrus) but a *kind* of ἔρως: the love of *fame* → the gods who became famous as artisans-artists, were indeed inspired by ἔρως, but not by ἔρως for bodily beauty but by the ἔρως for *fame*. The gods were the originators of civilisation, not indeed out of φιλανθρωπία {philanthropy} but out of φιλοτιμία.

Agathon is the first to transcend the level of bodily love—since ἔρως is on the highest level love of fame, ἔρως is in *harmony* with civilisation (≠ Aristophanes).

But: what about Agathon's *own* ἔργον {function}? He owes his *fame* as a poet to his *love* of fame—his poetry *itself*, his *wisdom* is not connected with ἔρως (cf. ad 196d6-e6): he has *no ἔρως for wisdom*.

Through "loving the beautiful things" all good things have arisen for both gods and men → via the *gods'* love of fame first? or was *human* love of fame sufficient?

197c1-3 Ἔρως being himself as the first most beautiful and most good, is thereafter responsible for the others' possessing other such like things (i.e. beautiful and good things)—prior to ἔρως, there were no beautiful and good things—the gods themselves were not beautiful and good.

c2: "the others" are human beings.

197c3-6 *The* poetic expression par exc.: ἔρως causes peace among *men* (*only* among men [≠ gods] - ≠ 195c5-6 and 197b8-9)—surely (ad 197b7-9), ἔρως as *human* love of fame is a sufficient motivation for establishing peace among men. But this limitation of ἔρως to *human* things is contradicted by the next 2 items: how can ἔρως be responsible for the quieting of winds and waves? Answer: *metaphorically*—if we compare the *passions* to strong seas etc. <32> The 4th & last item is again *human*—but not exactly a characteristic effect of ἔρως as either sexual desire or love of fame: the lie implied in the *metaphoric* description of the *true* effects of ἔρως leads to a lie regarding the effects of ἔρως.

197d1-5 ἔρως affects only human beings.

197d5-6 the gods are not wise [but ἔρως is wise: 196d5ff.] →

197e2, 4-5 ἔρως is *not* god. ἔρως the all-cheater, all-beguiler, all-enchanter—the inspirer in particular of Agathon, the *tragic* poet.

197e1-2: ἔρως not a στρατηγός {general}—as in Aristophanes' speech.

197d1-e5 Ἔρως *is* τὸ ἀγαθόν {the good}—not only *desire* for ἀγαθόν → Ἔρως is not ἔρως → Ἔρως is nothing.

197e6-8 Addressed to *Phaedrus* (cf. 194e1, 195a8, b6, c1): *I, Agathon, am the poet who has done what according to you no poet has done* (177a5-b1)—I have done my utmost (≠ Pausanias: what I could improvise 185c4-5; cf. also Eryximachus 188e1-4 and even Aristophanes 193d6-e3)

Summary of Agathon's speech

Starting point: he is a tragic poet → he *represents* tragic poetry—but he is not as a tragedian what Aristophanes is as a comedian—his vanity, his petty insincerities, his μαλακία {softness}: too obvious and for external κάλλος—the ἁπαλότης {tenderness} of his *speech*: nothing hard—the souls are μαλακωτάτοις {most soft} (195e3-4)—ἔρως harmonizes *everything* (195e3-4).—his speech is half *playful* (197e7), free from all *passion* because his ἔρως does not contain *suffering* (contrast with Aristophanes where there is passion in ἔρως because there is suffering in it)—his τέχνη is loveless (cf. ad 196d7-e1) and yet enchanting—shall we say that he is a *degenerate* tragic poet, an *epigonic* tragic poet? But: Agathon is closer to Socrates than any other speaker—he sits closest to him and he alone is awake at the end together with Socrates. And his doctrine: 1) ἔρως is ἔρως τοῦ *κάλλους* or τῶν καλῶν (not only of beautiful human beings nor of opposites nor of the ἀρχαία φύσις) and does not recognize anything superior to it which is alien to it. 2) ἔρως universal among the ζῷα (≠ Eryximachus? Aristophanes) (cf. ad 195b6-c6 in fine). 3) Agathon is the only one who raises the question regarding Ἔρως himself. → quâ epigonic tragic poet, he has undergone the influence of *philosophy*: he cannot take tragedy as seriously as the original tragic poets: but even in.its degeneracy, tragedy is superior to comedy—in which respect?

His praise of τέχναι {arts} (196d-197b) → he is not a rebel against νόμος {law}(ad 194d1, e5-6) (≠ comedy is such a rebellion)—in harmony with civilisation, with "κόσμος {cosmos}", for ἔρως is *also—above all* love of *fame* → silence about the cosmic gods (who lead back to chaos) and praise of the Olympian gods as originators of civilisation and as possessing νοῦς {mind} (→ silence about astronomy, the cosmic gods {LS' note on back:} implied in: Ἀνάγκη—cf. Empedocles B 116} and theoretic music).

Yet: he does not *believe* in the Olympian gods: he is the only one who makes the *being* of a god his *theme*—he *faces* that problem, whereas the others dismiss it. His primary thesis: Eros the *youngest* god and yet no parents → the *question* of his *origins*—no human shape—nothing self-subsisting: ἐρᾶν {loving}. The *youngest* god: the Olympian gods cannot have been *generated* → they have come into being out of nothing and through nothing if they are taken as they present themselves—but: they were *made* (*Phaedrus* 246a; cf. Simile on Cave): by *whom*? By *the* makers: the poets—i.e. the *tragic* poets—they are the makers of the gods of human shape: they *deify*—(Aristophanes [≠ Agathon] *makes Zeus speak*: but καταγέλαστως {ridiculous})—they create the gods because they are inspired by love of κάλλος: they "idealize" men—they do this in order to raise man's stature (beings looking like men but who are deathless etc.)—they are the true founders of civility → their *solemnity*—this is higher than comedy = (rebellion against the gods) provided that tragic poets *know* what they are doing, provided they are free from the spell which they create (as Agathon is): they *establish* τὸ καλόν ψεῦδος {the beautiful lie}—which the comic poet destroys.

Kinship between the gods and ἄρ. πολ. {short for "best regime"}—both are only λόγῳ {in speech} —but: the logos *leading up* to ... {sic} is suppressed (cf. 195a8-b5: the phenomenon ≠ hypothetical)

→ ἔρως (and the other gods) are mere objects of νοῦς {mind} (197e5): Agathon has *seen* Ἔρως.

Kinship between the gods and the *ideas*? Eros is desire but it does not desire—cf. the idea of a dog (= the dog itself) which is not a dog.

But: this superiority of tragedy is not *simply* true: both tragedy & comedy are *equally* necessary —

tragic—enchanting

comic—disenchanting (common sense—prosaic—cf. *Don Quixote* the clean shirts)

<33> Heraclitus fr. 32 ἓν μοῦνον σοφὸν {the one wise thing} it wishes and does not wish to be called Zeus - μανία {madness} it wishes → tragedy and φρόνησις {prudence} it does not wish → comedy to be called Zeus

→ tragedy superior to comedy not simply but due to the ὑπόθεσις {hypothesis} of *Symposium*.

1] the contest between philosophy and poetry. *Symposium*. Plato's *reply* to Aristophanes (his use of the *Frogs*) who had attacked Socrates and Euripides in the same breath—but: why was there a sympathy between Socrates and Euripides (tragedy) in the first place? what is the *principle* behind the antagonism of Socrates vs. Aristophanes? The philosopher not a tragic but a comic figure: philosopher presented only in comedy (≠ tragedy) and in the comedy necessarily from the point of view of ἔνδοξα {received opinions} → comedy *attacks* philosophy → comedy (≠ tragedy) *presents itself* as anti-philosophic.

ἔτι {besides}—τὸ γελοῖον {the ridiculous} ≠ τὸ σεμνόν {the solemn} or τὸ σπουδαῖον {the serious} → comedy presents the serious *beneath* τὸ γελοῖον: first impression is τὸ γελοῖον—not dignified.

Tragedy presents γελοῖον *beneath* the serious: the first impression is τὸ σπουδαῖον: dignified (εὐσχήμων {dignified})—philosophy must be εὐσχήμων and present *itself* as εὐσχήμων, if it is to fulfill its function.

2] Socrates's ὕβρις {hubris}—atheism = ideas (cf. *Euthyphro*) —abstraction from the soul = from the cosmic gods → esoterically ideas and exoterically Olympian gods = *recognition* of the Olympian gods = reenacting the ἔργον {function} of the tragic poets {LS note back of the page:} [P.{eter} H.{einrich} v.{on} Bl.{anckenhagen}: Aristophanes' speech preceded by φύσει {by nature} truth → taken care of by a physician → Aristophanes' theme is φύσις; Agathon's speech preceded by a νόμῳ {by convention} truth → taken care of by an αρχων {archon} → Agathon's theme is νόμος.]

Paus.{anias} & Eryx.{imachus} the perfect erotic ass'n {association} = noble ἔρως is a *combination* of *heterogeneous* elements: love of καλόν and love for bodily pleasures {in the line beneath:} opposition of the first: αἰσχρόν

Implies: ἔρως *proper* is directed towards bodily pleasure

≠ the 2 poets, inspired Ἔρως is single minded, not subject to something extraneous. Aristophanes: attacks love of καλόν—ἔρως → *embrace* —but: this means more than it seems → ἔρως τοῦ οἰκείου {eros of one's own} = αἰσχρόν {shameful/the ugly} → comedy the element of which is τὸ αἰσχρόν {the shameful/the ugly}

Agathon: ἔρως *only* love for καλόν {beautiful}—tragic poet: κάλλος {beauty} element of tragedy—visible, manifest beauty—(the orderliness of his presentation).

Transcript 5.3

LEO STRAUSS, TWO LETTERS
ON PLATO'S *SYMPOSIUM* (1959)

Editorial Note: These two letters addressed to Seth Benardete, one of Strauss's star students and the editor of Strauss's course on Plato's *Symposium*, are found in Leo Strauss Papers, box 18, folder 17, Special Collections Research Center, University of Chicago Library—the same folder that contains the n\otes on Plato's *Symposium* (transcript 5.1 in this volume). Numbers in the curly brackets refer to the page numbers of the typescript. Additions are all indicated by square brackets. The underlinings are replaced with italics.

{1} November 14, 1959
   Dear Mr. Benardete,
   I am now in the neighborhood of 205e. A question: Do you know of any other case where a woman says to a man "O comrade' (205e3)? I believe that Socrates appears here through the mask of Diotima and addresses his comrade Aristophanes.
   As for the work as a whole the key can be said to be 172b1 (Alcibiades) and c3ff. Alcibiades is again in Athens, i.e. 407, and the book gives the true story of the scandal of 416 (profanation or divulgation of the mysteries). Not Alcibiades divulged any mysteries, he came in after everything was over, but Socrates (and somehow Aristophanes (189d3-4)). The accuser Aristophanes was present at the blasphemy and participated in it. In brief, the work presents Socrates's ὕβρις [hybris]. It reminds of the *Frogs* (contest between two tragedians decided with a view to Alcibiades) but it surpasses the *Frogs* in comprehensiveness (the intra-tragic contest is

over, it is a contest between all forms of Athenian wisdom and the decision is made by Alcibiades). It is narrated by men other than Socrates and thus connected with the *Parmenides* and the *Phaedo*: the latter are the dialogues exhibiting the young Socrates who also was exhibited in the *Clouds* and Aristophanes is present in the *Symposium*: but above all the Socrates conversing with Diotima is the young Socrates. The title is in a way unique; ordinarily the title indicates a participant or in seven cases the subject matter (*Republic, Laws, Sophist, Statesman, Apology, Minos, Hipparchus*); the only title akin to that of the *Symposium* is that of the *Epinomis*. The *Symposium* is the only dialogue explicitly devoted to a god; the *Epinomis* is devoted to the cosmic gods. The *Symposium* abstracts from the cosmic gods; it leads therefore just as the *Euthyphron* to an atheistic conclusion (Socrates's ὕβρις [hybris]). For eros, the most plausible of the Olympian gods, even eros proves to be no god at all. The cosmic gods come up, though not explicitly as gods, only in Aristophanes' speech (original man looked like the cosmic gods and even moved like them (eros belongs here rather to the cosmic gods than to the Olympian gods)).

1) Phaedrus. 178b8-11. One must restore the ms. reading. Parmenides in the center because he praises eros most highly and he indicates the cause of eros. This praise of Parmenides is connected with the fact that Phaedrus's speech is unique, separated by a hiatus from the next speech; he realizes that the beloved is higher than the lover although or because the god is in the lover. He looks at eros from the point of view of the beloved (of himself), from the point of view of his gain. In all these points he anticipates Socrates. The first three speeches present eros as subordinate to something extraneous to it: gain, moral virtue, and techne [art]. The three last speeches present eros as "sovereign": love of αἶσχος [aischos = shame] love of καλός [kalos = beautiful], and love of the good.

2) Pausanias. This is the only deliberative speech occurring in Plato; in the guise of a praise of the Athenian νόμος [nomos = law] it is a proposal of a change of that νόμος (184c7-8). An elderly lover needs support by his respectability for his erotic success; he is the natural representative of the moralistic presentation of eros. Also, his presentation of the perfect erotic association is a parody of the polis which also has two heterogenous origins.

3) Eryximachus. The basis is Empedocles: love of the similar leads to chaos, love of the opposites to cosmos; in order to defend pederasty—for the defense of pederasty is the subject begun by Pausanias, continued by Eryximachus (185e6-186a1) and completed by Aristophanes; {2} in order to

defend pederasty Eryximachus must assert the superiority of love of the similar and this brings him into obvious difficulties especially since he also wishes to praise his τέχνη [techne = art](e.g. is it the task of medicine to cure men of heterosexuality or to bring about heterosexual relations, abhorred by nature, for the sake of the preservation of the species?). His pan-eroticism of Empedoclean origin leads just as in Empedocles himself (fr. 111) to the absolute rule of τέχνη [art]; for if love rules everything we humans must make a distinction between the right kind of love and the wrong kind (Heracleitus fr. 102).[1] We also must not forget that Empedocles' poem is addressed to Pausanias. Also Eryximachus's ending with a praise of μαντική [mantike = divination] reminds of Empedocles. Eryximachus's speech is in a way the central speech and therefore one may say that Empedocles is the target of the whole discussion.

4) Aristophanes. By nature men were simply cosmic beings; and the only link with the Olympian gods was the fact that they had genitals and we must add that they were not limited to mating seasons; the specificum is not rationality but sexiness. Not limited like the brutes by nature, man had to be limited by νόμος [nomos = law, convention]: the scission by Zeus (the beginning of Zeus' speech (190c7) is identical with the beginning of the whole work). Note also Apollo's blundering: he used up the skin of the whole for the half (hence the wrinkles), the other half skinless perished and therefore eros is hopelessly tragic. Incidentally, constant and through comparison of this story with Protagoras' story in the *Protagoras* is indispensable (the connection of the work as a whole with the *Protagoras* is obvious because of five of the characters). Eros is quest for one's own flesh and blood, most radically incestuous (cf. *Birds* and *Clouds*). More generally, love of one's own, and therefore also of the fatherland (cf. Euripides' *Phoenician Women* 350 or thereabouts). This is *the* alternative to Agathon according to whom love is quest for the beautiful. Abstraction from the former is characteristic of the *Symposium*.

5) Agathon. The most interesting passage in Agathon's speech is the verses in 197c5-6: eros' work limited to human beings (peace among *men*), the *metaphoric* extension of the effect of eros to winds and waves, i.e. human passions, and hence finally a non-metaphoric untrue statement about eros' effect (sleep). Agathon lets us see that eros as a self-subsisting being is nothing, since he has come to being out of nothing; he is only by virtue of the poet, i.e. the tragic poet, and this is true of all gods. I changed my mind regarding Plato's view of tragedy: tragedy is not the conflict between two opposite καλά [beautiful things], but rather reconciliation

through the gods; therefore the relation of comedy and tragedy is: construction of the gods and destruction of the gods, enchanting and disenchanting. Both are equally necessary but if the tragic poet knows what he is doing he is higher than the comic poet, because his construction includes the destruction (223d5; "by art," and the statement cannot be inverted). This does not do away with the fact that Aristophanes is superior as an individual to the individual Agathon: both Aristophanes and Socrates begin their speeches with the same words.

Aristophanes begins with a bodily predicament which is healed by a physician. Socrates begins with a moral predicament, an oath which embarrasses him now, which is healed by himself, for he is an Odysseus (198c2-5). With an unsurpassable insolence he makes clear in the same context (d) that his praise of eros will consist in being silent about its seamy side (i.e. about eros as love of one's own).

As for Socrates's speech, I would like say now only that 203dff. make it clear that eros has absolutely nothing to do with the gods: {3} he resembles only his mother, although he seems to resemble also his father. This is due to an ambiguity regarding Poverty. Is she sheer ignorance or dissatisfaction with ignorance? The problem was stated by Aristophanes in his *Plutus* (550–554). I just noted that in the Diotima section as distinguished from all other sections there is no reference to its being reported by Aristodemus or Apollodorus. This observation is a necessary but not a sufficient condition for understanding the strange goings-on regarding: "I said" (ἔφην, εἶπον, etc.); cf. in particular 202c5, 205c3, 10, d9. Mr. Gildin[2] who has been so good as to take down this dictation tells me that this lecture course will be typed pretty soon. Still, I believe that I have given you the highlights. With kindest regards,

Sincerely yours,

{1} November 30, 1959

Dear Mr. Benardete,

Socrates's speech in the *Banquet* consists of 7 parts (= to the number of speeches in the work). I Introduction on the true rhetoric (corresponds to Phaedrus's speech—foreshadows the *Phaedrus*). II Dialogue with Agathon. III Dialogue of the young Socrates with Diotima (the three dialogues narrated but not by Socrates (*Parmenides, Phaedo, Banquet*) are the only dialogues revealing the young Socrates). A) the nature of eros B) the human need for eros C) (207a5 to end) a) eros in procreation b) eros in ambition c) eros of the beautiful. The center is IIIB: eros is neither love of the beautiful (against Agathon) nor love of one's own (against Aristophanes): in IIIC both love of one's own and love of the beautiful are restored but the restoration takes place without the restoration of the gods: eros as love of one's own and love of the beautiful is the root of the Olympian gods (love of deathless beauty and love of one's own, i.e. the fatherland and dike [justice], hence the avenging gods). Diotima's speech effects a catharsis of eros. IIICb is a philosophic presentation of poetry and IIICc a poetic presentation of philosophy: Socrates wins the contest by being able to give these two presentations. I believe that Alcibiades's speech is a poetic presentation of Socrates, which is in one way utterly ridiculous: he proves that Socrates has hybris by proving that the has the greatest moderation; he speaks of the inner beauty of Socrates, of the fact that he alone knows Socrates's *pragma* [business], but in that famous night he did not discover in any way Socrates's secret teaching. The presentation of the poets—desire for immortal fame leads to immortal works—poses the question of Socrates's not writing. The answer I believe is that the perfect writing is tragedy containing comedy, not the other way round. And Socrates could not write tragedy (see *Gorgias*, the Callicles section). It is particularly amusing that Alcibiades presents Socrates as a kind of popular preacher of repentance, Savonarola style; if Socrates had been such a man he would have written.

One can figure out the personnel of the *Banquet* by considering that all combinations of the three following alternatives must be in. a) lover—beloved b) old—young c) cautious—soft—manly. The speeches not reported (end of Phaedrus's speech) are those of those combinations which are unworthy. This calculation is confirmed if one assumes that the total number of invited guests plus the host is nine, and there are two uninvited guests. Socrates represents two combinations: old—manly—lover and old—manly—beloved. Aristophanes I believe is old—soft—beloved—his lover is Plato.

As ever yours,
Leo Strauss

Notes

1. "To God all things are fair, good and just, but men suppose some things are unjust, some just" (Diels-Kranz 22 B 102).
2. Hilail Gildin (1928–2015), a student of Leo Strauss and a professor at Queens College, City University of New York.

SVETOZAR Y. MINKOV

Interpretative Essay

LEO STRAUSS ON AGATHON'S
THEOLOGY IN PLATO'S *SYMPOSIUM*

IN A LONG SUMMARY OF PLATO'S *SYMPOSIUM* sent to the philosophic classicist Seth Benardete,[1] Strauss remarks that "the *Symposium* is the only dialogue devoted to a god." Therefore, the *Symposium* contains "the Platonic theology" (*Laws* Book X and *Republic* Book II "belong[ing] to a non-theological context"). Agathon's speech may not seem a likely candidate for a thorough treatment of the theological theme. Agathon begins by saying he will focus on the nature of eros rather than on how it benefits humans. After claiming that eros is the youngest god, peacemaking and gentling, Agathon attributes the cardinal virtues (justice, moderation, courage, and wisdom) to eros. Besides, eros is the teacher of artisans, making them excel. We should then all follow the god Eros.

To accept this panegyric would be too anemic a response. One can easily imagine a more critical interpretation of Agathon's speech, according to which he subtly presents, and seriously believes in, a dark or cynical view of love, but obscures even from himself — in part through his rhetorical pyrotechnics and ability to conjure up images (or even create gods), in part because of the low intensity of his soul — whether this darkness is truly depressing for him or not. There is something to be said for this line of thought,[2] but one first needs to experience the full power and the undercurrent of philosophic excitement of Agathon's speech. And this is what I take up in these comments.

In fact, it may be that the whole dialogue is for the sake of Socrates's consultation with Agathon — for the sake of exploring whether Agathon can be Socrates's "Plato." That is, nonwriting Socrates (because his philosophic passion was not accompanied by the lower eros for writing, but only for having children[3]) needed a philosophic poet of the first rank to write him up and transmit his way of thought and life. On Strauss's reading, it proves remarkable how careful and subtle Agathon is, not to mention the keen interest Socrates must have when he sees the construction of the problem. Even if one still harbors suspicions about the extent to which Agathon understands the consequences of this construction, listening to Agathon's speech must have been for Socrates much like watching his own thought unfold in motion, enabling him to "diagram" it, to see how it begins, how it comes together, and where it leads. To anticipate, some indications of Agathon's greater rank include Agathon repeating gratuitously that the rule or monarchy of necessity has been overcome "now" that we have eros, that is, he subtly underscores the continued rule of necessity[4] (see the section on the second theological dimension below), as well as the fact that he is the last one to fall asleep, staying up with Socrates to the bittersweet end, at the drinking party, suggesting that he gets closer to the truth than the deep and passionate Aristophanes, with Socrates integrating and transcending the two poets.[5] Strauss enables us to see that the character of Agathon's speech is philosophical and theological (in the poetic and philosophical sense). While Strauss says that it was Socrates (or "Diotima")[6] who raises the question *quid sit deus?* ("what would be a god?") in the dialogue, he also remarks that Agathon "faces the issue" and comes at least very close to raising this all-important question.[7] Socrates's eagerness to attend Agathon's party (after Agathon won a tragedy competition) and engage Agathon — one-on-one, too, and in a gathering full of illustrious guests — begins to make sense.

This surprising vindication of Agathon becomes irresistible once one turns to Strauss's analysis of Agathon's speech. Strauss uncovers the unobtrusive but intransigent philosophical and theological dimensions of Agathon's speech, dimensions obscured if embellished by a tracery of charming refinements. In addition to the question of the "godness" of god[8] — the question of the best god or "what is a god? — that Agathon points to, Strauss detects two other theological dimensions in Agathon's speech: the implications of a history of imperfect beginnings and an account of the genesis of the gods is not obviously theological human passions; this account takes place despite or precisely because of the fact that Agathon begins his speech by saying that everyone before had only "blessed human beings for the goods for which the god is responsible":

Agathon will give an ultimately nontheological account of these goods. The three dimensions are interrelated. The question of the best god, or the best person as such, cannot be divorced from the question of what is materially or historically possible, and requires, at the end, the treatment of the poetic creation of gods. There are two main logical possibilities in play: either the gods are a species of self-subsisting intelligent beings or they are made; and if the gods are shown not to be self-subsisting beings, one needs an account of their origins; and if their origins prove incompatible with nature, or naturally impossible, then one has to show how they are generated by poets in conjunction with the passions of the human soul.

What follows below presents some of abundant evidence of Strauss's extraordinary attention to the *Symposium*. The complexity of the evidence is itself marvelous (notes, course delivery, letters, and so forth) and indicative of the attention Strauss lavished on this dialogue and its issues—despite not publishing a treatment of it (see Alex Priou's chapter in this volume). Indeed, it leads up to a consideration of what Strauss once called "his most important thought."

The Philosophical Character of Agathon's Speech: Its Combination of Seriousness and Play

Agathon is a tragic poet while the immediately preceding speaker, Aristophanes, is a comic poet. The question of the relative merits of tragedy and comedy remains central in Strauss's later work and may yet have undergone a transformation, but in 1959 Strauss reports a rethinking of the question. In the November 14, 1959 letter to Benardete included in this volume, Strauss announces: "I changed my mind[9] regarding Plato's view of tragedy: tragedy is not the conflict between two opposite καλά [beautiful things], but rather reconciliation through the gods; therefore the relation of comedy and tragedy is: construction of the gods and destruction of the gods, enchanting and disenchanting. Both are equally necessary but if the tragic poet knows what he is doing he is higher than the comic poet, because his construction includes the destruction (223d5; 'by art,' and *the statement cannot be inverted* [emphasis added])." This comprehensive construction-destruction suggests a broader knowledge by the tragedian of the pious part of the soul.

To indicate the breadth of what the tragic poet must know about the boundary between the impious and pious parts of the soul, Strauss quotes, in his notes prepared for his *Symposium* course, Heraclitus fr. 32: "ἓν μοῦνον σοφὸν {the one wise thing} wishes → tragedy and does not wish → comedy to be called Zeus." Agathon's speech is explicitly a combination of play and seriousness (*Symposium* 197e: "Let it be dedicated to the god, sharing, as far as I am able, partly in playfulness, partly in measured earnestness" [Benardete translation]). He is able to both construct and deconstruct the gods.[10]

The questioning, "destructive," or serious character of Agathon's speech may be in need of demonstration as much as its playful character. In his notes for the course, Strauss, in the context of *Symposium* 195a1-3, stresses "the *philosophic* character of [Agathon's] speech." We will see in the next section why Strauss stresses the *philosophic* character of Agathon's speech even though "quâ epigonic tragic poet, he has undergone the influence of *philosophy*: he cannot take tragedy as seriously as the original tragic poets": "even in its degeneracy tragedy seems to be superior to comedy." Strauss adds, however, that the "superiority of tragedy is not *simply* true: both tragedy and comedy are *equally* necessary." Tragedy is enchanting or constructive, comedy disenchanting or destructive (Strauss gives the example of the question of whether knights in *Don Quixote* carry clean shirts).

Strauss highlights Agathon's "praise of τέχναι [arts] (196d-197b)" and the consequent thought that "he is not a rebel against νόμος [law, convention] (ad 194d1, e5-6: (≠ comedy is such a rebellion) - in harmony with civilization, with "κόσμος [cosmos]" for ἔρως is *also - above all* love of *fame* → silence about the cosmic gods (who lead back to chaos) and praise of the Olympian gods as originators of civilization and as possessing νοῦς [mind] (→ silence about astronomy, the cosmic gods {implied in Ἀνάγκη [Necessity] - cf. Empedocles B 116}and theoretic music)." (As for ἀνάγκη [necessity], see the second theological section below.) Agathon's account of eros as love of fame, as a supporter of *nomos*, the arts, and a vision of the cosmos with beautiful, intelligent Olympians ruling (but deep down: ugly and unintelligent gods) is in harmony with civilization. The nondebunking, "harmonistic" attitude of Agathon is compatible with his radical unbelief. In fact, his praise of civility belongs to his understanding of the role of the poets in *creating* the gods. "Yet: he does not *believe* in the Olympian gods: he is the only one who makes the *being* of the god[s] his *theme* – he *faces* that problem, whereas the others dismiss it" (see the third theological section below). Simply put, the problem Agathon faces is: What are gods and where do they come from? And his answer is that they are not self-subsisting intelligent beings, but rather poetic creations, beautiful or terrifying images made by poets.

The First Theological Dimension: The Best God and Natural Theology

Agathon's theological approach, his focus on the question of the best qualities of the best person, his approximation of the *quid sit deus* question, is reflected in what Strauss calls Agathon's "primary thesis": "Eros as the *youngest* god and yet no parents → the *question* of his *origins* – no human shape – nothing self-subsisting – ἐρᾶν {loving}." We will see especially vividly in Agathon's "one-on-one" with Socrates the implied neediness in the gods' loving. "The *youngest* god: the Olympian gods cannot have been *generated* → they have come into being out of nothing and through nothing if they are taken as they present themselves." The question of the nature and qualities of the gods is perhaps too quickly connected with the poet's ability to *make* gods. Strauss notes about the Olympian gods: "but: they were *made* (*Phaedrus* 246a; cf. Simile of Cave): by *whom*? by *the makers: the poets* – i.e. the tragic poets – they are the makers of the gods of human shape: they *deify* – (Aristophanes [≠ Agathon] *makes Zeus speak* but καταγέλαστος {ridiculous})." The ridicule, to be sure, implies a standard of nonridiculousness, and even if the question of the godness of the god is not pronounced, it must be raised explicitly in order for an investigation to take place.

Yet the idealizing creation of gods still depends on a freedom from the spell cast by the new invention. The tragic poets "create the gods because they are inspired by love of κάλλος {beauty}: they 'idealize' men – they do this in order to raise man's stature (beings who look like men but are deathless, etc.) – they are the true founders of civility → their *solemnity* – this is higher than comedy (rebelling against the gods) provided the tragic poets *know* what they are doing, provided they are free from the spell which they create (as Agathon is) – they *establish* τὸ καλόν ψεῦδος {the beautiful lie}– which the comic poet destroys." The comic poet focuses on the burdensomeness or oppressiveness of the gods — and on the means for a liberation from that oppression in the name of pleasure.

It is the tragedian who comes *very close* to raising the *quid sit deus* question and shows the origination of the gods out of "nothing." Strauss adds this further explication and adverts to Agathon's freedom of mind: "Yet:

he does not *believe* in the Olympian gods: he is the only one who makes the *being* of the god[s] his *theme* – he *faces* that problem, whereas the others dismiss it." One has to add that Socrates, of course, does not dismiss it (and is in fact the first to raise the question strictly and directly) and "Aristophanes *almost* touched on that" (see On Plato's *Symposium*, 156; emphasis added).

In both the book and the notes, Strauss remarks, however, that "[t]he *eido*s, the essence, of Eros himself does not become the theme of Agathon" (*On Plato's Symposium*, 160). And with regards to 195a5-7 in his notes, Strauss writes, "*But*: he does not raise the *primary* question –of the τί ἐστι {what is} of ἔρως – i.e. quid sit deus {what is a god?}." Strauss's standard for what it means to raise that question must have been especially exacting as Agathon does raise the question of the class character of the gods (the criteria for inclusion in that class). Perhaps there is still something of the dogmatic in the way in which Agathon answers and even raises the question. As a result there may be a blurring between rigorous and demanding clarification of what "godness" is (what the best god/person is) and the civil theology of calling gods certain moving beautifications of human beings (perfect beauty, immortality) born out of our love of the beautiful, made by tragic poets, and effective on the passions (pity, fear, love of the beautiful, and attachment to justice). In that case, the question of the most perfect being is not raised or pursued with sufficient focus by Agathon.[11] And yet Agathon goes very far.

In *On Plato's Symposium* (168–69), Strauss says that as "an epigonic tragic poet [Agathon] has undergone the influence of philosophy." But being so "influenced" is compatible with at least implicitly raising the fundamental question: Agathon's "praise of ἔρως is necessarily a *critique of the other gods*: they all are less than perfect regarding beauty and goodness."

Strauss suggests that we "have to raise the question": "Will Agathon discuss the nature of eros or only his quality?" (page 156 of the book; in the audio recording, Strauss says, "not the nature," after "the question is raised, 'Of what quality is the god'."). In the notes, in reference to 194e6-195a5, Strauss writes: "For the first time, the *god himself* becomes the theme – not as something merely existing *in* the souls of men etc. but as *self-subsisting* – of *what quality* he is. *Aristophanes* had almost touched upon this (189d3-5): δύναμις {power} of ἔρως {eros} ≠ the human *nature*, not the *nature* of ἔρως → will Agathon discuss the *nature* of ἔρως?"

Aristophanes had spoken of the nature of man, but *not* of the nature — and not even of the quality — of eros.

If Agathon's praise of eros is necessarily "*a critique of the other gods*," Socrates's attention may have been heightened here, and perhaps the whole dialogue leads up to the one-on-one Socrates has with Agathon after the latter's speech. Socrates would have been intently focused on the suspenseful development: is Agathon raising with sufficient clarity the question "what is a god?"[12]

In 195a7-b5, we learn that "all other gods are more or less *oldy* {sic} and hence more or less *ugly*." This is one theological criterion, though it is immediately complicated in 195b6-c6 as "Agathon does {not} wish to blame Homer (→ d1) [the *oldest poet*: is there not a contrast between the blame of γῆρας {oldness} and the praise of Homer?]." Agathon has not (yet) risen to the issue. A little later (regarding 196e1-6), Strauss notes: "Ἔρως is wise *first* of all because he is a poet and the one who make others poetic [but does not say that ἔρως is indispensable for poetry → his τέχνη {art} is as love-less as Er[yximachus]. → the φύσει ἄριστοι {best by nature} who are genuinely ἄριστοι {best, pl.} precisely because they are *not* inspired by ἔρως, as *Phaedrus* said (179a9) – perhaps Homer was such a poet?" The reverence for Homer, but not qua old, is thus reconciled with the theology of the young and poetic-philosophic self-sufficiency. There is a kind of lovelessness in the seemingly most philanthropic arts, medicine (Eryximachus) and poetry here, which are seemingly most philanthropic. The highest activities are, in a way, loveless if eros is neediness.

Strauss adds a parenthetical remark about natural theology: "→ the gods other than ἔρως lack ἀρετή {virtue}." Agathon applies the standard of virtue to the gods. This is in line with the attempt to discover the class character of the gods. He will not be pushed around by authoritative-seeming gods who do not live up to a rational standard of virtue or to the standard of natural theology. The crucial theological implication is stated with regard to 197d5-6: "the gods are not wise [but ἔρως is wise: 196d5ff]." Yet even this needs to be immediately clarified in order to avoid the misunderstanding that eros itself is a god: "→ And then: 197e2, 4-5: ἔρως is *not* god. ἔρως, the all-cheater, all-beguiler, all-enchanter – the inspirer in particular of Agathon, the *tragic* poet." And with respect to 197e1-2, "ἔρως *not* a στρατηγός {general} – as in Aristophanes' speech." Agathon uses eros to critique all (other) gods as poor. But eros itself is not a god, but a beguiler, a cheater, and an enchanter. Eros is not a god;

eros is not even a general. The general is the poet himself (see the third theological dimension below).

The Second Theological Dimension: Imperfect Beginnings (the Rule of Necessity)

Even if the discussion of the "ideal" god packs theological and antitheological punch, it lacks teeth as long as it is not supplemented by a reflection on the actual historical situation of human beings — on the material conditions that limit the options lying before the attempt to know (the good) and to be good. To appreciate better what Strauss may have seen in Agathon's presentation regarding the role of terror and necessity in human history, it might help to consult first Strauss's treatment of the problem of "necessitous" beginnings elsewhere in his work.

In a footnote in *Natural Right and History* (150n24), Strauss develops the argument that "there cannot be true justice if there is no divine rule or providence." That is because one "would not reasonably expect much virtue or much justice of men who live habitually in a condition of extreme scarcity so that they have to fight with one another constantly for the sake of mere survival." "The cause of justice is infinitely strengthened if the condition of man as man, and hence especially the condition of man in the beginning (when he could not yet have been corrupted by false opinions), was one of nonscarcity. There is then a profound kinship between the notion of natural law and the notion of a perfect beginning: the golden age or the Garden of Eden." This reflection relates thematically back to page 97 of *Natural Right and History*: "if the philosophic life is indeed the right life or the life according to nature, man's beginnings were necessarily imperfect." In the immediately preceding paragraph 22 of chapter 3 of the book, Strauss has a note (n. 22) on "the combination of the assumption of savage beginnings with the acceptance of natural right" that he later, in the Cicero section, connects with n. 24 on page 150 (see the end of n. 30 on page 155).[13]

Strauss's review of Eric Havelock ("The Liberalism of Classical Political Philosophy" chapter in *Liberalism Ancient and Modern*) also revolves around that issue, especially in its implications for liberalism: "The opponents of liberalism seem to assert that man's nature does not change, that morality is timeless or a priori, and that man's beginnings were perfect. . . . But it is not clear, and it has not been made clear by Havelock, that there is a necessary connection between the assertion that man's nature does not change and the assertion that man's beginnings were perfect, that is, superior to the present" (34). "The first duty of civilized man is then to respect his past. This respect finds its exaggerated but effective expression in the belief that the ancestors—the Founding Fathers—were simply superior to the present generation and especially to the present youth, and mere 'logic' leads from this to the belief in perfect beginnings or in the age of Kronos" (41). But: "As regards the only state of things of which we possess firsthand knowledge, the philosopher says that there is in it no divine providence, no care of God or gods for men ([*Statesman*] 271d 3-6, 273a1, 274d3-6). The philosopher who indicates this thought, which is at variance with what other Platonic characters say elsewhere, is of course not Socrates, who merely listens in silence and refrains even at the end of the conversation from expressing his disagreement or agreement with what the strange philosopher had said. The stranger expresses a less disconcerting thought by saying that even if there were divine providence, human happiness would not be assured: the question of whether men led a blessed life under Kronos, when the gods took care of men, is left unanswered on the ground that we do not know whether men then used their freedom from care for philosophizing instead of telling one another myths; only a life dedicated to philosophy can be called happy (272b3-d4)."[14]

In Agathon's presentation, "Originally, Ἀνάγκη [Necessity] ruled over the gods, now Ἔρως rules (i.e. *not* Zeus is the king of the gods). If the stories told by Hesiod and Parmenides *are* true, ἔρως *vanquished* ἀνάγκη – yet ἔρως is the youngest god: he cannot always have ruled → ἀνάγκη must have ruled...→ the gods other than ἔρως lack ἀρετή {virtue}. Agathon tacitly opposes Aristophanes who implied that ἀνάγκη [necessity] is stronger than ἔρως [eros]." But this opposition on Agathon's part to Aristophanes's implication is not meant as a romantic rejection of the primary or original role of necessity (scarcity, human separateness, fundamental anxiety, death, and so forth), but it does point to the civilizing role of poetry. Poetry covers over "now" the primary terror, but that terror is not removed. "Savage beginnings → progress – i.e. good ≠ old – as Phaedrus implied and no one, not even Aristophanes contested (ἡ ἀρχαία φύσις {the *oldest* nature} is the model) – Agathon contests it (cf. *Legg.* III): the divination of ἀρχή = τέλος {*end*}. But Aristophanes contested already the assertion that ἔρως is the oldest god – implicitly → there is a progress of enlightenment, a progress of progress in the speeches: Ἔρως the oldest god; ἔρως younger than the Olympian gods; ἔρως explicitly the youngest god; ἔρως not a god at all." The "progress" here is tenuous and does not alter the fundamental fact of necessity and terror. The relative status and power of the low origins (cannibalism, incest, the rule of necessity, and so forth) and the high (poetry, the arts, the city, philosophy) remain to be adjudicated. And the question of the contribution of the poet to the improvement and protection of the human situation is still unresolved. This leads us directly into the third theological dimension of Agathon's speech.

The Third Theological Dimension: The Soul Replaces the Gods or the Human Genesis of the Gods

In *On Plato's Symposium* (159), Strauss says, "Agathon transforms Ate into Eros, something not beautiful into something beautiful. There is a parallel to that in Aristophanes' speech. For Aristophanes, the god who solves the riddle of the human soul is Hephaestus, the limping god who, in addition, was deceived by his wife." In the notes, the thought is presented in this way: "no longer 'guilt-ridden' and 'fear-ridden' → Agathon transforms Ἄτη into ἔρως – something not-beautiful into something beautiful. ≠ Aristophanes: the limping god Hephaestus, who was *deceived* by his wife, *alone* of the gods understands ἔρως." The limping and deceived god is, *and for that very reason*, the one who understands eros. Besides, we are reminded of the second theological dimension and the crucial role the technical arts play in clawing back against the ugly, original necessity. The obtrusive mention of Necessity, though apparently self-congratulatory, suggests that there are traces of necessity, of limping, and of the ugly, even in the period after poetry has legislated and brought in civilization. But what is the poet's understanding of his creative, civilizing role, that is, what is the basis of Agathon's constructive, harmonistic position?

In commenting on 197c3-6, Strauss speaks of "*the* poetic expression par excellence: ἔρως causes peace among *men* (*only* among men [≠ gods] - ≠ 195c5-6 and 197b8-9)." Strauss notes, "surely (ad 197b7-9), ἔρως as *human* love of fame is a sufficient motivation for establishing peace among men." But the real problem is this: the "limitation of ἔρως to human things is contradicted by the next 2 items: how can ἔρως be responsible for the quieting of winds and waves?," especially since we know from 197d1-5 that "ἔρως affects only human beings." The answer is: it can do that "*metaphorically* – if we compare the *passions* to strong seas, etc." "The 4th & last item is again *human* – but not exactly a characteristic effect of ἔρως as either sexual desire or love of fame: the lie implied in the *metaphoric* description of the *true* effects of ἔρως leads to a lie regarding the effects of ἔρως."¹⁵ (The four items being: human peace; calmness of the winds; the calmness of the waves; and the calming of human cares.) This is the part of Agathon's speech that Strauss characterizes, in his November 14, 1959 letter to Benardete, as "the most interesting passage," that is *Symposium* 197c5-6. Eros's work is "limited to human beings (peace among men), the metaphoric extension of the effect of eros to winds and waves, i.e. human passions, and hence finally a non-metaphoric untrue statement about eros' effect (sleep)." In other words, "Agathon lets us see that eros as a self-subsisting being is nothing, since he has come to being out of nothing; he is only by virtue of the poet, i.e. the tragic poet, and *this is true of all gods" (emphasis added).*¹⁶

Strauss notes that the idea of the gods is akin to the idea of the best regime: "Kinship between the gods and ἄρ. πολ. {short for "best regime"} – both are only λόγῳ {in speech} : but the λόγος [argument] *leading up to...* {sic} is suppressed (cf. 195a8-b5: the phenomenon ≠ hypothetical)." Part of that suppressed argument is that "ἔρως (and the other gods) are mere objects of νοῦς {mind} (197e5): Agathon has *seen* Ἔρως."¹⁷

Socrates's One-on-One with Agathon

In the course on the *Symposium*, Strauss speaks of a "constant reference to the fact of agreement" between Socrates and Agathon in their exchange (199c3-201c9; *On Plato's Symposium*, 179). Strauss suggests that this should be understood in light of the two kinds of conversations described in Xenophon's *Memorabilia* (IV.6.13-15): speaking to contradictors and speaking to noncontradictors. With Agathon, Socrates himself speaks as a noncontradictor while taking over the initiative of the conversation. But this means that the premise of Agathon's speech is preserved: love is of the beautiful, not of one's own. (Strauss refers to Bury's observation that Ficino translates καλῶς γε εἶπες at 201c1 as "recte dixisti" [correctly spoke] while Wolf as "praeclare dixisti" [beautifully spoke]).¹⁸ As a result, the conclusion of Socrates's exchange with Agathon is that there is no incestuous love, no love for the present or the available, no love for one's wife, nor for one's city, nor even for sexual gratification. Strauss points out that this decision offers a "perfect justification of Socrates' eros" (*On Plato's Symposium*, 183; cf. *Symposium* 212c4-6). It seems that Agathonic tragedy has overcome, much like philosophy, the love of one's own, all the while exoterically sacralizing the most venerable objects of that love.

In *On Plato's Symposium*, an important segment of Socrates's exchange with Agathon remains without comment ("[Gap in tape concerning 200a-201b]"). From Strauss's notes, we can highlight the following. Socrates had warned in advance that his truthful praise of eros will be silent about what is not most beautiful about eros. Is this why Socrates will be silent about love of one's own, love for one's family (let alone incest[19]) or one's fatherland (Aeschylus's *Agamemnon* 540), for any *polis* (Aristophanes's *Birds* 1316; Euripides's *Phoenissae* 358–359: "all men of necessity have eros for the fatherland"). Since generally love is toward what is *lacking* or *absent*, a desire for what one does have must mean a desire to possess it *in its fullness*. A beautiful being may wish to be still more beautiful and adorn itself. Moreover, because one can be beautiful *unwillingly* (a woman may *curse* her beauty because of the misfortunes it brought upon her), there can be a *willing* of one's beauty. If someone is present, one may still wish for the fullest possible embrace with that someone (in addition to enjoying their presence). At least, there are cases in which eros and possession, desire and satisfaction, are essentially *copresent* (*Gorgias* 496c6ff., 497c5ff.). If eros for the present were simply impossible, sexual gratification would not be present and hence would not be desired. Eros, *one way or another*, is directed toward something *lacking* (at 200e2-6, "what he does not possess" is in the center), but in his restatement, in order to draw up an agreement, at 200e6-8, Socrates drops "what he does not possess." One may possess something and still need it (e.g., a house). Concerning 201a2-7, Strauss points out an ambiguity "τοῖς θεοῖς κατεσκευάσθη τὰ πράγματα" [the gods have arranged these things]: if the dative is of agency, the meaning could be that the gods have arranged things as such; or the statement could mean that the gods have arranged *their* own things. Concerning 201a8, Strauss points out the difference between Agathon saying "εἶπον" ["said"] and Socrates using the present "λέγεις" and suggests that Socrates is directing Agathon to a change in the statement for his speech: it was the god eros *in* the gods, not simply the gods, that accounts for the ordering and establishing of things. This suggestion enables one to return to the implication from the first theological section above regarding the poverty of the gods: while 201b1-2 implies that eros is not beautiful (it desires beauty and so it must not have it), 201a5 extends the statement to *all* the gods. All the gods desire beauty and are therefore not beautiful. Moreover, "Love of the beautiful equals lack of beauty; beautiful equals good; therefore that which loves beauty is characterized by absence of beauty, which equals absence of good. The gods are also prompted by love of beauty" (*On Plato's Symposium*, 182). The question remains whether Agathon is willing to accept this conclusion about the ugliness and badness of all gods, including the gods he himself masterfully creates — whether he is able and willing to apply the criteria of goodness consistently to the objects of his longings.

Strauss's "Most Important Thought"

We have seen that Strauss detects the presence of at least three interrelated theological dimensions in Agathon's speech in Plato's *Symposium*: the *quid sit deus* question or the philosophic investigation of natural theology; the truth about the imperfect historical beginnings of human life; and the poetic-metaphoric genesis of belief (the poet's idealization of natural human passions and their objects).

But we also noted that, despite this comprehensiveness and depth of Agathon's treatment of the divine, Strauss says that tragedy is not simply superior to comedy. It is comedy, but not tragedy, that can represent (true) philosophy if only in light of the received opinions and under the guise of being antiphilosophic. One must also account for the fact that Aristophanes's speech is "much deeper and richer" than anyone else's speech, but also "the most wrong, because it goes in the false direction most passionately." It is "the opposite of Socrates' speech, but almost on the same level."[20]

The question of comedy's and tragedy's articulation of, and confrontation with, the question of the gods (in relation to "family and city, pleasure and justice, nature and convention, the ancient and the novel, the Muses, and fatherbeating"[21]) is the theme of Strauss's great *Socrates and Aristophanes*. The treatment of these themes is related to a suggestion Strauss makes with regard to the end of the *Symposium* and the relation among philosophy, comedy, and tragedy. In a June 3, 1964 letter to Benardete, Strauss writes, "In his introduction to *Herakles*, Wilamowitz has stated our task well enough: to bring out by induction the 'historical' concept of tragedy (and, I would add, comedy), as distinguished from the 'philosophic' concept (= *Poetics*)—in order then to try to understand [which is no longer a concern of Wil.{amowitz}] the changes effected by Aristotle—the reasons for those changes. I *hope* that I shall arrive at the ὅρος [definition] of the Aristophanean comedy. Part of the ὅρος would be that the comedy presents the transgression of a sacred limit (at least, a limit set by εὐσχημοσύνη [decorum])—but this is surely true of tragedy as well—and the προοίμια [preludes] of Homer → Homer and the Μοῦσαι present the truth by presenting a transcending of a sacred limit—this transgression may cause φόβος - ἔλεος [fear - pity] or else γέλως [laughter]. (Yet that which is closed off from those τέρατα [monsters] is the πόλις [city], the Cave–ergo....) Something of this kind may be meant by the end of the *Symposium*. I have the vague feeling that this thought which occurred to me a few days ago is the most important thought which ever occurred to me. Can you understand why I feel so?" Perhaps we cannot yet understand why Strauss felt so,[22] but his comments on Agathon's guilt-free transgression of sacred limits while protecting civilization may be part of the story. Agathon's debonair tragedy might make comedy appear narrow. Comedy does not thematize death, suffering, and love proper. But comedy may reply that these themes are not the highest. Besides, "Aristophanean comedy certainly presupposes tragedy; it builds on tragedy; in this sense, at any rate, it is higher than tragedy. It conjures up for us, within the limits of that possibility which it must respect, a simply pleasant falsehood: a life without war, law courts, terrors caused by gods and death, poverty, and coercion or restraint or nomos. The falsehood points to the truth; the truth is the inevitable suffering, coeval with man, that is caused by both physis and nomos."[23] If the greatest vice is boastfulness (based on spirited and vain self-importance), then comedy possesses the highest perspective. Tragedy requires that one take divine law seriously, which is not the same as taking the truth of it seriously. It seems that after comedy and tragedy transcend the city, philosophy resists all three.

Notes

1. See the forthcoming edition of the Strauss-Benardete correspondence, to be edited by Ronna Burger and Svetozar Y. Minkov and published with Mercer University Press. – I am grateful to Daniel Doneson and Rafael Major for their comments.

2. Christopher Bruell once remarked that Socrates combines Agathon's braininess and comprehensiveness with Aristophanes's deep passion and narrowness, but Agathon may even have a strong sense of that "one thing needful": Patrick Kernahan's notes from Bruell's fall 2008 course on the *Symposium* at Boston College.

3. See Strauss's comment in the 1968 "The Socratic Question" where he remarks, in the question-and-answer period: "Plato wrote books but he did

not generate children. Socrates generated children but he did not write books. And that is perhaps the peculiar purity of Socrates, that he did not write books. Now if we look, as we cannot help looking, at Jesus, we see that Jesus did not partake of either of the two lower forms of eros, generation of children and writing" (https://leostrausscenter.uchicago.edu/the-socratic-question-february-1968/).

4. See Strauss's "Restatement": "Warriors and workers of all countries, unite, while there is still time, to prevent the coming of 'the realm of freedom.' Defend with might and main, if it needs to be defended, 'the realm of necessity'" (*On Tyranny,* corrected and expanded edition, including the Strauss-Kojève correspondence, ed. Victor Gourevitch and Michael Roth [Chicago: University of Chicago Press, 2013], 210).

5. Strauss notes: "Agathon is awake when Aristophanes has already dozed off – but not simply: the technē tragedian [the tragedian by art] is also a comedian – the statement cannot be inverted." In a April 22, 1957 letter to Alexandre Kojève, Strauss wrote: "All the Dialogues are tragicomedies. (The tragedian is awake while the comedian is sleeping at the end of the Symp<osium>.) The dramatic hypothesis of the Symp<osium> is that Plato reveals what happened prior to the Sicilian expedition: not Alc<ibiades>, but Socrates divulges the mystery" (*On Tyranny,* 276). Rafael Major points out to me that Plato's *Phaedo* is the classic tragicomedy and a work that turns Socrates into a god. See also Franz Rosenzweig, *The Star of Redemption*: "In its content, all art is 'tragic,' a representation of suffering; even comedy lives from this sympathy for the everpresent poverty and defectiveness of existence. In its content, art is tragic, as in its form all art is comic, and even the most horrible—it represents with a certain romantic-ironic ease. Art as representation is that which is tragic and comic in one. And the great actor is truly comedian and tragedian at the same time, as it was handled by Agathon's banquet at daybreak)" (trans. Barbara Galli [Madison: University of Wisconsin Press, 2005], 400). In *On Plato's Symposium* (168): "Agathon's art is loveless; it is not inspired by eros and yet is enchanting. The sound and the rhythm are beautiful. Shall we then say that he is a degenerate tragic poet, an epigonic tragic poet? Perhaps. This would even be historically correct. One has only to read Aristotle's *Poetics* to get this impression. But Agathon is closer to Socrates than any other speaker. He sits closest to him and he alone is awake at the end together with Socrates, when everyone else is drunk. This applies not only to the fact that he can drink so well but also to his doctrine. It is Agathon who teaches that eros is eros of beauty or the beautiful things. He does not say, as some of the earlier speakers had said, that eros is love of beautiful human beings, or love of opposites, or love of the ancient nature. He is in agreement with Socrates' in saying that eros is love of the beautiful and he does not recognize anything superior to eros which is alien to eros."

6. Allan Bloom remarks that Agathon is "the first to the raise the question of form or use the word for Form or Idea, but his forms are insubstantial or

inessential" (*Plato's Symposium*, trans. Seth Benardete, with commentaries by Allan Bloom and Seth Benardete [Chicago: University of Chicago Press, 2001], 118). Yet this is too weak a way of characterizing Agathon's contribution.

7. See *The City and Man* (Chicago: Rand McNally, 1964), 241. Strauss wrote a preliminary version of his *Socrates and Aristophanes* book that he never published, commenting on each play (Strauss archive, Box 17, Folders 7–9); in that version, the question *quid sit deus*, underlined in red, appears on virtually every other page. The dialogue on this question is *The Symposium*.

8. See *Socrates and Aristophanes* (New York: Basic Books, 1966), 212, 313.

9. In the 1964 *The City and Man*, Strauss says, "We may . . . say that the Socratic conversation and hence the Platonic dialogue is slightly more akin to comedy than to tragedy" (61).

10. See *The City and Man*, 22, n. 22, as well as "Religion and the Commonweal in the Tradition of Political Philosophy: An Unpublished Lecture by Leo Strauss," below, 289-328; see also "Could Zeus have had the intention to make his subjects seek the countenance, not of Zeus, but of God?" ("How Farabi Read Plato's *Laws*," in *What Is Political Philosophy? And Other Studies* [Chicago: University of Chicago Press, 1959], 151).

11. Strauss says that Agathon is "a beautiful young man . . . with a not so beautiful inside" and that "[p]erhaps this applies to their [Agathon's and Socrates'] speeches too." But Strauss also points out immediately that one does not find "perfect beauty" *anywhere* in the dialogue; it is always "tainted, if only by a snub nose" (*On Plato's Symposium*, 155). Agathon's and Socrates's speeches are both exoteric-esoteric: with beautiful and pleasing edifying surface, but ugly internal, true meaning; the theological implications of this denial of perfect beauty may be seen in the *Phaedrus* as well as in Strauss's *Thoughts on Machiavelli* (Chicago: University of Chicago Press, 1958), 167, 190, 193.

12. Strauss's November 24, 1959 letter to Harry Jaffa: The *Symposium* "gives the inside dope of what happened in 416, the profanation of the mysteries of which Alcibiades was accused and which led first to his downfall and eventually to the downfall of Athens; the true version is that Alcibiades came in after everything was over; the real culprit was Socrates and to some extent Aristophanes. It appears that Socrates did not believe that the gods worshipped by the city exist; in addition the immortality of the individual is almost explicitly denied; the gods of the city prove to be the product of love of the beautiful on the one hand, and of love of one's own (the latter leading to the city, to justice and hence to the demand for avenging gods) on the other. The symposium also contains in a nutshell an explanation of why Socrates did not write: he did not write because the perfect writing is tragedy embodying comedy and he could not write tragedy because he was incapable of writing punitive speeches (cf. *Gorgias*)." Does Agathon stand for *both* love of the beautiful and love of one's own, both of which would be implied in his representing the construction of the gods of the city? Or does he stand for

love of the beautiful only? In that case, this would be the limit to his comprehensiveness.

13. See also *Thoughts on Machiavelli* 165 (through 167): the "primacy of Love" is replaced by the "primacy of Terror"; and 203: "The principle of authority finds its primary expression in the equating of the good and the ancestral. This equation implies the assumption of absolutely superior or perfect beginnings, of a golden age or of a Paradise. The ground or origin of the perfect beginning is the supremacy of the Good or of Love or, as we might also say, the rule of Providence. The origin of evil is a fall. Progress is return, betterment is restoration. To perfect oneself means to return to the beginning when men were good, to pre-historical beginnings. Especially if the pre-historical beginnings are assumed to be unknowable, one must rest satisfied with the imitation of a founder-captain who at least excels all other men, if he is not semi-divine or divine. These few words concerning the comprehensive theo-cosmological scheme implied in the principle of authority will suffice for the understanding of Machiavelli's thought."

14. See also *The Argument and the Action of Plato's Laws* (Chicago: University of Chicago Press, 1975), 39–40; see *Statesman* 272b8-c5; *The City and Man*, 38–39, on "original sin" (blaming man for willing the conditions under which he can be bad). See also *Guide of the Perplexed*; and *The Rebirth of Classical Political Rationalism*, ed. Thomas L. Pangle (Chicago: University of Chicago Press, 1988), 235: "precisely on the basis of the Bible the beginning cannot be imperfect." One could also consult Strauss's discussion of Thucydides's archaeology and "Diodotus" in *The City and Man*.

15. See Strauss's "How Farabi Read Plato's *Laws*": "In most of these cases 'divine' obviously designates a certain quality of human beings or of human achievements or of human pursuits, namely, their excellence. If one considers the fact that the divine laws are the work of a human legislator (8,18-10; 22,19; 29,15-17), there hardly remains a single example in which 'divine' has a meaning different from the one that we have indicated" (141; see also the thirty-third paragraph of "Farabi's *Plato*").

16. Benardete refers to this part of Agathon's speech in explaining Strauss's interpretive skill: "In a recent translation of the *Symposium*, the translator puts into a heroic couplet two lines of epic verse that Agathon made up in honor of Eros. Eros 'brings,' Agathon says, 'Sweet peace to men, and calm o'er all the deep.// Rest to the winds. to those who sorrow, sleep.' The translation seems flawless until one notices that 'rest' is not the same as *koite*, which means either 'sleep' or bedtime.' 'The sleep of the winds' points directly to Agathon's argument, that Eros is the god of poetic production, by whose agency the metaphorical becomes literal. It seems therefore almost inevitable that that translator introduces the couplet with the words '[Eros] brings,' and not with '[Eros] makes.' Perhaps one could come to understand Agathon even through a nonliteral translation; but Strauss alone, as far as l know, did understand him because he followed the argument down to and

from the details" ("Strauss on Plato," in *The Argument of the Action*, ed. Ronna Burger and Michael Davis [Chicago: University of Chicago Press, 2000], 415).

17. This discussion of the poetic production in Agathon prepares Strauss's later suggestion, in line with Gerhard Krüger's comment but in a very different spirit, that it is "not wrong" to say that eros, rather than Christ, is *the* mediator between gods and men (*On Plato's Symposium*, 191)" and that this is "really the difference between Plato and Christianity" (Krüger, *Einsicht and Leidenschaft* [Frankfurt am Main: Klostermann, 1939], 153–54 and 180–81).

18. R. G. Bury, *Plato's Symposium* (Cambridge: Heffer and sons, 1909), 93.

19. See *Symposium* 199d. See Steve Berg's *Eros and the Intoxications of Enlightenment* (Albany: State University of New York Press, 2010): Aristophanes "will show that Eryximachus' ambitions have their ground in the fundamental problem that is the ground of the Oedipal longing that Eryximachus pretends to resolve" (38); "Aristophanes would agree with Eryximachus that Oedipus is at the center of eros and so the problematical center of the city and man" (64) — "Speaking poetically, not Oedipus, but Odysseus is the problematic core of the human as such" (90) and Socrates "dismisses Aristophanes' claim that eros is the eros of tragedy and Oedipus the paradigmatic erotic man" (96); regarding Agathon's speech, "Eros is self-caused. He is the realization of the wildest dreams of Oedipus" (79).

20. *On Plato's Symposium*, 172, 180.

21. *Socrates and Aristophanes*, 53.

22. An initial pass at what this might mean is made by Benardete in his preface to his *Philebus* edition: "The stories of poetry center around foundational crimes, crimes that reveal what must not be violated if either man is to be man or the city is to be possible. The line between man's humanity and man's sociality, the poets seem to be saying, cannot be clearly drawn, for they show that the answer to the riddle of the Sphinx and Oedipus's incest and patricide are linked and that, in light of what Oedipus has done, Oedipus has to cease to be what he is. His knowledge cannot consist with his being, and he must shut out the world if he is to live with his crimes. Plato, on the other hand, has Socrates propose a city of Oedipuses, as if there were in principle no boundaries the transgression of which would deny to man his humanity, provided that knowledge or the love of knowledge still informed him" (*The Tragedy and Comedy of Life* [Chicago: University of Chicago Press, 1993], ix). R. G. Collingwood: "The Oedipus of Greek Philosophy Is Socrates" (*The Principles of History And Other Writings in Philosophy of History*, ed. W. H. Dray and W. J. van der Dussen [Oxford: Oxford University Press, 1999], 173). See also Benardete's "On Greek Tragedy" in *The Argument of the Action*. I have drawn on Benardete in part because the materials at hand were above all shared with him, but also because, while Strauss's "daimon" restrained him for the most part from dealing with Greek tragedy, Benardete took Strauss's indications as the starting point for his own work.

23. *Socrates and Aristophanes*, 312.

ALEX PRIOU

Interpretative Essay

LEO STRAUSS'S INTENTION
WITH PLATO'S *SYMPOSIUM*

READERS MIGHT BE CURIOUS why the transcript of Leo Strauss's 1959 seminar on Plato's *Symposium* was the first to be published by nearly two decades. This particular course was given "partly in honor of [Strauss's] friend, Peter Heinrich von Blanckenhagen," who had recently accepted the honor of a position at the Institute of Fine Arts at New York University.[1] But the course apparently also caused a stir among Strauss's students, who immediately sought his permission to prepare a transcript for publication. Strauss was, according to the transcript's editor, Seth Benardete, somewhat ambivalent about its publication but did eventually consent.[2] Only many decades later, in 2001, did a reliable and polished version of the manuscript, not without its lacunae, finally make its way into print. Its publication was something of an event, certainly among those who, like myself at the time, had heard of the transcripts of Strauss's courses yet had no access to them. For, until their online publication at the Leo Strauss Center's website, they were shared only privately, save for when copies would become available through online booksellers. The publication of the course thus offered many at the time, myself included, a rare glimpse into Strauss's teaching, even his thinking. Such was the impression, at least. For even a quick comparison of his other courses with the publications that emerged from them suffices to show that his remarks in class should never be taken as indicative of his final view, to say nothing of the necessary discrepancies between the presentation of his thought in public—whether provisional or final, in the classroom or in print—and that thought as Strauss understood it himself, in private.

233

Yet the case of the transcript on Plato's *Symposium* is a special one, in that Strauss did make some rather definite claims in his private correspondence with Benardete and even composed a sketch that, together with these letters, offers us a hazy glimpse or an intriguing fragment of what Strauss might have had to say, even thought, about the questions at issue in the dialogue. It is my hope that a comparison of the sources, supplemented by the fruits of Strauss's pregnant remarks, might aid us in demystifying somewhat Strauss's thinking on this text.

Our curiosity here need not be idle; it may have good grounds. Early in his career, Strauss argued for the inadequacy of the early modern critiques of premodern philosophy and of revealed religion, restoring thereby what he would eventually call the source of the "secret vitality" of the Western tradition, the original tension between reason and revelation, represented in the ancient cities of Jerusalem and Athens. This restoration took some time. In his early and pathbreaking work, *The Political Philosophy of Hobbes* (1935), Strauss had initially claimed Thomas Hobbes was the founder of modern political philosophy, while nevertheless quietly recognizing that he had yet to assess the place of Niccolò Machiavelli.[3] Seventeen years later, in 1952, when Strauss wrote a new preface to the book, he felt comfortable giving that title to Machiavelli.[4] This remark found support in two works from the late 1950s, *What Is Political Philosophy?* and, of course, *Thoughts on Machiavelli*. In the former, Strauss suggested that "the narrowing of the horizon which Machiavelli was the first to effect, was caused, or at least facilitated, by anti-theological ire."[5] Less elliptical is Strauss's remark about Machiavelli's unbelief, that it "takes seriously the claim to truth of revealed religion by regarding the question of its truth as all-important and which therefore is not, at any rate, a lukewarm unbelief."[6] Common to both, however, is a clear orientation toward the theological-political problem. More to the point, it was in the wake of his study of Machiavelli qua founder of modernity, in light of the theological-political problem, that Strauss finally "concentrated on the study of 'classic natural right,' and in particular on 'Socrates,'" that is, that Strauss applied himself with unprecedented concentration, and in a series of highly focused publications, to interpreting the presentation of Socrates in the works of Plato, Xenophon, and Aristophanes.[7] Prior to *The City and Man*, Strauss had published his interpretation of two non-Socratic works by Xenophon, review essays of contemporary scholars in which he commented on Plato's *Republic* and *Protagoras* in a cursory or preliminary fashion, and a highly rhetorical or exoteric account of "classic natural right" that suppressed distinctions between various premodern thinkers. But he had yet to publish any holistic interpretation of a Socratic work, such interpretations as would become the hallmark of his last decade. *The City and Man* was, therefore, as Strauss himself noted, a turning point in his written oeuvre.[8] More specifically, its central chapter on Plato's *Republic* was a first for Strauss. And so, fittingly, he opened the chapter with a penetrating, thirteen-paragraph discussion of how to read Plato, intended to challenge our basic assumptions about his supposed teaching. Similarly, Strauss begins his sketch of Plato's *Symposium* with remarkably similar reflections, especially as regards the twin fictions or noble lies of Platonic writing: the denial of chance and the apparent completeness of each dialogue.[9] Did Strauss intend his sketch on Plato's *Symposium* to be his first publication on a Socratic work of classical political philosophy? Or was it intended as a supplement to his interpretation of the *Republic*? Cases can be made for both views. But whatever the case, Strauss eventually abandoned this work, for reasons unknown to us. Why he did so appears to me to be among the most difficult and important questions to answer in our attempt to demystify his thinking on this text.

We can further grasp the potential significance of the *Symposium* for Strauss's thought by considering his account of its uniqueness or singularity among Plato's dialogues. In both the course and the sketch, Strauss begins by offering some interpretive observations directed at what he calls, in *The City and Man*, "the surface of the surface of [Plato's] work."[10] The uniqueness of the *Symposium* is, according to Strauss, threefold: in form, title, and theme. In form, the *Symposium* is among the ten narrated dialogues, six of which are narrated by someone other than Socrates.[11] It is unique, however, in that it is "*doubly* narrated *and* narrated for the *second time*."[12] The uniqueness of the form has to do with the emerging, even gossipy, interest in the gathering at Agathon's house, the wider dissemination of the story succeeding thanks in part to Apollodorus's "missionary zeal."[13] Here it is appropriate to note the uniqueness of the title, often translated by Strauss as *Banquet*: it is the only dialogue named after an occasion.[14] Why *this* occasion? Strauss elaborates that the gathering at Agathon's house took place in 416, just before the Sicilian Expedition, on the eve of which there was a sacrilegious crime, the mutilation of the Hermae, which in turn revealed an earlier sacrilege, the profanation of the Eleusinian mysteries. Thucydides mentions that the profanation of the mysteries took place in playful drunkenness (μετὰ παιδιᾶς καὶ οἴνου) and at private dwellings, out of arrogant pride or ὕβρις (ἐν οἰκίαις ἐφ' ὕβρει).[15] Underscoring this

Interpretative Essay

connection is the presence of no fewer than three of those accused of this crime, Pausanias, Eryximachus, and Alcibiades, at Agathon's gathering.[16] More to the point, however, Apollodorus in his narration recalls correcting Glaucon, who believed the party occurred recently, which is impossible, Apollodorus notes, because Agathon is no longer in town. Strauss observes that Apollodorus reveals ex silentio that Alcibiades *is* in town, that is, that he has returned and, further, now led the procession in honor of the very mysteries he was accused of profaning. This reconciliation between Athens and Alcibiades means, Strauss observes, that the story can finally be told. But what we witness in the *Symposium*, he also notes, is a different profanation, and the guilty party is not Alcibiades but his apparent corrupter, Socrates. We witness, that is, the ὕβρις of Socrates. This brings us to the uniqueness of the dialogue's theme: the *Symposium* is the only dialogue devoted to a god, the god Eros. The treatment of the gods in the *Republic* and *Laws* is no exception, since in each that treatment is subordinated to another theme, namely, justice and law, respectively.[17] It is rather in the *Symposium* that Socrates discusses a particular god, Eros, whose divinity he will ultimately deny. The uniqueness of the *Symposium*'s title, form, and theme ultimately leads us to conclude that Plato boldly, not to say entirely openly, poses, perhaps even answers, "the all-important question which is coeval with philosophy although the philosophers do not *frequently* pronounce it—the question *quid sit deus*."[18]

There is a second point of significance that the *Symposium* potentially bears within Strauss's oeuvre, and that concerns the figure to whom Strauss would devote his next work after *The City and Man*, namely, Aristophanes. Occasionally, Strauss would elevate figures underappreciated or even unappreciated in scholarship on the history of political philosophy, and among these is certainly Aristophanes, whom he does not call a philosopher, but whom he does bring alongside Nietzsche in his critique of Socrates, thus elevating him to a status typically not afforded him in the scholarship. The argument of *Socrates and Aristophanes* narrows the question of Aristophanes's critique of Socrates to the question of their respective views on the gods.[19] In this way, *Socrates and Aristophanes* poses, or comes to pose, the question with which *The City and Man* ends, *quid sit deus*, so that the earlier work introduces the later, more fundamental work, in which philosopher and comic poet confront one another on this question. Strauss actually confirms this relationship between the two works in a 1962 letter to Alexandre Kojève, in which he writes, "I am preparing for publication three lectures on the city and man, dealing with the *Politics*, the *Republic* and Thucydides. Only after these things have been finished will I be able to begin with *my real work*, an interpretation of Aristophanes."[20] Now, of the eleven extant plays by Aristophanes, all of which Strauss discusses, the *Birds* is that most clearly devoted to this question, and fittingly it's here that he mentions Plato's *Symposium*. Strauss argues that, according to Aristophanes, Socrates

> does not leave room for any things by nature beautiful or noble. The birds however, by asserting the primacy of Eros, assign an unassailable place to the naturally festive and golden. As a consequence of this, Aristophanes is more tolerant of Zeus and the other gods than is his Socrates. Socrates' doctrine is radically a-Music because it has no place for Eros; his being unerotic reflects, or corresponds to, the fact that his doctrine is silent on Eros. But the birds' doctrine is erotic and therefore Music. *If* Aristophanes had been compelled to choose between Socrates' doctrine and the birds' doctrine, he would have chosen the birds' doctrine, a doctrine that, with the help of Parmenides and Empedocles, could easily have been stated in philosophic terms. This entitles us perhaps to say that Aristophanes is not opposed to philosophy simply, but only to a philosophy that, disregarding Eros, has no link with poetry. This would help us to understand the fitness of Plato's reply to Aristophanes: The only Platonic dialogue in which Aristophanes occurs as a character or in which Socrates is presented as conversing with poets is devoted to Eros, and Socrates' doctrine is shown therein to be more profoundly erotic than Aristophanes' or any other poet's.[21]

Both Strauss's course and his sketch deliver on the central point here, in that he comments at length on what he calls Socrates's "poetic presentation of philosophy" and the religious air he cultivates about himself, as well as Plato's deep engagement with, and ultimately *love* for, Aristophanes. Indeed, in both his course and sketch, Strauss makes the relationships between Socrates and Aristophanes, on the one hand, and Plato and Aristophanes, on the other, quite central. For this reason, our goal in understanding Strauss's intention requires that we focus, both in the first and last place, on these relationships.

In both the course and the sketch, Strauss places the *Symposium* in a twofold relationship to the works of Aristophanes. The theme of Socrates's ὕβρις connects it to the *Clouds*, the first expression of this accusation against him.[22] According to that accusation, Socrates transcends the ephemeral, ordinary life of man, the merely human, and realizes the conventional character of those things which are regarded as sacred by all men. Although he is a teacher of rhetoric, he is unable to win the argument in the end—he cannot persuade the many. His "think tank," his school, is burned down. Philosophy, Aristophanes suggests, in contradistinction to poetry, is unable to persuade or to charm the multitude. Philosophy transcends the ephemeral, the mundane, the political. However, it cannot find its way back to it.[23]

Plato responds to this accusation in a number of places, but most directly in the *Symposium*. Echoing what he says in *Socrates and Aristophanes*, Strauss points out that "Socrates, far from being an unerotic man, is the erotician. It is not true that poetry is the capstone of philosophy. On the contrary, philosophy is the capstone of poetry. This means not merely, as we shall see in the *Symposium*, that philosophy defeats poetry in the contest for supremacy regarding wisdom, it means also that the right kind of philosophy is more truly poetic than poetry in the common sense of the term."[24] What Strauss means with this last claim will become somewhat clearer, when, in the next paragraph, we turn to his account of the structure of the *Symposium*. More immediately, Plato's task of responding to the *Clouds* requires that he stage a "contest for supremacy regarding wisdom," and for that the fitting model is Aristophanes's *Frogs*. In the course, Strauss remarks that the *Frogs* presents us with "a contest between two tragic poets which is decided by Dionysus, the god of wine, with a view to Alcibiades. That is the model for the *Symposium*. In the *Symposium* the contest between the tragic poets is over: Agathon has won. We have a contest, as will appear, between a tragic poet, a comic poet, and Socrates."[25] In the sketch, he goes somewhat further: "a contest between *all* forms of Athenian wisdom, rhetoric, medicine, comedy, tragedy, philosophy, in which Alcib[iades] as Dionysus is the judge. He crowns S[ocrates]."[26] (Strauss is silent on Phaedrus with this list.) Plato affirms Alcibiades's judgment, not to say his way to that judgment, by having Socrates survive the two poets on the battlefield of intoxication and dialectic.

Now, what does Strauss mean by the claim that "the right kind of philosophy is more truly poetic than poetry in the common sense of the term"? Strauss explains that both poet and philosopher focus on the human things and in their proper order, high as high and low as low. This includes the highest things simply, the nonhuman principle(s).

The poet differs, however, in that he "does not let us see, and cannot let us see, the principle becoming manifest in man above everything else, and become differently manifest in different men."[27] This is rather what Plato does. "Plato claims that by his understanding of the principle he is enabled to make the true principles transparent in human beings, in human action, in his characters," a manner of writing based in his opinion that "the human soul, and in a sense man, is, as it were, the concrescence, the growing together, of the highest principles. Therefore, if you have understood the soul in its essence, you can make these highest principles transparent in all human beings and all types of human beings."[28] Later, in a passage that deserves more careful treatment than we can possibly give it here, Strauss opens a session of the course with a further development of this thought, specifically as regards the necessary connection between attitude or opinion and character. Platonic writing "does not present the nature of the thing as that nature presents itself, but as hidden or half revealed or overlaid by opinion. Plato reproduces the natures of things as they first come to sight; he imitates them as they show themselves at first. This being the case, Plato always discusses, whatever he discusses, in a human context. Human beings talking about the phenomena at question."[29] Platonic writing thus compels the reader, eventually, to something like the Socratic turn: "Philosophic inquiry, speculation, theoria, is in danger of forgetting itself, of losing itself in the contemplation of the subject. By this very fact speculation becomes very unphilosophic. Philosophy, or whatever you call this pursuit, must always know what it is doing—it must always be self-knowledge—and therefore it must always entail reflection on the philosophizer."[30] Plato thus invents a literary form, the philosophic dialogue, that corrects for the defects of pre-Socratic philosophy, or at least the dogmatic schools thereof, on the one hand, and of nonphilosophic poetry, on the other, by showing the mutual influence and interdependence of the human and the principles, as well as the specific, various manifestations of the latter in the former. It is on the basis of this understanding of Platonic poetry that, in the course, Strauss occasionally articulates the structure of the *Symposium* by dividing its six speeches on ἔρως into uninspired and inspired speeches. And though he also plays with other divisions, it is this one that he chooses in the sketch. Now, as the course proceeds, Strauss's articulations of this division change.[31] Yet in each articulation he presents the principle, according to which both the speech and the character giving it are to be understood. In the sketch, Strauss presents Phaedrus,

Pausanias, and Eryximachus as uninspired speakers, because they subordinate ἔρως to "something extraneous to it," namely, "gain, virtue (= nomos), techne," respectively, while Aristophanes, Agathon, and Socrates are inspired because in their speeches ἔρως is "sovereign," that is, that to which ἔρως is subject is an end inherent to it, namely, "ugliness, beauty, the good," respectively.[32] We will here pass over the first three principles and take up instead the latter three, those intrinsic to ἔρως—ugliness, beauty, and the good.

Now, it appears strange, at first blush, that Strauss sees Aristophanes as positing "ugliness" as the end of ἔρως. We are rather inclined to say that for him love is always love of one's own, namely, one's own half. But because we usually understand ἔρως as of another and that other as one who is beautiful, defining it as love of one's own requires positing a prior or ancient nature that must be entirely different from man in form and hence ugly, relative to the beautiful beloved.[33] The ugliness of the spherical men, who possess the shape of the cosmic gods, manifests specifically in their assault on the Olympian gods, for which proud thoughts they are justly punished by being cut in half and thus remade into the image of the Olympian gods. Love emerges therefrom, culminating in coupling and intercourse, and for heterosexuals in reproduction, rather than in the unknowingly desired fusion with the beloved and thus return to one's prior and ugly unity. On this final point, Strauss proposes in the course, albeit with some hesitation, that, when Apollo cut the spherical men in half, he cast out the other half.[34] His hesitation seems to have subsided, however, as he includes it in the sketch, as well as in a letter to Benardete, concluding on this basis that our longing for unity is strictly speaking tragic.[35] He further connects love of one's own to love of the fatherland, which is sensible, but the precise nature of that connection is unclear.[36] Perhaps Strauss means us to supply a point he makes elsewhere, namely, that man, in not being limited by nature, must rather be limited by law.[37] At any rate, he ultimately connects such a concern with the fatherland to "*avenging* gods mediated by thymos."[38] Strauss notes both here and in the course that θυμός is never mentioned in the *Symposium*, that it is the essential feature from which the dialogue abstracts.[39] Strauss never puts all these pieces together, but as a summary account we propose the following: Aristophanes conceives of ἔρως as love of one's own, most fundamentally in the sense of an individual's longing for the transcendence of his fragmentary and artificial condition toward a higher, natural, and prior unity, over and against the restraints imposed by just and vengeful gods; these gods warn that such ἔρως is tragic and ugly, in its overreaching pride, and instead demand, on pains of (further) punishment, that it be restrained to one's own in a conventional sense, namely, to one's own fatherland and its laws and to the gods who supply or support those laws. As Strauss himself notes more than once, Aristophanes's position is strikingly similar, not to say identical, to the position of Jerusalem, so that Socrates's response to Aristophanes promises a rare glimpse into the dialogue between the twin sources of the "secret vitality" of the Western tradition. But to the degree that the positions of Aristophanes and Jerusalem are not identical, the glimpse is necessarily partial—perhaps even as regards the essential point of contention. I will return to this difficulty in the penultimate paragraph.

Strauss says nearly nothing of Agathon in the sketch, only "*Agathon*: eros of the *beautiful* (≠ one's own)."[40] Of course, he says much more in the course, offering many helpful insights and proposals, but why didn't he include them in the sketch? At a minimum, this brief remark shows that he planned to clarify the distinction between love of one's own and love of the beautiful. This distinction is relevant to the question of the gods. In the course, Strauss notes that Agathon presents a shift from the old poets and the old, avenging gods—namely, Homer and Ate or Deception—to the new or young poets and (he claims) the youngest of the gods—namely, Agathon and Eros.[41] But when he finally turns to the origin of Eros on Agathon's account, Strauss reaches the conclusion that "eros as a self-subsisting being is nothing, since he has come to being out of nothing: he is only by virtue of the poet."[42] He elaborates: the poets, and Strauss here means tragic poets, not comic poets,

> are the makers of the gods of human shape. They deify what in itself is not divine. They create the gods. Why? Because they are inspired by love of beauty. They idealize man, as we say. They do this out of love of beauty—the human beauty which they see does not satisfy them—and in doing so they raise the stature of man. They visualize something which looks like man but which is deathless and free from any other defect.[43]

Aristophanes had focused on the ultimate end of ἔρως and therefore its rebelliousness against the laws. Agathon, however, brings out its civilizing effect by focusing more specifically on the love of glory or fame, which is, on Strauss's view, "not even alluded to by Aristophanes."[44] In so venturing beyond Aristophanes, Agathon poses much more radically the question of the being of the gods, what a god is or might be—*quid sit deus*.[45]

Now, before turning to Socrates's speech, it is important to note that, though Aristophanes and Agathon both advance separate ends, namely, one's own (and ugliness) and the beautiful, respectively, these ends operate simultaneously to generate the gods of the city. Strauss explains:

> The [Olympian] gods are essentially related to eros.... The gods have been created by eros.... How? It is easiest to understand in the case of eros as love of the beautiful, why love of the beautiful should create the Olympian gods—eternal beauty, deathless youth, something man can never achieve and which he loves. Sempiternal strength and beauty of one's body. But what about love of one's own? The love of one's own leads to the polis.... The political society is, of course, always a closed society.... These gods, as the guardians of the polis, are primarily the guardians of right. They are the avenging gods. The union of the beautiful gods and the avenging gods, which appears directly in the mythical presentation, has its common root in eros, but in two different manifestations—the love of one's own, on the one hand, and the love of the beautiful, on the other.[46]

Let us tie the preceding together, so that we can appreciate more fully the significance of Strauss's analysis of Socrates's speech. In the wake of his study of Machiavelli on the theological-political problem, and thereby the completion of his study of modernity, Strauss finally took up the task of presenting his understanding of Socrates publicly. The first in a series of publications on this question, *The City and Man*, ends by posing the question, *quid sit deus*, which his next book, *Socrates and Aristophanes*, takes up more directly. In his analysis of Aristophanes's understanding of the gods, Strauss is eventually brought to the *Birds*, where the disagreement between Aristophanes and Socrates regarding the gods is brought into relation with Aristophanes's political psychology, specifically as regards ἔρως. In that discussion, Strauss indicates that, for the Socratic response, one must turn, reasonably enough, to the *Symposium*. His interpretation divides the speeches on ἔρως to show that the only speakers analyzing it with respect to its inherent ends are the poets Aristophanes and Agathon and the philosopher Socrates. The poets treat, separately, the twin passions out of which the gods of the city are generated, love of one's own and love of the beautiful, which Socrates then situates relative to a third form of ἔρως, as it were, the love of the good.

Now, it is in a way strange to say that the theme of Socrates's speech is love of the good, since its most famous part is an ascent up a ladder of ever-increasing, ever-expanding beauties. Strauss is well aware of this interpretive difficulty and explains it as follows:

> Socrates' whole speech is characterized by the following fact: It begins with a refutation of the assertion that love is love of the beautiful and it ends with an unbelievable reassertion that love is love of the beautiful. This massive contradiction is of course not done because Plato had a loose mind, but because he wanted to do something. He deliberately abstracted from the two forms of love—love of one's own and love of the beautiful—to see what comes out of it, a perfectly common scientific procedure, and then he restores them.[47]

In every source—the course, the sketch, and the letters to Benardete—Strauss structures Socrates's speech into seven parts, identifying the central section as that in which this abstraction occurs.[48] Socrates's return from this abstraction and restoration of the beautiful involve what Strauss terms a "philosophic presentation of poetry" and a "poetic presentation of philosophy," to which we turn shortly. In the central section, Diotima, with Socrates in agreement, subordinates the love of one's own and the love of the beautiful to the love of the good on the grounds that the ultimate end of all action is happiness. People readily give up their own when manifestly bad, for example, with a gangrenous limb, while the beautiful, and reproduction therein, can promise and deliver on happiness only inasmuch as reproduction guarantees "sempiternal possession of the good."[49] As regards reproduction, however, Strauss observes that "Socrates is somehow disappointed" with this addition to the argument.[50] Strauss therefore posits that ἔρως and the love, or rather desire, for the good are not identical but rather that Diotima pursues the conditions under which they might be assimilated to one another.[51] Then to what end is the assimilation introduced? The answer seems to be Agathon, though Strauss does not develop this fully. In addition to presenting the Socratic view, according to which the passions generating the gods of the city are subordinate to the ubiquitous human desire for the good, Strauss also develops, in three connected but separate passages, the conclusions Agathon would draw but we would be rash to attribute to Socrates.[52] The essential difference between the two is the proposal, to which Agathon readily assents, but which young Socrates rather resists, that the beautiful things are also good. For it is out of some skepticism regarding this proposal that Socrates resists the full assimilation of ἔρως to the desire for the good.

Strauss is clear in his sketch that what follows, the restoration of the beautiful, involves "no restoration of gods and immortality proper."[53] Strauss explains in the course:

> By the denial of eros of the beautiful, as well as eros of one's own, the Olympian gods lose their basis. The Olympian gods are products of eros, but of a certain kind of eros: of the love of the beautiful—they are simply beautiful beings; but in a more indirect way, as avenging gods they are products of the love of one's own. One's own, culminating in the polis, one's right, and, therefore, in the need for avenging gods. Therefore, the gods do not reappear anymore, whereas love of one's own and love of the beautiful reappear.[54]

The reappearance of the gods is impossible, thanks both to the preceding critique and to the subsequent "philosophic presentation of poetry" or "disenchanting presentation of poetry."[55] Philosophy disenchants poetry by showing it to be an attempt to assimilate ἔρως to the desire for the sempiternal possession of the good through a form of reproduction, namely, through the production of beautiful poems that promise everlasting fame and reputation. What takes the place of the gods and everlasting fame, even immortality proper, is the subsequent poetic presentation of philosophy, which enchants by presenting philosophy as though it is the highest assimilation of ἔρως to the desire for sempiternal possession of the good. Strauss is clear that no poet can give a philosophic presentation of poetry, disenchanting as it is with the poet's own activity, and that they can achieve (or have achieved) a poetic presentation of philosophy only in comedy, that is, only by making it ridiculous and thus disenchanting the audience with it. For a poetic presentation of philosophy that is enchanting, rather than disenchanting, a tragic poet is necessary, and not just any tragic poet, but one who produces his poems by art or τέχνη. For, in making his poems through artful contrivance rather than divine inspiration, such a poet would not be enchanted with his own productions; he would rather be capable of disenchanting one with his poems and thus capable of writing comedies. Strauss emphasizes that, conversely, the artful comic poet is not necessarily capable of enchantment, of writing tragedies, precisely because comedy presupposes, without incorporating, tragedy into its activity. Strauss wrote in his unpublished notes for his lectures: "Aristophanes [≠ Agathon] makes Zeus speak but καταγέλαστος." In other words, and to generalize, the comic poet can only make ridiculous gods, not enchanting gods.[56] Aristophanes could never become such a poet, though Agathon certainly has the potential: this is why, Strauss argues in both the course and the sketch, Aristophanes falls asleep before Agathon.[57] Strauss nevertheless insists that Aristophanes is superior as an individual to Agathon, who seems rather to resist becoming such a poet.[58]

But then who, if not Agathon, is this poet? In the sketch, Strauss claims that it is Socrates, only to add quickly at the end, as though interrupting himself, "—but is this true?"[59] This question leads him to remark, first, on Socrates's reasons for not writing and, second, to develop further his remarks on the character of Platonic writing. Strauss calls Socrates a rhetor but not a poet, for "he could not write punitive speeches."[60] His evidence here is Socrates's failure with Callicles. Strauss says more in the course, connecting this point to the earlier discussion of the gods: "In the part with Polus Socrates is successful—he can persuade him. In the Callicles part Socrates fails. Socrates puts his cards on the table: he says my rhetoric reaches so far. Why? Socrates can persuade Polus because he can persuade him by dialectic, by proofs. He cannot persuade Callicles truly because Callicles could not be persuaded truly without recourse to threats, without recourse to punitive speeches, to speeches which in the last resort appeal to *avenging gods*."[61] It is here that Socrates and Plato differ, and in both the course and the sketch Strauss reminds his audience of al-Farabi's remark regarding Plato, Socrates, and Thrasymachus: "Plato's great achievement beyond Socrates was that he was able to combine the way of Socrates, by which you can teach, dialectically, nice people, with the way of Thrasymachus, by which you can persuade non-docile people who must be frightened and terrified."[62] He thus concludes that "Socrates did not write because he could not write, more precisely, because he could not write on the highest level, and writing on the highest level includes the ability to write tragedy, the tragedy behind which are the avenging gods."[63] In these impressively pregnant and incisive remarks, which we can do little more here than present to and emphasize for the reader, Strauss boldly divulges the bearing Socrates's conversation with the poets has on Plato's manner of writing. Of course, we are left to wonder how the way of Thrasymachus manifests in Plato's art of writing, and what transfigured form, if any, the avenging gods take in this new genre. How does Plato's presentation of the good, according to its popular understanding, culminate in moral self-restraint?

These are some of the questions that remain after reading the various documents currently available to us for understanding Strauss's interpretation of the *Symposium*, a dialogue, I remind you, of great consequence for Strauss's thinking. But, to my mind, the greatest difficulty in Strauss's interpretation concerns his view of Aristophanes. For, on the one hand, Strauss interprets Aristophanes as representing the position of the avenging gods qua avenging, though not qua beautiful. But, on the other, he also interprets him as unable to make such gods. In other words, Aristophanes is representative of a position for which he is deemed unrepresentative. This difficulty is not insurmountable, though Strauss does not discuss it. Perhaps, we speculate, Aristophanes merely makes evident the *need* for such a writing. His Zeus may be ridiculous, but his speech nevertheless makes the case for a nonridiculous Zeus, a Zeus both punitive, and thus protective of one's own, and beautiful. But then must we not admit that Aristophanes cannot, finally, serve the role he seems to serve in this dialogue, as the representative of Jerusalem in Athens? In his unpublished course notes on the *Symposium*, Strauss observes that the cosmic gods in Aristophanes's speech are asexual and that there is no place for law, whereas in the Bible "the First Cause," that is, God, is the source of both the law and man's bisexuality, that is, his division into male and female. The principle of Aristophanes's speech, ugliness, cannot be the principle of human ἔρως in the Bible. Another way to put this is that, whereas in Aristophanes's speech the cosmic gods and the Olympian gods exist side-by-side, with our form changing from the former to the latter, in the biblical account the cosmic gods, or rather the cosmos simply and therefore the false gods based thereupon, are subordinated to the God in whose image we are made: in short, Aristophanes posits two alternatives or causes where the Bible clearly asserts one.[64] Speculations aside, we can safely say that Strauss harbored reservations about finding among the Greek poets a suitable foil for the biblical account. For these questions, Strauss ultimately turned, under the guidance of Avicenna, who knew the alternative much better than we, to Plato's *Laws*, to which he devoted what would become his final "Socratic" work,[65] published only posthumously. Perhaps for these reasons Strauss abandoned his intended work on the *Symposium*.

But there is another possibility worth considering, and here I ask my reader to forgive me for what is admittedly wild speculation. So many of the circumstances surrounding Strauss's thinking on the *Symposium* seem to echo the dialogue itself. There are the two enthusiastic students, Seth Benardete and Hilail Gildin, eager to get the word out. There is the occasion for the course, in honor of Strauss's friend and colleague, Peter Heinrich von Blanckenhagen, soon to depart from Chicago. There is, further, curiosity and intrigue about this and the other course transcripts, both within the Straussian school and beyond. And there are the many years that pass—decades, in this case—between the original occasion and its eventual publication. But above all there is the intimated suggestion that all the mysteries of Strauss's teaching will be revealed, promising as the course does, as well as the letters and the sketch, to exhibit Strauss's thinking on the theological-political problem in Plato. Perhaps, then, Strauss never intended to publish on the *Symposium* at all or thought it best to leave these documents incomplete and hand their eventual dissemination over to his students and literary executors. Perhaps! Whatever the case may be, it is nevertheless undeniable that his thinking on the *Symposium*'s themes evokes from us much the same reaction as the end of the *Symposium* itself, a strange mixture of perplexity and awe.

Notes

1. Leo Strauss, *On Plato's Symposium*, ed. Seth Benardete (Chicago: University of Chicago Press, 2001), vii.

2. Strauss, *On Plato's Symposium*, vii.

3. Leo Strauss, *The Political Philosophy of Hobbes: Its Basis and Its Genesis*, trans. Elsa M. Sinclair (Chicago: University of Chicago Press, 1996), viii with 88n5.

4. Strauss, *Political Philosophy of Hobbes*, xv–xvi.

5. Leo Strauss, *What Is Political Philosophy? And Other Studies* (Chicago: University of Chicago Press, 1988), 44.

6. Leo Strauss, *Thoughts on Machiavelli* (Chicago: University of Chicago Press, 1995), 51. I owe this contrast to Heinrich Meier, *Political Philosophy and the Challenge of Revealed Religion*, trans. Robert Berman (Chicago: University of Chicago Press, 2017), 37, 46–47. See, also, 60–64 and 71 (end).

7. Leo Strauss, *Natural Right and History* (Chicago: University of Chicago Press, 1971), vii.

8. See, again, Strauss, *Natural Right and History*, vii.

9. 191–92 with Leo Strauss, *The City and Man* (Chicago: University of Chicago Press, 1978), 60, 61–62.

10. Strauss, *City and Man*, 55.

11. Strauss, *On Plato's Symposium*, 13; compare Strauss, *City and Man*, 58.

12. 193.

13. Strauss, *On Plato's Symposium*, 24; see, also, 172b5–6. "Aristodemus is the source by way of which the older generation of Socratics informs the younger generation. Apollodorus is the only one who leaks that information to the outside public. This is somehow connected with the fact that Apollodorus is a very enthusiastic man and cannot keep back such an exciting story" (Strauss, *On Plato's Symposium*, 21).

14. Strauss, *On Plato's Symposium*, 12; 192 in the present volume.

15. VI.28.

16. Andocides, *On the Mysteries* 15, 35.

17. Strauss, *On Plato's Symposium*, 15–16; compare 8.

18. Strauss, *City and Man*, 241, emphasis added.

19. Leo Strauss, *Socrates and Aristophanes* (Chicago: University of Chicago Press, 1980), 52–53.

20. Leo Strauss, *On Tyranny: Corrected and Expanded Edition*, ed. Victor Gourevitch and Michael S. Roth (Chicago: University of Chicago Press, 2013), 309, emphasis added. This letter was brought to my attention by Devin Stauffer, "Leo Strauss's UnSocratic Aristophanes?," in *The Political Theory of Aristophanes*, ed. Jeremy J. Mhire and Bryan Paul Frost (Albany: State University of New York Press, 2014), 331–51, 351.

21. Strauss, *Socrates and Aristophanes*, 173, emphasis added.

22. Strauss, *On Plato's Symposium*, 8; 193 in the present volume.

23. Strauss, *On Plato's Symposium*, 6.

24. Strauss, *On Plato's Symposium*, 7.

25. Strauss, *On Plato's Symposium*, 26.

26. 193–194.

27. Strauss, *On Plato's Symposium*, 7.

28. Strauss, *On Plato's Symposium*, 7–8.

29. Strauss, *On Plato's Symposium*, 57.

30. Strauss, *On Plato's Symposium*, 57–58.

31. Compare, for example, Strauss, *On Plato's Symposium*, 54, 73–74, 121, 143.

32. 194, with Strauss, *On Plato's Symposium*, 54, 137. Strauss adds to Socrates's principle, "the good," the parenthetical remark "inspired by Diotima." See paragraph 10, below, on the assimilation of ἔρως to the desire for the good through reproduction.

33. Strauss, *On Plato's Symposium*, 134; compare 184.

34. Strauss, *On Plato's Symposium*, 130, 131, 135.

35. 194, 211.

36. Strauss, *On Plato's Symposium*, 241; 194, 211, 213 in the present volume.

37. Strauss, *On Plato's Symposium*, 133–34; 194, 211 in the present volume.

38. 195.

39. Strauss, *On Plato's Symposium*, 243; see, again, Strauss, *City and Man*, 61–62.

40. 194.

41. Strauss, *On Plato's Symposium*, 159.

42. 211; see Strauss, *On Plato's Symposium*, 165.
43. Strauss, *On Plato's Symposium*, 169; see, also, 257–58.
44. Strauss, *On Plato's Symposium*, 137.
45. I owe this observation to Svetozar Minkov.
46. Strauss, *On Plato's Symposium*, 209; see, also, 210, 217.
47. Strauss, *On Plato's Symposium*, 213.
48. 204c7–207a4; see Strauss, *On Plato's Symposium*, 206 with 198; 195, 212–213 in the present volume.
49. Strauss, *On Plato's Symposium*, 204 ff.
50. Strauss, *On Plato's Symposium*, 206.
51. See, for example, Strauss, *On Plato's Symposium*, 216–17.
52. See Strauss, *On Plato's Symposium*, 182, 189, 196.
53. 195.
54. Strauss, *On Plato's Symposium*, 240.
55. 195.
56. See Strauss, *Socrates and Aristophanes*, 192.
57. Strauss, *On Plato's Symposium*, 168; 196 in the present volume.
58. 212.
59. 196.
60. 196.
61. Strauss, *On Plato's Symposium*, 246, emphasis added.
62. Strauss, *On Plato's Symposium*, 246–47.
63. Strauss, *On Plato's Symposium*, 247.
64. See Leo Strauss, "On the Interpretation of Genesis," in Leo Strauss, *Jewish Philosophy and the Crisis of Modernity*, ed. Kenneth Hart Green (Albany: State University of New York Press, 1997), 359–76, 367–70.
65. See Leo Strauss, *The Argument and the Action of Plato's* Laws (Chicago: University of Chicago Press, 1975), 2.

PART SIX

Transcript 6

LEO STRAUSS, SELECTIONS FROM
"SEMINAR IN POLITICAL PHILOSOPHY:
ROUSSEAU" (1962)

Editorial Note: The following four passages are quoted from Leo Strauss, *1962 Course on Rousseau Offered at the University of Chicago*, ed. Jonathan Marks (Chicago: Leo Strauss Center, 2014). The numbers in the parentheses refer to the page numbers of the edition above. The passages are slightly edited to improve readability and the footnotes are added by the editors.

1. (296–297) Now here[1] we have a clear deviation of the Savoyard Vicar from the accepted doctrine. He does not assert the eternity of God alone. He leaves it open whether there cannot be eternity of matter. And now in the first statement of the question, he says: Is there a single principle of things (that could mean strict monotheism) or are there two or more? This could mean at first hearing: Is there not more than one god? After all, theoretically there could be a body of gods, an assembly of gods who could rule the universe, perhaps with a highest god. But he narrows it down later to the question of two principles: God and eternal matter. He does not assert it, but he does not exclude it; he says it is a question of no importance to him. Now this is of course a gross overstatement. It must be of the greatest importance to him. But what is the advantage of the eternity of matter? [...] [I]n the Garnier edition of the *Letter to Beaumont*, on page 462, [we read:] "The co-existence of these two principles seems to explain better the construction of the universe; and to remove difficulties which one removes without it not easily, as among others that of the

origin of evil."[2] That is the point. In other words, if there is one principle, God, then God would seem to be also the author of evil—of everything, and thus of evil. And then of course the monotheistic answer, as you know, is to say: No, the origin of evil is in creatures, angels or men. And this leads to further difficulties, whereas if you say that there is a second principle, matter, which limits the power of God, [then] therefore his work cannot be as good as he wills it. Now this was very famous traditionally as the Manichean doctrine, from Manes, in the early Christian centuries, if I remember well. But it goes back to Persian dualism, Zoroastrian, and it was reasserted as theoretically best by Bayle in his *Dictionary*,[3] to which I referred before, and reasserted in a somewhat subtle manner by Voltaire in his *Candide*, because there are two men, a Leibnizian [, Martin,] who is a monotheist and another man whose name is Pangloss. And [Pangloss] says everything is the best of all possible worlds [...] and then of course there are many evils, and you know that's very funnily described. The alternative is Martin; and Martin asserts a dualism, and so he can account for evil by tracing it to a special principle.[4] And Martin is, incidentally, a man who had worked for ten years for the booksellers in Amsterdam.[5] Now everyone at that time knew that this was Bayle. Bayle [...] was a Frenchman by birth but left France because of the Edict of Nantes and earned his living as a writer in Amsterdam—and so that was he. So this was at that time quite well known, this doctrine, to informed people. By the way, the ultimate origin of this doctrine in the philosophic tradition is Plato himself, in the tenth book of the *Laws*, in the demonstration of the existence of God and the discussion of teleology. Two souls are mentioned, a good soul and a bad soul.[6] And there are other remarks in Plato. Well, that is a simple story: in the creation of the universe in the *Timaeus*, the Artificer creates a universe out of something which is not called matter but which has ontologically the function of matter. So this is the view which he takes. Now the key implication is of course this: there are two. If everything that is as it were the joint work of a good and a bad principle, man cannot be simply good. I mean, if God leads him to virtue, there is something in him *as natural* which leads him to unqualified egoism. The second implication is this: If matter is eternal, there is an eternal obstacle to the goodness of man—an eternal one—and that can easily be thought to mean [that] man's beginnings were particularly imperfect and that all progress was reached beyond this period by man's efforts.

2. (303) [U]ltimately all passions, *all* passions, go back to self-love: *amour de soi*, self-preservation. And then there is a certain complication by

virtue of which *amour de soi* becomes *amour-propre*, and there *amour-propre* means nothing but a passion constituted by regarding other men. If you are hungry (take a simple case), that is strictly in you: no comparison is needed in order to be sure that you are hungry. I mean, the others may all be non-hungry; that doesn't do away with your hunger. But in other things, comparison with others is essential for constituting the passion concerned. That is equally true of pity as of pride. Pity is also, as we have seen last time, based on comparison with others: I am better off than he and so I can pity him. And now pity and pride—let us assume pride is bad and pity is good, for convenience's sake. So this stems from the same single root called self-preservation. Now Rousseau admits that pity is not universally good: there is a kind of foolish pity. But how are you enabled to distinguish between a reasonable pity and foolish pity? Answer: by generalization—you remember that, this passage which in many respects sounds so awkward: pity with the human race in general, and only in the light of this universal pity apply your pity in a particular case. In other words, you have a strictly monistic derivation of morality from the sole thing called *amour de soi*, self-love, the egoistic principle in itself. In other words, altruism is a modification of egoism. I mean, the moral teaching as presented prior to the Profession of Faith does not require two principles; and the Vicar presents the moral problem as requiring two principles: A principle of vice on the one hand, [and] of virtue on the other, and corresponding to the metaphysical dualism of body (merely myself) and soul (which can embrace the whole).

3. (307–8) How did Rousseau understand Protestantism? I think that appears rather clearly from the *Letters Written from the Mountain*, which is addressed to the Genevans. And the view of Protestantism is the one which I think we all learned in school (because I went to a school in a Protestant country), which is [that] the big thing which the Reformation made was the emancipation of the individual judgment, universal priesthood. That means that everyone has as much right to interpret the Bible as everyone else; there is no ecclesiastical authority proper. So still here in Protestantism, this was of course in Luther and Calvin, to say the least, bound up with the belief in the divine character of the biblical text. And then there came this development: Once you grant the principle of the individual, each Christian is as good a judge as everyone else. Then the other questions came up, for example, the text: Is the text reliable? You know, the variant readings and all the other things. Well, everyone can judge it. And what remained then? The Dutch had a proverb, *geen ketter*

sonder letter: no heretic without a letter—of the church. And finally it became simply that Protestantism proper changed into simple rationalism: Everyone is a judge by virtue of his natural reason, and whether he accepts the Bible or not depends again on the outcome of his reasoning—you know, whether the ordinary proofs, like miracles, reliable tradition and so on, hold up or not. This is a view which Rousseau takes for granted. [. . .] It is surely not the Protestantism of Calvin's *Institutes*. It has been watered down very much—I mean a large part of Protestantism at that time was, of course, rationalistic, more or less, but the key point, I believe, is this (that will appear when we look forward): Rousseau was in a way surely a democrat. Now democracy requiring, meaning equality, and in a way, as is indicated by the equality of the vote, equality of judgment, the right of judgment. In the strictly secular doctrine, it is very clear. When you take Hobbes, everyone is as entitled to pass judgment on the means to his self-preservation as everyone else, the fool as well as the prudent man. Now if this is formally the principle of democracy, this would apply of course to all other matters, all matters of public import, let me say. I mean, no one would say it regarding shoemaking or physics, but all matters of public import. Now religion is obviously a matter of public import, and therefore there cannot be any religious authorities. Therefore the primarily anti-Catholic implication, naturally, because of the existence of the magisterial. The Protestant ecclesiastical authorities, at least the continental forms of Protestants, Lutherism and Calvinism—you know, these were strictly speaking ecclesiastical authorities: the synods, and whatever they had. And this is of course a question alive up to the present day in this country, the question: Is democracy compatible with any authority not derivative from the people? Religious authority by definition is not derivative from the people. This is, I think, a point which one must keep in mind here. You[7] made a point which is connected with that, that natural religion creates the same problem eventually as revealed religion, if I understood you correctly. And I understood you to mean that because not all men will be convinced by natural religion, and let us take the clearest case, atheists: Do not atheists have the same right as the followers of the Vicar? So in other words, while the Vicar will be willing to tolerate all people who make additions to natural religion—Catholics, Protestants, Jews, or whatever it may be—must he not also tolerate people who make subtractions from it? Is this not the question you meant? And then you arrived at the view which is now of course very common: that political society has no right whatever regarding religious matters, no right whatever; and separation of Church and State in the most strict construction would be the consequence. This is true, but Rousseau would of course say this: natural religion is so much an evident necessity for civil society that what is true of revealed religion is not true of natural religion. You can have a decent society of deists as well as of Christians and, he would say, even more than of Christians. But you cannot have a decent society of atheists, and therefore civil society is entitled and even obliged to establish a civil religion, which is exactly what he says in the famous last chapter of the *Social Contract* on civil religion.

4. (354) I can only say there are two moralities: There is a morality which Rousseau presented prior to the Profession of Faith, which is surely atheistic; and there is the morality implied in the Profession of Faith, which is theistic. And this question we have been discussing all the time: Is the Profession of Faith Rousseau's own teaching, or is it only the teaching of the Savoyard Vicar? And as I understand Rousseau, this plea of conscience in the way in which the Savoyard Vicar raises it is not tenable, because interpreted, the conscience as Rousseau understands it means enlightened compassion. And that is a very complex thing whose origin we have discussed, but which [means], then, enlightened compassion, meaning mere compassion will not do. Then you have a compassion with a condemned criminal which is unenlightened because you do not take into consideration the victims of the criminal. The only thing one could say regarding the statement of Bayle is this, that Bayle admits what Rousseau doesn't mention here, that the concern with glory (and also, of course, glory of one's country) would be, could be as effective in atheists as in non-atheists, and therefore there could be a patriotic motive there as well.[8] But Rousseau's objection is probably that this desire for glory will not be effective in a sufficiently powerful way in the majority of men, and therefore if there are no religious sanctions for politically or socially good actions, they will not come forth.

Notes

1. "I believe therefore that the world is governed by a powerful and wise will. I see it or, rather, I sense it; and that is something important for me to know. But is this same world eternal or created? Is there a single principle of things? Or, are there two or many of them, and what is their nature? I know nothing about all this, and what does it matter to me? As soon as this knowledge has something to do with my interests, I shall make an effort to acquire

it. Until then I renounce idle questions which may agitate my *amour-propre* but are useless for my conduct and are beyond my reason." Jean-Jacques Rousseau, *Emile or On Education*, trans. Allan Bloom (New York: Basic Books, 1973), 276–77.

2. "For in addition, the coexistence of two Principles seems to explain the constitution of the universe better, and to remove difficulties that are hard to resolve without it, such as, among others, that of the origin of evil." Jean-Jacques Rousseau, *Letter to Beaumont, Letters Written from the Mountain, and Related Writings*, ed. Christopher Kelly and Eve Grace, trans. Christopher Kelly and Judith R. Bush (Hanover, NH: University Press of New England, 2001), 44.

3. See Remark D in the entry on the "Manicheans": Pierre Bayle, *Historical and Critical Dictionary: Selections*, trans. Richard H. Popkin (Indianapolis: Hackett, 1991), 144–52.

4. Voltaire, *Candide and Other Stories*, trans. Roger Pearson (Oxford: Oxford University Press, 2006), 52.

5. Voltaire, *Candide and Other Stories*, 51.

6. Plato, *Laws* 896d–e. See also Leo Strauss, *1959 Course on Plato's Laws Offered at the University of Chicago*, ed. Lorraine Smith Pangle (Chicago: Leo Strauss Center, 2016), 364; Leo Strauss, *1971–72 Course on Plato's Laws Offered at St. John's College*, ed. Lorraine Smith Pangle (Chicago: Leo Strauss Center, 2016), 586–87.

7. Strauss is referring to one of the students in class who gave a presentation.

8. Pierre Bayle, *Various Thoughts on the Occasion of a Comet*, trans. Robert C. Bartlett (Albany: State University of New York Press, 2000), 212–14 (sections 172 and 173).

RASOUL NAMAZI

Interpretative Essay

LEO STRAUSS AND JEAN-JACQUES ROUSSEAU:
ANCIENTS AND MODERNS, ESOTERICISM,
AND THE CHALLENGE OF RELIGION

IT WOULD NOT BE AN EXAGGERATION to say that Leo Strauss's view of Rousseau is perhaps his most puzzling encounter with modern political philosophers. It is puzzling because, on the one hand, every serious reader of Strauss and his writings on Rousseau must admit that there is a profound sympathy, not to say an agreement, between Strauss and Rousseau, an agreement that one can with difficulty claim to exist between Strauss and any other modern political philosopher.[1] On the other hand, and despite this profound concord between the two, Strauss consistently takes a highly critical position toward Rousseau. This perplexing character of Strauss's view of Rousseau has not failed to attract the attention of Strauss's serious readers who are also Rousseau scholars.[2] It is my intention here to illustrate this conflictual relationship between Strauss and Rousseau while concentrating on the question of religion in Strauss's thought. In order to do so, however, I must briefly discuss two other aspects of Strauss's reading of Rousseau before turning to the question of religion proper. I divide my discussion into three parts on the basis of the central importance of three issues in Strauss's writings: (1) the quarrel of the ancients and the moderns, (2) esotericism, and (3) the challenge of religion. I will discuss these three issues in Strauss's thought in their relation to his encounter with the philosophy of Rousseau.

1. *The Quarrel of the Ancients and the Moderns.* Strauss was, above all, a thinker of crisis and since the beginning of his intellectual odyssey subscribed to the idea that we are living a deep crisis, the crisis of modernity.

Strauss traced the origin of this crisis to deep changes in the history of political philosophy and a rupture in the way of thought that began in the early sixteenth century with Niccolò Machiavelli; this rupture was later accelerated by Machiavelli's successors and intellectual heirs. Modern political philosophy, in Strauss's view, was a conscious rejection of premodern political philosophy, or what he often called "classical political philosophy," represented by the Socratic school and mainly in the writings of Plato, Xenophon, and Aristotle but also their Roman and later medieval followers like Cicero, Alfarabi, Maimonides, and Marsilius of Padua. Strauss's intellectual enterprise, therefore, can be described as a lifelong project of rehabilitation and even a return to classical political philosophy. In this perspective, Strauss did not believe in the superiority of modern political philosophy over classical political philosophy and did not believe that the former has managed to rationally reject the latter. In other words, borrowing the sixteenth-century expression "the quarrel of the ancients and the moderns," Strauss did not believe that the debate between classical and modern political philosophies had been decided in favor of the moderns and claimed that a renewal of that debate is perfectly reasonable and necessary for overcoming the crisis of modernity.[3] In many of his writings, and in the most dramatic ways possible, Strauss took the side of the ancients against modern political Philosophy. Discussing the political philosophy of Machiavelli, the originator of modern political philosophy in Strauss's eyes, Strauss questions the legitimacy of the whole modern project and dramatically raises the question of whether "the Enlightenment" is the right word for describing what should be more properly described as "Obfuscation."[4] Elsewhere, Strauss speaks in clearer terms by going even so far as to claim that "the perfect political order, as Plato and Aristotle have sketched it, *is* the perfect political order" and that it is "*morally-politically* the most reasonable and most pleasing."[5] In this regard, Rousseau is clearly included in the camp of modern political philosophy, an intellectual heir of the movement initiated by Machiavelli, and on the side of those responsible for the crisis of modernity. On closer inspection, however, the place of Rousseau in Strauss's thought turns out to be more complicated. While Machiavelli is criticized by Strauss in the most consistent manner as the founding father of modern political philosophy,[6] Rousseau occupies a peculiar place in Strauss's grand narrative of modern political philosophy. Machiavelli, Thomas Hobbes, John Locke, and Montesquieu squarely belong together and form what Strauss, borrowing an expression from Socrates in the

Republic, calls the first wave of modernity. Rousseau, on his part, initiates the second wave of modernity, and Strauss is critical of Rousseau's contributions to the formation of modern political philosophy by injecting the ideas of the practically infinite malleability of humanity through history. But Strauss also saw something going in the opposite direction in Rousseau's thought. While Machiavelli and his immediate successors were unanimous in rejecting the premodern political philosophy and its lofty, unrealistic expectations from human beings and they, therefore, lowered the standards of human life by embracing an economic perspective on human life, "Rousseau protested in the name of virtue, of the genuine, nonutilitarian virtue of the classical republics against the degrading and enervating doctrines of his predecessors; he opposed both the stifling spirit of the absolute monarchy and the more or less cynical commercialism of the modern republics."[7] In other words, despite all the negative points Strauss raises against Rousseau, in the end, rather than being a simple heir of the modern project initiated by Machiavelli, Rousseau turns out to be a critic of modernity who opposes it in the name of classical political philosophy. Strauss claims that "Rousseau questions [the modern idea of] progress in the decisive respect."[8]

Whatever Strauss's final view of Rousseau was, one cannot but see a certain affinity between Strauss's interest in classical political philosophy as the remedy to the crisis of modernity and Rousseau's critique of modernity. Just like Strauss, Rousseau thought that "the modern venture was a radical error."[9] Indeed, one cannot ignore the fact that Strauss is critical of many aspects of Rousseau's thought; but interestingly, Strauss is reluctant to claim that the impact of Rousseau on the process of modernization of political philosophy, what he describes as an "advance of modernity," was what Rousseau *himself* desired. In other words, Rousseau's thought led to the acceleration of the modern project and its radicalization *unintentionally* and *despite* his real intention: Rousseau's real intention was rather to reverse the course of modernity toward classical political philosophy. Surprisingly, this claim of Strauss goes against one of the most cherished methodological principles of Strauss's whole thought. Strauss was emphatic that the work of a historian is to refrain from trying to understand an old author better than he understood himself. He argued that the sound historical method requires that the historian tries to understand an earlier philosopher exactly as he understood himself.[10] But the claim that Rousseau was unaware of the opposite effects of his ideas and their contribution to the radicalization of modernity is precisely to claim a better understanding of Rousseau's thought than what was available to Rousseau. It is therefore not surprising that Strauss vacillated between, on the one hand, attributing something that can be described as shortsightedness to Rousseau and making him responsible for the crisis of modernity, and on the other, attributing to him an "amazingly lucid vision." Strauss, therefore, claimed that Rousseau is an author who, just like Nietzsche, is not responsible for the "perversion of his teaching" by others.[11]

2. *Esotericism.* Before becoming part of the grand narrative of the decline of modernity in Strauss's *Natural Right and History* (1953) and "The Three Waves of Modernity" (1964),[12] Rousseau played a very different role in Strauss's thought as it is reflected in "On the Intention of Rousseau" (1947). In this first of two substantial writings of Strauss on Rousseau, the thought of the latter is connected with one of the fundamental and controversial aspects of Strauss's thought through a meticulous study of Rousseau's *Discourse on the Sciences and the Arts*: the question of esotericism. Strauss famously claimed that many philosophers throughout history did not advertise their genuine ideas in writing and concealed this most fundamental aspect of their thought or their *esoteric* teaching from their readers. Instead of this true esoteric teaching, Strauss claimed, one often finds only the *exoteric* doctrines and ideas in the writings of the past philosophers, the exoteric teachings that are at most conditionally true, often untrue, and to which such philosophers did not entirely subscribe. To discover the deepest teachings of these philosophers, the esoteric core of their thought, Strauss argued, one must learn how to read their writings between the lines and practice an esoteric art of reading that is designed to decipher the esoteric art of writing of those authors. Strauss's discovery of esotericism happened independently and prior to his studies on Rousseau.[13] Interestingly, however, Strauss's 1947 study on Rousseau is perhaps his most extensive and clearest discussion of what he considered to be one of the chief justifications for esoteric writing. Strauss argued that authors engage in esoteric writing for different reasons: they often practice esotericism and conceal their true teachings from the public to protect themselves against persecution. Living in nonliberal societies where freedom of expression is not recognized, according to Strauss, many thinkers who held nonorthodox positions about religion or politics tried to obscure their true views in their writings.[14] But this is not the only reason for the practice of esoteric writing in Strauss's view, nor is it the most controversial. Strauss famously claimed that

some philosophers throughout history practiced esotericism for more altruistic reasons. These thinkers believed in the existence of "dangerous truths" whose communication to the public would jeopardize the health and stability of the politico-social order. They concealed their true esoteric teachings from the public to protect society from radical questioning inherent in their philosophical thought and from ideas that might endanger the well-being of a political order and destabilize it.[15] "On the Intention of Rousseau" claims that this idea is Rousseau's core teaching in his *Discourse on the Sciences and the Arts*. In this essay, which made him famous, Rousseau claimed that scientific progress and the diffusion of knowledge, far from contributing to the happiness of humankind, have rather made their life miserable and led to the corruption of human societies. This famous and still shocking thesis of Rousseau went against the whole project of Enlightenment, which, as its name clearly indicates, saw ignorance as the root cause of the evils in human societies and promised the improvement of human life through the progress of sciences and their diffusion among human beings. In his intensive interpretation of Rousseau's singular thesis, Strauss rejected any interpretation of Rousseau's thesis that would explain it solely by recourse to Rousseau's quirks of character or his contrarian habits. Far from being an unreasonable suggestion, Strauss connected Rousseau's thesis to his own view of esotericism. Attacking the core of the modern Enlightenment, in Strauss's view, Rousseau is simply following an old tradition going back originally to classical political philosophy and Socrates.[16] Rousseau's antimodern thesis was his way of rejecting modernity and returning to premodern thought. Rousseau agrees with premodern esoteric philosophers who rejected the desirability of enlightenment since they believed that "the element of society is opinion" and "science, being the attempt to replace opinion by knowledge, essentially endangers society because it dissolves opinion."[17] As Rousseau believed in the opposition of science or philosophy and the preservation of a healthy society, he was in favor of concealing the fruits of science from the many. The point of view of Rousseau is so close to what Strauss found in the thought of his own classical role models that his interpretative essay on Rousseau contains some of the clearest expositions of esotericism in his whole work:

> Science presupposes and fosters doubt; it forbids assent in all cases in which the truth is not evidently known, and it is at least possible that the truth about the most important subjects is not evidently known. But society requires that its members be sure regarding certain

fundamentals. These certainties, "our dogmas," are not only not the acquisitions of science, but are essentially endangered by science: they become exposed to doubt because their lack of evidence is brought to light as soon as they are scientifically investigated.[18]

Strauss's exposition of Rousseau's ideas about the relationship between philosophy and society is so sympathetic that some of Strauss's readers refer to this essay for arguing that Strauss actually subscribed to similar ideas.[19] Incidentally, however, Strauss points here to a possible reason why he himself believed that the practice of esotericism in his own historical circumstances is not justified: Strauss, just like Rousseau, seems to have thought that he is not living under perfectly healthy regimes and he claims that, according to Rousseau, care for the incompatibility of science and society is required in healthy societies and not strictly speaking in corrupt societies where the scientific truth cannot worsen the already bad state of the people living in those societies.[20] This might be a reason why, contrary to his ideal classical political philosophers, Strauss had no reservation about speaking openly about many subjects that he claimed were the esoteric core of the writings of those political philosophers.

3. *The Challenge of Religion.* It would not be an exaggeration to say that an intensive reflection on religion and its different aspects is one of the constant elements of Strauss's whole intellectual project. Strauss's intellectual odyssey and his return to classical political philosophy and premodern Jewish and Islamic thought began with dissatisfaction with Spinoza's critique of religion.[21] Religion also played a prominent role in Strauss's understanding of esotericism. Many, if not all, authors who were considered and studied as esoteric writers by Strauss concealed their views at least partly for their unorthodox religious character and their fear of being persecuted for religious heterodoxy and heresy. Furthermore, as we shall see, Strauss believed that authors who considered even a false religion necessary for the well-being of society made sure to conceal the fictional character of those religious traditions from the public and had recourse to esotericism in order to prevent their radical views from undermining the popular religious beliefs of the citizens, the religious beliefs that they considered necessary for the preservation of public morality and order. Considering the prominent place that religion occupies in Strauss's thought, it would not be surprising to see that he also paid attention to Rousseau's reflections on religious themes and that this subject is discussed in his commentaries on Rousseau. Interest in

the theme of religion in Rousseau's writings, however, varies from writing to writing. In this regard, "The Three Waves of Modernity" and the transcript of the 1962 Course on Rousseau offered at the University of Chicago are two opposite poles. In the former, even a cursory discussion of Rousseau's reflections on religion is absent,[22] while in the latter work three sessions (11, 12, and 13) out of seventeen discuss the famous Profession of Faith of the Savoyard vicar in great detail.[23] In his comments on the Profession of Faith, Strauss does what he does often and best: showing how a theological system that to our modern eyes seems perfectly innocent is actually highly problematic and contains fundamentally heretical aspects. Strauss's discussion of the Profession of Faith is subtle and detailed; there is, however, one main point in Strauss's interpretation that is worthy of particular attention as it also appears in his other writings. Strauss finds in the Savoyard vicar's theology a denial of divine omnipotence because the vicar argues for the eternity of two entities, God and matter. In the vicar's perspective, God is not the only eternal principle, and therefore the existence of evil is attributed to matter and thereby acquires an existence independent of God. The same idea is also attributed by Strauss to Plato in the same transcript as well as to Averroes in his other writings.[24] This point is of particular importance because, according to Strauss, faith in revelation is strongly dependent on the belief in divine omnipotence: "There cannot be faith in God that is not faith in our being *absolutely* in the hands of God, and this means that is not faith in God's *omnipotence*, and therefore in the possibility of *miracles*."[25] The Savoyard vicar denies divine omnipotence to account for the existence of evil. But what are the advantages of attributing the existence of evil to a separate eternal source? First, Strauss claims that if evil has an eternal source, egoism of the individuals is seen as beyond their control and as natural, something for which they cannot be condemned. Second, to argue for the eternity of the source of evil is to argue for the imperfection of the beginnings of human beings and to attribute all the progress made since those imperfect beginnings to the efforts of human beings alone rather than to any divine assistance.[26]

The agreement between the Savoyard vicar and Rousseau seems to be the main question preoccupying Strauss, the question that he repeatedly raises in his commentaries.[27] To begin with, it seems that Strauss believed in a fundamental agreement between Rousseau and the Savoyard vicar: the religion presented in the Profession of Faith is a civil religion, that is, the "theology required for the existence and preservation of civil society." This is the famous civil theology also discussed in Rousseau's *Social Contract* whose general history is discussed in one of Strauss's most illuminating works.[28] Strauss emphasizes, however, that "this does not imply that the Profession of Faith is *true*," because some teachings can be salutary without being true, "something may be conducive to a pedagogic political purpose without being true."[29] In other words, Strauss claims that the theology of the Savoyard vicar is Rousseau's exoteric teaching, a "noble lie" necessary for Rousseau's republican regime: this civil theology bridges the gap between man and citizen, the private good and the common good by recourse to gods.

According to Strauss, Rousseau's adherence to the idea of civil religion does not mean that he is in full agreement with the Savoyard vicar on every point. Two differences between Rousseau and his fictional character are fundamental. First, to begin with, Rousseau rejects the vicar's Manichean view that attributes evil to matter because this would mean that the fundamental difficulties of life are due to the unavoidable effects of life on earth. Consequent to this idea is that no solution for the evils of life is imaginable as long as humans live on earth and therefore no political solution for the evils of human life is available. But Rousseau was a political thinker and therefore he believed in political remedies; he could not, therefore, agree with this aspect of the Profession of Faith.[30] Second, most importantly, in Strauss's view, Rousseau did not believe that the vicar's Manichean view is necessary to explain the human condition: the duality of God and matter for the vicar is translated into the duality of soul and body, which for him explains human altruism and egoism. Strauss claims, however, that Rousseau has no difficulty in explaining, with the help of a single principle, the human phenomena in their entirety without relying on anything resembling the Savoyard vicar's theology. In other words, according to Strauss, Rousseau's whole philosophical system has no dependence on any theological presupposition.[31] This point raises a much more controversial question: What did Strauss think about Rousseau's true religious beliefs? Granted that Rousseau advertised the theology of the Savoyard vicar as a beneficial civil theology, that is, as an untrue theological system suitable for the well-being of a republican regime similar to what is illustrated famously in the fourth book of the *Social Contract*. But if Rousseau did not believe in the truth of such a theology, did he believe in an alternative theology? What would that theology look like?

This question guides us toward one of the most controversial issues in Strauss's thought. Strauss is famous for picturing an antagonistic relationship between philosophy and religion, also depicted as a conflict between reason and revelation or Jerusalem and Athens. Strauss claimed that this opposition is irreconcilable and that a synthesis of reason and revelation, most famously argued in Thomistic thought, is impossible. In Strauss's view, in every synthesis of philosophy and religion, "however impressive, one of the two opposed elements is sacrificed, more or less subtly but in any event surely to the other."[32] Many Strauss scholars have found this formulation of eternal opposition of philosophy and religion, which might sound like a justification for decisionism and denial of the possibility of deciding rationally between these opposing camps, unsatisfactory. These scholars have, therefore, tried to find out whether this is Strauss's last word on the subject. Different hypotheses have been advanced. Some have argued that Strauss's thought paves the way for embracing the religious view as rationally superior to the philosophic view; others have claimed that Strauss did not believe that either the philosophic or the religious views can refute the other definitively and that one is bound to remain open, *zetetic*, to the claims of both without embracing or rejecting either; still others have claimed that Strauss actually believed that in the end philosophy is capable of refuting the claim of revelation and that it is only as a rhetorical strategy that Strauss depicted such an unresolvable antagonism and stand-off situation between philosophy and religion.[33] The question is: What do Strauss's writings on Rousseau add to the debate about Strauss's view of religion? One should not expect to find a clear statement in these writings to resolve this classic puzzle once and for all. There is, however, at least one passage in Strauss's writings on Rousseau that seem to be relevant to this debate. The importance of this passage comes from the fact that it is repeated, *almost* verbatim, in two different works, in "On the Intention of Rousseau" (the first statement) and in *Natural Right and History* (the second statement) (see table 6.1).

In view of the fact that Strauss believed that "in a good author a repetition always teaches us something we could not have learned from the first statement"[34] and that one must always closely study repetitions in the works of good authors by paying close attention to what is not repeated, added, or changed in a repeated statement, these two similar passages seem to be an invitation from Strauss to compare them. This is something that I cannot do here in an exhaustive manner, although I must point

Table 6.1. Comparison of "On the Intention of Rousseau" and *Natural Right and History*

"On The Intention of Rousseau"[1]	*Natural Right and History*[2]
We need not go into the question whether Rousseau himself **believed** in the religion he presented in the profession of faith of the Savoyard vicar, a question that cannot be answered by reference to what he said when he was persecuted on account of that profession. What is decisive is the fact that according to his explicit view of the relation of knowledge, faith and "the people," the citizen body **cannot have more than opinion regarding the truth of this or any other religion. One may even wonder whether any human being can have genuine knowledge in this respect since,** according to Rousseau's last word on the subject, there are "insoluble objections" to the religion preached by the Savoyard vicar. **Therefore every civil religion would seem to have, in the last analysis, the same character as the legislator's account of the origin of his code,** in so far as both **are essentially endangered by the "dangerous pyrrhonism" fostered** by the rigorous demands of philosophy or **science: the "insoluble objections," to which even the best of all religions is exposed, are dangerous truths.** Rousseau's personal horror, and impatience, of intolerance is primarily responsible for the fact that he did not dwell in his writings subsequent to the *Discours* on the consequences that this view entails.	We need not go into the question of whether Rousseau himself **fully subscribed to** the religion which he presented in the profession of faith of the Savoyard vicar, a question that cannot be answered by reference to what he said when he was persecuted on account of that profession. What is decisive is the fact that, according to his explicit views about the relation of knowledge, faith, and the people, the people **cannot have more than opinion regarding the truth of this or any other religion. One may even wonder whether any human being can have any genuine knowledge in this respect, since the religion preached by the Savoyard vicar** is exposed to "insoluble objections." **Therefore, every civil religion would seem, in the last analysis, to have the same character as the legislator's account of the origin of his code,** at least in so far as both **are essentially endangered by the "dangerous pyrrhonism" fostered by science; the "insoluble objections" to which even the best of all religions is exposed are dangerous truths.** Precisely a free society cannot exist if he who doubts the fundamental dogma of the civil religion does not outwardly conform.

1. Strauss, "On the Intention of Rousseau," 483–84.
2. Strauss, *Natural Right and History*, 288–89.

specifically to the different formulations coming at the end of these two passages as I believe they have a bearing on Strauss's own understanding of civil religion. Be that as it may, given the importance of these two passages, one should pay special attention to Strauss's statement that "the 'insoluble objections'" to which the Savoyard vicar's theology is exposed do not seem to be exclusive to the vicar's specific theological system or to any "civil religion." These "insoluble objections," which are somehow related to "the rigorous demands of philosophy or science" (in the first statement) seem to be of decisive character because they are said to concern "even the best of all religions" without any qualification. Does this mean that Rousseau did not "believe in" (in the first statement; cf. "fully subscribed to" in the second statement)the vicar's religion specifically, or in any religion at all, "even the best of all religions"? Is this why, curiously, Strauss decides to only briefly discuss the highest, not narrowly political, benefits of religion by Rousseau in his course and limits his remarks to saying that perhaps the same good virtues attributed to religious individuals by Rousseau can also exist among atheists?[35] In the last analysis and regardless of what this passage says about Strauss's own view of religion and revelation, Rousseau seems to have been included by Strauss alongside all other philosophers in his various commentaries whose unbelief goes as a matter of course.

Notes

1. An exception in this regard is Friedrich Nietzsche. Strauss claimed, however, that Nietzsche owed much to Rousseau without admitting his debt, what Strauss dramatically described as "perhaps the greatest historical injustice which Nietzsche committed!" Leo Strauss, *1962 Course on Rousseau Offered at the University of Chicago*, ed. Jonathan Marks (Chicago: Leo Strauss Center, 2014), 353.

2. See Heinrich Meier, "The History of Philosophy and the Intention of the Philosopher: Reflections on Leo Strauss," in *Leo Strauss and the Theologico-Political Problem*, trans. Marcus Brainard (Cambridge: Cambridge University Press, 2006), 53–75; Victor Gourevitch, "On Strauss on Rousseau," in *The Challenge of Rousseau*, ed. Christopher Kelly and Eve Grace (Cambridge: Cambridge University Press, 2012), 147–67.

3. Leo Strauss, "On the Basis of Hobbes' Political Philosophy," in *What Is Political Philosophy? And Other Studies* (Glencoe, IL: Free Press, 1959), 172; Susan Meld Shell, ed., *The Strauss-Krüger Correspondence. Returning to Plato through Kant* (Cham, Switzerland: Palgrave Macmillan, 2018), 47 (Letter to Gerhard Krüger on December 12, 1932).

4. Leo Strauss, *Thoughts on Machiavelli* (Glencoe, IL: Free Press, 1958), 173.

5. Leo Strauss and Karl Löwith, "Correspondence between Karl Löwith and Leo Strauss concerning Modernity," *Independent Journal of Philosophy* 4 (1988): 107 (Letter to Karl Löwith on August 15, 1946), 113 (Letter to Karl Löwith on August 20, 1946).

6. Although even the critical view of Strauss toward Machiavelli has been questioned: Heinrich Meier, *Political Philosophy and the Challenge of Revealed Religion*, trans. Robert Berman (Chicago: University of Chicago Press, 2017), chapter 2.

7. Leo Strauss, "The Three Waves of Modernity," in *An Introduction to Political Philosophy: Ten Essays*, ed. Hilail Gildin (Detroit, MI: Wayne State University Press, 1989), 89.

8. Strauss, *1962 Course on Rousseau Offered at the University of Chicago*, 360.

9. Leo Strauss, *Natural Right and History* (Chicago: University of Chicago Press, 1953), 252; Leo Strauss, "On the Intention of Rousseau," *Social Research* 14, no. 4 (1947): 485.

10. Leo Strauss, "How to Study Medieval Philosophy," *Interpretation: A Journal of Political Philosophy* 23, no. 3 (1996): 322; Leo Strauss, *1963 Spring Course on Vico Offered at the University of Chicago*, ed. Wayne Ambler (Chicago: Leo Strauss Center, 2016), 59 (Session 3, October 7, 1963).

11. Strauss, "On the Intention of Rousseau," 146; Strauss, "Three Waves of Modernity," 98.

12. The "Three Waves of Modernity" was originally a lecture given at Cornell University on March 25, 1964 that was published posthumously in 1975.

13. See Rasoul Namazi, *Leo Strauss and Islamic Political Thought* (Cambridge: Cambridge University Press, 2022), 13–19.

14. Leo Strauss, *Persecution and the Art of Writing* (Glencoe, IL: Free Press, 1952), 33–34.

15. Strauss, *Persecution and the Art of Writing*, 34–36, 110–11; Leo Strauss, "On a Forgotten Kind of Writing," in *What Is Political Philosophy? And Other Studies* (Glencoe, IL: Free Press, 1959), 221–22.

16. Strauss, "On the Intention of Rousseau," 456.

17. Strauss, "On the Intention of Rousseau," 473.

18. Strauss, "On the Intention of Rousseau," 472.

19. Shadia B. Drury, *The Political Ideas of Leo Strauss, Updated Edition with a New Introduction by the Author* (London: Palgrave Macmillan, 2005), 153.

20. Strauss, "On the Intention of Rousseau," 467. For Strauss's definitive rejection of esoteric writing for political purposes in the contemporary world, see Strauss, *Persecution and the Art of Writing*, 36.

21. See Leo Strauss, *Spinoza's Critique of Religion*, trans. Elsa M. Sinclair (New York: Schocken Books, 1965), 28–29; Steven Harvey, "The Story of a Twentieth-Century Jewish Scholar's Discovery of Plato's Political Philosophy in Tenth-Century Islam: Leo Strauss' Early Interest in the Islamic Falāsifa," in *Modern Jewish Scholarship on Islam in Context: Rationality, European Borders,*

and the Search for Belonging, ed. Ottfried Fraisse (Berlin: De Gruyter, 2018), 222 (Letter to Cecil Adler on November 30, 1933).

22. One indication for the unsatisfactory character of "The Three Waves of Modernity" is the fact that instead of the antagonism of classical political philosophy and the biblical faith, that is, one of Strauss's core ideas, in this text their harmony is emphasized. See Strauss, "Three Waves of Modernity," 86.

23. Strauss, *1962 Course on Rousseau Offered at the University of Chicago*, 275–371.

24. Strauss, *1962 Course on Rousseau*, 297; Leo Strauss, "Notes on Averroes's Commentary on Plato's Republic," in *Leo Strauss and Islamic Political Thought*, ed. Rasoul Namazi (Cambridge: Cambridge University Press, 2022), 212.

25. Leo Strauss, "Reason and Revelation (1948)," in *Leo Strauss and the Theologico-Political Problem*, ed. Heinrich Meier, trans. Marcus Brainard (Cambridge: Cambridge University Press, 2006), 158.

26. Strauss, *1962 Course on Rousseau Offered at the University of Chicago*, 297.

27. Cf. Strauss, *1962 Course on Rousseau*, 275, 321, 341, with the same question asked in Strauss, "On the Intention of Rousseau," 483; Strauss, *Natural Right and History*, 288.

28. Leo Strauss, "'Religion and the Commonweal in the Tradition of Political Philosophy.' An Unpublished Lecture by Leo Strauss," ed. Svetozar Minkov and Rasoul Namazi, *American Political Thought* 10, no. 1 (2021): 86–120.

29. Strauss, *1962 Course on Rousseau Offered at the University of Chicago*, 309, 339.

30. Strauss, *1962 Course on Rousseau*, 321.

31. Strauss, *1962 Course on Rousseau*, 317.

32. Strauss, *Natural Right and History*, 74–75; Leo Strauss, "Progress or Return?," in *The Rebirth of Classical Political Rationalism: An Introduction to the Thought of Leo Strauss*, ed. Thomas L. Pangle (Chicago: University of Chicago Press, 1989), 270.

33. For a good summary of the debate and the position of different scholars, see Michael Zuckert and Catherine Zuckert, *Leo Strauss and the Problem of Political Philosophy* (Chicago: University of Chicago Press, 2014), 313–27.

34. Leo Strauss, *Xenophon's Socratic Discourse: An Interpretation of the Oeconomicus* (Ithaca: Cornell University Press, 1970), 125–26.

35. Jean-Jacques Rousseau, *Emile or On Education*, trans. Allan Bloom (New York: Basic Books, 1973), 312–14 (Rousseau's long footnote. Cf. especially the beginning of Rousseau's footnote and Strauss's comments); Strauss, *1962 Course on Rousseau Offered at the University of Chicago*, 354 (note "I can only say" and "The only thing one could say").

JOHN RAY

Interpretative Essay

"TRULY A CIVIL RELIGION":
LEO STRAUSS TEACHES THE
PROFESSION OF FAITH

ALTHOUGH MY TEACHERS were all students of Leo Strauss, I have been only a casual reader of Strauss's oeuvre. As befits such a reader, I will keep this report on Strauss's three class sessions on the Profession of Faith brief. By letting Strauss speak for himself more than is typical, I hope to convey more directly something of the intellectual excitement of Strauss's seminar. Strauss's interpretation of the Profession of Faith is an original and significant contribution to understanding the indispensable role of religion in Jean-Jacques Rousseau's political philosophy. Yet, as readers of the Profession will recognize, at least some of Strauss's more emphatic conclusions are not the only ones that might be drawn from Rousseau's text. If at some moments Strauss exudes a confidence that leads him to dismisses interpretations that have validity, for the most part the transcript reveals the philosophic openness we expect from Strauss.

The Political Character of the Profession

What is most striking about Strauss's interpretation of the Profession of Faith is how thoroughly *political* it is. Strauss reads the Profession *exclusively* as a civil religion.[1] This is surprising because it is the possibility of individual happiness in an unjust world that seems to be the cause of the Vicar making his Profession to the young, embittered Rousseau in the first place. The Profession results from the Vicar's intensive introspection. In response to his private doubts about God and the goodness of human life, the Vicar appeals to his conscience as the "inner light" that guides his thinking. Certainly Rousseau's works cannot be said to be exclusively political, even if we use that word in its broadest signification to include morality. Rousseau is hugely preoccupied with reflection on the meaning of his most intensely private experiences. His thought is crowned by the "*sentiment* of existence."[2] Yet Strauss treats the Vicar's Profession as having a political intention to the exclusion of the private and personal.

Strauss stresses that the Profession is preceded and followed by two nonreligious moralities: generalized pity prior to the Profession and what he calls refined Epicureanism, or taste, after the Profession. These are both of course highly political in their nature and consequence. The existence of God plays no part in Emile's education before or after the Profession. Why then does Emile need to be told about God? In order to become a *citizen*. For Strauss, the distinction Rousseau makes between man and citizen, which are "two entirely different and incompatible things," is of critical importance. Rousseau describes "man" as a self-sufficient whole without prejudices (as having psychological unity[3]). The "citizen" necessarily has prejudices because each country has its customs and traditions, its particular preferences, which of course are different from those of other countries. Above all, each country will have a religion that teaches citizens that the fundamental laws of that country are in accordance with the divine will. Thus, whereas the education appropriate to a man is an education in goodness (follow your own good with no unnecessary harm to others), the education appropriate to a citizen is an education in virtue, meaning the civic virtues needed for a country (especially a small self-governing republic) to survive.[4]

Emile must be viewed against the fundamental distinction of man and citizen (to view something or someone *against* something or someone is characteristic of Strauss's interpretive method). Prior to the Profession, "Emile is educated as a man, and emphatically not as a citizen."[5] But he must now become a citizen. The problem is to reconcile as far as possible Emile the man with Emile the citizen, and to do this is *the* purpose of the Profession. To be a citizen is to put the common good first, which is against nature, according to Rousseau. Rousseau enhances the difficulty of reconciling "man" with "citizen" by using extreme rhetoric when speaking of the need to *denature* the citizen. It is not easy to make a citizen. It must be a question if the Profession is enough to make Emile more than the pleasant neighbor. Strauss says Emile "is meant to become a leader in a republican society."⁶ But a more plausible view sees him living only on the fringes of society.⁷

Strauss finds a "strict correspondence to the Profession of Faith in the *Social Contract*" such that the one should be read in light of the other.⁸ The dogmas of the social contract are as follows: "The existence of the powerful, intelligent, beneficent, prescient, and provident Divinity, the life to come, the happiness of the just, the punishment of the wicked, and sanctity of the social Contract and the Laws." To these positive dogmas, Rousseau adds a negative one: intolerance. Rousseau calls the dogmas of the civil religion "sentiments of sociability, without which it is impossible to be either a good Citizen or a loyal subject." The dogmas of the civil religion are of interest to the state or the community only insofar as they "bear on morality, and on the duties which anyone who professes it is bound to fulfill toward others." This makes it clear why Strauss regards the Profession as a political text, not just primarily but exclusively.⁹

If the Profession is for Emile and others like him, we need to ask what kind of man Strauss thinks Emile is. "Emile has the maximum perfection of reason possible in what Rousseau calls *un homme vulgaire*, a common man," "an ordinary man."¹⁰ Emile is the best of ordinary men. Above ordinary men are a small number of men of the "top drawer," of the highest intellectual distinction, for whom the antagonism between man and citizen remains. The primary difference between the two types is the easy acceptance by ordinary men of moral doctrines that rest more on sentiment than reason. The Profession claims to rely on reason, which is why it is called natural religion, but in fact it rests on certain sentiments of the heart related to human experience, such as the feeling that the universe is orderly and purposeful. Emile represents peak rationality for men of the common variety, yet he is sufficiently open to sentiment that he can accept the Profession's dogmas. Men of the top drawer reject the comforting illusions of the Profession. Because they cannot accept the dogmas of natural religion (it seems for Strauss to go without saying that they cannot accept the more demanding dogmas of any positive religion), top-drawer men cannot be good citizens. As for Rousseau himself, Strauss says he "is not accidentally a bad citizen or an unsatisfactory citizen, but essentially [so], because the center of his being is his private life.... But this eccentricity enables him accidentally ... to become the conscience of a society, to be *the* teacher of legislators."¹¹

We may wonder if Rousseau's famous "sentiment of existence" does not mean that sentiment rather than reason ultimately rules even Rousseau.

Strauss says that for Rousseau the sentiment of existence is "the highest passion" a human being is capable of experiencing and is "absolutely beyond practical political life."[12] A perceptive student asks Strauss, "What is the relationship between the sentiment of existence and the perfection of human reason?"

> You know, someone may have this feeling of existence lying somewhere in a meadow on a nice early summer day, and have it in fact; but it would be a passing experience, like any other. So the appreciation of the sentiment of existence is not the same as the experience of the sentiment of existence. Now the appreciation would require philosophy, presuppose philosophy. I mean, the whole message of this experience is grasped only on the basis of philosophy. That, I think … to that extent the perfection of reason is presupposed for the sentiment of existence.[13]

For Strauss the perfection of reason—philosophy—is the "highest level," not the (false but necessary) sentiments that are needed to teach an "individual as individual" to "prefer the *common* good to his own good."[14] Strauss concludes that in Rousseau's view the importance of religion to political life has nothing to do with the actual existence of God or the life hereafter, but *only* with the needs of political life and ultimately the political revolution on earth that would be needed to bring about just governance.

Rousseau's Nonagreement with the Vicar

There are two characters in the Profession of Faith: a "young juvenile delinquent" and the Savoyard Vicar. "This was a boy (Rousseau himself, you know) at the lowest grade of his morality ever, and the first thing this sensible educator did was to awaken in him what we would call self-respect. But self-respect is of course a modification of *amour-propre*, because self-respect always is based on some form of comparison." To the young Rousseau the Profession is intended as a hopeful teaching about the goodness of human life and God's existence and care for humanity. But the young Rousseau, even less a believer in God than the Vicar, does not as a mature thinker discover solutions to the "insoluble objections" he saw when young. For Strauss, as we have seen, the most fundamental defect of the Profession is that it is based on "sentiment as distinguished from reason." The Vicar admits that his opinions may be illusions. "In other words, he admits that his firmest opinions may be lies."[15]

In the first session on the Profession Strauss makes clear "what the Profession is about: it is a demonstration of the existence of God." He finds that to make the case for the existence of God Rousseau employs "the two most easily intelligible proofs," a "modified argument from motion plus the teleological proof" of the ordered universe, "order pointing to an intelligent orderer." Strauss regards all this as rhetorical and in no way successful in proving God's existence. The argument, he claims, is intended for ordinary minds and Strauss emphasizes it is supported only by sentiment.[16]

Despite the Profession being "about" the existence of God, Strauss's focus is elsewhere. The question that preoccupies Strauss over the three class sessions devoted to the Profession is instead, "Is Rousseau in agreement with the Savoyard Vicar or is he not?" Strauss begins to answer his question by emphasizing that the Profession of Faith is delivered by a character of Rousseau's creation, the Savoyard Vicar. "What are his moral and intellectual qualifications?" The Vicar is a man of "moral taint." He admits not to adultery but to fornication with unmarried young women. "I mean one can safely say that he was a questionable Catholic ... he is not a sincere Catholic." Rousseau, who himself had "a very irregular youth regarding sex," "didn't really accept this as a serious blemish on the man's character," yet "he has to reckon with his readers." Rousseau is here "talking as a responsible educator," not as "(how shall I say it?) a man of the drawing-room." Why does Rousseau choose to have the Profession of Faith presented by a man of lax morals? Surely it was not to undermine the teaching of the Profession. There is a parallel between the Vicar's sexual "infirmity" and Rousseau's own "irregular youth." "The infirmity of the Vicar is of course also the infirmity of Rousseau." But "the Vicar also has an infirmity which is very rare, and that is that he is a Catholic priest who is in his heart a Protestant." Is there a parallel here? Strauss observes that "Rousseau became a Catholic on no ground but convenience, you know, in his first trip to Italy. This is the same thing. But the deeper problem is not this switch between Protestantism and Catholicism or all of that, but that Rousseau asserts principles which he does not hold." This "insincerity" of both "the Vicar and in another way of Rousseau is a much more interesting moral problem than that of this sexual thing."[17]

Strauss's evaluation of the Vicar's intellectual abilities is no less severe than his estimation of the Vicar's moral character. Although Rousseau says the Vicar "lacked neither wit nor learning," Strauss immediately denigrates the Vicar's learning: "You see, this is not a very high praise; you must not give ... 'He was not without esprit, nor without letters.' Well, that is compatible with being barely literate, of course, and having some common sense; but surely not a philosopher." Strauss proclaims a wide gulf between the two men: Rousseau is philosophical, the Vicar is sub-philosophical. Two class sessions later Strauss again attacks the Vicar's intellectual abilities on the basis of a comment by the Vicar to the young Rousseau: "'I always remain as I am ... out of fear that insensibly the taste for contemplation becoming an idle passion makes me lukewarm regarding the exercise of my virtues, and from fear to fall again into my first Pyrrhonism,' i.e. skepticism, 'without finding again the force to leave it.' So the Vicar is surely not a contemplative man; he is not a philosopher. This is also clear."[18] The Vicar acknowledges a taste for contemplation, he fears it will make him less likely to do his duty as a priest, and that he will fall permanently into skepticism. From this admission Strauss concludes the Vicar is not a contemplative man. Does the Vicar's fear of permanent doubt disqualify him for philosophy in Strauss's view? Is the capacity to live indefinitely without illusions the critical difference between the philosopher and others?

Strauss restates his question in the next session: "Can you identify Rousseau with the Savoyard Vicar?" "Do you see?," he asks the class. "I mean, the theology of the Savoyard Vicar is based, say, more on sentiment than on reason. Does Rousseau agree with the view that a doctrine of this nature can be based on sentiment as distinguished from reason?" Strauss acknowledges that his effort to disassociate Rousseau from the Vicar on the basis of the distinction between reason and sentiment faces an interpretative challenge from the *Reveries* of *the Solitary Walker*. We cannot investigate this very complex matter here, but I would like to provide some of Strauss's comments on the *Reveries* as to whether that work contradicts his interpretation of the Profession. To be clear, let's quickly add that it is quite evident that Strauss himself does *not* believe this to be the case—still, it is an interesting interpretive problem and one he fully acknowledges.

In the *Reveries*, this later work, Rousseau reasserts (asserts even much more clearly than in the *Emile*) that he is substantially in agreement with the Savoyard Vicar. He says this first. Then you find a long discussion [about] whether one is obliged to say the truth.... And the solution is one must say the truth in every useful matter—in every useful matter. So in other words, if you say the truth about how many pebbles there are in a stream, if you deceive about that, that's not lying. Good. So it must be useful. But this means, of course, what Rousseau does not say here but it is implied: What about dangerous truth? Clearly, if the duty of veracity applies only to useful truth, then there is a moral obligation to conceal dangerous truth. And then the argument goes on, and there are certain points where the contradiction between the Savoyard Vicar's doctrine and what Rousseau says become quite manifest.[19]

A student quickly notes that "Rousseau said something very like this in one of the *Reveries*, when he says why he is not going to reason..." LS: "Yes, but in that part of the *Reveries*—the *Reveries* is a very complicated book—in that part where he identifies himself with the Profession of Faith. But the argument goes on, one cannot leave it at that. But this would take us too long now." Rousseau's identification in the *Reveries* with the Profession of Faith complicates matters for Strauss's claim that Rousseau doesn't agree with the Vicar. The discussion again shows Strauss is committed to the idea that philosophy means reason and not sentiment, or that sentiment is important for wisdom only when it is viewed in light of reason. If sentiment is important, it is because reason makes it so; even the sentiment of existence is not an independent source of wisdom. Unfortunately, Strauss is not able to develop his view of the relation between the two books during the 1962 seminar. He concludes the matter this way: "I would be satisfied if every one of you would regard it as possible, not more, that Rousseau's opinion may not be identical with the opinion of the Savoyard Vicar. You see afterwards, partly here [in the *Reveries*] and partly in the reply to the Archbishop of Paris and partly in the *Letters from the Mountain*, Rousseau identifies himself with the Profession of the Savoyard Vicar."[20]

Of course, Strauss's answer to his question does not turn on the Vicar's character or intelligence but on specific arguments, and of these the Vicar's account of human evil is for Strauss decisive. The critical element is the Vicar's belief in the eternity of matter, because this view leads, Strauss argues, to Rousseau and the Vicar giving quite different accounts of the origin of evil. Strauss seems to believe that Rousseau's understanding of unmodified self-love (*amour de soi* before its modification into latent *amour-propre*) as the basis of the natural goodness of man is incompatible with the Vicar's dualism (two substances rather than one) because dualism (more precisely the eternity of matter) means that human beings are necessarily and originally mixed with evil. However, as Strauss himself notes, the issue of what Rousseau believes is very much complicated by Rousseau's seeming endorsement of the Vicar's dualistic metaphysics. Strauss quotes from the *Letter to Beaumont*: "The co-existence of these two principles seems to explain better the construction of the universe; and to remove difficulties which one removes without it not easily, as among others that of the origin of evil."[21] So again, we have the problem that other writings of Rousseau seem to endorse at least part of the argument of the Profession. Since the Vicar's dualism is Strauss's strongest argument against the identification of the Vicar with Rousseau, let us see the argument in detail.

> LS: In brief, God is the thinking and willing and powerful being. Now here we have a clear deviation of the Savoyard Vicar from the accepted doctrine. He does not assert the eternity of God alone. He leaves it open whether there cannot be eternity of matter. And now in the first statement of the question, he says: Is there a single principle of things (that could mean strict monotheism) or are there two or more? This could mean at first hearing: Is there not more than one god? After all, theoretically there could be a body of gods, an assembly of gods who could rule the universe, perhaps with a highest god. But he narrows it down later to the question of two principles: God and eternal matter. He does not assert it, but he does not exclude it; he says it is a question of no importance to him. Now this is of course a gross overstatement. It must be of the greatest importance to him.[22]

We might ask if it is enough only to *imply* there are two eternal principles, God and matter, but as the argument develops there is in fact enough evidence to warrant the conclusion that the Vicar is a dualist. Strauss summarizes the issue: "Two principles: God and matter, let us call them; and this means of course that every being—in particular, man—is the product of both God and matter. Man cannot be by nature simply good because that non-good principle, matter, enters into his constitution. On the other hand, there is no need for explaining evil any further, because there is an evil principle, matter, there. And especially there is no basis for asserting original sin."[23] Strauss identifies two key implications of the

Vicar's dualism: first, "there is something in [man] *as natural* which leads him to unqualified egoism," and second, if matter is an *eternal* obstacle to the goodness of man, the progress men have made is due to their own efforts. Contrary to the Bible and to Rousseau, man's beginnings were "particularly imperfect."

Strauss frames the disagreement between the Vicar and Rousseau as follows:

> First, he [the Savoyard Vicar] has God and matter; and then we go down to the good will in man—let us call it goodness—and this is badness; and that means in practice altruism versus egoism. And this has to do with the fact that there are two substances in man, soul and body. So there is a consistent dualism, going up from man's actions—soul and body—to God and matter. This is clear. Now the difficulty is very simply this: Prior to the introduction of theology, Rousseau had shown that goodness, or virtue, is a modification of self-love or *amour-propre*; that is to say, he doesn't need an independent principle. He doesn't need two principles. Therefore this, I think, is for me at any rate sufficient proof of the fact that Rousseau did not himself accept this doctrine.[24]

The Vicar's dualism is at odds with Rousseau's teaching of the origin of evil, which results from a modification of *amour de soi* into *amour-propre*, that is, primitive self-love or self-preservation into vanity, yet also pride, and in all cases *amour-propre* refers to the self-love that makes comparisons of oneself to other human beings. Thus, Rousseau has one substance; the Vicar has two. Therefore, Rousseau cannot be in agreement with the Vicar. Strauss finds this "sufficient proof" that Rousseau did not agree with his character the Vicar.

Strauss's conclusion is by no means the only possible one. Roger D. Masters, for instance, does not find any incompatibility between dualistic metaphysics and Rousseau in his 1968 book on the political philosophy of Rousseau. Masters suggests that because "matter in itself is neither good nor bad," Rousseau's arguments about the origin of evil are not contradicted. Masters concludes "it would seem that the Savoyard Vicar's metaphysical dualism corresponds to Rousseau's own position."[25]

In addition to the issue of dualism, the Vicar and Rousseau disagree, if Strauss is right, on the status of the human conscience. Among the most hopeful passages in the Profession of Faith are the Vicar's statements on the human conscience as an innate "inner light" of moral guidance. Strauss responds with what he seems to believe is a decisive rhetorical blow against the Vicar's description of the conscience and perhaps to the Profession altogether:

> This is then the meaning—that is the peak, the end, the meaning of the Profession of Faith: there is a natural morality of utmost simplicity and unambiguity, the morality of the conscience. Now if this is natural and is as such available in every man, there is no difficulty in democracy. Every human being, as human being, is competent to judge morality; whereas from the point of view of the older view, there was a difference between the men who are truly prudent and those who are not truly prudent according ... all men are equally wise in the decisive respect. No one needs an authority by nature; and only accidentally he might need it.[26]

At a later point in the seminar a student tries to resurrect the conscience as a realistic moral guide and receives a rare rebuke:

> Student: I thought that Rousseau himself believes that there is a conscience which can tell a man what to do.

> LS: Since you say you believe it, I say I do not believe it. I think what Rousseau means by belief, that is ... what the Savoyard Vicar, especially, says. But this—for Rousseau, as I have tried to explain more than once, on the basis of what we have read, morality emerges through a transformation of self-preservation, *amour de soi*, via *amour-propre* and pity. You know, enlightened compassion. This is that. But enlightened compassion, this is not simply ... I mean, you have a criterion here: Is this really enlightened compassion which induces you to favor this action or not? I mean, you cannot merely say: My conscience tells me, period. That's impossible.[27]

If Strauss seems to lose patience here it is more with Rousseau than with the student. Yet Strauss's certitude that Rousseau does not—could not possibly—believe the conscience is innate may have blinded him to a more nuanced understanding of Rousseau altogether. At least some post-Strauss scholarship (that is yet friendly to Strauss) has taken Rousseau's assertions about the conscience in the Profession and elsewhere more seriously than Strauss does in his seminar.[28] If the conscience is a modification of *amour de soi*, why could it not then be called "innate"?

Reading the Transcript

Strauss insists that we face human existence without the illusions of the Profession of Faith. This is sad because atheism is not in any way comforting, but it seems to be Strauss's view that it is better to know the truth than to live with false if hopeful stories. Whether or not his students are "top drawer," Strauss treats them as if they are, and does not hesitate to expose them to his own "dangerous truth."

Readers may turn to the seminar transcript with extremely high expectations formed on the basis of Strauss's magisterial writing on Rousseau in *Natural Right and History*. The fact that the transcript is of a seminar must be kept in mind and comparison with Strauss's written work ought to be resisted. Here Strauss is *teaching* and his aim is to demonstrate how to read a text in addition to settling the meaning of this particular text. Strauss repeatedly calls attention to the limitations of time imposed by the seminar format and the need for further investigation of Rousseau and his intellectual sources and opponents. He pleads: "[P]lease don't misunderstand me: these things require a much closer study than we can possibly give here in a single seminar."[29] Much that would be necessary to know for a scholarly article or book cannot be pursued under the time constraints of the seminar. Therefore, to prevent an unintentional disservice to Strauss, we must not read the transcript of his spontaneously given classroom remarks as his definitive reading of the Profession on any given point. We simply do not know what Strauss might have concluded differently about the Profession in a published article or book.

Whether one agrees or not with Strauss's interpretation of the Profession, to read the transcript is itself an exciting treat. His classroom is alive with the need to know the truth about human existence and it is obvious even from a written transcript that his lucky students are more than a little mesmerized. At the peak of his powers, Strauss is able to convince students decades younger and from a quite different culture that the big concerns—human nature, God and creation, decent political life—matter more than anything else and therefore getting the old books by the greatest thinkers as close to right as possible is of the utmost urgency.

Most impressive is Strauss's ability to summarize a fundamental issue. At such moments his vast learning is on full display and yet he is typically open to student inquiries and quite at ease with give and take. He generously compliments students on their insights and formulations. If I were absolutely forced to make a criticism of these particular sessions on the

Profession of Faith it would be that while Strauss maintains that Rousseau "is not clear and unambiguous regarding the *whole* matter," meaning the Profession altogether, Strauss nonetheless is uninhibited in reaching unqualified conclusions on specific issues that on their face seem open to alternative interpretations.[30] Strauss is a bold thinker known for insisting on sharp dichotomies. In the sessions on the Profession he occasionally comes across, unintentionally I believe, as too confident in his conclusions. On the other hand, the firm positions Strauss takes are useful to readers of the Profession interested in pursuing alternative explanations.

Here's a partial list of Strauss's conclusions about the Profession of Faith: (1) for Rousseau *all* passions are derivative of self-love, of *amour de soi*, or self-preservation, and this is not the case for the Vicar; (2) Rousseau is not a dualist because for his account of evil he needs only the single principle of self-love (*amour de soi*), whereas the Vicar is a dualist with two substances or principles, and this means the Vicar and Rousseau offer radically different accounts of human evil; (3) the conscience is not for Rousseau as it is for the Vicar an innate prerational moral guide but rather a modification of pity, which is itself a modification of *amour-propre*; (4) the conscience does not for Rousseau as it does for the Vicar serve to overcome the tension between private interest and the common good; this is impossible; (5) Rousseau believes all societies need religion as the ultimate source of civic virtue but doctrines in addition to those of natural religion are unnecessary if not harmful; (6) between atheism and religious fanaticism, Rousseau prefers fanaticism because an atheistic society is necessarily insufficient in civic virtue and immoral; (7) for the Vicar, the union of body and soul is unnatural; (8) the Vicar is not a Christian; (9) Rousseau does not accept any positive religion as true; (10) Rousseau does not accept natural religion as true; (11) natural religion is not for those of the highest intellectual quality but can be useful to ordinary men properly prepared to receive it; (12) the Vicar's natural religion culminates in acceptance of life after death as the *theological* (*other-worldly*) solution to the human need for justice, whereas Rousseau's solution is *political* (*this-worldly*) and culminates in a proposal for just governance on earth.

Notes

1. Leo Strauss, *Strauss Course Rousseau 1962_0 pdf*, ed. Jonathan Marks (Chicago: Leo Strauss Center, 2014), 495. Hereafter cited as *Rousseau Course*. I am citing the page numbers of the PDF (rather confusingly, page numbers provided in the side toolbar of the online PDF are higher by twenty-one).

2. See especially *The Reveries of the Solitary Walker*, Fifth Walk.

3. On the distinction between man and citizen, see especially Jean-Jacques Rousseau, *Emile or on Education*, ed. Allan Bloom (New York: Basic Books, 1979), 40–41.

4. *Rousseau Course*, 495.

5. *Rousseau Course*, 495.

6. *Rousseau Course*, 310.

7. Clifford Orwin, "Montesquieu's Humanité and Rousseau's Pité," in *Montesquieu and His Legacy*, ed. Rebecca E. Kingston (Albany: State University of New York Press, 2008), 140.

8. *Rousseau Course*, 495.

9. Jean-Jacques Rousseau, *The Social Contract and Other Later Political Writings*, ed. Victor Gourevitch (Cambridge: Cambridge University Press, 1997), 150–51.

10. Strauss's use of "man" and "men" rather than, say, "human beings" accurately reflects the sexist thought of Rousseau. We must not assume that Strauss agrees with Rousseau.

11. *Rousseau Course*, 495, 311, 316.

12. *Rousseau Course*, 495.

13. *Rousseau Course*, 497.

14. *Rousseau Course*, 310, emphasis is original.

15. *Rousseau Course*, 282, 313, 332.

16. *Rousseau Course*, 293, 295.

17. *Rousseau Course*, 282, 283, 285, 288, 289.

18. *Rousseau Course*, 282, 350.

19. *Rousseau Course*, 313.

20. *Rousseau Course*, 333.

21. *Rousseau Course*, 296.

22. *Rousseau Course*, 296.

23. *Rousseau Course*, 317.

24. *Rousseau Course*, 297, 317.

25. Roger D. Masters, *The Political Philosophy of Rousseau* (Princeton, NJ: Princeton University Press, 1968), n. 52, 67–68 and 67.

26. *Rousseau Course*, 328

27. *Rousseau Course*, 353.

28. A thoughtful work on the subject is Laurence D. Cooper, *Rousseau, Nature, and the Problem of the Good Life* (University Park: Pennsylvania State University Press, 1999). See, especially, 80–99.

29. *Rousseau Course*, 333.

30. *Rousseau Course*, 365.

PART SEVEN

Transcript 7.1

"RELIGION AND THE COMMONWEAL IN
THE TRADITION OF POLITICAL PHILOSOPHY":
THE LECTURE (1963)

Editorial Note: The following transcript is of a 1963 lecture by Leo Strauss delivered at the Hillel House, University of Chicago. An early version of this lecture was previously published relying entirely on the surviving recording of the lecture.[1] Fortunately, since then the original manuscript of the lecture has been discovered.[2] This manuscript is of substantial importance for improving the transcript as it not only reflects Strauss's whole thought process but also clarifies some of the more obscure parts of the lecture. We have now entirely revised the transcript on the basis of the manuscript, added the supplementary information available in the manuscript but missing from the lecture, and clarified some aspects of the lecture with footnotes and similar editorial aids.

As the manuscript itself is of considerable importance and gives access to Strauss's personal reflections on the subject of the lecture, we have concluded that it is beneficial to provide a transcript of the manuscript after the lecture transcript as well so that the readers can consult both and compare them. To facilitate the comparison, the relevant paragraph numbers of the manuscript are added to the lecture transcript (¶ paragraph number). The reader should keep in mind, however, that in many cases, it is impossible to say with confidence where a new paragraph in the manuscript begins and ends and the editors had to rely on their judgment. The important point is that Strauss did not, unlike some of his other manuscripts, number his paragraphs, hence the division of the text into paragraphs does not seem to be crucial. Our editorial interventions are mostly present in the lecture transcript and we have kept the transcript of the manuscript intact by limiting the indispensable comments to the footnotes.

Acknowledgment: We thank Professor Nathan Tarcov for giving us permission on behalf of Jenny Strauss to publish these two transcripts in this volume. She retains all rights for further publication of the transcripts. The transcript were considerably improved by Nathan Tarcov, Gayle McKeen, and two anonymous reviewers of the journal of *American Political Thought*, to whom we are grateful.

Religion and the Commonweal Lecture, the Hillel Foundation, January 27, 1963

Moderator: I would like to welcome you all to Hillel this evening. When we have a series like this, there is always a tendency to multiply introducers. As host, I guess, I am happy to welcome you all and then very quickly to call upon Mr. George Anastaplo,[3] who helped arrange, or actually did arrange this evening series. Mr. Anastaplo, as is well known to you, is lecturer in liberal arts at the downtown center of the College, and he will introduce both the series and the speaker of this evening. Mr. Anastaplo!

Anastaplo: It is a privilege to have Mrs. Pekarsky here this evening, especially since this is a series dedicated to the memory of her late husband, and I like to think that this is a series that Rabbi Pekarsky particularly would have enjoyed.[4] We prepared several such as this in recent years, and this is one that he was working on, in fact, the last one that he was working on before he had to be taken to the hospital last summer. I should add that the preparation of the series is in large part due to Mr. Ralph Lerner[5] and to Mr. [Werner] Dannhauser,[6] who will be lecturing next Sunday evening, same time. Our program will consist of the talk, and then a question period, then tea or coffee afterward, and brochures can be gotten afterward for the remainder of the series. I turn now to the lecture of the evening. It is fitting and proper, I believe, that a distinguished professor of political philosophy who was regarded so highly by Rabbi Pekarsky during an association of almost a decade and a half, or almost two decades, should open this series on "Religion and Commonweal." Mr. Strauss will speak on the tradition of political philosophy.

[¶ 1] *Leo Strauss*: Ladies and gentlemen, Mrs. Pekarsky. This is the first time that I have the honor to give a lecture in Hillel House after the death of my friend Rabbi Maurice Pekarsky. Permit me to pay homage to his memory. The soul and substance of Rabbi Pekarsky was Jewish piety, simple old-fashioned, chaste, Jewish piety. He dedicated his life to keeping alive this holy fire, or to revive it. He knew very well how difficult this task was in the middle of the twentieth century, especially at a university like ours. He acted in this difficult situation with singular tact and prudence. He did not protest against those who tried to reduce Judaism to social ethics on the one hand, and to an ethnic culture on the other, since both parties retain a part, however small, of the ancient truth and since their very antagonism, the antagonism between the universal and the particular, points to the full truth: the chosen people, the people chosen to be witness of justice. He did not rebuff, nay he attracted those who were not as blessed as he was, who had not succeeded in finding a way of reconciling the old piety and the new science, for he was united with them in love of truth. This was indeed the limit of his tolerance and forbearance. He just tolerated, for he was a very polite man, those for whom the university is above all a place for promoting themselves. I believe, and after having heard Mr. Anastaplo, I know that he would have approved of the effort of Mr. Anastaplo and his friends, which is to explore how one can secure by human means the future of religion without infringing on the rights of man.

[¶ 2] I would like to say first a few words about how I plan to approach this subject. I speak, of course, as a social scientist. A social scientist is a man who is sworn to face and pronounce also unpleasant truths, truths unpleasant to himself.[7] There are two kinds of unpleasant truths: unpleasant truths which are at the same time pleasant, and simply unpleasant truths. I give an example of both. For example, it is not altogether unpleasant for a friend of big businesses to point out the vicious, the unpleasant power of the labor unions; nor for a friend of the labor unions to point out the unpleasant power of big businesses. These are pleasant facts for these people, facts on which they thrive. The truly unpleasant facts are those which render questionable one's party line. For example, like Yalta [Conference] for the professional liberal, and strong central government with a terrific defense budget for the professional conservative. It is in this spirit that I approach my subject: what does the tradition of political philosophy teach regarding religion and the commonweal?

[¶ 3] Voltaire has said "celui qui n'ose regarder fixement les deux pôles de la vie [humaine], la religion et le government n'est qu'un lâche."[8] He who doesn't dare to look straight at the two poles of life, religion and government, is only a coward. In the language of our time, the two poles of life are government, the subcultural, and religion, the supracultural. Two *stern* and exacting things, as distinguished from culture. If we understand politics and religion in terms of culture, we obscure the fundamental difficulty: government, the commonweal, is necessarily particular; religion is, at least according to its intention, universal, embracing all men. If we look at everything from the point of view of culture, we forget the universal, because culture is something used in the plural; we forget the universal, the truly human, for culture as the term is now used is essentially particular.

[¶ 4] Now if we were to follow this thought, we might be compelled to question the concept not only of culture, but even the concept of religion. "Religion" is not a Hebrew term nor a Greek term. It stems from Latin. Piety is indeed a universal term. But is religion the same as piety? That is a rather subtle question. When we say of a man he is religious, and when we say he is pious, I think we do not in all cases mean the same thing. For example, I do not believe that anyone ever called [Martin] Buber pious, whereas he is of course a religious man. But let us not appear to be pedantic. Let us say, as we are entitled to say by our[9] Western tradition, that religion simply means every human concern with a personal god, with a god who thinks and wills and is concerned with man, with every man, or, to use a current expression, a being who is a "Thou."[10]

[¶ 5] As for the political philosophy mentioned in the title of the lecture, I have made its meaning sufficiently clear for our present purpose by speaking of the *tradition* of political philosophy.[11] Political philosophy, I indicated, is something which is not precisely thriving in our age, not in spite but because of the fact that the word "philosophy," and "political philosophy," is used in our time, I believe every day, more than it was ever used in the past. This is one of the characteristics of our times. Just to illustrate what this means: the word "historic" is doubtless now used with great prodigality. Every day we read of another "historic" event, and these events prove to be worthy of a headline today but to be forgotten tomorrow, and surely not later than next year. So in other words, we suffer from a kind of inflation regarding these words, and this applies to the word "philosophy" too. Inflation must not deceive us about the *scarcity* of the real stuff, and this applies to political philosophy itself. Yet, however absent political philosophy may be from our age, all present-day discussions, for instance of the question of religion and the commonweal, are *based*, whether the discussants know it or not, on political philosophy. This is incidentally especially true of the so-called *liberal* position.

The liberal position regarding this issue is surely not based on religion (Jewish *or* Christian) but on the unassisted human mind alone, and hence on philosophy.

[¶ 7] Now one thing one may say while being reasonably certain that it will be permitted to pass by everyone is this: political philosophy emerged in Greece, and the classical document of Greek political philosophy is Aristotle's *Politics*. Let us then begin here: What do we learn from Aristotle on our subject? Somewhere in the seventh book of the *Politics*, he enumerates the functions, the works (ἔργα), essential to the commonweal.[12] He mentions six of them in ascending order: from food, below, to government, at the top; and in this enumeration there occurs the following strange expression: "fifth and first, the concern regarding the divine."[13] What does he mean by that? [¶ 8] In the first place, he means: no commonweal or city is possible without religion, without *established* religion, a *state* religion obligatory on all citizens. In the sole remark which Aristotle makes in his own name on natural right (τὸ φύσει δίκαιον), he indicates that sacrificing to the gods, and hence of course also praying, belongs to natural right (iure naturali). It is by nature just that the citizens pray and sacrifice.[14] Every society must have this concern with the divine as a *public* political concern. Now this concern is "the first in a way" (πως πρῶτον), Aristotle says "fifth and first." [¶ 9] It is the first because it is more necessary even than food, and at the same time it is higher even than the government. But in another respect it is not the first, therefore he says "*fifth* or first." The divine (τὸ θεῖον) in itself is surely higher than anything human (ἀνθρώπινον). But what Aristotle speaks of here, the political concern with the divine, this is not the highest. This political concern with the divine is something radically distinguished from *knowledge* of the divine, and knowledge of the divine would be, according to Aristotle, the highest human pursuit. This kind of concern, the political kind of concern, is neither the highest nor is it the most fundamental. Aristotle explains this in a passage of the *Metaphysics*, twelfth book,[15] very famous in the Middle Ages, in the Latin Middle Ages, [where Aristotle speaks of thinkers] at the beginning, and quote "the opinion of the fathers."[16] Now, what does he say there? He speaks there of the popular notions regarding the gods which underlie public established religion. These popular notions contain an element of truth, but they are not completely true: something untrue is added to them. Why? "For the persuasion of the many, and for use in regard to the laws and to the useful [i.e., the politically useful—LS]."[17] The laws, the ordinary political laws, need, in a sense, superhuman support. Laws as Aristotle understands them cannot be simply rational or reasonable, because the simply rational or reasonable does not have a great force. The reasonable is powerful in the arts, in medicine, shoemaking, strategy, or what have you, but it is not regarding laws. Laws owe their validity decisively to *custom*, to habituation, not to their intrinsic rationality, and therefore they need another support, a superhuman support.[18] Religion, in a word—if we translate Aristotle's term, "the concern with the divine" by religion, as we may—religion is *civil* religion, political religion, a part of the political establishment. We can also use another term, not occurring in Aristotle but somewhat later: we can say there is a "civil theology" as distinguished from the true philosophic theology. This term is best known from a quotation in Augustine, traced to some Stoics, but the thought is of course clearly in Aristotle.[19] [¶ 10] Now, this view is not peculiar to Aristotle. I mention a few points. Plato: Everyone knows the thesis of Plato's *Republic*: the rule of philosophers is *the* condition for public happiness. But if you read this in the context of the *sequel* of the *Republic*, the dialogue called *Timaeus*, you see that the rule of philosophers takes the place not simply of the rule of the people, or of the aristocrats, or of the kings, but especially it takes the place of the rule of *priests*.[20] The rule of philosophers is, as it were, the only adequate answer to the rule of the priests.

I will now only assert that something of this kind, religion as civil religion, is a teaching of all classical philosophers. [¶ 11] *The* example is the famous case of Socrates. Socrates was accused of having committed an unjust act by not worshiping the gods of the city. Now, what does this mean? Did he not bring the sacrifice or did not bring them in an orderly, law-prescribed manner? Plato's *interpretation* of the charge is this: Socrates did not believe that the gods worshiped by the city of Athens *exist*. This is infinitely graver than to omit occasionally a sacrifice, as he admits having omitted at the end of his life, when he says to Crito, "We have forgotten to bring a sacrifice to Asclepius."[21] You know this was not quite orthodox, and he gave this as a last injunction to his friend: "Bring that sacrifice tomorrow." Surely, Socrates did not *preach* that the gods worshiped by the city of Athens do not exist, which is much graver, but in his famous *Apology*, he does not meet that charge. When you read it, you see that he does not refute it. He lays a trap for the accuser, and the accuser, a fool, goes into the trap, and then Socrates is out of all difficulties. But it is surely not a refutation of the charge. Socrates somehow claims, of course, that he is not guilty as charged, and therewith by implication, after he is condemned, that he is *innocently* condemned.²² But this is a somewhat queer story. When someone, a very enthusiastic admirer of Socrates, says, "How terrible, Socrates, that you have been unjustly condemned," Socrates laughs—the only time he ever laughed—and says, "Would you prefer that I were justly condemned?"²³ [laughter] But there can be no question if you read the evidence that he was guilty as charged. Now, he cannot deny to the polis, to the city, the right to demand that every citizen believes in the existence of Zeus, Hera, and the whole lot (νομίζειν).²⁴ He makes only one reservation where he would refuse to obey the city: even if the city would enact legally a law forbidding philosophizing, he says he would disobey that law.²⁵ But such a law was not in existence, and would probably never have been enacted in these terms. What he does not, of course, speak about is the connection between the prohibition against philosophizing and the prohibition against not believing in the existence of the gods worshiped by the city of Athens. He goes so far in the *Apology* to say that his philosophizing is due to a straight command of a god, of Apollo, who had *commanded* him to philosophize. Now again, if you read it, you see that Apollo didn't do anything of this kind. When [Apollo was asked] the ambiguous question, when he was asked by another enthusiastic admirer of Socrates, "Is anyone wiser than Socrates?" Apollo or the priestess said, "No, no one is wiser than Socrates," which of course is not exactly a command: "Socrates, you must philosophize!" Socrates interpreted it to mean that he is wiser than the others according to the gods, because he knows that he knows nothing; and therefore in order to convince himself and others, he goes around in Athens and shows up everyone who *pretends* to be wise. And of course, that is not too difficult for him: he shows that these men who pretend to be wise are in fact very unwise. And then he gets very unpopular by that, and the end of it is the condemnation. But however large a view we may take of how oracles can be interpreted, it stretches the thing a bit to say that it was a clear injunction of Apollo.

[¶ 12] Now Plato, after the experience of Socrates, made an honest effort to solve that problem shown by Socrates's fate, namely, that he is a philosopher who as such cannot believe in the gods worshiped by the city of Athens, and philosophy and the city are incompatible. How can one make them compatible?²⁶ This is a great problem which Plato solved in the *Laws*, especially in the tenth book, where he shows what the proper legislation regarding religion would be, namely, to demand from every citizen belief in those gods whose existence can be demonstrated (the existence of Zeus and so on can never be demonstrated), and these are what we may call the cosmic gods, meaning the heavenly bodies which Plato thought were animate beings. And in this better city of the *Laws*, only this rational belief is demanded from every citizen, and of course then also legally enforced. And Socrates could have lived and died without any difficulty in such a city. The punishment for unbelief there is very complicated. One has first the impression that it is capital punishment in every case, but this is not quite true because if a man is just, has led a just life, and is not orthodox along the lines of this *rational* religion, he will not be condemned to death; this is made clear later on.[27]

This much about Aristotle and Plato. But some could say: but in all cases, there *must* be a public religion which every citizen must accept. [¶ 13] But one could say: were there no *radicals* in classical antiquity—*liberals*, as some people say? Now there are quite a few people today who assert that, and they refer to such people as Protagoras, who of course was not an Athenian citizen, but who lived in Athens for a while and got into troubles because his book began roughly with the sentence, "Whether the gods are or are not, I do not know. The difficulty or the remoteness of the subject matter and the brevity of my life prevent me from finding out the truth."[28] And he has been called an agnostic because he didn't formally deny but only expressed his doubt. But one must also say that—and there were such people—neither Protagoras nor any other man of whom we know something engaged in *propagating* this view. These were people who in very private circles of refined society said these things, and perhaps to some extent also in writing, but we have only fragments of these writings; we do not know how that thing looked in the whole book. It is always dangerous to judge on the basis of fragments. The view fostered in our age by some Marxist and crypto-Marxist authors that the lines were roughly drawn in antiquity as in our time: a right and a left, and the right were these cursed fellows Socrates, Plato, and Aristotle, the reactionaries; and the left were the precursors of John Dewey [laughter]—just, I mean, a piece of fiction which has no basis. The clear, very clear statement by Edmund Burke will help to clarify the situation. Burke said somewhere, "Boldness formerly was not the character of Atheists as such. They were even of a character nearly the reverse; they were formerly like the old Epicureans, rather an unenterprising race. But of late they are grown active, designing, turbulent, and seditious."[29] These old irreligious people were not an enterprising race, they were sometimes what we now call intellectuals, and in other cases a kind of bums [laughter] living at the margin of society (λάθε βιώσας), but that had no political importance.³⁰ We can safely say that the political philosophy which existed in classical antiquity is that of men like Socrates, Plato and Aristotle, and the Stoics. [¶ 14] The other people who could be regarded as precursors of modern liberalism were not *politically* interested. There was not a ghost of a chance of a hope that this kind of thought could become *politically* relevant. Good.

Now let me summarize then this point. No religion—I mean the view which Aristotle implies, and which Aristotle, Plato, and others imply. And please understand me: I take now religion in the precise sense as a translation of what Aristotle means by "the concern with the divine" as the fifth and the first, nothing more. But one must be somehow precise. I have heard people say in this country: Well, I am a religious man, I am a scientist! If you call any dedication religion, then of course one can say every dedicated man is religious, but I think this is a gross misuse of words. [¶ 15] Now if I state then the view of the classics coherently, I would say this: no religion is *true*, but *some* religion, *any* religion is politically necessary. Law and morality are insufficient for the large majority of men. Obedience to the law and to the moral rules is insufficient for making men happy—well, the well-known fact that [the] wicked are happy and the just live in misery. Law and morality are therefore in need of being *supplemented* by divine rewards and punishments. The *true* supplement to law and morality is, however, philosophy, but philosophy is essentially the preserve of *very few* men, because a special *nature* (φύσις) is required for becoming a philosopher. [¶ 16] Religion is here not meant to be the work of philosophers. None of these philosophers believed that he could *found* a religion. Religion is a work of the *founders* or legislators, and philosophy simply *finds* that and has to accept it. Yet philosophy can and should affect or modify religion. While it is indispensable to the city, religion also creates certain *dangers* to the city. Famous cases: earthquakes and eclipses interpreted as bad *omina*: panics in the army. Well, what do you do if you have an enlightened general, like Pericles, like Scipio? He will give a brief lecture to the army and tell them that has happened perfectly naturally and there is no omen in it. So [that is] an interesting question and the first book of Cicero's *Republic* is the most coherent discussion of that.³¹ Or another case: the famous naval battle of Arginusae, which the Athenians won, but there the generals or admirals didn't take care of picking up, not the shipwrecked soldiers, but the corpses. Now according to the Athenian religious notion, the corpses have to be brought *home* to be buried properly, and the generals were condemned to death.³² Now here there was another case where from the philosopher's point of view some information about the irrelevance of the mere corpse, as it is given for example in Plato's *Phaedo*, would have been helpful for the sake of humanity.[33]

Forgive me if I mention also an example from Jewish history: no fighting on Sabbath. You know, at the beginning of the Maccabean wars, no fighting on Sabbath; and then it simply had to be changed because it proved to be impossible.[34] Another example which goes *through* the ages from classical antiquity on: the institution of religious asylum. Someone touching an altar, a murderer, is protected by this very fact—an *irrational* practice which must be changed. The most urgent and famous question today of this nature is of course the question of birth control, as you all know. [¶ 17] The position in this respect of the philosophers was clearly indicated by the Jewish *pious* poet Judah Halevi, who said that the philosophers, in contradistinction to religion or Judaism in particular, do not recognize a single rule of action, of conduct which is universally valid. In other words, when the common good is in danger, there is no rule which cannot be disregarded.[35]

[¶ 18] Now, what was the actual influence of philosophy on religion in this respect? Well, one can say there was a fairly liberal religious practice, for example in Athens for some time, and that had to do with the fact that Pericles was under the influence of men like Anaxagoras, a philosopher, and other cases. There was also a very liberal practice in the Roman Empire to some extent. But this liberal practice is one thing, and *legal* protection is another. If we are concerned with *legal* protection, we must say classical antiquity philosophic, or non-philosophic was radically *illiberal*. There was nothing corresponding to the First Amendment. No freedom of religion was recognized in theory or in practice. To repeat, what happened was in certain cities for certain periods very liberal practice because of easygoing people, but when it came to a *test*, this liberalism could not be defended. [¶ 19] Now, the danger from this point of view was not that the polis represses religious *freedom*—this they did not even *desire*—but the undue influence of religion or priests on the city. About this, they were seriously concerned, but they did not demand in any way freedom of religion. Religious repression, or positively stated, religious uniformity, is a *need*; the *true* concern with the divine is *knowledge* in contradistinction to prayer and sacrifice. And the basis of that is, to elaborate one point I indicated before—the fundamental human fact, so to speak, is the gulf between the philosophers and nonphilosophers, whom they called the *demos*, the common people. The very *ends* of the philosophers and the nonphilosophers differ, and therefore the freedom which the philosophers can have cannot be had by anybody else.

But there is a point which is not altogether unimportant: the philosophers recognized the existence of an *intermediate* group between the philosophers and the *demos*, and these are the people whom they called the *educated* people (πεπαιδευμένοι), people who have *listened* to philosophers and have come under their influence. In more social terms, the gentlemen. A gentleman meant here an urban patrician. According to the orthodox doctrine, this urban patriciate had to derive its livelihood from agriculture, but as a matter of fact, it was largely commercial, and I think that the history of philosophy, viewed from the point of view of mere sociology of philosophy, is to a large extent the history of a commercial patriciate. This, I think, goes until the eighteenth century. This was the social basis of philosophy strictly understood.

[¶ 20] It is absolutely necessary that I say a word on what I have called political theology.[36] Now by political theology, I mean teachings based on divine revelation, like the Jewish, Christian, Muslim, and perhaps others. And from the point of view of any form of political theology, one particular religion is *the* true religion; whereas from the point of view of the philosophers, *no* religion is the true religion. Let us look for one moment at the difference between the three universal monotheistic religions. Judaism does not demand from all men that they become Jews: as you know, only those born from a Jewish mother. Christianity demands—Christianity in principle—from all men [to become Christians], but tolerates Jews with great disability. I am speaking now of course of the situation up to, what, 200 years ago. Islam tolerates Jews and Christians with considerable civil disabilities. Now, this had of course to do with the fact that Christians recognize Mosaic revelation and the Muslims recognize the Jewish and Christian revelation although they do not recognize the books. [¶ 21] Now does the Jewish position entail recognition of a right to be irreligious? This, I believe, is a question which we must raise with a view to the burning question of our time. I would say: No! The basis of traditional Jewish toleration, or however we might call it, is the famous sentence that the pious—or the righteous, as people say—among the nations of the world, i.e., amongst the non-Jews, have a share in the world to come,[37] which in Christian understanding means they will be *saved*.[38] But righteous is—the word is the pious—it goes without saying that is simply understood that these righteous men will of course believe in God. [¶ 22] Maimonides, who is generally regarded as the greatest Jewish authority in post-Talmudic times, *limits* this high position to non-Jews who recognize and perform the so-called seven Noahide commandments, the commandments which were already given according to the Bible not later than Noah's time, that is to say, after the Deluge, immediately after the Deluge. And they include such prohibitions against murder and theft, and so on, and of course also against idolatry. But Maimonides limits this toleration to non-Jews who recognize and perform these seven Noahide commandments *on the basis of the Mosaic revelation*. That is to say that anyone who abstains from these actions because he has a natural inclination towards that abstention, or because his reason has led him to abstain from them does not belong according to Maimonides to these pious among the gentiles. In practical terms, that means Maimonides limits this toleration to Christians and Muslims, because they of course by definition recognize the Mosaic revelation.[39] Pagans are excluded, and this creates some problem because one of the pagans was Aristotle, whom Maimonides admired very highly. [¶ 23] In the discussion about this decision of Maimonides, which became more and more shocking, the more the modern liberal notions prevailed within Judaism, a defender of Maimonides in the older view quoted from the 9th Psalm, verses which I may read in English translation: "the wicked shall be turned into hell and all nations that forget God ... Arise O Lord, let no man prevail, let the heathen be judged in thy sight."[40]

[¶ 24] I must mention one point because this becomes important later on. On the basis of political *theology*, in contradistinction to political philosophy, there is this fundamental difficulty. What is better: *no* religion or a *false* religion? I mean, given the fact that there will be people who will not have *the* true religion, what is better? In other words, what is better or worse: atheism or a living faith in a beast like Moloch? Because faith in Moloch is of course religion of a sort, and atheism clearly is not. [¶ 25] The *true* religion is known as such only by revelation, not by reason or nature, and therefore there cannot be a *natural* obligation to worship and to love God, *the* true God. This is recognized by Thomas Aquinas: not reason *simply*, but reason informed by *faith* teaches that God is to be loved and worshiped.[41] This means that—deviating from Aristotle, and deviating because for Thomas Aquinas [Christianity] is *the* true religion—Thomas teaches that divine worship is not strictly speaking an institute of natural right, for natural theology, i.e., the natural knowledge of God's existence and so on, does not lead to the insight that God *alone* must be worshiped, which is, of course, the principle of Christianity, as it is of Judaism and Islam. [¶ 26] Now natural theology does not lead to the insight that God alone must be worshiped, because the alternative being the Aristotelian view, the belief in the eternity of the world, and on this basis, the heavenly bodies, for example, are eternal and therefore can legitimately be called gods, as they are called by Aristotle, and then there is no reason why they shouldn't be worshiped. This much, I think, is clear.

[¶ 27] Now let me continue with my theme proper. Freedom of religion as a right, as it is recognized in the First Amendment, is something specifically *modern*, especially in that interpretation according to which freedom *of* religion includes the freedom of *irreligion*, and this is I think the only interesting case. But someone can say: Is not freedom of religion in the widest sense simply the right of the *conscience*, which includes the right of the *erring* conscience and therefore also in principle of atheism? This is a Christian view, to which I have to say first that conscience is not a philosophic conception but it stems from Christian theology, at least in this meaning. Hence this line of thought does not belong to the tradition of political philosophy. Secondly, however, I believe that the freedom of the erring conscience is not freedom for any false religion. I mean that the erring conscience is *excused* doesn't mean that the man of the erring conscience has a full *legal* right, for example, to *propagate* his false teaching. We also cannot entirely divorce the ecclesiastical teaching according to which the erring conscience *binds*—it binds, it doesn't give rights—from consideration of the ecclesiastical practice. [¶ 28] One can say, however, that freedom of religion is an indirect consequence of the Reformation, the whole story with which you are familiar since your grade school days: the Reformation, the religious wars, the ruin of Europe, the desire to stop that bloodshed and the devastation, tolerance. There is no question about this historical concatenation. One must also mention that there were certain *sects*, Christian sects from the very beginning of the Reformation who were in favor of toleration. But again I say, and that is not merely a verbal excuse, this is not political philosophy. These sectarians who wanted their freedom of religion on the basis of certain *Christian* notions of the conscience and of faith, these were surely not philosophers.

However, *prior* to the Reformation, or at any rate independently of it, certain *modifications* of classical political philosophy occurred within political philosophy. [¶ 29] I mention two names: The first is Sir Thomas More's *Utopia*, which is written fundamentally from a philosophic point of view, published in 1516, that is to say, one year before the outbreak of the Reformation. Now in this perfect commonwealth, *Utopia*, which is described there, the established—there is an established religion—is, however, *the* natural or rational religion, something which Plato had somehow *hinted* at in the *Laws*. But everyone is free to add to it of his own; for example, if he thinks he should worship, say, Mercury, the star [planet] Mercury, in addition to the one cause of everything, he is perfectly free to do so. No one can be *persecuted* on account of his religion. Everyone may follow the religion which he likes, except that no one who doesn't believe in the immortality of the souls and in providence can be a citizen. This is the absolute limit. So there *is* an established religion. No one may defend his religious views differing from the accepted views in *public*, but he may defend it before priests and serious men, grave men, *viri graves*.⁴² But again, there is no punishment for infraction. The public cult is uniform but does not violate anything peculiar to anyone's *private* religion. For example, there is no prayer which *everyone* could not speak—I think you are reminded of many contemporary facts by that;⁴³ it's very interesting, in 1516! In brief, a society united in and by *the* true religion of reason. It tolerates additions to it, but no *subtraction*.

[¶ 30] The contemporary of More who also made a considerable change in the traditional doctrine was Machiavelli, in his two great books which were written at about the same time as *Utopia* was. I mention only one point, the only point of epoch-making importance. Machiavelli teaches that a public religion is *indispensable*, as everyone else had taught before him, but he makes this qualification: for *republics*, not in absolute monarchy; there the strong arm of the prince can supply what religion otherwise gives. So this is a kind of inkling of the so-called *enlightened* despotism of the sixteenth, seventeenth, and eighteenth centuries. I do not know of any suggestion of this kind from earlier literature, but let us keep in mind the implication of Machiavelli: while an irreligious absolute monarchy, despotism, may be possible, an irreligious *republic* is not [SPINOZA].

[¶ 31] Now the change which was effected by Machiavelli—and the man who in these matters is his successor surely, Hobbes—is fundamental, because it concerns the relation of philosophy and the commonweal. I must, unfortunately, say a few words about that. The change, in brief, consists of two elements. [Strauss interrupts his talk and asks the moderator for more time: "Do I have 20 minutes?" "Yes, sir."] [¶ 32] The first is this: science is for the sake of power.⁴⁴ Science is not—and science means always philosophy, that is not different at this time—science is not for its own sake but for the sake of power, for the "relief of man's estate," as someone called it. ⁴⁵ That implies that from now on, the ultimate end of the philosopher and the end of the nonphilosophers are the *same*. There is no longer that gulf which existed in classical times; and the formula for that end, which is the best which was ever coined, was Locke's formulation: comfortable self-preservation.⁴⁶ [¶ 33] A second difference: the common people, the nonphilosophers, can become enlightened. The philosophic-scientific teaching does no longer remain a *preserve* of a so-called intellectual elite, but is spread, is broadcast, and transforms the whole citizen body. Science becomes for the first time a *public* power. It becomes a public power because it forms the minds of large masses of men.

[¶ 34] Now, what is the situation of our problem at this stage? Hobbes, whose construction is still the clearest and most lucid in existence, starts from a very massive fact which has very much to do with toleration, namely, fear of violent death, because persecution naturally culminates in killing people. Violent death is the greatest evil and this must be avoided by government, i.e., peace at all costs is a fundamental condition, and this of course requires strong government. I mean, whenever government is divided, there will be all kinds of frictions, legal delays, and so on. *Unqualified* sovereignty—and he preferred monarchy, i.e., absolute monarchy. Religion owes its legal power *only* to the uncontrolled and uncontrollable act of the sovereign. Say, if Christianity is an established religion in England, that is due to an act of British kings or kings and Parliament and not to any intrinsic truth which it might have. The sovereign can determine *which* religion is to be established as he sees fit. This means of course also that he can *disestablish* it as he sees fit. The Christian is obliged in conscience to commit idolatrous and blasphemous acts if his sovereign so commands because obedience to the sovereign is *the* fundamental duty.

And now comes the interesting turn: the sovereign may establish or disestablish any religion he pleases, but he is not *obliged* to establish *any* religion, any public worship which as such would be uniform. He *may*, as Hobbes puts it, allow "many sorts of worship." Many sorts of worship. In that case, however, he goes on, and it is extremely interesting, "it cannot be said that the commonwealth is of any religion at all."⁴⁷ Why? Because there is no public religion, no established religion. The consequence is that Hobbes admits at this passage—a unique passage in this work, but an important one—that an *irreligious* commonwealth is possible. Or to state it quite bluntly, an atheistic society is possible. This is one of the greatest events in the history of thought proper.

Three years after Hobbes's death, a French writer, Pierre Bayle, published a book, *Pensées diverses* [*sur la comète*], diverse thoughts on a certain comet which had appeared, and which spells out what in Hobbes is only once mentioned. I must say a few words about this book, which I think is one the most important works in this whole development. Bayle opposes the belief that comets are omens, a belief still very strong in the seventeenth century, but an issue which we would all regard as extremely trivial. Now, he gives eight reasons why comets are not [omens]—it's a large book, 400 or 500 pages. Eight reasons. The seventh[48] reason is a *theological* reason, and the only theological reason which he adduces against the belief in the comets. He argues as follows: if comets were evil omens, God would have made miracles in order to confirm *idolatry*. If they are omens, if they say something, then they are not merely natural events, they are miracles. And since comets were used in pagan antiquity and in China for idolatrous purposes, God—you see that is a very neat piece of theological reasoning—God would have made miracles in order to confirm idolatry. But then here comes an objection: but God might very well have confirmed idolatry because it is a *lesser* evil than *atheism*. That the Greeks or the Chinese are idolaters is better than that they were atheists. Then a response, Bayle's response, to this objection is the following: he denies that atheism is necessarily such an evil. Atheism does not necessarily lead to immorality. And in this connection he does something. He proves, or he attempts to prove, the possibility of an atheistic society. It is an enormous step. Atheism is altogether innocent. I can't suppress mentioning his theological argument proper, which is taken from the analogy of *human* jealousy. Opposed to idolatry is God's jealousy. He says a husband is less jealous if his wife does not love any man, including himself, than if she loves another man [laughter].[49] You know, he uses the old principle of analogy for his very novel purpose.

[¶ 35] Now this epoch-making event, which is connected with the names of Hobbes and Bayle, remained, however, *subterraneous* and did not in any way affect public policy or public discussions until the nineteenth century, when an open atheistic propagation with a political or social purpose came into [the] open, especially of course in socialism and communism. But something took place, say, between 1670 roughly and the French Revolution, which met the eye and the grounds of which were not discerned by everyone, but the men who were responsible for it knew it very well. In other words, that part of the iceberg which became visible was a technique, the technique of the enlightenment of these philosophers. Two rules: *multiply* sects, and *deflect* the attention of men from the otherworldly goals to this-worldly goals. The empirical basis, the Dutch Republic, which was the model, regarded as the model, because of religious tolerance: every sect can have freedom in Holland and they are getting richer and richer, whereas the Spanish monarchy gets poorer and poorer from day to day [laughter]. So there is a connection, a connection between these two things: multiplication of sects plus economics, we can say. That was the technique of these men who steered this big conspiracy, I think we can say, of the late seventeenth century and the eighteenth century.

Now the great political philosophers of that age (of the seventeenth and eighteenth centuries), apart from Hobbes, do not of course go so far as Hobbes and Bayle do. I mention these three names: Locke, famous fighter for tolerance, but severe limitation—surely no tolerance for atheists, explicitly. In his case, not even for Catholics. That had of course to do with the British settlement. Spinoza: a state religion in a republic, absolutely necessary. The state religion must be based on either the Old Testament or the Old and New Testaments taken together, so the Jews and Christians are all right. Naturally, he gives an extremely great freedom of interpretation—for example, everyone must believe that God exists; but he may just say that *matter* is God; then he complies. In other words, it is almost zero but still, legally no toleration for atheists. That's important. And the last great man of this tradition, Rousseau, who as everyone knows demanded a *civil* religion as absolutely necessary, and he has been accused by some people who know nothing *prior* to Rousseau, and know only nineteenth-century liberalism, that he was a terrible totalitarian and I don't know what, whereas he was in this respect only the last relic, so to say, of the older view.[50] Good.

So in other words, in this great period, the formative period of modern times, there is a considerable modification of the overall understanding but clearly no freedom of irreligion. Tolerance means for all practical purposes tolerance for every religion, but not for *irreligion*. I believe one has to take this into account if one wants to understand the First Amendment because the First Amendment and the American Constitution altogether are after all a product of the eighteenth century, or the great authorities there; the philosophical authorities are all men of the eighteenth century. I believe one has to consider this very seriously. The question of what all individuals responsible for the Constitution, for the Federalist Papers, but for the Constitution as a whole, thought privately is utterly uninteresting; the point is what they could publicly defend. This would have to be considered. Now of course in the nineteenth century, it seems, freedom became *unlimited*, unlimited, and this is a tradition to which people defer.

[¶ 36] Now let us look for one moment at the greatest representative of free libertarianism in the nineteenth century, and that is, as I believe everyone would admit, John Stuart Mill. But let us not look at *On Liberty*; let us look at his *Autobiography*. I must bore you with a few quotations:

I was brought up from the first without any religious belief, in the ordinary acceptation of the term. My father, educated in the creed of Scotch Presbyterianism, had by his own studies and reflections been early led to reject not only the belief in revelation, but the foundations of what is commonly called Natural Religion....

[His father's] aversion to religion, in the sense usually attached to the term [LS: Do you see the hedging? I am not simply irreligious only in the sense usually attached to the term] was of the same kind with that of Lucretius: he regarded it with the feelings due not to a mere mental delusion, but to a great moral evil. He looked upon it as the greatest enemy of morality. I am thus one of the very few examples, in this country, of one who has, not thrown off religious belief, but never had it [laughter]. I grew up in a negative state in relation to it. [LS: Obviously even in England he will not be so rare today.] This point in my early education had, however, incidentally one bad consequence deserving notice. In giving me an opinion contrary to that of the world, my father thought it necessary to give it as one which could not prudently be avowed to the world. This lesson of keeping my thoughts to myself, at that early age, was attended with some moral disadvantages [in the original: "could not but be morally prejudicial"].[51]

One more point, and then I am through with these quotations and almost through with my lecture, when he was running for Parliament, much later, of course:

A well-known literary man was heard to say that the Almighty himself would have no chance of being elected on such a programme [LS: That on which he ran]. I strictly adhered to it, neither spending money nor canvassing, nor did I take any personal part in the election, until about a week preceding the day of nomination, when I attended a few public meetings to state my principles and give answers to any questions which the electors might exercise their just right of putting to me for their own guidance, answers as plain and unreserved as my Address. On one subject only, my religious opinions, I announced from the beginning that I would answer no questions; a determination which appeared to be completely approved by those who attended the meetings.[52] [laughter]

Exceedingly interesting, how the freedom of religion—or from religion, rather—which Mill exercised as distinguished from what he demanded in his *On Liberty*, was still along the lines of Locke, Spinoza, and Rousseau, rather than of John Dewey.

[¶ 37] I'll summarize that point. What is *the* issue? The issue seems to be this: Does the commonwealth require religion for its well-being, and may it therefore legitimately demand from every citizen that he has *some* religion, i.e., that he believes in God? Or can an atheistic society be a good society? I would like to define atheistic society lest there be any doubt. Of course, there is no society in which all members are atheists. [¶ 38] An atheistic society is a "society in which no public governmental act and no publicly supported act has any reference whatsoever to god—this is a clear case in the USSR—or in which no man suffers from *any* politically relevant disability, as distinguished from a mere legal disability, on the ground of his professed atheism."[53]

[¶ 39] What is uppermost in our minds is a question, a question of American constitutional law, namely, the correct interpretation of the First Amendment. Does the freedom of religion mean freedom for all *religions*, but *only* for them, or does it give an equal freedom *from* all religions? I believe that it is impossible to settle this legal question of utmost gravity if one does not settle first the theoretical question, the discussion of which we have begun tonight. This is all I have.

[Applause] [Tape change]

Strauss: And just not standing on ceremony, he or she who has a ready question, indicate so by any means short of firecrackers [laughter].

Student: Do you believe that a public support of religion can be as influential today when there are so many sources of irreligion in society? Do you believe that a public support of religion can be effective today as compared to, let's say the past, where society was quite different?

Strauss: This is a very complicated question, but I believe it is not the first question. The first question is: Is it desirable? And that is the question that one must really have before one's mind's eye: an atheistic society as defined, and a nonatheistic society. And say, let it—well, of course, we take a nonatheistic society as we *wish* it, not necessarily like one in the past which may have been defective on a thousand grounds. That is the question. And then the question of whether any legal compulsion, whether any use, is an entirely different [one]—but there are—for example, in this question the famous case which I do not wish to touch, not being a trained constitutional lawyer, I mean the prayer in public schools, this is an example of what the practical issues are.[54] You see, it was an old maxim of wise men of the past that legislation can only follow a certain state of preparedness of public opinion. By public opinion, I don't mean what the Gallup Poll means, but the settled convictions, not necessarily coming out in questionnaires, on which people habitually act. You know?

Same Student: It would seem to be desirable to support religion publicly, and that—it would—working on that premise, the gravity of the question would depend—well, the gravity of the issue of whether religion should be publicly supported or not depends in part on the effectiveness of the public support of religion, and there are many people who would deny that the school prayer or something of this sort can have real effect on the training of children when there are so many other things—

Strauss: These things cannot be weighed, they cannot be measured. No one can know what a certain phrase heard, stated drowsily, repeated drowsily, but remembered in a key moment of one's life, would mean. Now if this phrase was never heard, it will not be remembered. Even Stalin remembered—in a conversation with Churchill, I remember—when they spoke about the Great War situation, and he said something like this, "God helps!"[55] Well, he of course had gone even to a priest seminary and so had a more than ordinary religious education. But you know what I mean; I am speaking now not exactly of habitual and thoughtless use, but in certain moments, if there is such an expression, any others I don't want to do that but I think I tried ... the imagination of every one of you. That is unfathomable, unpredictable even, because these are all seeds, and whether the seeds will go up depends not only on the soil, also on the weather, and who can know that? I believe that all these methods, the quantitative methods, I don't think they make any allowance for these depths, although they even have now I hear depth interview [laughter]. But this depth is of course a relative depth, maybe what depth psychology means by depth. That may not be true depth. So that one cannot say. I think one must face first this question whether—I know there are people who would say if there were no religion whatever anymore, no one would go to any synagogue or church and no one would ever pray and one ... and bless births and wedding and burial would be—would be a relief for the world. I am sure that Lord [Bertrand] Russell thinks along these lines. And he is not the only one, quite a few people. But all right! But one must really figure it out. One must look at it detachedly and soberly: How would this affect human beings, and all kinds of human beings?

And the other way—and if this is not a desirable thing, if this is not a desirable thing, then one must see: Well, what can one do? Is it possible that any governmental action in the widest sense—not necessarily legal actions; you know there are also certain things which are simply done in statements by leading statesmen and so on, as what could be done, what could be implemented. In any case, the decision, either way, has effects in unexpected quarters. Unexpected quarters. And that I would say is the primary question. This raises questions of immense practical importance but as with all practical questions, it presupposes somehow a theoretical decision. Mr. [Donald] Reinken?[56]

Reinken: To ask what is perhaps the other half of that gentleman's question: Where would the area of the greatest expense and cost be, if it is taken seriously, of reestablishing a state-established religion believing in a providential god?

Strauss: The established religion—religion in the strict sense, as you mean it when you speak of established, means of course a *particular* religion. To mention the two examples in this country, Christianity and Judaism—because I think we can disregard Islam in spite of the Black Muslims.

Student: No, I didn't mean putting Cardinal Spellman[57] in the White House, but something milder, taking—we already have "In God We Trust" on the currency. God is known to be Mammon, by the religious people (Strauss: inaudible [laughter]) but reversing the trend away from the prayers in the public functions to make it essentially politically impossible for people to succeed in public life without avowing a trust in a providential god—what some have called the "first church of your choice" religion.

Strauss: But still, whatever this may be—I mean, if it is a religion, it is surely a belief in a providential god, isn't it? And the question is simply not the question of the establishment of any *particular* religion, it is a question of, to what extent—I think the simplest statement of the problem as it has frequently been stated is: Does the First Amendment mean freedom for *all* religions, or does it also include freedom *from* religion? That is the question. Of course, there is another point—I should have looked it up, remind me, Mr. Anastaplo, even admitting that it means only freedom *for* religion, what about the freedom of *speech*? Maybe the freedom of speech would protect irreligious speech as much as religious speech, and therefore we would be up against a similar difficulty, that is quite true. Yes?

Student: Doctor, I wonder if, once we accept the principle that freedom of religion, meaning freedom to practice any religion in a state—I wonder if perhaps—

Strauss: By the way, with some qualifications. Mormons. But they are trivial, they are not ...

Same Student: I wonder if that does not imply that in the eyes of the state, that one religion is as good as another. This isn't the implication of that?

Strauss: I believe that at the moment that is abandoned, I believe the state would then cease to be a liberal state proper. I mean, that I believe is really meant from the very beginning, that there must not be any identification of the state with any particular religion.

Same Student: Well, if that is the case, doesn't it follow logically, or does it follow logically that freedom of religion, implying that in the eyes of the state one religion is the equal of another, doesn't that follow that it is freedom from religion?

Strauss: No. Because the example, for example, of Thomas More already prior to the modern development proper shows that. There can be something which one can loosely call (but sufficiently precise for practical purposes) a rational religion. You know, today the term has become discredited, and today people speak of the Hebrew-Christian tradition. That is a historical term roughly for this. Perhaps naturally the term religion would also have included quite a few pagans who did not share in the Hebrew-Christian tradition. That I think is the practical issue today. I believe no one has the intention of establishing any religion, even Christianity in general—you know, as distinguished from the difference between Catholicism on the one hand, and any Protestant variety on the other. This is not the issue.

Well, of course, I deliberately didn't go into one very big question which indeed belongs to a theoretical consideration but not to the constitutional consideration. And that is whatever the law, including the constitutional law, may say, the state of mind of the citizen is at least as important. You know? So that, for example, in say, around—in 1800 there would be no question that the overwhelming majority of American citizens were practicing Christians. While not a *legal* fact, it was politically immensely important. Well, if you remember the last election, when for the first time a non-Protestant became president of the United States. And you know how politically relevant the nonlegal—I mean not the illegal, but the nonlegal—facts are. I mean, that is, I believe, what political sociology is concerned with, you know, these kinds of things which do not appear in law but are very powerful politically. Into this, I didn't go; which of course we should also consider. But I suppose that today the fact that a *considerable* minority of the American people is no longer either Christian or Jewish in any religiously relevant sense of course has created this underlying present situation. I mean, I don't believe that you can state these things very clearly in statistical terms, but this is, I think, the basis, something again, a nonlegal fact, a nonlegal fact as possible under the Constitution, as in the other cases the whole population would adhere to one and the same particular religion—which is of course equally possible legally, and yet it would give society an entirely different character than it has in the two cases. One has surely to consider both possibilities: what one might call the religiously homogenous liberal democracy, and an atheistic liberal democracy. Both are theoretically possible. One should consider that. Although in fact, I believe, the liberal democracies are all in countries which are not religiously homogenous. Is it not true? Or did I forget anything? Surely Holland has a considerable Catholic minority, Britain has a smaller one, but on the other hand a large variety of Protestant sects—where do you, pardon?

Reinken: Scandinavia, where the church—

Strauss: That is correct. Scandinavian countries are so to speak religiously homogenous—Protestant, Lutheran.

Reinken: But very diluted, they are almost gone now.

Strauss: But there because a large part of the population is no longer *really* Christian. And that would be an interesting object of study, how this change occurred—you know, not political change in the narrower sense of the term but of course decisive for the character of the society. Yes? Oh no, this lady was first, I'm sorry.

Student: What theoretical difficulty would you see in a position that it's possible to have a well-ordered and viable society which has ... a public ethics assisting, without—the obligation of which lies solely and strictly in teleological goals decided upon by the society at large, a strictly—an ethics that is only good so long as the society could decide on certain goals, and which would be changed if the goals were altered.

Strauss: But what kind of goals? Cannibalism?

Same Student: No, let us say a society were to form goals that are very much similar to the goals many people say our nation has got now.

Strauss: So you say decent goals. That's a great difference. All right. But let us assume decent goals; but then the question is this: Is the dedication of the society to decent goals and I suppose also of the *serious* part of the population—otherwise society consists of individuals—is this sufficient, humanly sufficient? You doubtless have heard, and probably know much more about this than I do, about the fact which is sometimes called insecurity—insecurity, which even decent people have—and loneliness—you know, loneliness and this kind of thing. So I think in order to be realistic you would have to say: dedication to decent goals plus psychiatry, because psychiatry would then be the only way in which these problems of the individual, which are not solved by this dedication to decent goals, would be solved. Now I don't say that this is a *complete* picture, but I believe it is somewhat more complete than the one that you drew: decent goals, say, social welfare, socialism or, you know, welfare state plus psychiatry. This we have to some extent; we are on the way to it.[58] But again the question is: "Is this what one can be *satisfied* with?" would be the question. One would have to face that.

Same Student: Could one add that perhaps a public ethics based on mutual goals with the addition that there is a complete and total freedom to be both religious and irreligious ...

Strauss: I couldn't hear the last part of it.

Same Student: Adding that one could have whatever religion privately one chose to one's personal—

Strauss: But this is I believe not the question because that is understood according to any interpretation of the First Amendment, that the Constitution does not prescribe to any individual which religion he or she has. There are other questions which are more subtle into which I cannot go; there is a limit to every discussion. For example, there are people who say that Buddhism, for example, strictly understood is an atheistic religion. I mean, in other words, it is not mere—how shall I say?—spiritual emptiness, but it is something spiritual and yet it is atheistic. That I have heard. Now, this would have to be considered, this kind of thing; and especially I hear there is now in some circles in the United States a great movement, numerically probably not very strong, in favor of Zen Buddhism. Have you heard of that? I have heard of it [laughter]. But still, if one wants to have a complete picture, one must without any fastidiousness take into consideration all these kinds of things. My promise was a very limited one: to state what the fundamental issue is which one has to face if one wants to reach clarity about a seemingly purely legal constitutional law question. If I may repeat this once more, the interpretation of the Constitution, as I learned from a very thorough study by Mr. Anastaplo, which I had the pleasure to read, comes always up against the question: What was in the minds of the founding fathers? Now, this can be *partly* established of course by their explicit utterances, but since they were not strictly speaking theoretical men, then one must find that out to some extent by studying the theorists who influenced them. Well, Locke is of course always mentioned in this connection, but perhaps others also have to be considered. In brief, the state of political philosophy and its latitudes which were limited in the late eighteenth century. You agree with that, don't you? And this is what I tried to supply to some extent. Mr. [Charles] Butterworth.[59]

Butterworth: What would be, if any, the grounds for reconciliation between the philosophical view that says "no one religion is true" and the religious view which says "our religious view is the truth"?

Strauss: No—practical reconciliation, practical forbearance, no theoretical reconciliation, as I believe. I mean, there are all kinds of things—for example, take perhaps the most famous case: Hegel who said *the* philosophic system has shown *the* truth of the Christian dogma. But by this very fact, of course, he transformed the Christian dogma into a philosophic theorem where all nonphilosophic things were dismissed as merely imaginary irrelevancies. You know? There are also Jews who have done the same thing. But this, I think, conceals the issue. The older view, the simple older view, that there is natural reason and there is suprarational revelation, which of course would not be accepted by [the] philosopher as suprarational, but yet by virtue of the clear distinction keeps at least alive the problem and doesn't *conceal* it by a sham identification. Yes?

Student: An extension of that question: if the political philosopher is in principle a nonbeliever, yet on the other hand somehow in principle has governing responsibilities in the society, doesn't his status, so to speak, as a nonbeliever point the way for an atheistic society? Is there some kind of unbridgeable gap between the political philosopher and the—

Strauss: That is a long question. In practice, all kinds of combinations are possible. But this may very well be due to the human and all-too-human desire to eat the cake and have it. But if we speak now about serious men—I mean men who take *intellectual* responsibility—I think that is perfectly clear that the philosopher—I mean, I refer you to Thomas Aquinas himself—that philosophy as philosophy is not dependent on faith. I mean, that is a kind of *fideistic* view which Pascal may have had and other people, but which surely is not the Thomistic view. There is a sphere in which human reason can exert itself, and that is of course meant by the word "philosophy" or "science" and political philosophy is a part of it. Now the key controversy is this: Is the sphere of philosophy so *essentially incomplete*, while being autonomous in itself, that it *points* toward its completion in revelation? And if I understand Thomas well, he says that's the case, it is incomplete and points toward this completion. But by the fact that Thomas teaches that and acts on that teaching also theoretically, he is a theologian who uses philosophy, and one can perhaps say he is a better philosopher than other philosophers are. That is probably what you would say. But it is still something which is no longer possible on the basis of philosophy as such, and since even all proof of the defects of philosophy, the defectiveness of philosophy, are of no great help if you do not get the supplement, and since this supplement is accessible *only* on the basis of faith, the conclusion follows.

Same Student: Assuming that you don't get this supplement, I think, I got the impression in your lecture that you suggest that political philosophy as such implies nonbelief. Admitting that Thomistic philosophy suggests—points to something more, and you don't get that something more; and also assuming that the political philosopher has some governing responsibility to the community.

Strauss: But he can fulfill that only on the basis of human reason. And I would say that, and I believe that Thomas Aquinas would say, that the guidance which political philosophy gives for the commonweal is genuine guidance as far as it goes, I mean for this-worldly ends.

Same Student: But won't that guidance necessarily be in conflict with the civil religion, assuming the political philosopher is a nonbeliever and this is a principle?

Strauss: Why should that be? Well, if you take even the doctrine of Rousseau, what does it amount to? That there are sanctions, superhuman sanctions for morality; the content of the morality is entirely determined by human reason. I mean, I do not wish to—the very contrary, I wish to make as clear as possible that there are real questions there, but I would say *these* are the real questions, not some which are ordinarily discussed. And I would like to add one point, which I said already at the beginning: some of you may have seen that I am not a 100% liberal. But the liberal position is today, at least in modern academic circles, almost omnipotent. Now, this position, the liberal position surely, is based on philosophy alone—I mean, they don't call it philosophy anymore, but if you use the term unassisted human mind alone. I mean, the social sciences are not in any way based on revelation in any sense; I believe there is a universal agreement on this point. And therefore, for this reason alone, I would have been compelled to take up the issue, on this basis alone. Because otherwise one simply says: Well, you have your beliefs that are your private prejudices, these prejudices may be nice or they may be obnoxious, but this has no *standing* in academic discussion; that you would hear. I believe someone there raised his hand or finger. No?

Well, if we have exhausted the subject [laughter], there is no reason why we should not have tea.

[Applause]

Notes

1. Leo Strauss, "'Religion and the Commonweal in the Tradition of Political Philosophy.' An Unpublished Lecture by Leo Strauss," ed. Svetozar Minkov and Rasoul Namazi, *American Political Thought* 10, no. 1 (2021): 86–120. The recording is available on the Leo Strauss Center website: https://leostrausscenter.uchicago.edu.

2. Leo Strauss Papers, box 18, folder 13, Special Collections Research Center, University of Chicago Library.

3. George Anastaplo (1925–2014) was a professor at Loyola University Law School and in the Basic Program in the Liberal Arts at the University of Chicago. He appealed the refusal of the Illinois Bar's Committee on Character and Fitness to admit him all the way to the US Supreme Court (losing by a 5–4 decision In re Anastaplo 366 U.S. 82 1961). The "thorough study" Strauss refers to in the Q&A period is Anastaplo's PhD dissertation, "Notes on the First Amendment to the Constitution of the United States of America" (University of Chicago, 1964), published as George Anastaplo, *The Constitutionalist: Notes on the First Amendment* (Lanham, MD: Lexington, 2005).

4. Rabbi Maurice B. Pekarsky (1905–1962) was director of the Hillel Foundation at the University of Chicago.

5. Ralph Lerner is the Benjamin Franklin Emeritus Professor at the University of Chicago and author of works on medieval political philosophy, the Enlightenment, and American political thought, including *Naïve Readings: Reveilles Political and Philosophic* (Chicago: University of Chicago Press, 2016).

6. Werner J. Dannhauser (1929–2014) was professor at Cornell University and Michigan State University and the author of *Nietzsche's View of Socrates* (Ithaca, NY: Cornell University Press, 1974).

7. Max Weber, "Science as a Vocation," in *The Vocation Lectures*, ed. David Owen and Tracy B. Strong, trans. Rodney Livingstone (Indianapolis: Hackett, 2004), 22.

8. The complete quotation, including the first sentence that Strauss drops here, is as follows: "Le partage du brave homme est d'expliquer librement ses pensées. Celui qui n'ose regarder fixément les deux pôles de la vie humaine,

la religion et le gouvernement, n'est qu'un lâche." (The lot of a good man is to explain his thoughts freely. He who does not dare to keep his eyes on the two poles of human life, religion and government, is only a coward.) The complete quotation appears as the epigraph of Strauss's 1939 manuscript entitled "Exoteric Teaching." Leo Strauss, "Exoteric Teaching," in *Reorientation: Leo Strauss in the 1930s*, ed. Hannes Kerber, Martin D. Yaffe, and Richard S. Ruderman (New York: Palgrave Macmillan, 2014), 275. Strauss's source is the 1782 essay titled "Something Lessing Said" by Friedrich Heinrich Jacobi, who quotes this passage with some alterations at the end of his work. The passage is originally from Voltaire's *L'A, B, C, ou Dialogues entre A, B, C*. See Voltaire, "The A B C, or Dialogues between A B C," in *Voltaire: Political Writings*, trans. David Williams (Cambridge: Cambridge University Press, 1994), 142; Friedrich Heinrich Jacobi, "Something Lessing Said: A Commentary on Journeys of the Popes," in *What Is Enlightenment? Eighteenth-Century Answers and Twentieth-Century Questions*, ed. James Schmidt (Berkeley: University of California Press, 1996), 209.

9. In the ms. "our" is crossed out and replaced with "the."

10. See Martin Buber, *I and Thou*, trans. Walter Kaufmann (New York: Scribner's, 1970).

11. For a discussion of the difference between philosophy proper and a philosophic "tradition" and critique of tradition as something petrified and dead as distinguished from vibrant and alive, see Leo Strauss, *On Tyranny: Including the Strauss-Kojève Correspondence. Corrected and Expanded Edition*, ed. Victor Gourevitch and Michael Roth (Chicago: University of Chicago Press, 2013), 195–97; Susan Meld Shell, ed., *The Strauss-Krüger Correspondence. Returning to Plato through Kant* (Cham, Switzerland: Palgrave Macmillan, 2018), 39–40 (letter to Gerhard Krüger on November 17, 1932); Leo Strauss, "The Living Issues of German Postwar Philosophy (1940)," in *Leo Strauss and the Theologico-Political Problem*, ed. Heinrich Meier (Cambridge: Cambridge University Press, 2006), 123–24.

12. "πόλις" in the manuscript. In the manuscript, apart from the title, Strauss uses the Greek term "πόλις" ten times while the term "commonwealth" is used four times. In the lecture, "polis" appears only twice. These two terms seem to be synonymous on this occasion.

13. Aristotle, *Politics* 1328b11–12.

14. Aristotle, *Nicomachean Ethics* 1134b23–25. For more details on this famous passage and the interpretative difficulties involved, see Leo Strauss, "On Natural Law," in *Studies in Platonic Political Philosophy*, ed. Thomas L. Pangle (Chicago: University of Chicago Press, 1983), 140; Leo Strauss, *Natural Right and History* (Chicago: University of Chicago Press, 1953), 156–63.

15. In the manuscript, Strauss uses the Hebrew expression "Sefer" instead of "book."

16. Aristotle, *Metaphysics* 1074b13 (πά τριος δό ξα).

17. Aristotle, *Metaphysics* 1074b4–5.

18. As is clear from the manuscript ("*Politics* II on Hippodamus"), Strauss is referring to Aristotle, *Politics* 1267b21–1269a27 especially 1269a20–21. For a

detailed discussion of this point, see Leo Strauss, *The City and Man* (Charlottesville: University of Virginia Press, 1964), 17–19.

19. Augustine, *The City of God* 4.27. See also Leo Strauss, *1959 Course on Plato's Laws Offered at the University of Chicago*, ed. Lorraine Smith Pangle (Chicago: Leo Strauss Center, 2016), 339 (Session 13 on February 26, 1959).

20. Plato, *Timaeus* 24a–b. See Leo Strauss, *Thoughts on Machiavelli* (Glencoe, IL: Free Press, 1958), 184–85; Leo Strauss, "Marsilius of Padua," in *History of Political Philosophy*, 3rd ed. (Chicago: University of Chicago Press, 1987), 252–57; Leo Strauss, "Literary Character of the Guide for the Perplexed," in *Persecution and the Art of Writing* (Glencoe, IL: Free Press, 1952), 91n156.

21. Plato, *Phaedo* 118a.

22. Leo Strauss, "On Plato's Apology of Socrates and Crito," in *Studies in Platonic Political Philosophy*, ed. Thomas L. Pangle (Chicago: University of Chicago Press, 1983), 39–41.

23. Xenophon, *Apology of Socrates* 28. For the other instance of Socrates laughing see Plato, *Phaedo* 115c5, and Strauss, *The City and Man*, 61.

24. "νομίζειν" is from the manuscript. The term refers to Socrates's reformulation of the charge against himself in Plato's *Apology* (26a). *Nomizein* can mean "to believe" in but it is also related to the term *nomos* (law), hence "to believe" in the gods of the city might also mean to acknowledge them according to the laws through the outward performance of religious duties. See Leo Strauss, *1966 Course on Plato's Apology of Socrates and Crito Offered in the Autumn Quarter at the University of Chicago*, ed. David Janssens (Chicago: Leo Strauss Center, 2016), 92 (Session 5 on November 1, 1966).

25. Plato, *Apology of Socrates* 29d.

26. In the manuscript, two answers are given to this question. Only the second is also mentioned in the lecture. The first solution is described as "a) the philosopher-kings."

27. Leo Strauss, *The Argument and the Action of Plato's Laws* (Chicago: University of Chicago Press, 1975), 155–56; Leo Strauss, *1971–72 Course on Plato's Laws Offered at St. John's College*, ed. Lorraine Smith Pangle (Chicago: Leo Strauss Center, 2016), 587 (Session 26).

28. Protagoras's most famous saying quoted wholly in part by other authors. The following is from a scholium on Plato's *Republic* by Hesychius: "[Protagoras's] books were burned by the Athenians because he said, Concerning the gods, I cannot ascertain whether they exist or whether they do not." Daniel W. Graham, ed., *The Texts of Early Greek Philosophy: The Complete Fragments and Selected Testimonies of the Major Presocratics* (Cambridge: Cambridge University Press, 2010), 2:697 (DK 80 A3). See also Diogenes Laertius, *Vitae*, 9.51.

29. Edmund Burke, "Thoughts on French Affairs," in *The Works of the Right Honorable Edmund Burke*, vol. 4 (Boston: Little and Brown, 1881), 355.

30. The Greek term *lathe biosas* appears only in the manuscript. An Epicurean maxim meaning "live unnoticed," "unknown," or "in obscurity," is an invitation to those living a philosophic life to avoid political power and

fame and according to Strauss clearly shows the unpolitical character of the Epicurean philosophy. See Leo Strauss, *1962 Course on Rousseau Offered at the University of Chicago*, ed. Jonathan Marks (Chicago: University of Chicago Press, 2014), 77 (session 4).

31. Cicero, *Republic* 24. The story is told by Scipio Africanus the Younger in the dialogue. This eclipse is mentioned by Thucydides as well: *History of the Peloponnesian War* 2.28. See also Strauss, *Thoughts on Machiavelli*, 208.

32. Xenophon, *Hellenica* I.6–7. See also Plato, *Apology of Socrates* 32a–c; Xenophon, *Memorabilia* 1.1.18, 4.4.2; Leo Strauss, "Greek Historians," *Review of Metaphysics* 21, no. 4 (1968): 656–66.

33. See Plato, *Phaedo* 115c–e.

34. First Maccabees 2:41.

35. See Leo Strauss, "The Law of Reason in the *Kuzari*," in *Persecution and the Art of Writing* (Glencoe, IL: Free Press, 1952), 95–142.

36. Leo Strauss, "What Is Political Philosophy?," in *What Is Political Philosophy? And Other Studies* (Glencoe, Illinois: Free Press, 1959), 13.

37. This is a central issue in the first-century debate between Rabbi Eliezer and Rabbi Joshua b. Hananiah. The famous sentence is the position of Rabbi Joshua. See *Tosefta Sanhedrin* 13:2.

38. In the manuscript, Strauss contrasts this more inclusive view of salvation with the orthodox Catholic position and quotes "nulla salus extra Ecclesiam" (no salvation outside the Church).

39. *Hilchot Melachim* 8:11.

40. Psalms 9:17 and 9:19.

41. *Summa Theologica*, I–II, q. 104, art. 1.

42. See the section, "On the religions of the Utopians," in book II of Thomas More's *Utopia*.

43. This seems to be a reference to the US Supreme Court ruling in *Engel v. Vitale* 370 U.S. 421, which took place on June 25, 1962, when, in a 6–1 decision, the Supreme Court held that voluntary prayer in public schools was unconstitutional, violating the Establishment Clause of the First Amendment. Strauss's lecture on January 27, 1963, was delivered seven months after this landmark decision, reiterating *Everson v. Board of Education* 330 U.S. 1 (1947), which applied the Establishment Clause in the country's Bill of Rights to state law. We are grateful to an anonymous reviewer of *American Political Thought* who drew our attention to this point.

44. In the manuscript, the Latin phrase "scientia propter potentiam" from the Latin edition of Hobbes's *Leviathan* is quoted.

45. Francis Bacon, *The Advancement of Learning* 1.5.8.

46. *First Treatise*, § 87.

47. *Leviathan*, chapter 31.

48. Number seven is underlined in the manuscript.

49. Pierre Bayle, *Various Thoughts on the Occasion of a Comet*, trans. Robert C. Bartlett (Albany: State University of New York Press, 2000), 75–97, 134–36 (§§ 57–78, 103).

50. Robert A. Nisbet, "Rousseau and Totalitarianism," *Journal of Politics* 5, no. 2 (1943): 93-114.

51. Selections from chapter 2 ("Moral Influences in Early Youth. My Father's Character and Opinions") in John Stuart Mill, "Autobiography," in *Collected Works of John Stuart Mill*, vol. 1 (Toronto: University of Toronto Press, 1981), 41-44.

52. Chapter 7 ("General View of the Remainder of My Life") in Mill, "Autobiography," 274.

53. As can be deduced from the manuscript, Strauss seems to be giving a definition of the atheistic society.

54. *Engel v. Vitale*, 370 U.S. 421 (June 25, 1962).

55. "May God help this enterprise to succeed!"—Stalin to Churchill, Moscow, August 12, 1942, in Robert E. Sherwood, *The White House Papers of Harry L. Hopkins: An Intimate History*, vol. 2 (London: Eyre & Spittiswoode, 1949), 618. Sherwood continues, "(The translation of this remark, as given by Churchill to Roosevelt, was: 'May God prosper this undertaking!') I have been told that it was by no means unusual for Stalin, who had been educated for a time in a religious seminary, to invoke the aid of the Deity." (Strauss thought highly of this book and made a gift of it to Joseph Cropsey.)

56. Donald Reinken (1934-2018) held a PhD in mathematics and served as a reader of the text under consideration in many of Strauss's courses.

57. Francis Joseph Spellman (1889-1967), an American bishop and cardinal of the Catholic Church.

58. Leo Strauss, *1971-72 Course on Nietzsche's Beyond Good and Evil Offered at St. John's College*, ed. Mark Blitz (Chicago: Leo Strauss Center, 2014), 5 (Session 1, October 6, 1971); Leo Strauss, *On Nietzsche's "Thus Spoke Zarathustra,"* ed. Richard Velkley (Chicago: University of Chicago Press, 2017), 98.

59. Charles E. Butterworth is professor emeritus at the University of Maryland, College Park, author of works on medieval Islamic political philosophy and translator of Alfarabi, Averroes, and Jean-Jacques Rousseau, most recently of Alfarabi, *The Political Writings: Volume II Political Regime and Summary of Plato's Laws*, trans. Charles E. Butterworth (Ithaca: Cornell University Press, 2015).

Transcript 7.2

LEO STRAUSS, "RELIGION
AND THE COMMONWEAL":
THE MANUSCRIPT (1963)

Editorial Note: This transcript is an edited version of a manuscript found in the Leo Strauss Papers.[1] Numbers in square brackets, inserted by the editors, refer to the page numbers of the manuscript, numbers in square brackets preceded by ¶, also inserted by the editors, refer to the paragraph numbers; all underlined words have been converted to italics; crossed out words and handwritten insertions are mentioned in the footnotes; the abbreviated title of the books and names are everywhere replaced by their full forms.

[1] *Religion and the Commonweal* lecture to be delivered at Hillel on 27.1.1963

1.[2] This is the first time that I have the honor to give a lecture in Hillel House after the death of my friend Rabbi Maurice Pekarsky. Permit me to pay homage to his memory. The soul and substance of Rabbi Pekarsky was Jewish piety, simple old-fashioned, chaste, Jewish piety. He dedicated his life to keeping alive this holy fire, or to revive[3] it. He knew very well how difficult this task was in the middle of the twentieth century—especially at a university like ours. He acted in this difficult situation with singular tact and prudence. He did not protest against those who tried to reduce Judaism to social ethics on the one hand, and to an ethnic culture on the other, since both parties retain a part, however small, of the ancient truth and since their very antagonism—the antagonism between the universal and the particular points to the full truth: the chosen people, the people chosen to be witness of justice. He did not rebuff, nay he attracted those who were not as blessed as he was, who had not succeeded in finding a way of reconciling the old piety and the new science, for he was united with them in love of truth. This was indeed the limit of his tolerance and forbearance: He barely tolerated (for he was a very polite man) those for whom the university is above all a place for promoting themselves. I believe that he would have approved of the effort of Mr. Anastaplo and his friends—which is to explore how one can secure, by human means, the future of religion without infringing on the rights of man.

2. I speak as a social scientist. A social scientist is a man who is sworn to face and pronounce also unpleasant truths—unpleasant to himself. There are two kinds of unpleasant truths, unpleasant truths which are at the same time pleasant, and simply unpleasant truths. As for the former: it is not altogether unpleasant for a friend of big businesses to point out the unpleasant power of the labor unions, nor for a friend of the labor unions to point out the unpleasant power of big businesses: these are pleasant facts for them, facts on which they thrive. The truly unpleasant facts are those which render questionable one's party line—like Yalta for the professional liberal and strong central government with a terrific defense budget for the professional conservative. It is in this spirit that I approach my subject: what does the tradition of political philosophy teach regarding religion and the commonweal.

3. Voltaire has said: celui qui n'ose regarder fixement les deux pôles de la vie, la religion et le government, n'est qu'un lâche. In the language of our time: the two poles of life are the *sub*-cultural, and the *supra*-cultural: two *stern* things, as *distinguished* from culture. If we understand politics and religion in *terms* of culture, we obscure the fundamental difficulty. Government is necessarily particular—religion at least according to its intention universal. By looking at everything from the point of view of culture, we forget the universal, the truly human, for culture, as now used, is essentially particular.

4. If we were to follow this thought, we might be compelled to question the concept of religion too. "Religion" is not a Hebrew term nor a Greek term—piety is—but is religion the same as piety? But let us not be, or appear to be, pedantic. Let us say, as we are entitled to say by the[4] Western tradition, that religion is all human concern with a personal God, with a God who thinks and wills and is concerned with man, with every man, or to use a current felicitous[5] phrase, who is a Thou.

5. As for the political philosophy in the title of my lecture, I have made its meaning sufficiently clear for our present purpose[6] by speaking of the

tradition of political philosophy; it is something which is not exactly thriving in our age—not in spite but because of the fact that the word is more frequently used today than it was ever in the past. (Cf. "historic event" = events which make headlines today but prove to be utterly irrelevant the next year or at best next year)

6. Yet: the present discussions are *based*, whether the discussants are aware of it or not, on political philosophy—this is true especially of the *liberal* position: the liberal position is based not on *religion* (Jewish *or* Christian) *but* on the unassisted human mind alone—and hence philosophy.

[2] 7. One thing one can say while being reasonably certain that it will be permitted to pass by everyone is this: political philosophy emerged in Greece, and the classical document of Greek political philosophy is Aristotle's *Politics*. What do we learn from *Aristotle* on our subject? *Politics* VII (1328b): ἔργα essential to the πόλις—6 of them in ascending order—from food up to government—"fifth—first: the concern regarding the divine."

8. Implies: 1) no πόλις possible without religion, without *established* religion—*state*-religion obligatory for all citizens. Cf. EN V τὸ φύσει δίκαιον → sacrifice and prayer de iure naturali—

9. 2) This is πως πρῶτον: more necessary even than food (or higher even than human government)—but in other respects is *not* the first— τὸ θεῖον is merely higher than anything ἀνθρώπινον—but: this *kind* of concern (≠ *knowledge* of the divine) is *not* the highest nor the most fundamental—explained in Sefer lambda: the popular notions contain an element of truth—but: *additions* to pure truth "for the persuasion of the many and for the use in regard to the laws and useful"—the laws need a kind of superhuman support—they cannot be simply rational or reasonable (≠ τέχνη—*Politics* II on Hippodamus)—religion is *civil* religion—or: *civil* theology (≠ philosophic theology)

10. This view not peculiar to Aristotle—Cf. Plato (*Republic* and *Timaeus*): rule of *philosophers* (≠ rule of *priests*)—and all other classic philosophers—

11. The example: the case of Socrates—the charge—how interpreted by Plato: the gods worshiped by the city *are not*—Socrates did not *preach* that—and: he does not meet the charge—he somehow claims that he is *not* guilty as charged—that he is innocently condemned (his laughing remark to Apollodorus)—but he *is* guilty as charged: he cannot deny the πόλις the right to demand that νομίζειν—his *sole* reservation: he will not obey a ban of πόλις prohibiting him to *philosophize*—his justification: *Apollo* has *commanded* him to philosophize—but what did Apollo truly say?

12. Plato's attempt to solve the problem of harmonizing philosophy and πόλις—a) the philosopher-kings b) *Leges* 7: the cosmic gods ≠ the Olympian gods

13. But were there not *radicals* among the classical philosophers? *Liberals*? Some people say that they were—e.g. *agnostic* Protagoras—but: he did not engage in propagating this view—or Epicurus-Burke: "Boldness formerly was not the character of Atheists as such. They were even of a character nearly the reverse; they were formerly like the old Epicureans, rather an unenterprising race. But of late they are grown active, designing, turbulent, and seditious."

14. λάθε βιώσας—no political philosophy proper, for no public spiritedness.

15. Summary on classical political philosophy: no religion is true but some religion *any* religion is necessary—law and morality are insufficient for the large majority of men—obedience to the law and morality are insufficient for making men happy (the happiness of the wicked, the misery of the just): need for supplementation by divine reward and publishment—the *true* supplement is philosophy—but philosophy is essentially a preserve of the few: special φύσις required

16. Religion is not the work of philosophers but of founders-legislators—yet philosophy can, and should, influence or modify religion—while indispensable to πόλις, religion also creates *dangers* to πόλις—e.g. earthquakes etc. as omina → panics in armies (Cicero, *Republic* I)—or: generals at the battle of Arginusae (not the shipwrecked but the corpses)—no fighting on Sabbath—asylum to murderers [at temple] and altar—today: birth control

17. Yehuda Halevi: the philosophers (≠ religion) do not recognize a single rule of conduct which is universally valid—

18. Influence of philosophy on religion: fairly liberal religious policies in practice (cf. Pericles ~ Anaxagoras) but: no *legal* guarantee (= *freedom* of religion)

19. The danger is not the πόλις repressing religious freedom (this they do not even desire) but undue influence of religion or priests of πόλις—religious repression, i.e. uniformity is a *need—true* concern with the θεὶς is *knowledge* of the whole (≠ prayers and sacrifices)—gulf between philosopher and δῆμος: their τέλη differ—intermediate group between philosopher and δῆμος: the πεπαιδευμένοι, the gentlemen: *urban patrician* →[7]

[3] 20. A word on political *theology*—quid sit [the footnote attached to "quid sit" written below the page:] *one* particular religion is the *true* religion—Judaism: does not demand of all men to become Jews but only those born from a Jewish mother—Christianity: demands from all men but tolerates Jews with great disabilities—Islam: tolerates Jews and Christians with considerable civil disabilities—

21. Does the Jewish position entail recognition of the right to be *ir*religious:

חסיד אומות העולם[8]

They have a share in the world to come (=are saved)

(≠ nulla salus extra Ecclesiam)

22. Rambam: limits it to non-Jews who recognize and perform the 7 Noahide commandments *on the basis of Mosaic revelation*, i.e. Christians and Muslims—(≠ Pagans, including pagan philosophers)

23. Cf. Psalms 9: "The wicked shall be turned into hell, and all the nations that forget God ... Arise, O LORD – let not man prevail – let the heathen be judged in thy sight."

24. The fundamental difficulty from this basis: what is better, *no* religion or a *false* religion? Atheism or a living faith in Moloch?

25. The *true* religion is known as such only by revelation (≠ reason or nature) → no natural obligation to worship and to love God—Thomas Aquinas: not reason simply but reason informed by faith teaches that God should be loved and worshiped—

26. Thomas (≠ Aristotle): divine worship is *not* de iure naturali—for: natural theology (= natural *knowledge* of god's existence etc.) does not lead to the insight that God *alone* must be worshipped—(for: eternity of the world, the heavenly bodies—= cosmic gods)

27. Freedom of religion as a right, as it is recognized in the First Amendment is something specifically *modern*—especially in the interpretation according to which freedom of religion includes the freedom of *ir*religion. But is not freedom of religion in the *widest* meaning simply the right of the conscience, which includes the right of the *erring* conscience? a) "conscience" is not a *philosophic* conception but stems from Christian theology—hence does not belong to tradition of political philosophy—b) freedom of erring conscience ≠ freedom of the false religion = full legal right for it, including its propagation—and: one must entirely divorce the ecclesiastical teaching according to which the erring conscience *binds* (≠ gives rights) from consideration of ecclesiastical practice.

28. One can say however that freedom of religion is an *indirect* consequence of Reformation—religious wars etc. → toleration—also: certain *sects* from the very beginning—but this is not political *philosophy*—but *prior* to Reformation or at any rate independently of it, certain modifications of classical political philosophy—

29. Thomas More's *Utopia* (1516)—the established religion is *the* natural or rational religion—but everyone is free to add to it of his own—no one can be persecuted on the account of his religion, everyone may follow the religion which he likes except that no one who does not believe in the immortality of souls and in providence can be a citizen—nor may he defend his views in public coram vulgo (≠ priests, viri graves)—but no punishment for this—the public cult is uniform but does not violate anything peculiar to any man's private religion (e.g. no prayers which cannot be said by everyone) → the society united in and by *the* true religion of reason—tolerates additions to it but no subtraction

30. *Machiavelli*—public religion indispensable for *republics* but in absolute monarchy: the power of the prince may supply to the want of religion—an irreligious republic is impossible (→ Spinoza) → enlightened despotism: whose descendant is *Hobbes*.

[4] 31. The change effected by Machiavelli and Hobbes is fundamental; it concerns *the relation of philosophy and πόλις—*

32. a) scientia propter potentiam—the relief of man's estate → the τέλος of the philosopher and the δῆμος is identical ("comfortable self-preservation"[9])

33. b) the δῆμος can be *enlightened—diffusion* of scientific knowledge—science becomes a public *power*

34. The difficulty in Hobbes: danger of violent death as the greatest evil → peace at all costs → unqualified sovereignty, preferably absolute monarchy—religion owes its legal power *only* to the uncontrolled act of the sovereign—he can determine *which* religion is to be established as he sees fit—but: he can *dis*establish it—the Christian is obliged in his conscience to commit idolatrous and blasphemous acts if his sovereign so commands—but: the sovereign is not *obliged* to establish any public worship which as such is uniform—he *may* allow "many sorts of worship": in that case "It cannot be said that the commonwealth is of any religion at all"—→ an irreligious commonwealth is possible—an *atheistic* society is possible. Bayle, *Pensées Diverses*—1682 explicitly against the belief that comets are omena—8 reasons—the 7th[10] reason is the only *theological* reason: if comets were evil omens, God would have made miracles in order

to confirm *idolatry*—an objection: but God might have confirmed idolatry because it is greater [*sic*; recte: lesser] evil than atheism—response to that objection: atheism does not necessarily lead to immorality → *proof of possibility of atheistic society*—atheism is altogether innocent—the theological argument proper: taken from the analogy of *human* jealousy: the husband is less jealous if his wife does not love any man including himself than if she loves another man (God).

35. This epoch making event remained *subterraneous* until 19th century (especially socialism)—but the *visible* thing—[11] the teachings of enlightenment of the philosophers: multiplication of sects (—toleration, Dutch example) plus economics (= this worldly goals to be preferred to those of the other world)—the greatest political philosophers do not go as far as Hobbes-Bayle: Locke (toleration excludes Catholics, atheists), Spinoza (the 7 dogmas—but liberty of interpretation—e.g. God exists = matter exists), JJ: religion civile

36. John Stuart Mill—perfect freedom in theory—what about practice? What about *his* practice? *Autobiography* 32, 34. 36, 37, 240

37. *The* issue: does the commonwealth require religion for its wellbeing and may it therefore legitimately demand from every citizen that he has some religion, or that he believes in God *or* can an atheistic society be a good society?

38. An atheist society—"[12]society in which no public (governmental) act and no publicly supported act has any reference whatever to God (cf. USSR) or in which no man suffers from any politically relevant discrimination (≠ legal discrimination) on the ground of his professed atheism"

39. What is uppermost in our minds is the question of American constitutional law—the correct interpretation of the First Amendment—does the freedom of religion mean freedom for *all* religions but only for them—or does it give freedom *from* all religion? I believe that it is impossible to settle this legal question if we do not settle first the *theoretical* question, the discussion of which we begin tonight.

Notes

1. Leo Strauss Papers, box 18, folder 13, Special Collections Research Center, University of Chicago Library.

2. In many cases, it is impossible to say with confidence where a new paragraph begins and ends in the ms. and the editors had to rely on their fallible judgment. The important point is that Strauss did not, unlike many of his other mss., number his paragraphs, hence the division of the text into paragraphs does not seem to be crucial.

3. "awaken" is crossed out and replaced with "revive."

4. In the ms. "our" is crossed out and replaced with "the."

5. The term "felicitous" is difficult to read.

6. "for our present purpose" is added over the sentence.

7. An illegible word after the arrow is crossed out.

8. In "ḥasidei ummot ha'olam," the first word "ḥasidei" (the pious, righteous) is underlined.

9. The closing quotation mark is not in the ms.

10. "7" is underlined.

11. The dash seems to mean "is."

12. The opening quotation mark is illegible but it seems to be necessary from the closing quotation mark. Strauss seems to be giving a definition of the atheistic society.

NATHAN TARCOV

Interpretative Essay

LEO STRAUSS ON RELIGION
AND THE COMMONWEAL

I WILL DISCUSS A PRACTICALLY UNKNOWN TEXT, a talk Strauss gave as part of a series on "Religion and the Commonweal" at the Hillel Foundation at the University of Chicago on January 27, 1963, rather than any of the well-known texts of Strauss on the relation of religion and philosophy.[1] This lecture by Strauss focuses not directly on the relation between religion and *philosophy* but on the relation between religion and *politics*, an issue Strauss rarely dealt with thematically. Strauss's lifelong concern with what he called "the theologico-political problem" was *not* primarily concerned, as one might expect from that phrase, with the relation between theology and politics but rather with the relation between theology *and philosophy*, or between faith in revelation and unassisted human reason. One might be tempted to ask why he did not therefore call it instead "the theologico-*philosophical* problem." It would seem he preferred to call it "the theologico-*political* problem" because he saw the connection between theology or religion *and politics* as so close that philosophic questioning of the gods of the city put philosophy at odds with both religion and the political community, facing a challenge that was both theological and political. Furthermore, philosophy had to deal with the theoretical and existential challenge of revelation by understanding revelation or religion *politically*. But if the premise of this view is the close connection between religion and the political community or commonweal, then examining that relation and considering whether religion *is* essential to the political community becomes crucial. And so I turn to that talk Strauss gave on that issue.

Strauss's talk starts with a tribute to his friend Rabbi Maurice Pekarsky. Rabbi Pekarsky, the director of the Hillel Foundation who had brought Strauss to speak there numerous times, died in 1962 and the series of which Strauss's lecture was a part was dedicated to him. Strauss's homage to the memory of Rabbi Pekarsky expresses Strauss's stance toward Jewish piety and is worth quoting from at some length:

> The soul and substance of Rabbi Pekarsky were Jewish piety, simple old-fashioned, chaste, Jewish piety. He dedicated his life to keeping alive this holy fire or to revive it. He knew very well how difficult this task was in the middle of the twentieth-century, especially at a university like ours. He acted in this difficult situation with singular tact and prudence. He did not protest against those who tried to reduce Judaism to social ethics on the one hand, and to an ethnic culture on the other, since both parties retain a part, however small, of the ancient truth and since their very antagonism, the antagonism between the universal and the particular, points to the full truth: the chosen people, the people chosen to be witness of justice. He did not rebuff, nay he attracted those who were not as blessed as he was, who had not succeeded in finding a way of reconciling the old piety and the new science, for he was united with them in love of truth. This was indeed the limit of his tolerance and forbearance.

Finally, Strauss adds that he knows Rabbi Pekarsky approved the effort "to explore how one can secure by human means the future of religion without infringing on the rights of man."

Although Strauss here rejects the reduction of Judaism to either *universal* social ethics or a *particular* ethnic culture, he sees those opposed reductions as an expression of the tension between the *universal* message of Judaism and the *particular* people chosen to witness it. Thus Strauss's homage to his pious friend may serve as a gloss to the striking passage in Strauss's 1962 preface to *Spinoza's Critique of Religion* in which he wrote that "it looks as if the Jewish people were the chosen people in the sense, at least that the Jewish problem is the most manifest symbol of the human problem as a social or political problem," indicating that problem may be understood as the tension between the *universal* aspirations of *thought* whether *religious or philosophic* and the *particular* character of political life.[2] (In paragraph 3 Strauss says "government, the commonweal, is necessarily particular; religion is, at least according to its intention, universal, embracing all men.") I assume Strauss counted himself among those who were "not as blessed" as Rabbi Pekarsky was, those who had "not succeeded in finding a way of reconciling the old piety and the new science," but he declared that the pious rabbi and the scientist or philosopher were united in their love of truth despite the different ways they attempted to understand and access truth.

After this striking homage to his pious friend, Strauss started the lecture itself by declaring that he approached the subject of religion and the commonweal "as a social scientist," who as such is sworn to pronounce unpleasant truths. He delineates his subject more precisely as "what *the tradition of political philosophy* teaches regarding religion and the commonweal," which appears from this and from Anastaplo's introduction to be the title of Strauss's lecture. Since Strauss thus approaches the issue of the relation between religion and politics from the standpoint of political philosophy or at least from that of a student or historian of the tradition of political philosophy, his lecture necessarily but indirectly also engages the relation of philosophy to both religion and politics. He defines religion according to the Western tradition as "every human concern with a personal god, with a god who thinks and wills and is concerned with man, with every man." Thus he excludes from religion in the sense he is discussing, for example, concern with a god like that of Aristotle's *Metaphysics* and similar natural theologies concerned with an impersonal god unconcerned with human beings. Strauss claims that all present-day discussions for instance of the question of religion and the commonweal, whether the discussants know it or not, especially the liberal position, are based on political philosophy, on the unassisted human mind, and hence on philosophy, not on religion.

Since Strauss approaches the issue through what he calls the *tradition* of political philosophy, his approach is largely chronological. He starts with Aristotle's *Politics*, in particular with Aristotle's odd remark that among the necessary parts of the polis "the concern regarding the divine" is "fifth and first." Aristotle does not say why he calls it both fifth and first or make explicit what the numbering of the parts indicates, though the sixth and last named, deciding about the advantageous and the just, is called most necessary. Strauss asserts that by calling the city's concern with the divine a necessary part of the polis Aristotle means that "no commonweal or city is possible without religion, without established religion, a state religion obligatory on all citizens," which Strauss says may also be called civil religion, political religion, or civil theology as distinguished from the true philosophic theology. Strauss further contends that the concern with the divine is called *first* because it is more necessary even than food and higher even than the government. But in another respect, although the divine is higher than the human, the political concern with the divine is not concern with *knowledge* of the divine, which according to Aristotle is the highest human pursuit. Strauss notes that the popular notions regarding the gods underlying public established religion, according to a passage in Aristotle's *Metaphysics,* are only for the persuasion of the many and for use in regard to the laws and the politically useful. In support of his claim that an established religion is necessary for the polis, Strauss adduces the passage in the discussion of natural right in the *Nicomachean Ethics* where Aristotle says that sacrificing (and Strauss adds therefore praying) belongs to natural right, although what should be sacrificed belongs to legal or conventional right (see the manuscript regarding these points).

The final piece of evidence Strauss adduces in support of his claim that Aristotle views an established religion as necessary to the polis appears to refer to Aristotle's critique of Hippodamus's proposal for honoring those who propose changes to the laws in book 2 of the *Politics*, where Aristotle argues that, unlike the arts, laws depend for their force on habit and so should not be lightly changed or even improved. Aristotle leaves it at that but Strauss adds something Aristotle does not say there: "Laws owe their validity decisively to custom, to habituation, not to their intrinsic rationality, and therefore they need another support, *a superhuman support*." Strauss seems eager to strengthen the case for attributing to Aristotle a teaching of the necessity for an established or civil religion.

For some reason, Strauss starts with Aristotle and only after that turns to Plato. He begins by inferring from Plato's *Timaeus* that the rule of the philosopher-kings in Plato's *Republic* is meant to take the place of rule by priests. Strauss says no more and does not explain exactly how this shows that Plato shares Aristotle's teaching of the necessity of a civil religion. I presume he means that the philosophers would rule through a civil religion although a different one from that of the priests. Perhaps he had in mind the theology of book 2 of the *Republic*, although the theology of book 2 is introduced *before* the introduction of rule by philosophers in book 5. In arguing that civil religion is a teaching of *all* classical philosophers, Strauss points out that in Plato's *Apology* although Socrates was guilty of not believing in the gods of the city, he does not deny to the city the right to demand that every citizen believe in the existence of the gods of the city. Strauss says that Plato solved the problem shown by Socrates's fate, that a philosopher as such cannot believe in the gods worshiped by the city of Athens, and philosophy and the city are incompatible, in the tenth book of the *Laws* where he shows the proper legislation regarding religion would be to demand from every citizen the rational belief in those gods whose existence can be demonstrated: the heavenly bodies, which Plato thought were animate beings.

Strauss concludes his discussion of the view of the issue of religion and commonweal *implied* (he does not say stated) by the classical political philosophers as follows: "[N]o religion is *true*, but *some* religion, *any* religion is politically necessary. Law and morality are insufficient for the large majority of men. Obedience to the law and the moral rules is insufficient for making men happy ... are therefore in need of being *supplemented* by divine rewards and punishments. The *true* supplement to law and morality is, however, philosophy, but philosophy is essentially the preserve of very few men."

Given Strauss's general respect and sympathy for what he calls classical political philosophy, one can hardly help asking whether Strauss agrees with the view of religion and the commonwealth he attributes to the classical political philosophers. Strauss does not explicitly state such an agreement in this lecture. The closest he comes to doing so that I can think of is in the chapter on "The Law of Reason in the *Kuzari*" in *Persecution and the Art of Writing*, where he writes, "To deny that religion is essential to society is difficult for a man of Halevi's piety, and, we venture to add, for *anyone who puts any trust in the accumulated experience of the human race.*" Apart from whether Strauss could in some sense share in Halevi's piety, we may venture to ask how much trust Strauss put in "the accumulated experience of the human race." Even if the answer to the historical question is that every society that has long endured in the past has had some religion, that would not unequivocally prove the necessity of religion and resolve what Strauss calls in that passage "the *philosophic* question of the basis of any and every society." The presence of *some religion* in enduring societies would also fall short of proving the view he attributes to Aristotle in this lecture, that "no commonweal or city is possible without *established* religion, a *state* religion obligatory on all citizens." Strauss refers numerous times later in the lecture and the ensuing discussion period to the First Amendment to the Constitution of the United States of America, which expressly forbids Congress from passing any law respecting an establishment of religion or abridging its free exercise.

Interpretative Essay

Strauss adds that the classical political philosophers did not believe philosophers could found a religion; instead, they had to accept the existing religions, though they could affect or modify the religion of their society. For even though they regarded religion as indispensable to the city, they recognized that religion or priests could sometimes be dangerous to society by interfering with prudent political or military action. Thus, there is a tension between theology and politics as well as one between theology and philosophy, and philosophy can drive a wedge between theology or religion and politics so as not to face a united adversary. Strauss suggests that philosophy contributed to the fairly liberal religious practice in Athens and Rome, though it fell short of religious freedom. Strauss suggests that the influence of philosophy in those cases, an influence exercised across what he calls "the gulf between the philosophers and non-philosophers, whom they called the demos, the common people," was owing to the existence of an intermediate group, the educated people or gentlemen, who had come under the influence of philosophers, in practice a commercial urban patriciate. Strauss remarks here that "the history of philosophy, viewed from the point of view of mere sociology of philosophy, is to a large extent the history of a commercial patriciate." This echoes his earlier statement in *Natural Right and History* that "it is an experience of many centuries in greatly different natural and moral climates that there was one and only one class which was habitually sympathetic to philosophy ... and this was the urban patriciate."[3] Classical political philosophers were "radically illiberal": they were concerned with particular dangers religion posed to the commonweal; they were not concerned with freedom of religion or of irreligion or opposed to the establishment of religion. This may be one of the unpleasant truths Strauss pronounces.

Strauss then distinguishes political philosophy from political theology, by which he means teachings based on divine revelation, including teachings about religious toleration, before continuing with his theme of the teachings of the tradition of political philosophy. He shows that Jewish, Christian, and Muslim political theology limited toleration in various ways and did not recognize a right to be irreligious. This may be another of the unpleasant truths Strauss pronounces.

Finally, Strauss turns to modern political philosophy. He declares that freedom of religion *as a right* is specifically modern, especially in the interpretation that includes freedom of irreligion. Freedom *of conscience*, which includes the erring conscience and therefore in principle atheism, however, stems from Christian theology and does not belong to the tradition of political philosophy.

Machiavelli made a considerable change in the traditional doctrine regarding religion and the commonweal. He taught that a public religion is indispensable for republics but in absolute monarchy the strong arm of the prince can supply what religion otherwise provides. Alluding to Francis Bacon, Strauss notes that a change took place in the relation of philosophy and the commonweal: first, science or philosophy is not for its own sake but for the sake of power so the ends of the philosophers and the nonphilosophers are the same. There is no longer that gulf between them that existed in classical political philosophy. And, second, the nonphilosophers can become enlightened so that science or philosophy becomes a public power.

Thomas Hobbes for the sake of peace and the avoidance of violent death insisted on unqualified sovereignty. His sovereign may establish or disestablish any religion he pleases, but is not obliged to establish any religion, in which case Hobbes writes, "it cannot be said that the commonwealth is of any religion at all." Strauss restates this bluntly as "an atheistic society is possible," and comments that "this is one of the greatest events in the history of thought proper." Strauss adds that shortly afterward Pierre Bayle attempted to prove the possibility of an atheistic society.

Strauss notes, however, that this epoch-making event did not in any way affect public policy or public discussions until the nineteenth century. John Locke, Baruch Spinoza, and Jean-Jacques Rousseau did not go as far as Hobbes and Bayle. Locke argued for toleration but excluded atheists and Catholics. Spinoza insisted on a state religion. Rousseau demanded a civil religion. Even John Stuart Mill, Strauss notes, who had no religious belief, could not publicly avow that.

Finally, Strauss summarizes the issue as follows. "Does the commonwealth require religion for its well-being, and may it therefore legitimately demand from every citizen that he has *some* religion, that he believes in God? Or can an atheistic society be a good society?" By an atheistic society he meant one where no public governmental act has any reference to God as in the Soviet Union or no one suffers from any political disability for his professed atheism. Strauss then shifts to a question of American constitutional law, does the freedom of religion protected by the First Amendment mean freedom only for all *religions* without identifying the state with any particular religion or does it give an equal freedom *from* all religion? He declares it cannot be settled without settling the theoretical question he addressed in the lecture of the basis of society, whether it depends on religion or whether an atheistic society can be a good society.

Strauss's lecture was followed by a lively discussion. I cannot go into every point that was raised, but I should mention that Strauss makes clear that the establishment of any one particular religion or even Christianity in general would be out of the question in the United States and incompatible with any liberal state. Strauss was asked about the possibility of a reconciliation between the philosophic view and the religious view. He conceded the possibility of *practical* reconciliation, practical forbearance, but not a theoretical reconciliation. With a nod to Thomas Aquinas, Strauss admits that the key controversy is the following: "Is the sphere of philosophy so essentially incomplete, while being autonomous in itself, that it points toward its completion in revelation?" Strauss responds, "all proof of the defects of philosophy ... are of no great help if you do not get the supplement ... accessible only on the basis of faith."

Notes

1. This essay is a revised version of a talk given at a conference on Leo Strauss on religion and philosophy organized by Raimondo Cubeddu and Marco Menon at the University of Pisa, November 18, 2017, on the occasion of the publication of Leo Strauss, *Scritti su filosofia e religion,* ed. Raimondo Cubeddu and Marco Menon (Pisa: Edizioni ETS, 2017), a collection of Strauss's writings on that subject translated by Marco Menon.

2. Leo Strauss, *Spinoza's Critique of Religion,* trans. E. M. Sinclair (Chicago: University of Chicago Press, 1965), 6.

3. Leo Strauss, *Natural Right and History* (Chicago: University of Chicago Press, 1953), 143.

PHILIPP VON WUSSOW

Interpretative Essay

LEO STRAUSS ON CIVIL RELIGION

IT IS NOTORIOUSLY DIFFICULT for Strauss scholars to determine where he stands. Strauss speaks to all sides in debates on religion and politics, but he rarely states his own position. His uncanny ability to mimic the voices of others—even those he despised—often makes it difficult to identify his own voice in the text.[1] The 1963 lecture "Religion and the Commonweal," a survey of civil religion in the tradition of political philosophy, is no exception. Strauss appears to favor some version of civil religion and bemoan its demise, but he does not seem to state his own position on civil religion. We are on safe ground if we assume that we initially do not know where he stands.

Does Strauss argue for a renewal of civic religion as a counterbalance to the corrosive effects of modern democracy? At least a few remarks, both in the lecture and in the subsequent discussion, suggest otherwise. Does he even advocate for an authoritarian theo-political order to control the masses, as a certain subsection of Strauss scholarship argues? Strauss does not claim that philosophers could found a religious or political order. Rather they find this order and have to "accept it." To the extent they can seek to "affect or modify" it, the modification occurs solely by philosophical means (297).[2]

Other reservations against an unqualified embrace of civil religion are not as easily visible. To come to a more precise understanding of Strauss's intention, it is crucial to face a certain ambiguity in his stance on civil religion. The place in the lecture where this ambiguity is best visible is the juxtaposition of two different views on the relation of religion and politics, designated as *political philosophy* and *political theology*. Whereas political philosophy is the view in favor of civil religion, political theology represents the theological objection—the passionate reaction to the indifference of civil religion to the truth of religion. Both views are well documented in Strauss's oeuvre and can be said to be genuinely his own.

Precedents

The topic of civil religion is not without precedent in Strauss's writings. In his first book *Die Religions-Kritik Spinozas* (1930) he explicates the Averroist view that "civil government, which regulates and supervises only external human actions, is not in itself sufficient for orderly corporate life within society. Religion is a regulator of order in social life. It bears on the life of the populace. It is not a necessary and spontaneous product of the life of the many, but a code of law prescribed for the many by higher intelligences (prophets). Religion is not by nature but by institution."[3] Strauss contrasts this major line of philosophical thinking on religion to the Epicurean view, which sought to abandon religion for the sake of tranquility.[4]

The most extensive written discussion of civil religion, or "the religion of the philosophers," prior to the lecture occurs in his article "The Law of Reason in the *Kuzari*" (1943), which later became the fourth chapter of *Persecution and the Art of Writing*. Judah Halevi's *Kuzari*, a great work of medieval Spanish Jewish thought, is devised as a defense of Judaism against philosophy. The dialogue between the Khazar king and a Jewish scholar leads to the conversion of the king and his entire nation to Judaism.

In his interpretation Strauss explicates the difference between rational law and revealed law—a topic that reveals a deep ambiguity in the notion of civil religion. Rational law, or rational *nomoi*, may refer to the philosopher's law or to political law. Whereas the political law is binding for all men, the philosophical *nomoi* are set up with regard to the needs of man as man but are not obligatory.[5] Strauss explains how Halevi uses the term "rational *nomoi*" for two different things and why he chooses to retain the ambiguity that could easily have been avoided. As he recounts, Halevi understood that the religion of the philosophers is actually "governmental." The philosopher, a lover of truth, proposes a teaching he must consider untrue—an exoteric teaching that serves to govern the lower by the higher.[6] Halevi contrasts these rational *nomoi*, which are of human origin, with the *nomos* that originates in divine knowledge.[7] In another mention, the rational *nomoi* are said to be known independently of divine knowledge as regards the general rules, but not as regards their measure.[8] In any case, for Halevi "even a merely governmental code, if it is to be good for the community, must be the work of revelation. [...] We are driven to the conclusion that no society which is not ruled by a revealed code, can last, or, that not only religion, but revealed religion, is essential for the lasting of any society."[9]

This view is apt for Halevi's figure of the Jewish scholar, for whom "only the Jewish nation is eternal, all other nations are perishable."[10] It is contrasted by the philosophical view: "The philosopher has no attachment to society: his soul is elsewhere. Accordingly, the philosopher's rules of social conduct do not go beyond the minimum moral requirements of living together." The rules are not obligatory and "only hypothetically valid."[11] According to Strauss, the principal argument between Judaism and philosophy in the *Kuzari* exposes the fundamental weakness of the philosophical position and provides that law must be revealed law. Halevi's defense of Judaism against philosophy defends "morality itself and therewith the cause, not only of Judaism, but of mankind at large."[12]

In his lecture Strauss mentions Judah Halevi's position on philosophy in passing (298). The philosophical view described here resembles Strauss's own position on the validity of rules in the fourth chapter of *Natural Right and History*.[13] But Strauss also retains the key distinction between the two views in his lecture, rephrasing them as political theology and political philosophy. Again, we do not know where he stands, but we have reason to believe he was far more interested in the conflict than in a proper solution.

Another major reference in Strauss's understanding of civil religion is Jean-Jacques Rousseau, who coined the term in the second to last chapter of his *Contrat Social*. Rousseau understands civil religion in purely political terms: "It is a kind of theocracy, in which there ought to be no pontiff but the Prince, no other priests than the magistrates." Rousseau notices that civil religion was "based on error and falsehood, it deceives men, renders them credulous and superstitious, and obscures the true worship of the Deity with superficial rituals,"[14] but he is uninterested in the truth of religion. His concern is with a proper foundation of the state, which requires "that every citizen should have a religion which may make him delight in his duties" without specifying the dogmas of this religion. "There is, therefore, a purely civil profession of faith, the articles of which it is the duty of the sovereign to determine, not exactly as dogmas of religion, but as sentiments of sociability, without which it is impossible to be a good citizen or a faithful subject."[15]

This position is not altogether different from what Spinoza had demanded in chapter 14 of the *Theologico-Political Treatise*. But Spinoza had moved from theological and biblical analyses toward the political function of religion, showing that revelation is compatible with democracy and freedom. Rousseau moves from politics to theology. He asks first which beliefs are necessary for a republic and then provides them with a theological garb.[16] Spinoza outlines the theological minimum of the faith of the people, who may otherwise believe whatever they want. Rousseau outlines this minimum without recourse to theology, and only with regard to its social usefulness: "Without having power to compel any one to believe them, the sovereign may banish from the State whoever does not believe them; it may banish him not as impious, but as unsociable, as incapable of sincerely loving the law, justice and of sacrificing, if need be, his life to his duty. But if any one, after publicly acknowledging these dogmas, behaves like an unbeliever in them, he should be punished with death; he has committed the greatest of crimes, he has lied before the laws."[17]

Strauss briefly mentions religion "considered merely as a social bond" in his article "On the Intention of Rousseau" (1947), at a key place in the text, albeit only to illustrate a point on the relation of philosophy and society.[18] In his Rousseau seminar in 1962, an immediate precursor to the talk at the Hillel House, civil religion is front and center. Strauss describes how Rousseau became a source both for the "worship of Reason" in the French Revolution and for liberal democracy,[19] but he strongly emphasizes his ties to the tradition of political philosophy. This strategy is still visible in his lecture, where he appears to downplay the totalitarian implications of Rousseau's view on religion. As he maintains, Rousseau is "only the last relic [...] of the older view" (305), and he discounts the extent to which Rousseau also radicalized this older view.

Reservations

Given that the theme was already well established in Strauss's published work, it is crucial to see how it relates to another great theme, namely, the conflict (and possible agreement) of Athens and Jerusalem. He had maintained early on that the alternative of divine guidance or human guidance was not only the most important topic of philosophy but also the most serious question of humankind.[20] When the topic reappeared in his thought in the late 1940s it often took on the form of self-assurance.[21] Strauss had chosen the philosophical life and opted against the life of obedience to God, but he could never make sure that the choice was right. He also could not return to Judaism, although he outlined the epistemic possibility of returning more than any other twentieth-century thinker.[22] This dilemma is at the bottom of the quest to explore the conflict between Jerusalem and Athens.

Compared to this strain of thought, one can hardly avoid the impression that Strauss does not speak his mind when talking about civil religion. Does he mimic the social scientist to bury a conflict in his own stance on religion? In any case, the proposition that religion is necessary for the well-being of society is, at best, the exoteric teaching on religion. Following Strauss's outline of civil religion in *Persecution and the Art of Writing*, the 1962 lecture constitutes his exoteric speech on the political necessity of religion: "A man who has become a philosopher, may adhere in his deeds and speeches to a religion to which he does not adhere in his thoughts."[23] But the burden of proof that Strauss practices exotericism is high, and theories that would support the suspicion may be misleading.

There are other reasons why we cannot leave it at that. According to Strauss's own words, the teaching of civil religion is essentially untrue, even as it may be useful for society; but he is genuinely concerned with the truth of religion. Does Strauss simply accept the degradation of religion to its political function? Furthermore, modern advocates of civil religion tend to downplay the theological details. As they maintain, a few basic "beliefs" without the specifics of each particular religion would be best for the well-being of society. Strauss knew of this sentiment. He mentions John Dewey several times in his lecture to evoke laughter from his audience. Dewey, who proposed some sort of religiosity as a healthy median position between the belief in a personal God and atheism (*A Common Faith*, 1933), marks the utmost depravation of religion. The problem with this sort of religiosity is always the same: none of its beliefs are rooted in a tradition of unconditional authority, and hence it is not binding (unless it is also provided with political or clerical power).

Strauss's contempt for this all-too-human understanding of religion is well documented. He had written in his first publication against the abolishment of God in Martin Buber's *Addresses on Judaism*.[24] His semi-autobiographical preface to the English translation of his Spinoza book, written in the second half of 1962, strongly emphasizes divine revelation as a theological key concept.[25] Here he also reiterates his early commitment to biblical atheism[26]—a strain of thought that is utterly incompatible with civil religion. In his *Thoughts on Machiavelli* he addresses the theological objection to civil religion most directly. He cites a predominant view, according to which "Machiavelli was a friend of religion because he stressed the useful and the indispensable character of religion." In reality, however, "his praise of religion is only the reverse side of what one might provisionally call his complete indifference to the truth of religion."[27] The concern with the truth of religion provides the antidote to an unqualified embrace of civil religion.

In this lecture Strauss opens up this line of thought when he asks bluntly: "What is better: no religion or a false religion?" (300). At this point he seeks to explore the view of political theology "in contradistinction to political philosophy" (300). The generic term "political theology" as employed here clearly corresponds to what Strauss famously called the "theological-political problem."[28] Hence there are two different answers to the question: for political theology, no religion is better than a false religion; but for civil religion, any religion will do. Strauss appears to prop up the view of civil religion against political theology, pointing out that it does not demand to worship God alone (300–1). How does this view match with the assertion in the subsequent discussion that "if it is a religion, it is surely a belief in a providential god"? (309).

It seems as if a political or sociological view and a philosophical *or* theological view on religion exist side by side in the lecture. But in matters of gravest concern, two diametrically opposed views cannot just coexist peacefully side by side. There must be some link between the two different views on religion—or at least there must be some argument as to why the conflict cannot be resolved. Strauss alludes to a partial solution in the discussion, stating that there can only be a "practical reconciliation," but no "theoretical reconciliation," between the two views that no religion is true and that only one religion is the true religion (313). But he closes the lecture with the remark that "the theoretical question" must be settled before the legal question can be settled. On a theoretical level, neither a solution nor a nonsolution is viable. This suspicion is further confirmed by some of Strauss's initial remarks.

How to Begin

Strauss often begins his articles and lectures by outlining how he plans to approach his subject. These remarks seem too marginal and almost trivial to catch the attention of most readers, but they are indispensable for a proper understanding of the argument. A typical element of these introductory remarks is a brief discussion of "culture"—a theme that pops up in various writings, mostly at the beginning and without much elaboration, but serves as a gateway to the things that matter. In particular, they lead to what Strauss called the "theological-political problem." Scholars have treated this phrase as a key to Strauss's thought, but it has remained somewhat enigmatic. The present lecture helps to both narrow and broaden our understanding. In the first place, the theological-political problem is the problem of the relation of religion and politics. Religion and politics—the "two poles of life"—are diametrically opposed and inseparably intertwined. The relation of religion and politics, Strauss suggests, is obfuscated by an inconspicuous third, namely, by the notion of "culture." First and foremost, then, the theologico-political problem is the problem of how religion and politics cannot be understood in terms of "culture."

Strauss is not always very clear about the way in which culture, or the cultural understanding of politics and religion, makes their respective claims incomprehensible. His lecture is no exception here. Strauss speaks of politics, government, and the commonweal almost interchangeably. This is in part due to the terminology of the Voltaire quote at the beginning: "He who doesn't dare to look straight at the two poles of life, religion and government, is only a coward." It is in part due to the topic of the lecture series, Religion and the Commonweal. Hence Strauss speaks of politics and religion *or* of government and religion, almost as if politics and government were the same. But in the main distinction of government and religion, government cannot be substituted by politics: "government, the commonweal, is necessarily particular, religion is, at least according to its intention, universal, embracing all men" (292).

The same cannot be said about politics and religion, for at least in some respect, politics concern all men.[29] Government may be particular as far as it concerns a particular group of people, but it raises a claim to regulate all human affairs according to Strauss's own view. On the other hand, religion may be universal according to its own intention, but it must eventually come to terms with its particularity as *a* religion. Each religion raises a claim to universality, but each claim to universality is refuted by the fact that there are other religions, each raising a claim to universality in its own right.

Interpretative Essay

The distinction between the particularism of politics and the universalism of religion does not seem to last. It appears to fade away once Strauss explains his objection to the notion of culture: "If we look at everything from the point of view of culture, we forget the universal, because culture is something used in the plural; we forget the universal, the truly human, for culture as the term is now used is essentially particular" (292). Strauss still has the reader confused at this point. One cannot overlook that the objection applies to politics as well as to religion, both of which cannot be properly understood "from the point of view of culture." Universalism and particularism are inseparably intertwined.

Furthermore, "culture" had not always been used in the plural. This usage (*a* culture) largely emerged during the 1930s in the field of cultural anthropology, and Strauss often pointed out how the older notion of culture, stemming from German philosophy, still reverberated in these more recent usages.[30] According to *Philosophy and Law* the problem with culture is not its particularism. The objection here is twofold: first, philosophy of culture understands by "culture" the spontaneous product of man, but religion—which has its basis in divine revelation—cannot be understood in this way. Second, philosophy of culture understands religion as a domain of truth among others, but religion raises a claim to universality. "The claim to universality on the part of 'culture,' which in its own view rests on spontaneous production, seems to be opposed by the claim to universality on the part of religion, which in its own view is not produced by man but *given* to him."[31] Strauss generalizes this claim to the extent that it also applies to "the fact of the political," hence opposing both religion and politics to culture: "'Religion' and 'politics' are *the* facts that transcend 'culture,' or, to speak more precisely, the original facts."[32]

After his 1935 book Strauss rehearsed these criticisms whenever he approached the conflict of religion and politics. While the arguments may seem repetitive, their function varies from text to text. Why, then, does Strauss insert the remarks on "culture" into his lecture? The new transcription of Strauss's prepared lecture notes shows that these words are not some offhand remarks. They were devised in advance as a bridge between the introduction of his subject matter and an explanation of the terms "religion" and "political philosophy." They serve to highlight the conflict between politics and religion, whereas "culture" had allegedly brought politics and religion into a false harmony. But why is it so important to reiterate these criticisms in a lecture on civil religion? In civil religion, it seems that the conflict has already been settled by integrating religion into the framework of politics.

It appears that the section has a specific function in the "action" of the lecture as opposed to the "argument." Strauss deliberately chooses to include a section on "culture" that does little as a theoretical argument. The section indicates that the conflict between religion and politics—"two *stern* and exacting things, as distinguished from culture" (292)—cannot be resolved. Civil religion, then, is a problem and not a solution. It may be useful for society, but it cannot account for the "two poles of life" of religion and politics.

Social Science and Judaism

Strauss explains that the concept of religion does not deserve the same scrutiny as the concept of culture, despite the fact that only Christianity is a religion in the strict sense. Judaism *became* a religion only in the nineteenth century,[33] being remodeled into a confession along the lines of Protestantism. Strauss knows these and other conceptual difficulties, but he maintains that questioning the term "religion" would be "pedantic." A simple, common-sense definition would be sufficient: "religion simply means every human concern with a personal god" (292).

Strauss indicates at the beginning that he will speak "as a social scientist" (291). This is not a matter of course for a lecture at the Hillel House in Chicago, an institution of Jewish outreach and Jewish learning. Strauss gave a number of talks at the same venue in which he spoke more directly as a Jew and with regard to Judaism ("Jerusalem and Athens," 1950; "Progress or Return?," 1952; "Freud on Moses and Monotheism," 1958; "Introduction to Maimonides' *The Guide of the Perplexed*," 1960; "Why We Remain Jews," 1962), albeit with similar occasional caveats.[34] These speeches on Jewish topics, addressed to a predominantly Jewish audience, may be said to be "esoteric," whereas the speech on the social science (or "political sociology," as Strauss called the approach in the discussion) of religion is "exoteric."

The statement may be somewhat tongue-in-cheek, but it is not merely ironic. Strauss indicates that he neither speaks as a philosopher nor simply as a Jew. He honors Judaism by not speaking about civil religion as a Jew. However, the prohibition is difficult to follow, and a few moments later Strauss asks his audience to forgive him for mentioning an example from Jewish history. He then continues to speak about Judaism, now without any disclaimer, while rephrasing a key statement on Judaism as a mere example of what he called "the three universal monotheistic religions" (299). Strauss then reiterates the Maimonidean notion that non-Jews who respect the seven Noahide commandments—but not the Jewish atheist—have a share in the world to come. Pagans are excluded, but there appears to be an exception for Aristotle, and hence possibly for philosophers in general, as Strauss hastens to add. The section holds an important clue to the overall lecture: Strauss honors the Jewish notion that an atheist cannot be a righteous man, but he seeks to carve out a niche for the philosopher.

As a social scientist, Strauss treats religion with regard to its social or political function. "Religion [...] is civil religion political religion, a part of the political establishment" (294). He takes his cues from Aristotle's statement that the concern with the divine is "fifth or first."[35] Religion is essential for the commonweal or the city, but it is not the highest human pursuit (293). Civil religion thus understood is incompatible with Judaism. Strauss's identification as a social scientist therefore serves to explicate the difference between the political treatment and the pious treatment of religion. Balancing social science and Judaism, Strauss shows that the deviation from the pious treatment must be respectful.

The brief section on Judaism creates an interlude between the sections on Greek and modern political philosophy, but it also serves to develop a broader argument as to "the burning question of our time" (299). Strauss introduces the view of political theology (i.e., on Judaism) expecting that "this becomes important later on" (300). The only place in the lecture where this becomes important later on is the closing section, where Strauss raises the legal issue of the freedom of irreligion. The link between the two sections of the lecture provides a clear answer: Judaism does not recognize a right to be irreligious. It is not immediately clear, though, what this means for the burning question of the time. What can be inferred from political theology to civil religion, or from the Jewish tradition to the future of religion in America?

Strauss's Argument

Historically speaking, the proposition that religion as civil religion "is a teaching of all classical philosophers" is a provocation. The great variety of philosophical positions on religion seems to prove otherwise.

Furthermore, even within the tradition of "civil religion" the exact positions on religion are vastly different. Strauss is certainly aware of the differences, but he chooses to disregard most of them and present a continuous line of tradition—from Plato and Aristotle to the medieval Islamic and Jewish Enlightenment and all the way to Niccolò Machiavelli, Spinoza, and Rousseau (and possibly Friedrich Nietzsche). This is not altogether surprising. Strauss understood that the tradition he spoke about was insufficiently known. As he declares, political philosophy "is something which is not precisely thriving in our age," despite the "inflation" of the term (292). The greatest challenge for his audience, though, was not political philosophy per se. Far less common was the treatment of religion in political philosophy, rather than in philosophy of religion. As Strauss states the view of political philosophy, "No religion is *true*, but *some* religion, *any* religion is politically necessary." Law and morality are insufficient for most people and must be supplemented by religion. The true supplement to law and morality is philosophy, but only a few people can be philosophers (297).

Strauss's assertion that civil religion, or the treatment of religion as civil religion, is the classical philosophical teaching on religion is open to a number of objections. At least initially, this teaching also appears to contradict itself, especially when it comes to the philosophers. Civil religion is not entirely true but nevertheless binding for everyone but the philosophers. Even philosophers must respect civil religion in one way or another, but they may indicate between the lines that they do not fully believe it. Can it be justified that only the philosophers should be exempt from accepting the premise, that is, from being religious? Strauss holds that the very ends of the philosophers and the nonphilosophers differ, so that the philosophers can have greater freedom than "anybody else" (299). But he cannot expect the city to honor this special place of the philosophers. At last, why do they require an exemption? Strauss emphasizes that the demands of civil religion only specify the minimum requirements of social life. Is it too much to demand from the philosopher, then, to adhere to the few basic beliefs of civil religion?

We may not go as far as to claim that Strauss could accept or embrace civil religion on the condition that he, as a philosopher, is exempt from its demands. Strauss did not count himself among the philosophers. Just as he wrote on Judah Halevi, he preferred to speak of philosophers as if he did not belong to them: "He presents himself as an interpreter of, or as a messenger from, the philosophers rather than as a philosopher."[36] The situation resembles Plato's *Republic*, in which philosophers should become kings but almost nobody—except for maybe one or two in every generation—can legitimately be called a philosopher.[37]

Strauss's concern with an exemption for the philosophers is striking, but it can only be understood on the basis of his claim that philosophers are atheists. However, even if *all* classical philosophers proposed some variation of civil religion, does that necessarily mean that all of them were atheists? Strauss himself changed his views in this respect over the course of his work, most notably on Maimonides. Is Maimonides the keeper of the Jewish faith, similar to what Thomas Aquinas is for Christianity, or is he a radical philosopher? And if he is both, what is the connection between the two unequal pursuits?[38]

Strauss had good reason to pass over most medieval philosophers here, who had a more complicated view on philosophy and religion. But even on the basis of antiquity, does the philosophers' embrace of civil religion mean in any case that they are atheists? Civil religion views religiosity as a social behavior, but is it in any case a *mere* social behavior without any religious substance? Strauss's own examples show mixed results. As he recounts Socrates's last words to Crito before his death, quoting from memory: "We have forgotten to bring a sacrifice to Asclepius. [...] Bring that sacrifice tomorrow" (294). Strauss recounts the story almost as a joke. The phrasing in Plato's *Phaedo*, however, also allows for the interpretation that Socrates's concern regarding the missed sacrifice was genuine.[39] But if making up for the missed sacrifice on the next day was of utmost importance to Socrates, what was so important about it when he no longer had to fear persecution?

Strauss recounts how, in the tenth book of the *Laws*, Plato sought to "solve that problem" demonstrated by the fate of Socrates (295). Book 10 of the *Laws* is notorious for the proposition that the profession of atheism will be punished by death. In his *The Argument and the Action of Plato's Laws* Strauss recounts this dialogue as if it describes the natural order of society, but he claims that it is incomplete. He pays great attention to a possible exception for the philosopher who may believe in the cosmic gods but not in the Olympian gods. Furthermore, he asked, "What happens to the atheist who is a just man and does not ridicule others because they sacrifice and pray and who to this extent is a dissembler?" As Strauss suspects, "He will become guilty if he frankly expresses his unbelief—but what if he expresses it only to sensible friends?"[40] In his lecture Strauss indicates that he consents to the solution of the *Laws* since Socrates would not have been sentenced to death. The bar for punishment is so high that the exemption almost becomes the norm (296).

Strauss largely omits the medieval Islamic and Jewish sources that had informed his view of civil religion. Instead he focused on Thomas More, Machiavelli, Thomas Hobbes, and Pierre Bayle while also briefly mentioning John Locke, Spinoza, and Rousseau. And whereas Rousseau was the last of the older tradition, Hobbes and Bayle announced the possibility of an openly atheistic society. Strauss locates the decisive break in the nineteenth century, especially in John Stuart Mill, who represents both the older view and the new understanding of unlimited freedom of irreligion (306-307).

Civil Religion in America

The sociological approach to religion was well established in American thought at the time, even though Robert Bellah's seminal article "Civil Religion in America" was published only in 1967. An unqualified embrace of civil religion would have amounted to little more than preaching to the choir.

Strauss posed the question at a time when the freedom from all religion was largely a matter of course in liberal democracies around the world. Religion was still enshrined in various constitutions, but atheists were no longer persecuted. As Strauss stated in the discussion after his lecture, "a *considerable* minority of the American people is no longer either Christian or Jewish in any religiously relevant sense" (311). Atheism was about to become the default setting for academics and intellectuals, and irreligious speech was covered by the right to free speech. Constitutional issues continued to arise when religious beliefs were at odds with secular beliefs (Strauss alludes to the issue of prayer in public schools [308]), but here religion was no longer the norm: the focus had begun to shift toward the persistence of religious beliefs and attitudes in a secular or atheist society.

But people had second thoughts. Was the freedom of religion, now including the freedom from all religion, a good thing? The increased freedom from oppressive religious institutions appeared to come with a decline in social coherence. A return to some variant of civil religion seemed like a way out. But can civil religion bring back the alleged social coherence of old once its lack of theological merit has been established? Can civil religion still maintain its social usefulness if it does not convey anything that could not be known without religion? And, most importantly, can one bring it back without imposing it, which would inevitably be at odds with the First Amendment? Western men lived in a double bind: they could not live without civil religion but they also could not reestablish it.

Strauss is well aware of these difficulties. As he rephrases the effort of the lecture series, the question is "how one can secure, by human means, the future of religion without infringing on the rights of man" (291). The Constitution certainly posed a limit on the future of civil religion in America. But that is hardly the only or even the most severe problem Strauss faces. He leaves open the question of whether an atheistic society could be a good society. He combines two vastly different definitions of an atheistic society, linking them by the inconspicuous word "or" as if they were the same. The first refers to a state without any reference to god, such as the Soviet Union, whereas the second refers to the lack of any political disability for the profession of atheism, as in liberal democracies (311). As a matter of course, the two are not the same. But Strauss saw that the future of religion was threatened by two political systems.

Civil religion, however, could do little to counter the corrosive effects of socialism and liberal democracy. And Strauss sees clearly how the theoretical question and the legal question are intertwined here. Asked in the discussion about the possibility of "a public ethics" in which society "decides" on certain goals, he replies with a plethora of references to cannibalism, socialism, and psychiatry, thereby suggesting that an atheistic society would lack a proper moral fundament (311–312). But he also alludes to the difficulties of "legitimately demand[ing] from each citizen that he has some religion" (327). He ends his lecture by stating that "first the theoretical question" must be settled before the legal question could be settled (307). But as he aptly demonstrates throughout the lecture, the theoretical question could not be settled.

Notes

1. Michael P. Zuckert and Catherine H. Zuckert, *Leo Strauss and the Problem of Political Philosophy* (Chicago: University of Chicago Press 2014), 228: "Rather than standing outside the author and offering an interpretation of his words supported by quotations, Strauss attempts to replicate the thought of the author and present it in the author's own voice. As a result, Strauss's restatement of the thought of the thinker he is interpreting is often taken to be a statement of Strauss's own thought."

2. All numbers in brackets refer to transcripts 7.1 and 7.2 in this volume.

3. Strauss, *Spinoza's Critique of Religion* (New York: Schocken 1965), 47.

4. As to Epicureanism, see also *Spinoza's Critique of Religion*, 29–30; *Philosophy and Law: Contributions to the Understanding of Maimonides and His Predecessors*, trans. Eve Adler (Albany: State University of New York Press, 1995), 35–37; "Die Religionskritik des Hobbes: Ein Beitrag zum Verständnis der Aufklärung," *Gesammelte Schriften*, vol. 3, ed. Heinrich/Wiebke Meier, 2nd ed. (Stuttgart/Weimar: Metzler 2008), 315–22; letter to Krüger, *Gesammelte Schriften*, vol. 3, 379–81.

5. Strauss, *Persecution and the Art of Writing* (Chicago: University of Chicago Press 1988), 116–17. When paraphrasing Strauss this article uses Strauss's terminology, including terms such as "man" and "mankind" that today may be considered as gender-biased.

6. Strauss, *Persecution and the Art of Writing*, 119–21.

7. Strauss, *Persecution and the Art of Writing*, 122.

8. Strauss, *Persecution and the Art of Writing*, 127.

9. Strauss, *Persecution and the Art of Writing*, 134.

10. Strauss, *Persecution and the Art of Writing*, 134.

11. Strauss, *Persecution and the Art of Writing*, 139.

12. Strauss, *Persecution and the Art of Writing*, 141.

13. Strauss, *Natural Right and History* (Chicago: University of Chicago Press, 1965), 156–64.

14. Jean-Jacques Rousseau, *The Social Contract and the First and Second Discourses*, ed. Susan Dunn (New Haven: Yale University Press 2002), 250.

15. Rousseau, *The Social Contract*, 252–53.

16. Steven Frankel and Martin D. Yaffe, eds., *Civil Religion in Modern Political Philosophy: Machiavelli to Tocqueville* (University Park: State University of Pennsylvania Press, 2020), introduction.

17. Rousseau, *The Social Contract and the First and Second Discourses*, 253.

18. Strauss, "On the Intention of Rousseau," *Social Research* 14, no. 4 (December 1947): 455–87: 461, cf. 483–84; see also *Natural Right and History*, 288–89.

19. Strauss, *Rousseau, Autumn 1962*, ed. Jonathan Marks, Leo Strauss Transcripts, https://leostrausscenter.uchicago.edu/rousseau-autumn-1962/, 317.

20. Strauss, *The Early Writings (1921–1932)*, ed. Michael Zank (Albany: State University of New York Press, 2002), 204.

21. See his personal note, written in 1946, quoted in Heinrich Meier, *Leo Strauss and the Theologico-Political Problem* (New York: Cambridge University Press 2006), 29n1; "Reason and Revelation," in Meier, *Leo Strauss and the Theologico-Political Problem*, 141–80; "'Jerusalem and Athens' (1950): Three Lectures Delivered at Hillel House, Chicago," ed. Laurenz Denker, Hannes Kerber, David Kretz, *Journal for the History of Modern Theology/Zeitschrift für neuere Theologiegeschichte* 29, no. 1 (2022): 133–73; "Jerusalem and Athens," in *Jewish Philosophy and the Crisis of Modernity: Essays and Lectures in Modern Jewish Thought*, ed. Kenneth Hart Green (Albany: State University of New York Press, 1997), 377–405.

22. Cf. Philipp von Wussow, "Leo Strauss on Returning: Some Methodological Aspects," *Philosophical Readings* 9 (2017): 1, 18–24.

23. Strauss, *Persecution and the Art of Writing*, 139.

24. Strauss, *The Early Writings*, 67. For particulars, see my chapter "Martin Buber and Leo Strauss: Notes on a Strained Relationship," in *Martin Buber: His Intellectual and Scholarly Legacy*, ed. Sam Berrin Shonkoff (Leiden: Brill 2018), 194–211.

25. Strauss, *Spinoza's Critique of Religion*, 8–13, 28–30.

26. Strauss, *Spinoza's Critique of Religion*, 30; cf. *Philosophy and Law*, 36–38.

27. Leo Strauss, *Thoughts on Machiavelli* (Chicago: University of Chicago Press, 1978), 12.

28. Strauss, "Preface to *Hobbes' Politische Wissenschaft*," in *Jewish Philosophy and the Crisis of Modernity*, 453. The term "political theology" is generic inasmuch as it neither follows Carl Schmitt (*Politische Theologie*, 1922) nor Varro and Saint Augustine's distinction of three kinds of theology (mythical, physical or natural, and political theology). "Political theology" in the sense of Varro and Saint Augustine is closer to civil religion than "natural theology." According to Saint Augustine's paraphrase of Varro, this is the kind of theology "which the people, and particularly the priests, in the cities ought to know and practice. It belongs to this theology to explain what gods should be worshiped in public and by what rites and sacrifices each one should do this." Whereas natural theology is suitable "for the world," political theology is suitable "for the city" (Saint Augustine, *The City of God, Books I-VII* [Washington, DC: Catholic University of America Press, 1962], 317). Strauss was aware of this terminological peculiarity. In his Rousseau seminar he reproduced the three theologies as poetic, civil, and philosophic, hence substituting civil theology for political theology and philosophical theology for physical or natural theology: "Poetic, that is what the poets say about the gods; civil, what the legislators teach; and the philosophic, what the philosophers teach [...]. Civil theology is the theology required for the existence and preservation of civil society." (Leo Strauss, *Rousseau, Autumn 1962*, 339.)

29. Strauss, "Notes on Carl Schmitt, The Concept of the Political," in Heinrich Meier, *Carl Schmitt & Leo Strauss: The Hidden Dialogue* (Chicago: University of Chicago Press, 1995), 91–119.

30. See Philipp von Wussow, *Leo Strauss and the Theopolitics of Culture* (Albany: State University of New York Press, 2020).

31. Leo Strauss, *Philosophy and Law*, 42.

32. Strauss, *Philosophy and Law*, 139n2.

33. Leora Batnitzky, *How Judaism Became a Religion: An Introduction to Modern Jewish Thought* (Princeton: Princeton University Press, 2011).

34. Strauss opened his lecture "Why We Remain Jews" with the claim that "my specialty is (to use a very broad and nonspecialist name) social science rather than divinity" (*Jewish Philosophy and the Crisis of Modernity*, 312). In "Jerusalem and Athens" (1950) he ventured that he would "speak here as a social

scientist," but he would "deviate" from the approach of most social scientists because they "would speak of two cultures" ("'Jerusalem and Athens' [1950]: Three Lectures Delivered at Hillel House," 136). Strauss did not use the persona of a social scientist in the other Hillel House lectures.

35. Aristotle, *Politics* 1289a20-23.

36. Strauss, *Persecution and the Art of Writing*, 113.

37. Plato, *Republic*, 473c-496d; cf. al-Farabi's *Book of the Opinions of the Inhabitants of the Virtuous City*, chapter 15, especially §13: "Now it is difficult to find all these qualities united in one man, and, therefore, men endowed with this nature will be found one at a time only, such men being altogether very rare." *Al-Farabi on the Perfect State*, ed. Richard Walzer (Oxford: Clarendon Press, 1985), 249.

38. Cf. *Leo Strauss on Maimonides: The Complete Writings*, ed. Kenneth Hart Green (Chicago: University of Chicago Press, 2013).

39. Plato, *Phaedo* 118a. Strauss briefly mentioned the phrase "We still owe Aesculapius a cock" in "On the *Euthyphron*," *The Rebirth of Classical Political Rationalism: An Introduction to the Thought of Leo Strauss*, ed. Thomas L. Pangle (Chicago: University of Chicago Press, 1989), 205.

40. Strauss, *The Argument and the Action of Plato's Laws* (Chicago: University of Chicago Press, 1975), 156.

Svetozar Y. Minkov

Appendix

STRAUSS'S CONFRONTATION WITH PASCAL

A VOLUME ON STRAUSS ON RELIGION would no doubt profit from a consideration of Strauss's study of St. Augustine, Thomas Aquinas, John Calvin, Martin Luther, Blaise Pascal, Søren Kierkegaard, and other luminaries of religious thought (one could add here, on the Christian side alone, Marsilius of Padua, Thomas More, Niccolò Machiavelli, Thomas Hobbes, St. Newman, C. S. Lewis). This could easily become the subject of several other volumes. As a kind of appetizer, we include below Strauss's confrontation with Pascal. The notes belong to a period when Strauss was teaching and studying Pascal, partly with a view to writing another book on Baruch Spinoza, so that Strauss could develop his discussion of the alleged "moral superficiality" of the philosophers or their blindness to the meaning of diversion or distraction, as well as the issue of causality and nature as divine "habit" or "custom."

As will become clear in the transcript below, the word for Strauss's engagement with Pascal should indeed be "confrontation." Such a confrontation is, to be sure, only possible on the basis of very high regard: see this remark in the spring 1959 course on Cicero: "There was a man called Pascal, who lived with the notion that there are abysses right here where he sits. Neurotic? Well, to which one might very well say (and I believe one must say) that while this may have been in the literal sense exaggerated, Pascal's was a much healthier mind than those who do not see abysses anywhere, because he faced the crisis; whereas a kind of mental health which is based on the assumption that crises do not happen, or that they will not happen to me, or this kind of thing, is of course a very superficial health."[1] In the same course, there are two other significant references to Pascal, one of which is as follows: in raising "the very long question" of "what misery can exist in the pursuit of truth," Strauss remarks, "It is good from this point of view to look occasionally at Pascal, where the case against the theoretical ideal is presented with great strength."[2] Strauss faults Hobbes for allowing the "experience, as well as the legitimate anticipation, of unheard-of progress" to render him "insensitive" to what Pascal called "the eternal silence of those infinite spaces."[3]

The references to Pascal made in print by Strauss himself are rare but pregnant. Strauss states that "[t]he classics did not regard the conflict between philosophy and the city as tragic. Xenophon at any rate seems to have viewed that conflict in the light of Socrates' relation to Xanthippe. At least at this point, there appears then something like an agreement between Xenophon and Pascal. For the classics, the conflict between philosophy and the city is as little tragic as the death of Socrates."[4] In his "Restatement on Xenophon's *Hiero*," Strauss notes that "[w]hat Pascal said with antiphilosophic intent about the impotence of both dogmatism and skepticism, is the only possible justification of philosophy."[5] Which Pascal fragment Strauss has in mind may be a little unclear, one possibility being Brunschvicg fr. 434, but the reference to "impotence" suggests that Strauss means fr. 395 (see fig. A.1).[6]

Figure A.1. This extract reads: "Nous avons une impuissance de prouver invincible à tout le dogmatisme. Nous avons une idée de la vérité invincible à tout le pyrrhonisme." *Source*: Bibliothèque Nationale de France, public domain. [alt text=The image shows a handwritten page that reads in French: "Nous avons une impuissance de prouver invincible à tout le dogmatisme. Nous avons une idée de la vérité invincible à tout le pyrrhonisme."]

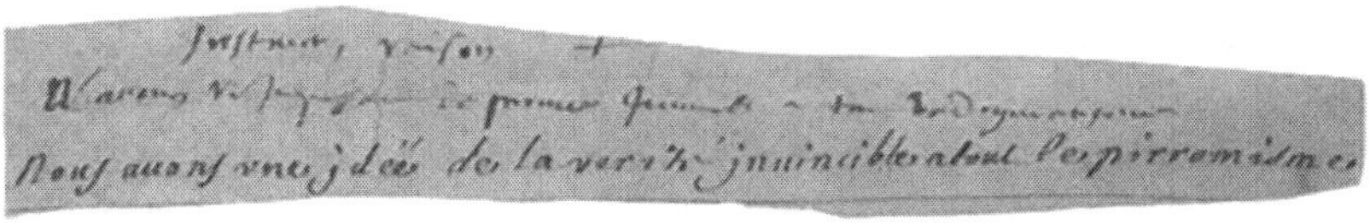

In *The City and Man*, Pascal is brought in to testify, going "much beyond Aristotle," that while "there are things which are by nature just . . . they can[not] be known to unassisted man owing to original sin."[7] Finally, in *Natural Right and History*, Strauss refers to Pascal (along with Maimonides) for the thought that "[w]hen 'nature' is denied, 'custom' is restored to its original place."[8]

Philippe Bénéton's "Strauss and Pascal: Is Discussion Possible?" (in *Leo Strauss and His Catholic Readers*, ed. Geoffrey M. Vaughan [Catholic University Press, 2018]) is a start, but it has not benefited from Strauss's extensive discussion of Pascal available in the archive. The most substantial, but still extremely brief, engagement of Strauss with Pascal that has been previously published is found in "Reason and Revelation," in *Leo Strauss and the Theologico-Political Problem*.[9]

Before we present the notes themselves, we might point out the crucial argument or challenge that Pascal poses on Strauss's reading: it is that the philosophical life is not permitted, is even sinful, and is not able to get a hold of unchangeable necessity. Strauss's twofold response is that Pascal's thought itself depends on and presupposes modern science, just as it depends on and presupposes biblical morality: the whole analysis of *divertissement* (1) presupposes an *intelligible* necessity (though in Pascal's case a necessity understood in the slanting light of modern mathematical physics)—viz., that a finite being that *knows* of its finiteness cannot possibly find its happiness in itself; (2) presupposes biblical morality—that pride is bad and sinful. Because Strauss sees this moral implication as playing a crucial role in Pascal's position, he wonders if Pascal's Pyrrhonism regarding knowledge of justice—his claim that we are ignorant of justice, a claim Pascal needs in order to defend the possibility that eternal damnation is compatible with divine justice—endangers Pascal's own argument.

Leo Strauss's Notes on Pascal (1947)

Editorial Note: This transcript is an edited version of a manuscript found in the Leo Strauss Papers.[10] Editorial notes are added in curly brackets. The underlinings are replaced with italics. The edition of Pascal Strauss used was *Pensées et opuscules* (5e édition revue), ed. M. Léon Brunschvicg (Paris: Hachette, 1909). The notes are related to Strauss's Fall 1947 course on "Reason and Revelation" at the New School for Social Research. The syllabus is shown in fig. A.2.

Appendix

Figure A.2. Syllabus for Strauss's Fall 1947 course on "Reason and Revelation." *Source:* Leo Strauss Archive, University of Chicago. [alt text=A syllabus for a course taught by Leo Strauss at the New School for Social Research, which includes readings of Maimonides's *Guide for the Perplexed,* Thomas Aquinas's *Basic Writings,* Calvin's *Institutes of the Christian Religion,* Pascal's *Pensées,* Newman's *Essay in Aid of Grammar of Assent,* Kierkegaard's *Philosophical Fragments,* and Brunner's *Revelation and Reason*]

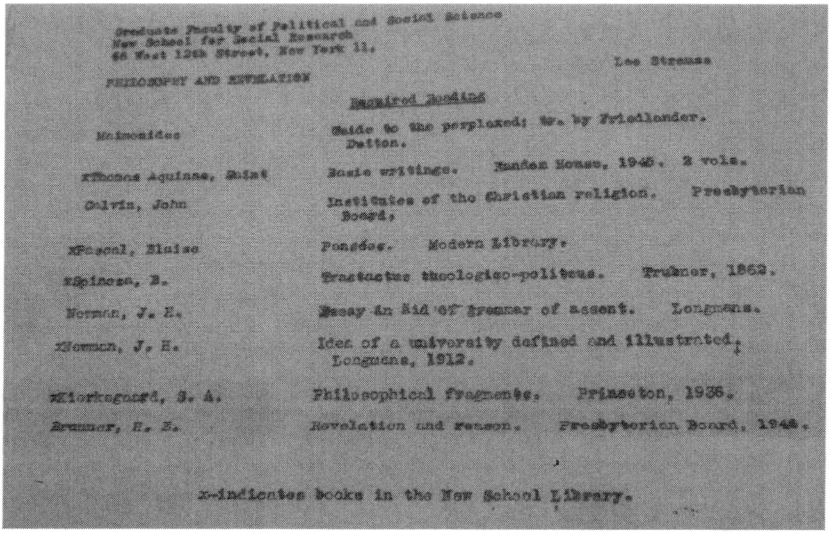

Pascal's critique of the philosophy {Seven arguments and counterarguments – ed.}

The apparent self-contradiction: that use of reason for fighting reason—actually this:

1′) reason can show the insufficiency of reason for solving the human problem, for understanding man, to say nothing of the universe, and to say still less of God.

2′) reason can refute the *objections* to faith

Reason confronts us with the alternative of despair and faith—faith is the gift of God.—[The *real* self-contradiction—see re عادة {ʿāda—habit, custom}]

However much P. may insist on the uncertainty of reason, he cannot but admit the *greater* uncertainty of faith—we do not "know" what is believed in the same way in which we "know" that we exist e.g. Still, it is sufficient for him that there is no *absolute* certainty of knowledge: the two positions, belief and unbelief, are uncertain. Now, uncertainty is an objection to what claims to be knowledge; it is *no* objection to faith (fr. 194, p. 415).

[Nor, we shall say, is it a *proof*—may the insistence on the mysteriousness of revelation and on the hiddenness of God be due to the awareness of the problematic character of the *basic* assertion of faith, viz. divine gov't of man? Cf. Eth. {Spinoza's *Ethics*} I app.]

[There must be *some* kind of *positive* argument—cf. *demonstration*]—the *demonstrable* misery of man without God, and hence of the philosophers, and hence the demonstrative refutation of the claim of the philosophers that philosophy, and philosophy alone, leads to happiness.

1) Philosophy does not lead to happiness - fr.425 (p. 518) - {LS:} but: Socrates
    fr. 82: imagination rather than thought leads to happiness—{LS:} mistakes "contentment" for true happiness.
    fr. 67: science does not help in afflictions—{LS:} in some it does.
    fr. 129: no repose possible for man, or man cannot find his happiness in repose {LS:} but the *progress* in understanding

Still, philosophy presupposes that man *can* understand by his own efforts—but:
2) The radical insufficiency of human understanding
    a) man's incapacity to grasp the infinite, i.e. the true principles of the whole—fr. 72 (p. 350–355) {LS:} - but does he not *know* the true principles of the whole are the infinite? [But does not the finite have principles of its own? Are there no πρῶτα πρὸς ἡμᾶς {prota pros hemas; things first for us}? [or they may have the proportionateness to *human* understanding which is required for understanding the universe.]
    b) عادة {'āda—habit, custom}: necessity is a precarious *assumption* cf. fr. 194 (p. 418, p. 4-p. 419, p. 1], 208, 339 (see separate sheet)—{LS:} without it Pascal's argument would break down
    c) man cannot understand *himself* in his contradictoriness, fr. 139 (page 392f.) etc. fr. 420

His self-contradiction: similar to God and to worms: fr. 432, 435 {LS:} but: ζῷον λόγον ἔχον {zoon logon echon; the animal that has logos: speech/reason}—fr. 358, 366, 418.

Cf. also the statement on "flies"—fr. 358—{LS:} ἡ ἀνθρώπιων φύσις πολλαχῇ δούλη {he anthropine physis pollahē gar hē physisdoulē tōn anthrōpōn; for the nature of human is enslaved in many ways; a version of Aristotle, Metaphysics 982b20}

[Obvious insufficiency of philosophic happiness: the need for diversion and the distraction.] [Human inability to understand oneself in one's natural desires.(A human being is neither an angel nor a beast, and unhappiness would have it that he who wants to be like an angel will act like a beast) with "human nature is often enslaved" in Plato.]

d) the demonstrable insufficiency of philosophic psychology: (divertissement—proves original sin)

fr. 194 (page 420)

his inability to become happy *and* his desire for happiness proves original sin: fr. 425 (p. 518f.), 434 (532), 445, 477, 489 end—{LS:} obviously not—cf. e.g. Rousseau's criticism of the intellectual development of man: the happiness of the savages: does P. not take his bearings by the misery of *civilised* man?

e) dogmatism refuted by pyrrhonism and vice versa but so that pyrrhonism has the edge: the first principles are *true* but not *believed*—{LS:} but: a) distinction between λόγος {logos; reason} and νόησις {noesis; intellection}; he who seeks λόγος for everything, ἀναιρέι λόγον {anairei logon; removes reason}; b) doubt of existence of external world based on delusions of senses and dreams: not sufficient consider fr. 434 (p. 529 p. 2), fr. 386.

3) Assuming equal uncertainty of both philosophy & faith: the wager
The last doubt: eternal annihilation or eternal damnation—we do not *know* which expects us—we lose nothing by assuming eternal damnation and therefore reforming our lives, refraining from pursuit of pleasure, submitting to ecclesiastical authority—fr. 194 (417 p. 3, 419 p. 2), 233 (p. 437–441)

{LS:} but: a) wager *presupposes* that eternal damnation is a *possibility*—is it?—incompatible with divine justice—we do not know what justice is?—Insufficiency of Pascal's argument; b) we abando*n nothing*? is there *no* earthly happiness, both individual and collective? is death the greatest evil? cf. fr. 194 (417 u.)

(Above all: s'embêtir {to be bored}: p. 441) cf. Anatole France's *Thaïs*
Pascal's critique of the philosophers -- continued

4) The fundamental argument: mind → infinite
heart → lovable
{connected by a bracket to both arrow-statements above:} the conflict between mind & heart can be resolved only by a *lovable* infinite-eternal—cf. fr. 205f.
{LS:} *but*: is this *wish* not due to desire for *comfort*? does it not lead to *illusory* comfort, — hence to misery? must we not sacrifice *all* our heart's wishes to our mind's desire for clarity? and is clarity not the only *solid* happiness? In other words, if the *heart* loves only knowledge, the problem is resolved —cf. {Spinoza's} Tr{actatus Theologico-Politicus}. IV.12f.

No infinite or eternal good would be required, if man could love a finite good without suffering for its loss or the prospect of its loss—*fr. 181:* {LS:} But: there is a finite good which we cannot love without *not* wishing its eternity—this finite good is our progress in knowledge.

Implied: we cannot be happy without being loved—being loved is an essential ingredient of happiness—{LS:} Is not being admired more than being loved? No nearness in space & time required; no services required: we may admire the victories of an enemy although we cannot love him. Love has no relation to excellence, whereas admiration has. Love has no criteria of its relevance outside of itself, whereas admiration has. The κάλλιστος κόσμος {*kallistos kosmos*; the most beautiful universe} is an object of admiration rather than of love.

5) Philosophy does not attack self-love—fr. 455 beg.; it encourages *pride* —fr. 430 (p. 522), 461-463)
   {LS}: *presupposes* Biblical morality

6) Philosophy asserts that God cannot take care of man—but we do not know what God is—fr. 430 (p. 525)—we cannot set limits to God's mercy {connected by a bracket to the first statement under point 6:} {LS:} all right—but this means merely that both assertions are a matter of *faith* only. Still, P. admits that a real *proof* of the *fact* of revelation is required—fr. 430 (p. 525u {bottom}-526, p. 1).

Yet: the proof must not be absolutely *clear*—to expect more, would not be *just* fr. 430 (526 p. 2-3) {LS:} but we know nothing of justice?
the argument based on the Bible—the principle: fr. 66, 289-291.

7) *The* argument as stated in *Theol. and Pol.*[11] I B.

Ad Pascal
His extreme scepticism—endangering his whole argument—
his alternative: dogmatism—pyrrhonism—the truth is *beyond*—
also عادة {ʿāda—habit, custom}—but his knowledge of human nature →
esprit de la finesse—its superiority in regard to depth & relevance to esprit géométrique—why not *return* to esprit de finesse as the *common basis* of dogmatism & pyrrhonism rather than *go beyond* them?

Connection with general problem of modern philosophy:
    Biblical theology—Greek cosmology no truth scepticism
    truth scepticism reinforced by Biblical theology
    Descartes: cosmology on *the basis* of extreme scepticism → epistemology
    philosophy of culture = human productivity—anthropology (existentialist philosophy).
    The latest things are correction of extremes—why not *return* to the original position

Ad *metaphysical criticism*—consider Sp.{inoza}'s denial of possibility of any trans-rational "knowledge" in the light of Pascal's argument

    [Spinoza and Pascal]
Critique of Sp.[inoza]'s critique – on the basis of Pascal's Pensées
Sp's argument leads up to: uncertainty of revelation – certainty = mathematical certainty = truth. (cf. Tr.{actatus Theologico-Politicus} XV with letter to Burgh). Man has no access to the truth but reason: cor {heart}= mens {mind} = intellectus {intellect} (Tr. XII 2).

But no mathematical argument in Tr. – even the mathematical argument of *Ethics* is deceptive: exotericism

Pensées I directed in fact against these two essential features of Sp.'s critique (a) geometric method, b) exotericism or unnatural way of writing).

1) the limitations of geometric spirit. cf. Pascal's de l'esprit géométrique.

Geometry	Finesse
Few principles	*many* principles —but: fr. 2.
Clear & "grossieres" principles → they are <u>seen</u>	subtle & delicate principles → they are felt rather than seen.
The *irreducibility* of precepts: fr. 20	they *are not accessible or available.* fr.
---------------------- of truths: fr. 21.	1, 3, 4. fr. 72 (p. 351 p.{aragraph} 2).

Esprit de finesse: instinctive tact in <u>moral</u> matters – no <u>science</u> outside the sphere of the geometric spirit : science is <u>mathematical</u> science (cf. criticism of Aristotle in de l'esprit géométrique).
Morality <u>more important</u> than speculation and <u>independent</u> of speculation: fr. 67-68.
(The question: why science? in a seemingly Socratic sense).

2) l'esprit de finesse & l'art de persuader {the art of persuasion}
The language of the heart: natural presentation of the passions (fr. 11).
Natural discussion = speech of the <u>gentleman</u> – its <u>sincerity</u> – opposed to academic – pedantic – specialistic as well as to rhetorical-bombastic speech – the true language of the heart, of tactful and refined feelings: fr. 14, 16, 25, 29, 30, 34-38.

Connection with <u>Montaigne</u> – but Pascal <u>criticizes</u> Montaigne (fr. 62-65) [implicitly a criticism of exotericism.] But cf. fr. 336.

One has to consider l'amour propre {vanity/pride} of the addressee : fr. 9-10, 16. p. 270. Cf. p. 195. fr. 189
Superiority of gentlemanship = morality to book learning: fr. 67-68.
The <u>danger</u> of l'esprit de la finesse → <u>divertissement</u> (fr. 11) (l'esprit de la finesse is only the <u>point of contact</u> of theological argument)

Pensées II {fr. 60-183}
Rational argument in favor of revelation: Misère de l'homme sans Dieu {misery of man without God}(fr. 60) *cf. fr. 242-243.* Cf. fr. 185.

Not based on physics: fr. 67-68. Cf. p. 361u {fr. 77, end}: nature is "mute," does not lead to God {LS note:}[no *proof of the existence of God*: fr. 233 (p.

436); [the wager fr.]. The argument addressed to *moral* men: fr. 187 cf. fr. 67-68 on *primacy* of morality.

The *radical insufficiency of human understanding* -- fr. 72 {Disproportion de l'homme} (cf. fr. 73 beginning) :{Mais peut-être que ce sujet passe la portée de la raison . . . .}

[The boast of unbelieving man is science—but science does no help in *serious* situations, in afflictions (fr. 67) {Vanité des sciences. La science des choses extérieures ne me consolera pas de l'ignorance de la morale au temps d'affliction, mais la science des mœurs me consolera toujours de l'ignorance des sciences extérieures: The vanity of sciences. The knowledge of external things will not console me for the ignorance of ethics in times of distress, but the knowledge of morals will always console me for the ignorance of external sciences.}—more than that: it is precisely science that teaches man that man is radically & always in an extremely serious situation: science reveals to man his misery, without giving him *any* remedy whatever.] The *double* infinity—the two abysses: man has no support in the universe for his self-consciousness. If there were only the infinitely great, le silence éternel de ces espaces infinis will frighten him (fr. 206), but man could withdraw to his own finite substantiality, to his *indivisible* substantiality: but the infinitely small—the finite surrounded by *two* infinities (cf. p. 354) {fr. 72} More precisely perhaps: all grant that the infinitely great is incomprehensible—but we mentally control it through its *principles*, the "small elements"—but these elements again lead into the infinite (p. 352, p. 3) {fr. 72}

Both infinites transcend absolutely, not only man's understanding, but his imagination as well.

The *disproportion* between human understanding and reality (cf. 350u-351o) {still fr. 72}

(cf. Hobbes[12] → construction of models. But *cf. fr. 121*.). {Idealistic interpretation of the "infinite" (Urteil des Ursprungs {judgment of the origin; Herman Cohen - ed. as an apparent way out.}

But does not the finite have principles of its own? Are there no πρῶτα πρὸς ἡμᾶς {*prōta pros hēmas*; first for us}? [or they may have the proportionateness to *human* understanding which is required for understanding the universe.]

They are rejected as derivative & inexact (351 p. 2) {fr. 72 again}

[Criticism of Plato-Aristotle on the basis of a) scepticism, b) modern mathematical physics is the basis of Pascal's argument. Science is *mathematical* science—but mathematical science is a) hypothetical and b) limited to corporeal world—ergo: science does not make intelligible reality.

As *far* as science teaches us anything, it teaches us the misery of man. Pascal, *Pensées II contin.*
[Still: man is the only being in the universe that *thinks*—in his *thinking* man finds his *happiness*—it is his *thinking* that *establishes* the two infinites.] (fr. 339. 346 347, 348—but: 365ff.]

Not reason, but foolish imagination leads to happiness: fr. 82 (363-364 p. 1)

The *weakness* of reason : fr. 82 (p. 364 p.4}. {Le plus grand philosophe du monde, sur une planche plus large qu'il ne faut, s'il y a au-dessous un précipice, quoique sa raison le convainque de sa sûreté, son imagination prévaudra. Plusieurs n'en sauraient soutenir la pensée sans pâlir et suer: "The greatest philosopher in the world on a plank wider than necessary, if there is a precipice below, although his reason convinces him of his safety, his imagination will prevail. Many could not bear the thought without turning pale and sweating."} → the precariousness of man's thinking and hence of his happiness. {The role of τύχη {*tuchē* ; chance} : fr. 97 {La chose la plus importante à toute la vie est le choix du métier, le hasard en dispose . . . . : "The most important thing in life is the choice of profession ; chance determines it"}

[The *precariousness* of man's happiness would not do away with the fact that only thinking constitutes man's happiness—it is not necessary to assert that man's thinking can *guarantee* the *conditions* of its actualization: εὐημερία {*euēmeria* cf. EN Nicomachean Ethics 1099b8, 1178b33: "sunshine"/equipment/success; see "Reason and Revelation," p. 148: "*euemeria*, sunshine in the shape of food, shelter, health, freedom and friendship – a sunshine that is not produced by philosophy, is required for philosophizing and hence happiness, although it does not constitute happiness.].] Cf. fr. 181: the highest pleasure leads to "amor fati".

The *radical* doubt : *the doubt of* φύσις {*physis* ; nature, عادة ʿāda—habit, custom} fr. 93 (cf. fr. 90-95).

Geometric necessity would not dispose of this ("logical" and "real" possibility)
But : fr. 81, 97, 99 beg.—yet : *due to free creation*. Fr. 208, *222, 233*[13] (p. 3750 {top; page 435 top}: Notre âme est jetée dans le corps où elle trouve nombre, temps, dimensions, elle raisonne là-dessus et appelle cela nature, nécessité, et ne peut croire autre chose: «Our soul is cast into the body, where it finds number, time, dimensions; it reasons upon these things and calls this nature, necessity, and cannot believe anything else."}, *339.*

[Still: does not the whole analysis of *divertissement* presuppose an *intelligible* necessity—*viz.,* that a finite being which *knows* of its finiteness cannot possibly find its happiness in itself?]

Impossibility of human happiness—of a state of repose (cf. Bacon, Hobbes) (cf. fr. 129: Notre nature est dans le mouvement, le repos entier est la mort.)

"Divertissement": fr. 135, 139 (pp. 392, 393, 396).

Pascal's starting-point is: the basic reason of man's restlessness is that man does not want to think of *himself*—of his imperfection, nothingness, mortality—the right life is *meditatio mortis*—his implicit objection to Sp.{inoza} is that his psychology does not fathom the depths of man *because* Sp. denies the *meditatio mortis* {"A free man" (by which he means "one who lives according to the dictate of reason alone") "thinks of nothing less than death, and his wisdom is a meditation on life, not on death." Ethics, IV, prop. 67}—fr. 139 (392, p. 3; 393 p. 2-3)

[The question is whether Pascal's analysis of divertissement is really adequate. No sufficient clarification of man's *natural* needs as impulses to activity and his natural need *for* activity as actualisation of his possibility—his natural need for *relaxation*. Pascal traces both Caesar's love of glory (→ conquest of the world) and the courtier's gambling or hunting to the *same* root: are the *qualitative* differences not decisive precisely from the point of view of morality?]

Many phenomena which Pascal describes as divertissement, can be understood *better* in a different way. Still, there is such a thing as distraction —*especially* in *our* world: radio, love of noise, etc.—I believe there is no ancient term for boredom (Langeweile): taedet me alicuius rei {"I am bored of something"}the unnatural character of *modern* life—how? the *necessity* of work, the *praiseworthy* character of certain *kinds* of ἔργα {*erga;* works}— unpleasantness of πόνος {*ponos;* toil}, the ἡδονη [*the pleasure*] of laziness (lazzarone). Cf. 396n. fr. 142 (p. 398), fr. 151, fr. 152. Connection between *distraction* and *vanity*: we are running away from ourselves, fearing the contemplation on what we are— we want to *preserve* our high opinion of ourselves: confirmation by others → vanity—fr. 147. (The analysis *presupposes* the religious "ideal.") (Why did the *philosophers* disregard the phenomenon put into the center by Pascal? Were they blind or superficial? They knew of course that, if εὐδαιμονία {*eudaimonia;* happiness} = θεωρία {theoria; contemplation}, the large majority of men are unhappy, because they seek happiness in the wrong things, in perishable things— how the average man reacts when he becomes aware of the futility of his aims, is much less important for the philosopher to know than a) what their aims are, and b) why they are futile. Above all: according to *the* philosophers, the typical reaction to the futility of the imaginative and affective aims is: *superstition. The analysis of superstition is the counterpart, in Sp. teaching, to Pascal's analysis of divertissement. More generally expressed: the analysis of false religion. Divertissement becomes a central subject if (large groups of) of non-philosophers become consciously irreligious.* {LS note:} And such non-philosophers are *the* addressees of the *Pensées.*)

Connection between distraction and *fear of death*: fr. 183, e.g. [We necessarily fear death as summum malum—but is this fear *reasonable*? Do we not *admire* certain dead people more than many living people?]

Connection between death and vanity: fr. 211.
{in pencil:} *Sp*'s position - a modification of *the* philos. position: philosophy being the attempt to replace opinion by knowledge is the highest human possibility: it is the *only* way in which man can be truly happy. For: man is incomplete - he must attach himself to something else to become complete: he must love. If the beloved object is perishable, *love* leads to madness → attachment to the *eternal* - to the *truly* eternal, to the *known* eternal. Difficulty of *knowing* it: the *liberating* effect of the *quest* - the increasing clarity about the *complexity* of reality as the greatest

enjoyment and achievement of which man is capable. *Disputation*, about decisive character, of true philosophy: understanding of the problems rather than the answer. {added in pen:} Cf. Pascal fr. 181: the good is the coherent account – its breakdown is a source of pleasure to the philosopher {LS' note:} "Cf. Brunschvicg, p. 297."
Dissatisfaction with this – with σκέψις {skepsis/examination} → science on the *basis* of extreme doubt: *mathematical* certainty as actually achievable – limitation of investigation to mathematical aspect of reality: the clear & distinct account of the whole is *possible* – it makes irrelevant the confused accounts whose claims to divine origin are, in addition, absolutely uncertain.

{in pen:}
Pascal: 1) the clear & distinct account of the whole is not *the* true account, because it is not an account of the *whole*: a whole *dimension* is inaccessible to mathematical method (esprit de finesse + esprit géométrique): the *dimension* of morality (fr. 67, 68). Mathematics > external world (object of physics) ≠ the *heart* (which Sp. identifies with the intellect). fr. 277, 278, 282.

2) The Socratic question: why science?—the *possibility* of this question shows that man is *primarily* concerned, not with science, but with happiness. How can man become happy? Without God, man is radically miserable: the experience, the honest admission, and the understanding of this misery leads him to *seek* God, to *desire* that there is a God, or that the religious message is true.

But, the philosophers object, man can find his happiness in *understanding*, in science.

Yes—α) science does not help in *afflictions* (fr. 67).—not reason, but imagination or folly leads to happiness.
   β) precisely science reveals the misery of man: the two abysses of the two infinites; science destroys the securities of pre-scientific man.
   γ) science does not lead to understanding at all: our ignorance of the true principles (disproportion of human understanding and reality).
   The problem of *physis* {nature}—عادة {'āda—habit, custom}) (cf. fr. 222).
→ the fundamental problem: is τύχη {tuchē; chance} at the bottom of ἀνάγκη {anankē; necessity}, or vice versa?
   γ') science is unable to account for the facts of human life (distraction)

The argument of Pensées II can be stated as follows: the philosophers admit that the life of non-philosophers is fundamentally miserable; the only problem therefore is the happiness of the philosopher. But philosophy cannot lead to, or constitute, happiness, because of the radical uncertainty of the principles of being: while the principles of being are uncertain, the misery of man is certain.

Pensées III {fr. 184-241}—

Reason or science is insufficient to give an adequate account of the whole: it cannot show that the whole is intelligible without God and thus refute the theistic assertion. While reason is uncertain, it is certain that man is miserable without God: man will *seek* God, he will *desire* that God exists, or that the religious message is true—provided that he is *sensible*.

Yet: the apparent *uncertainty* of religion: this is so far from being an *objection* to religion that it is the *contention* of religion (Deus absconditus): religion *must* be uncertain so that *full* devotion or faith is required for certainty. fr. 194 (p. 415), fr. 229, fr. 233 (p. 437 p. 2).

In other words:
I) Revelation cannot be *refuted*: impossibility of "system." Religion is then *possibly* true: the unbeliever cannot have certainty, but only *doubt*.
II) Revelation cannot be rejected as *uncertain—suspense of judgment is impossible*: the atheist position would require *absolute* clarity or certainty (fr. 221).
for—a) it is reasonable that the most important knowledge should not be *certain* knowledge (God wants *faith*)
b) it can be shown that the most important question is not capable of a *certain* answer.

The most important question: in the case of the unbeliever, the misery and shortness of this life is followed by either eternal damnation or eternal annihilation—neither is *certain*, but one is *necessary*.

The unbeliever confronted with this situation can either *face* this situation or try to *evade* it.

Let us assume that he *evades* it → *divertissement*: this is so fantastic, so *unreasonable* that it amounts to a proof of original sin (fr. 200, 211). fr. 194 (p. 420).

Appendix

{The next sentence is emphasized with two vertical lines in the left-hand margin.} [Not the fact of foolish diversions, hatred of solitude etc., proves insufficiency of philosophic psychology, but the fact that man seeks distraction *although he is faced by this absolute uncertainty regarding the most important subject.* {LS' note:} as to importance of this argument, cf. fr. 560 end.)

But is man faced by this uncertainty "par nature" {by nature} and not rather on the *basis* of revelation? And is it not natural or reasonable therefore that natural man *assumes* eternal annihilation, clings to life and seeks the only happiness possible, in the fragile happiness of *this* life?]

The atheist has then to *face* the dilemma: he has to admit the *possibility* of eternal damnation (and eternal bliss). One cannot *suspend* one's judgment between eternal life and eternal annihilation: "il faut parier; cela n'est pas volontaire, vous êtes embarqué"—p. 437u. {paragraph 11 of fr. 233[14]}—you are *headed* either for one or for the other—suspending judgment means betting {on} "annihilation." *There is no neutral position.*[15]

Philosophy asserts that one has to suspend his judgment in all cases of uncertainty—but one *cannot* suspend his judgment on all matters of life & death—fr. 194 (p. 416) and fr. 234—hence philosophy *presupposes* that all matters of life and death are settled in *advance* or that "suspense of judgment" is *the* good life in philosophy: based on the *insight* that the philos. Life is the good life. But this cannot be an *insight* if revelation is *possible*, as it is *admitted* to be: philosophy rests on an arbitrary decision: on a wager.

The question is: whether the wager is *reasonable*. Reasonable choice is guided by 2 considerations: the true and the good. Consideration of truth is out, because we do not *know*. Hence the reasonable choice is limited to the desirable.
 We have nothing to lose and everything to gain. We risk nothing (the negligible or non-existent happiness of this life) for an infinitely great good: if we lose, we lose nothing (we will be annihilated); if we gain, we gain everything (eternal bliss).
 But if we bet on the atheistic proposition, we risk nothing for an infinitely great evil: if we lose, we "gain" eternal damnation (lose everything), and if we gain, we gain nothing (annihilation). Fr. 233 (pp. 437-440).

[Presupposed: that it is *reasonable* to assume possibility of eternal damnation (and immortality of the soul); doubts lead to *investigation*, the θεοφιλέστατον {*theophilestaton*; most beloved by god}: God is not a gentleman who resents it if his word is not trusted or if he is not believed on his word (*Cyropaedia* {VII.2.15-17}). Cf. p. 425 p. 2 {fr. 195, paragraph 6}, 436u. {bottom} {fr. 233, paragraphs 8-9}, fr. 202, *390* (& parallels).

That it is reasonable to order one's whole life with a view to an uncertain, and even improbable, possibility—s'abêtir {make oneself a beast/stupid]—for nothing? Cf. P. 441 {final three paragraphs of fr. 233} (cf. Anatole France *Thaïs*). Is the consideration of earthly felicity—the only felicity of which we know anything—both individual and social altogether irrelevant?]

[As to *impossibility of neutrality*—cf. Marxism: the non-Marxists are capitalist-fascists.)

Admiration → ambition, glory → admiration of *oneself*: self-satisfaction is ἥδιστον {*hediston*; most pleasant} (Spinoza, cf. Tr.pol. VII 6; cf. κάλλιστος κόσμος {*kallistos kosmos*; most beautiful cosmos} —Timaeus etc.: object of *admiration* rather than love. Also *Banquet:* ambition higher than love of persons)

Pascal on the problem of love (fr. 323): one never loves persons, but qualities (one loves persons, not on account of themselves, but on account of qualities—e.g. my *child*) (the same would apply to admiration]

The only *thing* which one loves, is oneself (fr. 483, 485)—(but, if this is so, are the qualities for which one *admires* men not fundamentally different from those for which one *loves* men?)

Follows *here* : Pensées VI on "orgueil" {pride; see below}

Pensées IV {fr. 242-290}
Survey of the argument
   1) The atheists pretend that they have given a demonstrative refutation of the Christian faith: they are utterly mistaken a) the limitations of l'esprit géométrique—the hypothetical character of the definitions—the clear & distinct account following from these definitions is not the true

account, because it necessarily leaves out decisive parts of reality (e.g. no analysis of divertissement; the whole realm of l'esprit de finesse: the heart). b) عادة {ʿāda—habit, custom}

→ the atheistic position is itself uncertain.

2) The Christian position too is uncertain (Deus absconditus)—but Christianity admits this and even explains it.

The Christian religion not based on natural theology (cf. عادة {ʿāda—habit, custom})—fr. 242 (446 p. 2), 243 f.

both positions are unequally uncertain → *wager.*

3) Yet there are proofs by reason of the Christian religion—fr. 185, 242 (446 p. 1), 245, 252 (450u.), 253f., 259f., 282 (460 p. 3), 287

4) What are these proofs? Reason realizes its own insufficiency: fr. 267-270, *272, 273-275.*

The superiority of sentiment & the heart: fr. 252 (p. 450), *277, 278, 282*

[Still, this could be taken care by restoration of νόησις {*noēsis*; intellection} ≠ διάνοια {*dianoia*; discursive reason}]

fr. 60. Decisive: man cannot solve his problem by his own means: man is miserable without God (i.e. Christ). More precisely: man's misery cannot be understood but on the basis of faith. fr.230, Brunschvicg's note.

The crucial example: *divertissement* —not the fact of foolish diversions, hatred of solitude etc. proves insufficiency of philosophic psychology, but the fact that man seeks distraction *although he is faced by absolute uncertainty regarding the most important subject* (his eternal fate) fr. 200, 211, 194 (p. 420), 202

Man's radical problem: man needs an eternal, an infinite which he can love absolutely {LS note:}: cf. Brunschvicg, 197]—His *mind* leads him to the infinite (and thus destroys all security derived from finite things), but this infinite is not lovable (fr. 206). His *heart* leads him to lovable things, but finite ones.

[Consider this problem for {LS discussion of} "Biblical and philosophic morality" {Spinoza's} Tr.{actatus Theologico-Politicus} IV.12 f.]

Pensées IV *continued*
Is this not a real refutation of the philosophic position? Philosophy asserts that man can become happy through philosophizing and *only* through philosophizing. But how can this be if there is no a priori certainty that the object of contemplation is absolutely lovable? For happiness requires that man loves something eternal. But if the eternal which philosophy

discovers is repulsive rather than lovable (fr. 206)? Is {there} therefore not a hopeless conflict between the mind and the heart?

Why must man have an *eternal* good (= eternal lovable)? Because every temporal or finite good will be *lost*. *If man could love a finite good without suffering from its loss, no infinite or eternal good would be required.* fr. 181. That this is so, is asserted by Plato (*Philebus* 51ff.) with regard to the ἡδέα {*hēdea*; pleasant things}. There is a finite good which we cannot love without *not* wishing its eternity: this is *our* progress in knowledge.

Let us assume that the finite good is the improvement of the mind, or as continuous understanding as possible, an understanding aiming at coherent and clear account: the philosopher enjoys the coherent account at which he arrived. But the account will be *refuted*. He enjoys that too: he *learns* something through this.

But the graver danger: the philosopher knows that, however high he may rise, he will fall again (death, senility, forgetting due to illness). *The more he enjoys his understanding, the more he will be troubled by his error and ignorance.* But: he will not expect, and therefore not wish, more than that degree of understanding of which he is really capable. *His insight into the necessity of the finite character of his knowledge will prevent him from suffering from these shortcomings.* Man's misery is due to his desires? for unattainable ends, for the *impossible*. This desire is due to *ignorance* (Tr. theol.pol., praef. beg.).

Ergo: *insight into necessity essential for happiness* → عادة {ʿāda—habit, custom}) (cf. fr. 222).

But: *when* he forgets, when he sickens, one will no longer *see* the necessity and be unhappy. Yet, philosophy does not *claim* that it can guarantee the εὐημερία{*euēmeria*; "sunshine"/equipment/success}—

Pascal assumes that the eternal or infinite must be lovable if man is to be happy—i.e. that love of another *being* (i.e. love simply) is an essential ingredient of happiness. But what is love? For what *reasons* do we love someone or something? Is not admiration more than love? No nearness in space & time required, no services required. We may admire the virtues of an enemy although we cannot love him. *Love has no relation to excellence, whereas admiration has. Love has no criteria of its relevance outside of itself, whereas admiration has.*

Pensées V {fr. 291-338}
cf. fr. 434 (p. 532), fr. 445, fr. 477, 489 end, 502

Wager > eternal damnation. Cf. p. 425 p. 2, 436u {bottom}.

The objection which P. has to meet: a just God would not condemn man to eternal pain, just as a just man would not take savage revenge. P.'s answer: man does not know what justice is. (fr. 390).

The proof: the purely conventional character of justice (fr. 291ff.)
    a) δίκαιον {*dikaion*; just} = νόμιμον {*nomimon*; legal}[but this *follows* from δίκαιον = not to hurt others or to serve others → peace, not violence, legality rather than antinomianism; cf. fr. 299 end, 313, 319, 320, 332f.]
    b) rule of *custom* based on rule of *force* (of the many) – fr. 301-303, 298f. [From the fact that only a very imperfect justice is *practicable* among men, it does not follow that we do not have the true *principles* of justice or their knowledge]
    [Connection with عادة {'āda—habit, custom}-problem]

(The real objection would be this: the σόφος {*sophos*; wise one} does know what justice is—but his refusal to make everything dependent on justice or to identify justice with *the* ἀρετή {*aretē*; virtue} of man, leads to *indifference* to justice—his critique of eternal damnation is due to *indulgence*, ultimately *self*-indulgence: to his feeling that if demands of justice were taken seriously, he would deserve eternal damnation.

The philosophic answer: it can be shown that perfect justice—purity of heart—is impossible (the very prayers [ליבנו טהר {taher libenu "purify our hearts"}] prove it) and therefore cannot justly be demanded.—But: the maximum effort?)

[Sp. does not deny Pascal's thesis—ius naturale {natural right} = potentia naturalis {natural power} etc.—Sp.'s argument against eternal damnation is implied in denial of freewill of both God & man].

[The mixture of obscurity & clarity makes impossible stringent proof—but it also makes impossible stringent proof of untruth of the assertions of faith. Presupposed is *some* clarity. The clarity of the inner experience (call) does not suffice—for it does not account for *the* historical revelation—there must be at least *some* link between the inner experience and the fact of the past (Kierkegaard: the mere notice that the apostles believed that God has become man and resurrection—does not suffice. {The confrontation with Kierkegaard will be published in a subsequent volume}). Cf. fr. 758.—Furthermore, the mere fact that there is no stringent proof on either side, decides in favor of the faith; for faith asserts that, and explains why, this is so and *must* be so (*need* for faith, for full devotion) (fr. 795; {LS note:} cf. fr. 194 [p. 415], 226). [Is there no explanation of the fact of uncertain clarity on the basis of unbelief? The uncertainty due to the imaginary character; the clarity due to the direction of feeling of the human heart which yearns for a comforting principle of the universe]

[Apply this to preliminary argument: of course we do not know whether there is revelation, and hence whether philosophy may not be ultimately insignificant or even meaningless—but, we cannot possibly assent to a mere suggestion of even millions and millions of people contested by millions of other people—we have to *investigate*—a) the oldest book and the authenticity of the Bible.—? b) the fulfillment of the prophecies—yet they are as obscure as miracles—cf. fr. 758—; c) the impossibility to understand man without recourse to original sin; d) the need of the heart: the first cause that loves and is lovable—the desire for comfort—*this* is the reason why theological and historical demonstrations did play a decisive role. But do they not take away the possibility of faith?]

[As for *the* argument in favor of revelation (—philosophy, the quest for evident knowledge, rests itself on an unevident basis if there is a possibility of revelation) —this is true only if stated in general terms, and not if stated ἀκριβῶς {*akribōs*; precisely} [the question is: is revelation *really* possible?]—for: for all we know, knowledge is best; certainly, superhuman knowledge would be better; but the difficulty is that superhuman knowledge as such cannot be or become human knowledge; it will always remain dubitable; and this applies, not merely to the content of revelation, but to the fact of revelation as well. A wise God will therefore not make acceptance of revelation the condition of salvation.

The clarity of that knowledge will take away the necessity or the merit of faith? Not at all—as little as the clarity of my knowledge that this is my neighbor, takes away the decisive difficulty of *loving* him.

The *particular* revelation becomes intelligible if there is liberum arbitrium {free will} as *the* cause of divine response: Abraham is the first and sole man who responded to the call – he is *therefore* elected – but does not his election precede his response? Does not the whole story start with לך לך {"Go forth," in *Genesis* 12:1}? Besides, should there never have been a man in China e.g. who did the same thing?

Either the reason of particular revelation is due to unpredictable choice of human beings (but this is {inkblot – ed.}) or it is due to the mystery of God's choice (and this makes God's action absolutely arbitrary and hence unjust). {LS note:} the question is: is revelation *really* possible?

Pensées VIII-IX {fr. 556-641}
Historical objections to revelation
(*previously*: a) the weakness of reason → impossibility of *refuting* revelation
  b) man's ignorance of justice → impossibility to assert that eternal damnation is incompatible with divine justice.
  c) inability of mortality to account for misery of man (divertissement)
  d) man's quest for a lovable eternal – [but is this not due to unreasonable desire for *comfort*?])
The contradiction between the assertions of faith and the statements of the Bible: e.g. the Christian interpretation of the O.T. prophecies and the actual meaning of the passages in question.
Pascal's answer: a) distinction between spiritual and carnal understanding fr. 571 (fr.588).
  b) אמר ה' לשכון בערפל {I *Kings* 8:12 and II *Chronicles* 6:1, "the Lord has chosen to abide in a thick cloud" (NJPS), "the Lord hath said he would abide (or dwell) in a thick darkness" (JPS 1917) – ed.}: fr. 568, 578, 581, 585
  the obscurity an argument in *favor* of revelation. Cf. Sp.{inoza}'s principle of starting from the *clear* passages [LS' note: e.g. it is clear that temporal felicity is promised – is it really? is its clarity not *endangered* by command to love God with all one's heart, all one's soul and all one's power!]

The *fundamental* consideration: the uncertainty, or lack of evidence, of the assertions of faith is admitted: the *same* uncertainty is ascribed to unbelief – cf. fr. 564f.

Knowledge is *certain, but* limitation to what man knows and disregards (suspense of judgment) regarding the object of faith is *uncertain*. Hence Pascal does not seem to be compelled to assert the uncertainty of knowledge (pyrrhonism) – it would suffice for him to assert the *limited* character of knowledge. This would seem to make the *crucial* argument clearer. *But:* the *contrast* between the dimension of certain and evident knowledge and the dimension of *mere* belief. And: the danger that *progress* of knowledge e.g. might lead to a conquest of many strongholds of belief. Or: human knowledge, while being essentially limited, might be strong enough to realize the contrast between divine justice and eternal damnation → Pyrrhonism – but does this not endanger Pascal's *own* argument? He contradicts the Catholic teaching by denying natural theology and knowledge of natural law: does he not implicitly admit the strength of the unbelieving position by insisting on the untenability of natural theology and knowledge of the natural law? does he not despair of maintaining faith if there is any kind of important *knowledge*?

Does he not really *wish* to *prove* the divinity of Christianity? Cf. fr. 594-598 (poor apologetics > Grotius), above all 614, 619, 620, 622, 624-626, 628, 634. Cf. fr. 711, fr. 817 end.

Pensées X {fr. 642-692}—cf. p. 308 p. 2

fr. 642 (p. 621)—the idea of the whole (cf. e.g. fr. 652)—the doubtful character of the argument {connected by a symbol to "The *obscurity* of Bible ... "}

fr. *645* {fr.} —*675* P's answer to the merely temporal character of O.{ld} T.{estament} (→ empirical disproof of the fact of providence: suffering of just and happiness of wicked—based on belief that sensible goods are *the* goods—this belief apparently borne out of O.T.—but: Pascal's argument).

fr. *645*—the difficulties of the Gospel-text.

.... ad عادة {'āda—habit, custom}]

{Pascal XI – XIII}

The *obscurity* of the Bible—the *silly* things—cf. fr. 675, 680, 684, 691. But: *758*.

[the argument is *not* conclusive: the *carnal* promises connected with the thirst for the establishment of the kingdom of God on *earth*. הַהוּא בַּיּוֹם, {אֶחָד וּשְׁמוֹ--אֶחָד יְהוָה יִהְיֶה{"in that day shall the Lord be One, and His name one"—Zechariah 14:9}] [also: *both* circumcision of the flesh and of the heart]—cf. fr. 698 end. cf. fr. 671, 646, 860—how is this connected with basic problem?

The Christians' exclusive concern with spiritual glory—and yet: they rule—they defend themselves against the Turk etc. etc. Is the Jewish teaching not much more *sincere*? But??. for the *sake* of spiritual welfare one must *work*, and *pray*, for sensible goods? "the daily bread".

fr. 547 The proof {LS note:}[fr. 706, 710. Cf. 711: the assumption of authenticity]: *the* proof are the prophets of the OT whose *authenticity* is guaranteed by the Jews who are absolutely unsuspect because they are enemies of Christianity. {inserted above the line by LS} fr. 737,745,749,750 {LS note:} [*the* objection: the Jews do not believe in Jesus as the Messiah—answer: their unbelief is the much stronger argument in favor of Jesus than would be their belief.] But if one questions the authenticity of the OT?—cf. the doubtful apologetics of Pensées IX—; → the prophets or rather the Jews were deceived deceivers who expected the coming of a Messiah who actually came!—But did he actually come? Could not the prophetic or Jewish delusion incite a man and his disciples to believe that he is the Messiah ...)

Miracles
  Importance: fr. 808, 851, 806, 811-813, 829, 838, 839.
  Proof of miracles:
  there would not be false miracles if there were not true miracles—fr. 817, 818—consider fr. 817 end, fr. 818 end ....
    (................... prophets ....prophets)
    (................... witches, ...witches—
but are there witches?)
    (................... oracles, ...oracles—but
what are the true oracles?)

Philosophy - ἐδιζησάμην ἐμεωυτόν {*edizēsamēn emeōton*, "I sought for myself"/"I consulted myself" - Heraclitus B101 DK; or: ἐζητήσαμεν ἐμαυτούς [*exētēsamen emautous*/"we sought ourselves"] - perhaps Meno 86d}
What is a miracle? a strange event, a super-human fact, an event beyond human expectations—are not the *true* miracles the facts of nature?
  there would not be false X but for the fact that there are true X
    .... ψευδή {*pseudē*; false} .... ψευδή)

Pascal's more precise argument: fr. 817 end, 818 end: the false miracles *imitations* of the true ones—his poor proof—

How to make the argument good: *assuming* the fact of true miracles, false miracles are necessary (Deus absconditus—God *tempts* man.)

Miracles are not recognized but by faith: fr. 194 (p. 415), fr. 823-826
    but—fr. 852 cf. page 285 {from "Testament de Pascal," paragraphs 11-14}

The Biblical Jews had no doubt in the historicity of the lasting accounts of their past nor in the existence of God—but they did not have faith in the promises. cf. also the antagonism between Pascal and the Jesuits on *the basis* of Christian belief.
    e) The impossibility of explaining the faith—but will anything said by the philosopher about love ever satisfy the lovers? e.g. the mature man realizing the doubtful character of the eternity of "first love"—

Kalām-argument: there will not be false miracles but for the true miracles—the former deceitful imitations permitted by God of the latter—fr. 817f. (there would not be false X but for the fact that there are true X)
.... ψευδή {*pseudē*; false} .... ψευδή)

Apply Ad Pascal—the φύσις [*physis*; nature]- عادة {*'āda—habit, custom*}-problem
    φύσις is a problematic *interpretation* of regularity—that regularity *may* be nothing but عادة {*'āda—habit, custom*}. → radical scepticism. Or: idealistic legitimation of φύσις as a condition of the human mind (Hobbes, Kant). (Cf. Heidegger: coevity of truth and man, denies eternal truths as well as Demonstration überhaupt {demonstration generally}; he admits that beings [Seiendes] are *not* coeval with Dasein; as to the manner of being of beings in so far they antedate Dasein, it cannot be "eternity"—for only through Dasein is there the principle ex nihilo nihil fit: the *possibility* that prior to Dasein there was *nothing*: Dasein jumped into being out of nowhere, out of nothing; but on the basis of its understanding of the world "in" which Dasein is, Dasein has to *postulate* that ex nihilo nihil fit and that Seiendes precede Dasein.)
    Can there be on that basis existentialist analytics? or, for that matter, Pascal's analysis of human nature? Man is able to realize that what constitutes his essence is that he is a finite & mortal corporeal being that possesses reason or understanding—such a being *necessarily* will seek

happiness (not merely the pleasant here & now) and can find happiness only in connection with the eternal—or else Heidegger's metaphysics—

These statements are true of man as man, and hence of *all* men: they are necessary and universally valid {LS note:}[fr. 222: "Pourquoi une vierge ne peut-elle enfanter?" pourquoi l'homme ne peut être heureux sans Dieu? Analysis of human nature—analysis of the process of generation. Ad hominem: God created everything *wisely*.]

But they do not do away with a radical *contingency*—the *contingent* fact that there are men. Why *must* there be men? Or dogs?

a) simple teleology: how does it contribute to beauty of the whole that there are men, dogs ...

b) Aristotle: demonstration of the necessity of the eternity of the *visible* world *en bloc*.—

If both are inaccessible, we have to admit the radical contingency of the world → ex nihilo omnia fiunt ~ a nihilo omnia fiunt. {from nothing all things come into being ~ by nothing all things come into being}

{LS note:} fr. 654: the necessity *in* God—[but: we do *not know that* God is— *as* knowledge it is hypothetical knowledge, like geometry].

fr. 803, 816: the supranatural character of miracles presupposes *knowledge* of *nature*

cf. fr. 194 (p. 418 p. 4—419 p. 1). fr. 208, 339

Notes

1. Leo Strauss, *1959 Course on Cicero Offered at the University of Chicago*, ed. James H. Nichols (Chicago: Leo Strauss Center, 2016), 216. https://wslamp70.s3.amazonaws.com/leostrauss/s3fs-public/pdf/Cicero_1959_1.pdf. See, however, the letter to Karl Löwith from July 19, 1951: "Übrigens würde ich an Ihrer Stelle Kierkegaard Pascal vorziehen. K. scheint mir sowohl philosophisch wie theologisch der grössere Denker zu sein. Es ist kein Zufall, dass Pascal ein 'scientist' und nie ein Philosoph war" ["By the way, I would prefer Kierkegaard over Pascal if I were you. K. seems to me to be the greater thinker both philosophically and theologically. It is no coincidence that Pascal was a 'scientist' and never a philosopher"] (*Gesammelte Schriften*, edited by Heinrich Meier, 3:676).

2. Strauss, *1959 Course on Cicero*, 102. For the other reference, see Strauss, 1959 Course on Cicero, 184. See also the references to Pascal in Strauss's course on Plato's Gorgias and on Nietzsche: Leo Strauss, *1957 Course on Plato's Gorgias Offered at the University of Chicago*, ed. Devin Stauffer (Chicago: Leo Strauss Center, 2014), 4; Leo Strauss, *1963 Course on Plato's Gorgias Offered at the*

University of Chicago, ed. Devin Stauffer (Chicago: Leo Strauss Center, 2014), 80; Leo Strauss, *1971-72 Course on Nietzsche's Beyond Good and Evil Offered at the University of Chicago*, ed. Mark Blitz (Chicago: Leo Strauss Center, 2014), 21, 151, 153.

3. Leo Strauss, *Natural Right and History* (Chicago: University of Chicago Press, 1953), 175. See also *What Is Political Philosophy? And Other Studies* (Chicago: University of Chicago Press, 1959), 181.

4. Leo Strauss, *What Is Political Philosophy?*, 127. The reference to Pascal is to Brunschvicg fr. 331; the edition of Pascal Strauss used was *Pensées et opuscules* (5e édition revue), ed. M. Léon Brunschvicg (Paris: Hachette, 1909). The easiest way to find the corresponding numbers in the Faugère, Havet, Lafuma, Le Guern, Michaut, Sellier, and Tourneur editions is to consult https://pensees depascal.fr/. To look up the page references in Brunschvicg's edition, visit https://gallica.bnf.fr/ark:/12148/bpt6k56034742.

5. *What Is Political Philosophy*, 115–16; see also *On Plato's Symposium*, 4, where Strauss paraphrases Pascal's thought—calling it a "remarkable statement"; elsewhere a "true and beautiful sentence," audio at the end of "the classical solution" in the "What Is Political Philosophy" lecture [https://wslamp70.s3.amazonaws.com/leostrauss/s3fs-public/courses/01%20What%20Is%20Political%20Philosophy_%201955-01.mp3: 42:45-end]—as "we know too little to be dogmatists and too much to be skeptics."

6. The original autograph of Pascal's *Pensées* from *Recueil des originaux*, 489-2, kept at the Bibliothèque Nationale de France and accessible at http://www.penseesdepascal.fr/RO-extraits/RO489-2.pdf.

7. Leo Strauss, *The City and Man* (Chicago: University of Chicago Press, 1977), 18.

8. Leo Strauss, *Natural Right and History* (Chicago: University of Chicago Press, 1953), 83n3. See also *Studies in Platonic Political Philosophy* (Chicago: University of Chicago Press, 1983), 195n9, and the references to ʿāda (habit, custom) below in the transcript.

9. Author and editor Heinrich Meier (Cambridge: Cambridge University Press, 2006), 161–62.

10. Leo Strauss Papers, box 20, folder 20, Special Collections Research Center, University of Chicago Library.

11. A work, primarily on Spinoza, that Strauss had begun in the 1940s.

12. See *Hobbes's Critique of Religion and Related Writings*, tr. and ed. Gabriel Bartlett and Svetozar Y. Minkov (Chicago: Chicago University Press, 2009), 29n9.

13. Double underlined in the original.

14. Cf. Karl Löwith's "Man between Infinites" in *Karl Löwith: Wissen, Glaube und Skepsis*, vol. 3 of *Sämtliche Schriften* (Stuttgart: J. B. Metzlersche Verlagsbuchhandlung, 1985), 171–85; cf. Löwith's "Voltaires Bemerkungen zu Pascals *Pensées* in vol. 1 of his *Sämtliche Schriften* (1981), 426–49.

15. Double underlined in the original.

NOTES ON CONTRIBUTORS

Steven Frankel is a professor of philosophy at Xavier University, Cincinnati, Ohio. His work has appeared in journals including the *Review of Metaphysics, Interpretation, Archiv für Geschichte der Philosophie*, the *Review of Politics, International Philosophical Quarterly, Teaching Philosophy*, and the *Journal of Jewish Thought and Philosophy* and various collected volumes. His most recent book, with Martin Yaffe, is *Civil Religion in Modern Political Philosophy: Machiavelli to Tocqueville* (2020).

Yehuda Halper is a senior lecturer at Bar-Ilan University, Ramat Gan, Israel. His work has appeared in journals including *Jewish Quarterly Review, Arabic Sciences and Philosophy, Jewish Studies Quarterly, Quaestio, Zutot, Aleph, Studia Neoaristotelica*, and various collected volumes. His most recent book is *Jewish Socratic Questions in an Age without Plato: Permitting and Forbidding Open Inquiry in 12-15th Century Europe and North Africa* (2021).

Hannes Kerber is responsible for the Carl Friedrich von Siemens Foundation's Academic Lecture Program and teaches at the University of Munich's philosophy department. His articles have been published in, among others, the *Journal for the History of Modern Theology, Interpretation, International Yearbook of Hermeneutics*, and *Philosophisches Jahrbuch*. He is the author of *Die Aufklärung der Aufklärung: Lessing und die Herausforderung des Christentums* (The Enlightenment of the Enlightenment: Lessing and the Challenge of Christianity) (2021).

Till Kinzel received his Dr. phil. (2002) and Habilitation (2005) from the Technical University of Berlin; he has published books on Allan Bloom (*Platonische Kulturkritik in Amerika*; 2002), Nicolás Gómez Dávila (*Nicolás Gómez Dávila: Parteigänger verlorener Sachen*, 5th ed., 2023), Philip Roth (*Die Tragödie und Komödie des amerikanischen Lebens*, 2006), and Michael Oakeshott (*Michael Oakeshott: Philosoph der Politik*, 2007); and coedited volumes on imaginary dialogues (2012, 2014, 2017), audionarratology (2016), Edward Gibbon (2015), as well as on the German Enlightenment. His most recent books are *Johann Georg Hamann: Zu Leben und Werk* (2019), a German translation of Sir Walter Scott's essay on E. T. A. Hoffmann (2022), as well as a new edition of an eighteenth-century German translation of Oliver Goldsmith's *The Vicar of Wakefield* (2023).

Ralph Lerner is the Benjamin Franklin Emeritus Professor at the University of Chicago and author of works on medieval political philosophy, the Enlightenment, and American political thought, including *Naïve Readings: Reveilles Political and Philosophic, Playing the Food: Subversive Laughter in Troubled Times*, and *Maimonides' Empire of Light: Popular Enlightenment in an Age of Belief*.

Svetozar Y. Minkov is a professor of philosophy at Roosevelt University, Chicago, and president of the Leo Strauss Foundation. His work has appeared in journals including the *Review of Metaphysics*, the *Review of Politics, Interpretation, American Political Thought, Zeitschrift für Neuere Theologiegeschichte*, and various collected volumes. His most recent books are *Toward "Natural Right and History": Lectures and Essays by Leo Strauss, 1937-1946* (2018) and *Leo Strauss on Plato's Euthyphro: The 1948 Notebook, with Lectures and Critical Writings* (2023).

Rasoul Namazi is an assistant professor of political theory at Duke Kunshan University, Kunshan, Jiangsu, China. His publications include *Leo Strauss and Islamic Political Thought* (2022). His work has appeared in journals including the *Journal of Religion, Comparative Political Theory, Perspectives on Political Science, American Political Thought, Iranian Studies, Interpretation*, the *Review of Politics, Renaissance & Reformation, Eurorient*, and various collected volumes.

Alexander Orwin is an associate professor of political science at Louisiana State University and a graduate of the Committee on Social Thought at the University of Chicago. He authored *Redefining the Muslim Community: Ethnicity, Religion, and Politics in the Thought of Alfarabi* and, most recently, edited *Plato's "Republic" in the Islamic Context: New Perspectives on Averroes's Commentary*.

Joshua Parens is a professor of philosophy and politics at the University of Dallas, Irving, Texas. His work has appeared in journals including the *American Political Science Review, Polity, PS: Political Science & Politics, Philosophy & Theology*, the *Journal of Jewish Thought and Philosophy, Philosophy and Theology, American Catholic Philosophical Quarterly, Perspectives on Political Science*, and various collected volumes. His most recent book is *Leo Strauss and the Recovery of Medieval Political Philosophy* (2016).

Alex Priou is associate professor of political theory at the University of Austin. He is the author of *Becoming Socrates: Political Philosophy in Plato's Parmenides* (2018), *Musings on Plato's Symposium* (2023), and *Defending Socrates: Political Philosophy before the Tribunal of Science* (2023). His work has also appeared in various journals, including the *Review of Metaphysics*, *Epoché*, and *Polis*.

Andrea Ray is a PhD candidate at the Committee on Social Thought, University of Chicago.

John A. Ray is an associate professor of political science at Xavier University, Cincinnati, Ohio. His work has appeared in journals including *Mediterranean Studies*, *Presidential Studies Quarterly*, *Interpretation*, *Lincoln Law Review*, and various collected volumes. His publications include *French Studies: Literature, Culture, and Politics* with Steven Frankel (2014).

Nathan Tarcov is Karl J. Weintraub Professor at the University of Chicago, Chicago. His work has appeared in journals including *Social Research*, *Klesis—Revue Philosophique*, the *Review of Politics*, the *Good Society*, *Perspectives on Political Science*, *Political Science Reviewer*, the *Public Interest*, *Polity*, *Ethics*, and various collected volumes. His publications include *The Legacy of Rousseau* with Clifford Orwin (1996).

Philipp von Wussow is a senior researcher at Goethe University of Frankfurt, Germany. He specializes in political philosophy, philosophy of religion, and modern Jewish thought. After obtaining his PhD from Düsseldorf University he has held positions at the Hebrew University of Jerusalem, Leipzig University, and the University of Pennsylvania. His publications include *Leo Strauss and the Theopolitics of Culture* (2020).

Martin D. Yaffe is a professor of philosophy and religion at the University of North Texas, Denton, Texas. His work has appeared in journals including *Perspectives on Political Science*, *Jewish Political Studies Review*, the *Review of Politics*, *Telos*, *Philosophy in Review*, *International Philosophical Quarterly*, *Journal of Religious Ethics*, *Hebrew Studies*, and various collected volumes. His latest book is *Emil Fackenheim's Post-Holocaust Thought and Its Philosophical Sources* (2021).

INDEX

Abraham (Bible), xvi, 109-11, 113-24, 124n2, 129-37, 140n5, 141n16, 142n31, 376
Adorno, Theodor, 21, 32n2
Aesop, 24-25
Al-Ḥarizi, Judah, 127n29
Alfarabi, Abu Nasr Muhammad, 13n6, 74, 92-101, 101n2, 102n7, 103nn13-14, 103n18, 104n27, 104n34, 105n44, 105n53, 105n55, 141n10, 196, 230n10, 231n15, 245, 260, 353n37; his *Art of Dialectic*, 126n9; his *Enumeration of the Sciences*, 67; his *Philosophy of Plato and Aristotle*, 103n14, 104n25, 106n58; his "Summary of Plato's *Laws*," 104n28, 104n36-37, 105n40, 105n46, 105n49
Al-Ghazali, Abu Hamid Muhammad ibn Muhammad, 74-75, 102n2
Altmann, Alexander, 22, 32n6, 54n17
Anders/Stern, Günther, 21
Aquinas, Thomas, 10, 50, 74-75, 102n2, 195, 314, 325, 336, 348, 355, 358
Arendt, Hannah, xxvin10, 21, 32n2
Aristotle, xiii-xiv, xxi, 55n20, 56n31, 94, 99, 110, 119, 133, 137-39, 147, 192, 227, 260, 293-94, 296-97, 300, 301, 323, 325, 331-33, 346-47, 357, 363, 365, 380; his *Metaphysics*, 139, 198n3, 316nn16-17, 331, 360; his *Nicomachean Ethics*, 17n45, 114, 141n13, 198n4, 316n14; his *Parts of Animals*, 17n43; his *Poetics*, 229n5; his *Politics*, 141n17, 293-94, 316n13, 316n18, 323, 331-32, 346, 353n35; Aristotelian, 74, 125, 130, 166, 301; Maimonides on Aristotle's *Metaphysics*, 111-12, 134, 142; Maimonides on Aristotle's *Physics*, 111, 134, 142
Augustine of Hippo, 294, 352n28, 355; his *City of God*, 317n19
Averroes, 10, 13n6, 50, 74, 91-94, 102n2, 103n8, 103n19, 265, 271n24, 319, 338; Averroist/Averroism, 4, 56; his "Commentary on Plato's *Republic*," 93

Bacon, Francis, 318n45, 335, 366; Baconian, 151
Bayle, Pierre, 3, 54n15, 59n55, 254, 257, 258n3, 258n8, 303-305, 318n49, 326, 327n35, 335, 349
Bialik, Chaim Nachman, 87
Bloom, Allan, 229n6
Bruell, Christopher, 228n2
Buber, Martin, 112, 125, 138, 292, 316n10, 341, 352n24
Burke, Edmund, 150, 296, 317n29, 324n13

Cassirer, Ernst, 25, 33n16
Cicero, Marcus Tullius, 147, 150, 154n2
Cropsey, 319n55
Churchill, Winston, 308

387

David (Bible), 5, 47, 86
Descartes, René, 38, 45, 56n30, 151, 362
Dewey, John, 296, 307, 341
Diotima (character in Plato's *Symposium*), 192, 194–95, 197, 209–10, 212–13, 216, 243, 248n32

Elise, Reimarus, 26, 53n9
Empedocles, 206, 210–11, 218, 237
Epicurus, 324; Epicurean/Epicureanism, 65–66, 274, 296, 317n30, 324, 338, 351
Ernst, Simon, 22
Euripides, 17n44, 207; his *Ion*, 9; his *Phoenician Women/Phoenissae*, 211, 226

Fittbogen, Gottfried, 12, 18n53, 29
Frederick II of Hohenstaufen, 13n6
Frederick the Great (Friedrich II), 14n16, 57n39
Frederick the Wise (Friedrich III), 14n15, 57n39

Galileo, Galilei (Galilean), 172n19
Gibbon, Edward, 86–87, 89n24
Goethe, Johann Wolfgang von, 22

Halevi, Judah/Yehuda, 68–92, 100, 109, 121–22, 129–30, 298, 324, 333, 338–39, 347
Hamann, Johann Georg, 32, 34n28
Hegel, Georg Wilhelm Friedrich, xvii, 148, 313
Heidegger, Martin, xii, 380
Heraclitus, 17n, 198, 207, 211, 218, 378
Hobbes, Thomas, xxi, 44–45, 148, 150, 152, 158–60, 162, 167, 169n1, 234, 256, 260, 302–305, 318n44, 326–27, 335, 349, 355–56, 364, 366, 379
Horkheimer, Max, 21

Isaac (Bible), xvi, 109, 112, 120, 124, 127n39, 129–32

Jacob (Bible), xvi

Jacobi, Friedrich Heinrich, 5, 12, 14n18, 18n54, 18nn56–57, 22, 29, 34n28, 38–41, 44–45, 47, 52, 53n4, 53n9, 55n28, 316n8
Jaspers, Karl, xvin10, 32n4
Job (Biblical figure), 137

Kant, Immanuel, 150, 154, 379
Kierkegaard, Søren, 355, 358, 375, 380
Klein, Jacob, xiv, xxn3, xxiv, xxvn3, 13n6, 104n26

Leibniz, Gottfried Wilhelm, 4, 11, 13, 18, 24–25, 38, 40–45, 51–52, 54–56, 59–60
Lessing, Gotthold Ephraim, xxiv, 3–61, 103n15
Locke, John, 81, 260, 303, 305, 307, 313, 327, 335, 349

Machiavelli, Niccolò, xi, xxiv, 81, 147–50, 159, 167, 170n2, 231n13, 234, 242, 260–61, 270n6, 302, 326, 335, 342, 347, 349, 355
Maimonides, Moses (RMbM), xi, xvii–xviii, xxiv, 4, 10–11, 18n52, 50, 68–69, 71n10, 74–76, 80–82, 86, 92, 95–96, 99, 105n50, 109–43, 260, 299–300, 345–46, 348, 357–58
Mannheim, Karl, 21–22
Marxist/Marxism, 22, 296, 371
Mendelssohn, Moses, 11–12, 22, 29, 31, 38
Mill, John Stuart, 306–307, 335, 349; his *Autobiography*, 306, 319nn51–52, 327
Michaelis, Johann David, 11, 17n51
More, Thomas (his *Utopia*), 301–302, 318n42, 326, 349, 355
Moses (Bible), 13, 110, 113–18, 120, 132–33, 135, 140n5, 142n30, 149, 178, 185n12

Nietzsche, Friedrich, 41, 54n14, 236, 262, 269n1, 315n6, 319n58, 347, 380n2

Parmenides, 192, 200–201, 204, 210, 223, 237

Pascal, Blaise, xvii, xxiv, 313, 355–81

Plato, xii, xiv, xxiii, 56, 73, 94–106, 112, 139, 147, 150, 161–62, 165–70, 179–80, 254, 260, 265, 295–97, 323–24, 347, 360, 365; his *Alcibiades I*, 125n4; his *Apology of Socrates*, 294, 317nn24–25, 318n32, 332–33; his *Euthyphro*, 17n50, 208, 210; his *Gorgias*, 43, 94; his *Laws*, 141n18, 258n6, 295–96, 302, 323–24, 332–33, 348; his *Phaedo*, 94, 150, 192, 210, 212, 229, 298, 317n23, 318n33, 348, 353n39; his *Parmenides*, 192, 212; his *Philebus*, 373; his *Protagoras*, 55n23; his *Republic*, 59n55, 60n56, 295–96, 348, 353n37; his *Statesman/Politikos*, 151; his *Symposium*, xxiv, 191–241; his *Theaetetus*, 55n23; his *Timaeus*, 254, 294, 317n20, 323, 332–33; his exotericism, 42, 55n19; Mendelssohn's updating of his *Phaedo*, 54n16

Reimarus, Hermann Samuel, 24, 26, 28, 53n10

Richardson, Samuel, 24–25

Robespierre, Maximilien, 45

Rousseau, Jean-Jacques, xxiv, 44–45, 153, 164, 253–90, 305, 307, 314, 319n50, 335, 339–40, 347, 349, 351n14, 315n17, 360; influence of Ferguson's mitigated Rousseauism on Lessing, 55n27

Samuel Ibn Tibbon, 117, 127n29

Schmitt, Carl, 159, 352nn28–29

Simon, Ernst, 22

Socrates, 12, 43, 68, 95, 139, 192–98, 206–10, 212–13, 215–16, 219–22, 223–230, 232n19, 233n22, 234–49, 260, 263, 294–97, 317n24, 323, 332, 348–49, 356, 359, 363, 368

Solomon (Bible), 5, 47, 110

Speier, Hans, 21

Spinoza, Baruch/Benedict, xxiv, xxvin10, 4, 12, 18n54, 18nn56–67, 19n58, 29, 38–41, 45, 81, 147–87, 264, 302, 305, 307, 326–27, 335, 340, 347, 349, 355, 359, 361–62, 371–72; Spinozan pantheism, 32; Spinozism, 53n9

Spitz, David, xxii, xxvin10, xxvin12

Tchernichovski, Saul, 87

Thucydides, xi, xiv, 231n14, 235, 237, 318n31

Toland, John, 24, 33n13

Varro, Marcus Terentius, 352n28

Voltaire, François-Marie Arouet, 3, 41, 54n15, 60n67, 74, 254, 258nn4–5, 291, 316n8, 322, 343

Xenophon, 95, 195–96, 204, 225, 234, 260, 317n23, 356; his *Memorabilia*, xxiv, 204, 225, 318n32; his *On Hunting*, 195